The Ledgers of Merit and Demerit

The Ledgers of Merit and Demerit

SOCIAL CHANGE AND MORAL ORDER IN LATE IMPERIAL CHINA

Cynthia J. Brokaw

PRINCETON UNIVERSITY PRESS

PRINCETON, NEW JERSEY

Copyright © 1991 by Princeton University Press
Published by Princeton University Press, 41 William Street,
Princeton, New Jersey 08540
In the United Kingdom: Princeton University Press, Oxford

Library of Congress Cataloging-in-Publication Data

Brokaw, Cynthia Joanne.
The ledgers of merit and demerit : social change and moral order in late imperial China /
Cynthia J. Brokaw.
    p.   cm.
Revision of the author's thesis (Ph.D.)—Harvard University, 1984.
Includes bibliographical references and index.
1. Ethics, Chinese—History—16th century. 2. Ethics, Chinese—History—17th century. 3.
Moral education—China—History. 4. China—Social conditions—960–1644.
5. Merit (Ethics). I. Title.
BJ117.B76   1991   170'.951'09031—dc20   90-9059 CIP

ISBN 0-691-05543-2 (alk. paper)

This book has been composed in Linotron Sabon

Princeton University Press books are printed on acid-free paper,
and meet the guidelines for permanence and durability of the
Committee on Production Guidelines for Book Longevity of the
Council on Library Resources

Printed in the United States of America by Princeton University Press,
Princeton, New Jersey

10 9 8 7 6 5 4 3 2 1

FOR MY PARENTS

Edith and Alfred Brokaw

Contents

Acknowledgments

MANY PEOPLE have assisted in the completion of this study. I would like to thank the members of my dissertation committee, Benjamin I. Schwartz, Philip A. Kuhn, and Yü Ying-shih, for their advice and encouragement. I am very grateful to those who read and commented at some length on the dissertation: Timothy Brook, Paul Cohen, Prasenjit Duara, Joanna Handlin, Joseph McDermott, Susan Naquin, Daniel Overmyer, and Willard Peterson. I have not been able to incorporate all their suggestions and answer all their criticisms, but their ideas significantly guided my revision of the dissertation. The final manuscript was enriched by the criticisms and contributions of Joseph Esherick, who consistently urged me to strengthen the links between intellectual and social change; Valerie Hansen, who energetically but sympathetically tried to streamline my arguments; and Wei-ming Tu, who, through several discussions on Liu Zongzhou, considerably deepened my understanding of that thinker. I reserve my most profound thanks for Daniel K. Gardner, who has been with this project almost as long as I have. An utterly trustworthy critic, he has been tireless, if not always patient, in badgering me to clarify my arguments, refine my language, and reexamine my logic. That I did not always take his advice is doubtless the source of the many flaws remaining in the manuscript.

I owe a special debt to Sakai Tadao and Okuzaki Hiroshi, both of whom were extraordinarily generous with their time and their extensive knowledge of the morality-book literature when I was doing research in Japan from 1979 to 1982. This study clearly owes a great deal to their written work on the morality books; here I want to express my gratitude for their personal kindness.

Research for this study was conducted at libraries in both the United States and Japan. I am grateful to George Potter, Ho Chien, and Timothy Conner of the Harvard-Yenching Library; Diane Perushek of the Gest Oriental Library at Princeton University; Mi Chu Weins at the Library of Congress; and the staff of the East Asian Library at the University of California at Berkeley for their assistance and patience. In Japan, I relied heavily on the libraries of the Tōyō Bunka Kenkyūjo (Tokyo University) and the Jinbun Kagaku Kenkyūjo (Kyoto University), the Tōyō Bunko, the Naikaku Bunko, and the Sonkeikaku Bunko. At each I met with unfailing patience, good humor, and helpfulness.

Finally, I would like to thank the American Council of Learned Societies and the Mary Ingraham Bunting Institute of Radcliffe College for support during the 1986–1987 academic year, when the bulk of this manuscript was written.

Portions of the text have been published in "Yuan Huang (1533–1606) and the Ledgers of Merit and Demerit," *Harvard Journal of Asiatic Studies* 47.1 (June 1987), and are reprinted here with the permission of the editor.

Abbreviations

HY Refers to the serial number assigned to 1476 titles in the Daoist Canon according to the *Daozang zimu yinde* (Harvard-Yenching Institute Sinological Index Series Number 25)

LMP *Liming pian* (by Yuan Huang)

LZQS *Liuzi quanshu* (by Liu Zongzhou)

TSGYP *Taishang ganying pian*

YSCS *Yuanshi congshu* (edited by Yuan Huang)

Full bibliographical information is supplied in *Sources Cited*.

The Ledgers of Merit and Demerit

Introduction

THE SIXTEENTH and seventeenth centuries were times of considerable political, economic, social, and intellectual insecurity in China. The corruption in the central government, the rapid growth of the commercial economy, the breakdown of preexisting rural status relationships, the widespread questioning of Neo-Confucian orthodoxy—all made the Ming-Qing transition a period of both great opportunities and great anxieties. The magnitude of these changes was by no means lost on contemporary observers: gazetteers, letters, essays, and even poetry from the period often wistfully contrast the order, calm, and stability of life before the Jiajing era (1521–1566)—apparently the major dividing line—with the upsets, increased competition, and uncertainty of life thereafter.

No contemporary genre of texts reflects more sensitively or more richly both the social and moral confusion of the period than the ledgers of merit and demerit (*gongguoge*). Handbooks purporting to aid men in the mastery of their fate, the ledgers of the late Ming and early Qing provide precise guidelines for proper (and profitable) behavior during a time of high mobility, shifting values, and uncertain beliefs. As such, they reveal in unusual detail the nature of elite responses to the changes of the day. And, through the explanations the texts give of the mechanisms of fate manipulation, they offer insights into the cosmological beliefs of the elite, particularly the assumption that cosmic forces, as they were influenced by human actions, determined the stability of the social and political orders.

The ledgers of merit and demerit are a category of morality book (*shanshu*, literally, "good books"), a genre of literature that as a whole became very popular in the sixteenth and seventeenth centuries. Morality books can be defined simply as texts that teach people to do good and avoid evil.[1] The ledgers, like all morality books, are founded on the belief in supernatural retribution—that is, the faith that heaven and the gods will reward men who do good and punish those who do evil. What distinguishes the ledgers from other "good books" is their form. As lists of good and bad deeds, the ledgers are "how-to" books, describing quite

---

[1] For a general introduction to morality books, see Sakai Tadao, *Chūgoku zensho no kenkyū*, pp. 1–3; and Okuzaki Hiroshi, *Chūgoku kyōshin jinushi no kenkyū*, pp. 19–31. The ledgers, at least the ones treated here, should be distinguished from precious scrolls (*baojuan*), books that also provided moral and religious instruction. The precious scrolls were very closely tied to popular religious sects, in many cases forming part of the sacred literature of these "heterodox" groups. See Okuzaki, *Chūgoku kyōshin jinushi*, pp. 27–29.

specifically what deeds one should do to earn reward, and what deeds one should avoid doing to escape punishment. Most, but not all, of the ledgers quantify the deeds they list, assigning a certain number of merit or demerit points to each. For example, one seventeenth-century ledger allots one hundred merit points to a man who saves the life of another, but deducts one hundred from the account of a man who "hoards rice rather than distributing it to the needy in times of famine."[2] Ledgers usually include a simple one-month calendar, on which the user is to record his daily tally. If, then, in the course of one day a man spends five hundred cash on gifts of medicine or clothing for the poor, worth five merits (one for each one hundred cash spent), and on the same day also spreads slanders about a man, worth thirty demerits, his score for that day will be twenty-five demerits. His monthly balance helps him measure his moral progress, and at year's end his total score indicates whether he can expect good or bad fortune from the gods in the year ahead.

The ledgers that have survived from the Ming-Qing transition period tend to be rather complex works, at least in comparison to the brief, simple, and cheaply produced works available in Taiwan today.[3] The authors of these earlier ledgers came from all levels of the scholar-to-official hierarchy: some were obscure scholars who failed to pass any examinations at all, others were lower-level degree holders (*shengyuan* or *gongsheng*), while yet a few others were distinguished officials. The great center of ledger production was southeast China, particularly those areas that experienced the most profound economic changes and social upheavals in the late sixteenth and early seventeenth centuries—that is, Jiangxi, Zhejiang, Southern Zhili (Jiangsu and Anhui in the Qing), Fujian, and Guangdong. While some ledgers were later published in other areas—one as far north as Manchuria—for the most part the texts were a phenomenon of the south. In this study the ledgers are used as vehicles for the analysis of elite responses to the major problems and changes within the society of southern China during the Ming-Qing transition period: the corruption and inefficiency of central political authority in the late Ming, the social effects of increased commercialization (particularly changes in rural land relationships and merchant status), and the breakdown of Neo-Confucian intellectual consensus.

THE SIXTEENTH- AND SEVENTEENTH-CENTURY CONTEXT

Certainly the central government offered little assistance or relief to its people from the uncertainties and disorder that marked the period from the mid-sixteenth through the seventeenth centuries. By the late sixteenth

---

[2] Chen Xigu, *Huizuan gongguoge*, 7.37b.
[3] See Gary Seaman, *Temple Organization in a Chinese Village*, pp. 51–62.

century at the latest, factional struggles within the bureaucracy and the negligence of the bored and cynical Wanli emperor (r. 1572–1620) had weakened the effectiveness of the central government. Even after the fall of the notorious eunuch "emperor" Wei Zhongxian (1568–1627), the government, plagued by the great peasant rebellions of Li Zicheng (1605?–1645) and Zhang Xianzhong (c. 1605–1647), was unable to recover effective control of the country. Although the Manchu seizure of Beijing in 1644 gave China new rulers devoted to the pacification and unification of the country, it did not end the uncertainty and unrest: Manchu consolidation of power, in the face of both scattered incidents of loyalist resistance and the large-scale rebellion of the Three Feudatories, was not really assured until the end of the century.

No less profound were the economic and concommitant social changes of the period. Perhaps the most striking change of the sixteenth century was the commercialization of the economy, particularly in the Lower Yangzi (Jiangnan) and southeast coastal areas. The high foreign demand for Chinese luxury items, particularly silk and porcelain, stimulated the export trade and brought a much-needed influx of silver into China from Japan, the Philippines, and Europe. This influx of bullion made possible the monetization of economic exchange, spurred the growth of commercial agriculture and handicraft industries, and encouraged the expansion of interregional trade networks and the market system.[4]

Expanding economic opportunities had a profound impact on the social structure, both upsetting conventional definitions of the hierarchy and intensifying tensions between classes. Most noticeable was the elevation of the status of merchants. With the commercial growth of the period and the increasingly obvious power of money, merchants, though consigned in Confucian social theory to the bottom of the social scale, in fact enjoyed considerable power and social respectability. Wealthy merchants could now marry easily into gentry families and often formed close political and economic alliances with scholar-officials. They began to purchase estates and adopt the interests, attitudes, and customs of the rural gentry. In his biographies of famous merchants, Wang Daokun (1525–1593), a scholar-official descendant from a mercantile family, described how they might gain acceptance within rural communities through land investment and the performance of local charitable activities.[5] They could become members of the gentry more directly by purchasing the *shengyuan* or *jiansheng* degree, by making a hefty contribution to the imperial treasury, or by purchasing the genealogy of a gentry family fallen on hard times.[6]

4 William Atwell, "Notes on Silver, Foreign Trade, and the Late Ming Economy," p. 5.
5 Wang Daokun, *Taihan fumo*, 13.21a–23b.
6 Angela Ning-Jy Sun Hsi, "Social and Economic Status of the Merchant Class of the Ming Dynasty, 1368–1644," pp. 138, 140–142.

To some degree merchant status was now glorified as a positive achievement in itself, one that might well rival possession of the *jinshi* degree in terms of real power and social usefulness. Perhaps it is not surprising that the great Huizhou salt merchants valued trade over civil service, but even scholar-officials, in the face of the real power of late-Ming merchants, began to modify their traditional hostility to mercantile activity, and to emphasize the importance of merchants to society.[7] He Xinyin (1517–1579), a follower of the Wang Yangming school, changed the traditional ranking of social and occupational statuses, placing merchants above peasants and craftsmen (though still below scholars) on the social scale.[8] Many scholars were now willing to admit that commerce made a positive contribution to society; thus, merchants should no longer be considered parasitic or "secondary" in the social order.[9]

Merchants were not the only ones to benefit from the commercial advances of the late sixteenth and early seventeenth centuries. Members of the rural gentry (that is, landowners with official rank, who, depending on the degree they held, were exempt from certain corvée services) and wealthy commoner landowners took advantage of the new economic opportunities and invested their profits from office-holding or rents in commercial enterprises and moneylending activities. For example, the notorious Dong family of Huzhou, one of the richest of the Jiangnan gentry families, increased its wealth in part by investing in pawnshops or local stores and by lending money, usually at usurious interest rates, to handicraft producers in need of capital or commoners trying to pay the expenses of the corvée imposition.[10] Xie Zhaozhe (1567–1624) reported that many *jinshi* degree-holders in his native Fujian involved themselves in the salt trade while still in office and then, after retirement, devoted themselves exclusively to business.[11] Frequently, gentry families moved off their rural estates, leaving them in charge of a family member or a servant-manager, into the nearest large market town or city, so as to have more direct access to both the new commercial activities and the greater pleasures of urban life.

But the gentry by no means lost interest in their landholdings in the countryside. If anything, the size of gentry estates tended to increase in the late Ming. With the breakdown of the *lijia* system (a network of intravillage units, headed in rotation by local leaders, appointed to super-

---

[7] Hsi, "Merchant Class," p. 143.

[8] Liang Ruyuan (He Xinyin), *He Xinyin ji*, p. 53.

[9] Li Zhi, *Cang shu*, vol. 3, p. 587; cited in Hsi, "Merchant Class," p. 183.

[10] Saeki Yūichi, "Minmatsu Tōshi no hen—iwayuru 'nuhen' no seikaku ni kanren shite—," pp. 30–35; Fu Yiling, *Mingdai Jiangnan shimin jingji shitan*, pp. 31–51; and Chin Shih, "Peasant Economy and Rural Society in the Lake Tai Area, 1368–1840," pp. 52–68.

[11] Xie Zhaozhe, *Wuza zu*, 15.51b; cited in Hsi, "Merchant Class," p. 185.

vise tax collection and corvée service) and the implementation of tax reforms in the sixteenth century, gentry households were left relatively free of close official regulation. Taking advantage of this freedom, they manipulated their corvée exemption privileges to build up vast, though often geographically scattered, estates. Poor peasants unable to bear the corvée burden might renounce their independent status and commend themselves and their land to a gentry household, or wealthy commoner landlords might falsely register their land under the name of an official household to escape full tax payment.[12]

Landlords did not form a united bloc, however. Different styles of agricultural management created different groups within the landlord class. As a result of the commercial and fiscal changes of the sixteenth century, more and more landlords became absentee or rentier landlords. There did remain a small group of managerial landlords, usually holding only twenty to a hundred *mu* of land, who personally engaged in farming, supervising and assisting their agricultural laborers. Unlike absentee and rentier landlords, they expressed a moral commitment to the maintenance of close ties of mutual dependence and cooperation between landlords and agricultural workers.[13] Zhang Lixiang (1611–1674), a model managerial landlord, attacked contemporary gentry rentier landlords for ignoring these ties, indeed, for ignoring the whole process of agricultural production: "Nowadays the gentry (*qingshi*) do not think of going out in the rain or hot sun, or of walking out into the fields. They let the poor suffer cold, heat, and rain, and leave them to worry about flood, drought, locusts, and pests. . . . They cannot tell apart glutinous millet, rice plants, legumes and wheat. . . . They sit at ease in their homes, waiting for the harvest. They almost do not know what sowing and reaping are about;

[12] Tsurumi Naohiro, "Rural Control in the Ming Dynasty," pp. 266–273; Liang Fang-chung, *The Single Whip Method of Taxation in China*, pp. 16–17, 19–26; and Yamane Yukio, "Reforms in the Service Levy System in the Fifteenth and Sixteenth Centuries," pp. 297–306. The tax reforms of the sixteenth century—the "ten sections" (*shiduan jinfa*) and the single-whip (*yitiao bianfa*) methods, to mention the most famous—were attempts to correct some of the inequities of the system, largely by gradually merging land and corvée taxes into one tax, to be assessed according to landownership. But, by abandoning the *lijia* system and merging the two payments, the government was in effect sacrificing some of its own authority over landlord-tenant relationships. No longer involved in the supervision of either the *lijia* system or the conscription of corvée laborers, the government (in the guise of the local district magistrate) had little incentive to regulate this relationship very closely. In short, in the process of rationalizing the tax system and ensuring state revenues, the government ceded primary control over land-tenure relationships to the great landlords. See Linda Grove and Joseph Esherick, "From Feudalism to Capitalism: Japanese Scholarship on the Transformation of Chinese Rural Society," p. 409.

[13] Mi Chu Wiens, "Socioeconomic Change during the Ming Dynasty in the Kiangnan Area," pp. 203, 206–227.

nor who those people with darkly tanned faces and calloused feet are."[14] The phenomenon Zhang described had, by the early Qing, become the major trend: scholars have estimated that by the eighteenth century, up to 80 to 90 percent of Jiangnan landlords were absentee landlords, living in market towns and cities.[15]

The growth in commercialization and the consolidation of the landlord system naturally altered the relationships of agricultural labor in the Jiangnan area in the sixteenth and seventeenth centuries. The number of bondservants—that is, men and women indentured to a household to perform certain duties for a set period—increased considerably. In the early Ming, bondservants had usually been war captives or criminals (or members of their families) granted to high officials by the emperor, but as the dynasty progressed, more men and women commended themselves or their children to a master out of economic calculation or desperation. Well-to-do commoners might willingly take on the status to escape corvée service, while poor peasants might be driven into servitude to pay off debts or simply to avoid starvation. By law only official households were allowed to hold bondservants, but wealthy commoners frequently got around this restriction by "adopting" into their families men and women (or "adopted sons," yi'nan, and "adopted daughters," yi'nü) who served in fact as bondservants.[16] At the same time, large gentry families continued to accumulate bondservants—Gu Yanwu (1613–1682) estimated that some landlords of the Taihu basin had as many as two thousand bondservants.[17]

At worst these bondservants, who, as "base people" (jianmin), occupied a very low status in Ming law, might be more or less at the mercy of their masters, with no recourse to justice in the face of brutal exploitation. Zhang Lixiang described the kind of harsh treatment bondservants, usually those employed as field laborers, might be subject to: "I see that mas-

[14] Zhang Lixiang, Yangyuan xiansheng quanji, 19.21a–b; cited in Wiens, "Socioeconomic Change," p. 148.

[15] Wiens, "Socioeconomic Change," p. 206.

[16] Jing Junjian, "Guanyu Qingdai nubi zhidu de fange wenti," pp. 60–64. For general discussions of bondservitude, see Nishimura Kazuyo, "Mindai no doboku," pp. 24–50; Joseph McDermott, "Bondservants in the T'ai-hu Basin During the Late Ming: A Case of Mistaken Identities," pp. 675–685; and Wei Qingyuan, Wu Qiyan, and Lu Su, Qingdai nubi zhidu, pp. 1–135.

Just as there was a wide range of motives for entry into bondservant status, so too was there considerable variation in the terms and conditions of bondservitude. Some servants were bound to the soil, while others were not; some committed themselves and their families to permanent and hereditary servitude, while others had shorter contracts of service; some were promised payment and full care in return for their labor, while others (usually wealthy commoners trying to escape the corvée tax) were offered neither payment nor care.

[17] McDermott, "Bondservants in the T'ai-hu Basin," p. 685n.79.

ters are not treating their bondservants as people. They do not sympathize with their hunger, cold, and bitter labor. What is worse, they do not allow them to mourn their parents' death. Still worse, they rape their wives and daughters, as if this were proper, and seize the property of and kill those who protest. No one dares to bring them to court for these private murders and acts of destruction."[18]

But there was a type of bondservant who managed to thrive in the status, despite its low social and legal standing, and who may indeed have seen bondservitude as an opportunity for economic advance on the coattails of wealthy and powerful masters. Often employed as estate managers by absentee or rentier landlords, unscrupulous bondservants might use their masters' wealth or gentry status to bully and intimidate tenants, peasants, and local officials in order to accumulate land or other forms of wealth for themselves. Some bondservants were charged with managing their masters' commercial investments or with running shops or industries funded by their masters; these channels presented bondservants with yet other means of gaining wealth on their own.[19]

As a result, there was a small group of bondservants whose real wealth and power in late-Ming and early-Qing society contradicted their low legal status as base people. One description from the early Qing describes the status advances that could be made by bondservants associated with wealthy commercial and landowning families of the Jiangnan area:

> The Wang and Wu of Huizhou, and the Yao, Zhang, Zuo, and Ma of Tong-cheng are all big lineages. They have always purchased bondservants, using them to manage businesses or to cultivate the fields. Once these bondservants accumulate some wealth, they stop doing the dirty work with the other bond-servants. Their sons and younger brothers study for the examinations, or enter official service through the purchase of degrees, and their masters do not forbid these ambitions. It is the custom for indentured servants to take their masters' surnames, but when these servants become prosperous, they are not called servants, nor do they call their masters "master." They call their masters "uncle."[20]

Thus, by the late Ming, just as some merchants overstepped the status boundaries prescribed for them in Confucian orthodoxy and imperial law, so too some bondservants commanded a wealth and a social authority incommensurate with their low legal status.

[18] Zhang Lixiang, *Yangyuan xiansheng quanji*, 25a–b; cited in Wiens, "Socioeconomic Change," p. 149. It is not clear, however, that the courts would have offered much protection in any event, for bondservants occupied an inferior status in law. See Jing, "Guanyu Qingdai nubi," pp. 66–70.

[19] McDermott, "Bondservants in the T'ai-hu Basin," pp. 691–698.

[20] Xu Ke, *Qingbai leichao*, vol. 10, 82.2–3; cited in Wiens, "Socioeconomic Change," pp. 254–255.

Tenants, the major category of agricultural worker in the late Ming and Qing, were perhaps even more heavily influenced by the commercial expansion of the period.[21] The new crops (most notably maize, peanuts, and sweet potatoes) introduced into the Yangzi delta in the fifteenth century and the higher demands for both staple and cash crops that accompanied the growth of commerce and trade gave tenants opportunities for profit greater than those that had existed in the early Ming.[22] And tenants did earn some degree of independence from landlord domination through participation in rural handicraft industries.[23] Indeed, as tenants began to flee their fields for employment in manufacturing towns and cities, there gradually developed a shortage of tenant laborers. Desperate for peasants to rent their land, many landlords were forced to offer greater concessions to tenants.[24] The system of multiple landownership (*yitian liangzhu*), to some extent a product of this situation, often gave tenants virtual possession of the land they farmed, and thus significantly increased their economic power vis-à-vis their landlords.[25]

By the late sixteenth century, or the early seventeenth century at the latest, then, there were clear signs that the economic relationships and social statuses of the early and mid-Ming were undergoing severe and

[21] Wiens, "Socioeconomic Change," pp. 285–287. Tenants enjoyed a higher legal status than bondservants (they were considered commoners, not base people), but they were subject to financial exactions not imposed upon bondservants. In the Jiangnan area, most tenants paid a fixed rent, anywhere from 40 to 80 percent of the expected harvest. They might also be subject to subsidiary rent charges (the "winter gift," for example), charges for contract revision or renewal, and demands for rent deposits and bailiffs' fees, sometimes totaling 30 percent of the rent payment.

[22] Evelyn Rawski, *Agricultural Change and the Peasant Economy of South China*, p. 147.

[23] Mi Chu Wiens, "Lord and Peasant: The Sixteenth to the Eighteenth Century," pp. 13–14. The benefits of this independence certainly should not be exaggerated: while cotton and silk weaving allowed tenants to supplement their income, the structure of the rural handicraft industries encouraged a new dependence on brokers, merchant middlemen, and complex market forces beyond tenants' easy comprehension. As one scholar has remarked, tenants and, indeed, most rural laborers, "benefitted by a growing capacity to choose among potential exploiters, playing one off against the other," yet at the same time "suffered for an incapacity to control or regulate any one of them." (See Jerry Dennerline, *The Chia-ting Loyalists: Confucian Leadership and Social Change in Seventeenth-Century China*, p. 130.) Nonetheless, the increased commercialization of the late sixteenth century, by offering tenants in the Jiangnan area options for economic diversification, weakened the ties that had subordinated them strictly to landlord control.

[24] Wiens, "Lord and Peasant," pp. 15, 20–21.

[25] Ibid., pp. 12–16, 29–34. Under the multiple landownership system, the absentee or rentier landlord might still own the land itself—the so-called subsoil right—and be obligated to pay the taxes on it, while his tenant would own the topsoil or cultivation right—that is, the right to farm the land. Ownership of the cultivation right gradually came to be interpreted as a right of permanent tenancy, including the right to sell or further sublease the topsoil right. This new arrangement clearly benefited the tenant, for it gave him what amounted to part ownership in the land he cultivated.

wide-ranging changes, impelled in large part by the commercial advances of the period. A host of crises in the early seventeenth century, particularly the decades of the 1630s and 1640s, further accelerated the pace of social and economic change. A sharp decline in foreign trade caused a sharp reduction in silver imports, resulting in "severe economic contractions" in Southern Zhili, Zhejiang, Jiangxi, and Fujian.[26] Natural disaster exacerbated the economic depression: a series of droughts, floods, and finally locust attacks struck Southern Zhili and northern Zhejiang in the late 1630s and early 1640s, severely reducing grain yields. The famine and epidemics attending these natural disasters radically reduced the population, perhaps by as much as 40 percent.[27] The government, weakened by bureaucratic infighting, incompetent leadership, and eunuch intrigues, was unable, even under the relatively vigorous Chongzhen emperor (r. 1627–1644), to ease food shortages, stabilize rising prices, relieve suffering from famine and disease, much less subdue the great peasant rebellions of Li Zicheng and Zhang Xiancheng, or meet the Manchu military threat.

It was toward the end of this period of crisis that many of the tensions between landowners and tenants and contradictions between assigned status and real power within the bondservant class emerged in sharp relief. Tenants, emboldened by their new power, expressed their dissatisfaction with landlord control through a series of rent revolts, which were particularly intense in the 1630s and 1640s. In 1631, for example, tenants in Taicang county, Southern Zhili, turned against their landlords, refusing to pay their rents, burning their landlords' homes, and threatening their lives. At about the same time, tenants in several counties of southern Fujian banded together in a "bushel-measure society" (*doulao hui*) and threatened their landlords with violence if they did not adopt a uniform measure for the calculation of rents. Throughout the early Qing, southern China (in particular Jiangsu, Zhejiang, Fujian, Anhui, and Hunan) was also plagued with tenant revolts against what were claimed to be unfair tenancy contracts, the imposition of rent surcharges, and the use of unequal measures.[28]

Bondservant revolts were another source of social disorder, particularly during the early years of Qing rule, before Manchu power was fully consolidated. Jiading, Kunshan, Wusong, Nanxiang, Shanghai, Chongde, Liyang, Taizhou, Taicang (Jiangsu), Huizhou (Anhui), Quanzhou (Fujian), Guangshan, Shangcheng, Gushi (Henan), Shunde, and Xinhui

---

[26] Atwell, "Notes on Silver," pp. 10–16.

[27] Helen Dunstan, "The Late Ming Epidemics: A Preliminary Survey," pp. 1–59. See also Frederic Wakeman, Jr., "China and the Seventeenth-Century Crisis," pp. 5–6.

[28] Tanaka Masatoshi, "Popular Uprisings, Rent Resistance, and Bondservant Rebellions in the Late Ming," pp. 205–210.

(Guangdong) all suffered from bondservant rebellions.[29] These included two distinct types of uprisings: the seizure of a master's property by "brazen" bondservants (*haonu*) whose wealth and power exceeded their status, and the rebellion of poor bondservants attempting to destroy their contracts of servitude. It was the participants in this latter form of struggle who made the most far-reaching social claims. Song Qi, the leader of one such rebellion, argued, for example, that with the change of emperor there should also be a change, indeed a reversal, of status relations: "Our masters . . . should become servants and serve us."[30]

Perhaps the clearest long-term effect of both types of uprisings was a decline in the use of bondservants as either estate managers or agricultural laborers in the Qing. The frequent usurpation of a master's wealth by "brazen" bondservants must have made the dangers of employing bondservants as estate managers obvious to absentee landlords. Other factors clearly played a role in the decline in bondservitude as well: the rebellions of bondservants demanding freedom from hereditary servitude, the attempts of the early Qing emperors to regulate bondservitude, and, of course, the greater economic independence accessible to peasants through participation in handicraft industries. All of these factors tended to reduce the managerial and agricultural roles of bondservants in the early Qing.[31] By the eighteenth century the wealthy chose to use bondservants primarily as household servants, leaving agricultural labor to tenants and wage workers, and estate management to a new group of professional managers.[32]

Large landlords continued, then, to distance themselves, in the course of the seventeenth and eighteenth centuries, from estate management and agricultural labor. At the same time, as they moved away from their estates into market towns and cities, they retreated from their responsibilities for the maintenance of local social order. In the fifteenth and sixteenth centuries, local gentry often initiated and led famine relief efforts and charitable institutions; but in the very late Ming and early Qing, there was a considerable decline in the amount of care they offered their tenants, bondservants, hired laborers, and other members of the community. Certainly there were exceptions to this trend; as we shall see, the moral-

[29] Mori Masao, *Nuhen to kōso*, pp. 113–178; see also Xie Guozhen, *Qingchu nongmin qiyi ziliao jilu*, pp. 121–154; and James Tong, "Collective Violence in a Premodern Society: Rebellions and Banditry in the Ming Dynasty (1368–1644)," vol. 1, pp. 201–202.

[30] Tanaka, "Popular Uprisings," p. 195.

[31] Oyama Masaaki, "Large Landownership in the Jiangnan Delta Region during the Late Ming–Early Qing Period," pp. 136–147. See also Shih, "Peasant Economy," pp. 167–177; and Wei Qingyuan et al., *Qingdai nubi zhidu*, pp. 164–188. For a fuller treatment of this point, see Hosono Kōji, "Minmatsu Shinsho Kōnan ni okeru jinushi doboku kankei— kakun ni mirareru sono shintenkai o megutte—."

[32] Shih, "Peasant Economy," p. 173; Wiens, "Lord and Peasant," pp. 30–31.

ity-book authors of the day remained interested and active in the maintenance of local order. Generally speaking, however, over this period the gentry gradually surrendered the initiative for local action to the government. By the late eighteenth century the state had assumed much of the responsibility for famine relief and other local welfare projects. As Mori Masao explains, the Qing gentry elite was "essentially private in nature," lacking interest in the welfare of their local communities.[33]

ELITE RESPONSES TO SOCIAL CHANGE

The intense changes of the sixteenth and seventeenth centuries profoundly affected the economic and social security of the elite. On the one hand, new opportunities for enrichment offered themselves: both the gentry and literati (holders of an examination degree who had not earned official posting) could participate with profit in the commercial boom of the late Ming. But as a consequence of these same expanded economic opportunities, they also faced much more intense competition for elite status. Wealthy merchants, traditionally the objects of literati contempt, might be in a better economic position now to purchase examination degrees and official posts. And they could easily indulge in such elite activities as collecting books, painting, calligraphy, and organizing local charities and religious festivals. Even some lowly bondservants were able to accumulate wealth and power, often exceeding the fortunes of their own masters. Furthermore, the increased availability of books and expanding educational opportunities in the late Ming and early Qing meant that men of nonliterati backgrounds could aspire to literacy and even participation in the civil service examinations.[34] As more people tried to pass the examinations, the civil service system, traditionally the preserve of a small elite, became much more competitive.

Scholars today are still arguing about the nature, extent, and significance of all the changes summarized above, but no matter what their final conclusions, one fact remains clear: the Chinese themselves, at least those who left a record of their thoughts, felt that they were living through a period of economic and social upheaval. A few elite observers actually rejoiced in the new opportunities the changes brought. He Xinyin, from a wealthy family of Yongfeng county, Jiangxi, argued in favor of social ambition: each man should work to transcend the status into which·

---

[33] Mori Masao, "The Gentry in the Late Ming—An Outline of the Relations Between the *Shih-ta-fu* and Local Society," p. 52, and "Jūroku-jūkaseiki ni okeru kōsei to jinushi denko kankei."

[34] Evelyn Rawski discusses these developments in *Education and Popular Literacy in Ch'ing China*; for a briefer discussion, see her article, "Economic and Social Foundations of Late Imperial Culture," pp. 17–28.

he had been born and move up the social scale by mastering the principles of the next higher position.[35] Others encouraged upward mobility by writing educational handbooks—encyclopedias, guides to the Classics, and model examination essays—thereby giving commoners of non-literati background access to the knowledge required in the examination system.[36]

But much more common in the written record are the complaints of writers resentful of the changes wrought by commercialization and increased social mobility. Li Dami, lamenting moral decline in his native Jingshan county, Hubei, attributed the change to the urbanization and commercialization of the early sixteenth century, when "Jingshan became closely linked with the prefectural city," and "merchants and peddlars became rich with little effort, and all types of crafts gathered together."[37] An anonymous scholar from Huizhou, writing in the late sixteenth century, blamed the increased reliance on trade for the growing gap between rich and poor: "By the end of the Jiajing era and during the Longqing era [1567–1672], . . . the number of those who gained wealth from trade increased, while the number of those who gained wealth from land decreased. The rich became richer, and the poor, poorer. . . . Thirty years have passed since then, and . . . the rich represent only one in a hundred while the poor, nine out of ten. The poor, although many, cannot rival the rich, but the rich, though few, can control the many. It is the god of gold who rules heaven and the god of money who rules the earth."[38] Almost a generation later, the censor Li Banghua (1574–1644) complained about the effects of the new wealth on the pretensions of the commoner-residents of cities like Beijing: "Gold and pearls adorn the heads of the lowly, and the wives of ordinary commoners wear the dragon robes of officials."[39]

Most literati and gentry were quite fearful of the social unease that resulted when power and wealth were no longer correlated to legal status. Gui Youguang (1507–1571), the late-Ming scholar and well-known prose stylist, worried about the confusion of functions in contemporary society: "In ancient times the four orders of the people had their distinct functions, but in later times the status distinctions between scholars, peas-

[35] Liang Ruyuan, *He Xinyin ji*, pp. 53–54.

[36] Sakai Tadao, "Confucianism and Popular Educational Works," pp. 331–338.

[37] *Gujin tushu jicheng, Zhifang dian*, 1142.38a (vol. 10, p. 415b); cited in Mark Elvin, *The Pattern of the Chinese Past*, p. 244.

[38] Gu Yanwu, *Tianxia junguo libing shu, ce* 9.76 a–b; cited in Hsi, "Merchant Class," pp. 150–151.

[39] Li Banghua, *Huangming Li Zhongwen xiansheng ji*, 6.54b; cited in Albert Chan, *The Glory and Fall of the Ming Dynasty*, p. 314.

ants, and merchants have become blurred."[40] Xie Zhaozhe was keenly aware of the new social power of wealthy bondservants—he observed that many such men were able to marry into prominent gentry families once they had purchased their freedom. Many former masters, now suffering a decline in fortune, were forced to bow to the sons of their former bondservants.[41] Naturally, scholars were particularly disturbed by abuses in the educational system, their own preserve. Wu Yuancui, an educational intendant for Zhejiang in the late Ming, described in some consternation the ease with which bondservants' sons were admitted to prefectural schools in Suzhou: "Formerly there were one or two bondservant sons in the prefectural seat who entered the schools. Crowds of people then expressed shock and lamented their admission. Recently, the number of bondservant students has been increasing. Whenever I go to a school, there are several men who profess to be blasé about them and do not consider their admission strange."[42]

Elite writings from the period reflect a keen awareness of what this more open society meant for those of high status. One writer warned his descendants of the inevitable decline in store for a wealthy family undeserving of its privileges: "Whenever a family has been rich for a long time, it will decline and collapse. This comes of eating food produced by others without having the merit to justify doing so. Now eating food produced by others without having the merit to justify doing so is called 'oppressing the people to nourish yourself.' Whenever you oppress the people to nourish yourself, there is retribution from heaven. Therefore, after riches and ease have long been enjoyed, decline and collapse will ensue. Worse yet, you will become serfs or oxen, and your sons and nephews will have no choice but to toil at farming."[43] Thus, the new economic opportunities, while providing gentry and literati with new channels for enrichment, also created a much more competitive society—they now had to struggle harder to maintain their elite status.

There was, too, a growing awareness that new social and economic conditions necessitated new codes of conduct, particularly new codes for the regulation of status relationships. Landowners were most sharply and regretfully aware of the disruption of what they perceived as the traditional, paternalistic relationship of landlord to tenant or master to servant. One author described the closeness, generosity, and reciprocal cour-

[40] Gui Youguang, *Zhenchuan xiansheng ji*, 13.2a–b; cited in Ho Ping-ti, *The Ladder of Success in Late Imperial China*, p. 73.
[41] Xie Zhaozhe, *Wuza zu*, 14.31b–32a; cited in Hsi, "Merchant Class," p. 142.
[42] Wu Yuancui, *Manlu pingzheng, qianji*, 2.5a; translation (with minor changes) from McDermott, "Bondservants in the T'ai-hu Basin," p. 694.
[43] Huo Tao, "Huixun," 1.28a–b, *Huo Weiya jiaxun*; cited in Hosono, "Minmatsu Shinshu Kōnan," p. 4.

tesy that marked, in his own mind at least, the traditional form of this relationship:

> [Formerly] when the rent-collection time came, landlords always came to the field to collect rent in person. The amount of rent collected depended on the extent of the harvest. The tenant customarily provided a meal, with the landlord as the guest of honor and the elderly members of the tenant's family sitting next to him. They toasted the landlord's health. Sometimes rural gentry joined the dinner and talked about things of farm interest. After paying off the rent, the tenant would give a chicken and some delicacies to the landlord as parting gifts. The landlord would give some small presents such as a hand fan in return. Landlords and tenants treated each other with propriety.[44]

In this idealized vision, landlords were also responsible for the welfare of their tenants and servants during periods of famine; they lent them "life-saving rice" to get them through poor harvests, drought, and flood.[45]

But, in late-Ming Jiangnan, as landlords moved out of the villages into the cities, and as tenants and servants found other sources of income in handicraft industries, this model of reciprocal support was no longer applicable. Xu Jie (1503–1583), a chief grand secretary in the mid-sixteenth century, commented on the changes in the code governing the landlord-tenant relationship in his native Songjiang: "Recently . . . the so-called mutual support and mutual assistance of earlier times has begun to change to mutual suspicion and mutual enmity. Not only is it impossible to collect on loans, but rents are also largely in arrears. The fact that loans cannot be collected at first seemed to harm only the great houses, and no one understood that if tenants have no one to rely on for aid, they cannot escape disaster."[46] Thus, Xu lamented the waning of landlord authority over tenants and warned that this change not only weakened the "great houses," but also endangered the welfare of the tenants themselves.

By the next century, landlords were keenly, if not very happily, aware of the need to make concessions in their treatment of tenants. For example, Ji Maoxun, a Huzhou landlord in the early seventeenth century, instructed his family to deal generously with their tenants: "It is best to treat tenant farmers leniently. I have seen the landlords in the upper part of the county call their tenant farmers 'rent relatives' (zuqin). It is because landlords and tenant farmers are interdependent in their labor. Essentially, there is no distinction of superior and inferior between them. If we treat them with propriety, they will not have the heart to cheat us. When

---

[44] *Quanzhou fuzhi*, 20.13b; citation and translation from Wiens, "Lord and Peasant," pp. 12–13.

[45] Wiens, "Lord and Peasant," p. 13.

[46] Xu Jie, *Shijing tangji*, 22.21a–22b; citation from Dennerline, *The Chia-ting Loyalists*, pp. 82–83.

it happens that one or two of our tenants are obstinate, we should simply replace them gradually. Aren't they all our companions here in the countryside? How can we bear to have them hate us on account of a bit of rice?"[47] Complaints from less flexible landlords about the untrustworthiness, laziness, and outright wickedness of bondservants, tenants, and hired wage laborers in the late sixteenth and seventeenth centuries reflect elite uneasiness about the new and growing economic power and independence of these groups, and about their refusal to accept the terms of the old superior-inferior relationship, based on a Confucian ideal of reciprocity within a familial hierarchy.[48]

In short, men at the top of the traditional social hierarchy—officials, large gentry landlords, and literati—were certainly aware that they were facing increased competition from merchants, peasants, and even bondservants for the prizes of wealth and status. They were aware, too, that the rules of their game had changed: the standards regulating status relationships were no longer effective in the more fluid social and economic context of the sixteenth and seventeenth centuries. In particular, relations between landowners and their agricultural workers, previously dictated by a paternalistic code emphasizing the subordination of the worker to a landlord or master who directed his labor and (in theory at least) also cared for him and his family, came in the course of the seventeenth century to be regulated more and more by contract, a mode that gave the laborer new advantages vis-à-vis the landowner.[49]

INTELLECTUAL LIFE: CHALLENGES TO NEO-CONFUCIAN ORTHODOXY

At the same time that the economic and social changes of the late Ming were undermining elite claims to social dominance, certain literati were questioning some of the philosophical assumptions, derived from the orthodox Neo-Confucianism of the Cheng-Zhu school,[50] that had long

---

[47] *Nanxun zhi*, 53.4a–b; cited in Shih, "Peasant Economy," p. 168.

[48] Hosono, "Minmatsu Shinsho Kōnan," pp. 11–32.

[49] Wiens, "Socioeconomic Change," pp. 235–236.

[50] I am using the terms "orthodox Neo-Confucianism" and "Neo-Confucian orthodoxy" here to cover two different, but overlapping, meanings. First, they may refer to the philosophy of Cheng Yi (1033–1108) and Zhu Xi (1130–1200)—the Cheng-Zhu school—as it had come to be interpreted by scholars in the Ming. Second, they may also refer to Cheng-Zhu school thought as it had been institutionalized in the civil service examination system. Neither meaning should be identified precisely with the ideas of Cheng Yi and Zhu Xi as they were expressed during the Song. The first meaning emphasizes the general scholarly consensus in the Ming on what Cheng-Zhu Neo-Confucianism signified; the second, the interpretation of the school sanctioned and supported by the state. Clearly, each interpretation changed somewhat over time; just as clearly, each influenced the other. It should be obvious from context which meaning is being emphasized here.

been cherished as the intellectual foundations of elite authority. In fact, the challenge to this orthodoxy (based on the teachings of the great Song thinkers Cheng Yi and Zhu Xi) was issued well before the effects of the economic and social changes mentioned above had been felt. Wang Yangming (1472–1529), as early as the late fifteenth century, was already expressing doubts about the validity of the orthodox mode of self-cultivation as a means of training a moral elite. Certain of Wang Yangming's immediate followers, active in the early sixteenth century, made more direct attacks on elite claims to moral and intellectual superiority. Wang Gen (1483–1541), for example, vigorously asserted the equal access of ignorant commoners to moral perfection. The real social changes of the mid- and late-sixteenth century served to undermine faith in the commonly drawn correlation, so flattering to the scholar-official elite, between moral worth and social place. With mercantile wealth frequently honored now over scholarly attainments, and with greater tenant and bondservant demands for economic independence and higher social status, thoughtful men had even greater reason to reexamine this principle, particularly as it was expressed through the civil service examination system, the primary channel to high status. They began to wonder: did the scholastic education in the Classics institutionalized in the examination system necessarily produce good men and worthy officials? Indeed, was official service even to be considered the necessary goal of the good man?

But no new late-Ming consensus was ever reached on these points; perhaps the most striking general fact about the intellectual life of the period was its diversity and contentiousness. Stimulated to some degree by the freer economic environment, late-Ming literati, particularly those from the Jiangnan area, seem to have felt a greater intellectual independence from the state-sponsored orthodoxy; this independence was no doubt further encouraged by the widespread awareness of political corruption.

It was Wang Yangming, the most renowned Neo-Confucian thinker of the Ming, who set forth the principles that provided the philosophical justification for this assertion of independence. By the early sixteenth century Wang had already challenged the method of self-cultivation upheld in the orthodox mode of education—that is, the education designed to ensure success in the civil service examinations, based on a rigid version of Zhu Xi's Neo-Confucian curriculum. Wang's greatest contribution was to identify a new source for moral knowledge. Orthodox Neo-Confucianism dictated that goodness was to be found through an exhaustive search for principle (*li*) in the outside world and in the texts of the Classics. Questioning the efficiency of this method, Wang claimed that principle was best sought in the self, in the inborn knowledge of the good (*liangzhi*) in every man's mind. While not by any means rejecting the va-

lidity of external rules and standards, he simply insisted that these rules
and standards could be properly and sincerely fulfilled only as products
of the individual's own innate knowledge of the good.[51]

Wang's stand undermined some of the basic assumptions of the orthodox approach to study and self-cultivation. For a follower of Wang
Yangming, the Classics could no longer be accepted necessarily as the
final authorities on the Way; rather, these previously sacred texts had to
be measured against the dictates of the individual's innate knowledge of
what was good: "If words are examined in the mind and found to be
wrong, although they have come from the mouth of Confucius, I dare not
accept them as correct."[52] It was not so much the Classics themselves that
Wang called into question here, but the whole tradition of study, sanctioned by the state, that had shaped elite moral and professional concerns
since the Yuan. Implicit, too, in his concept of *liangzhi* was the idea that
anyone—not just the learned scholar—could with the proper discipline
perfect himself, to become a sage. If intensive study of a limited body of
relatively inaccessible texts was no longer a prerequisite for moral perfection, what was to prevent the petty shopkeeper in the city or the bondservant in the countryside from realizing the pure goodness within himself
and achieving the status of sage or official?[53]

It was Wang Yangming's followers who drew out these and other more
"dangerous" elements in his thinking. Wang Ji (1498–1583), developing
one of Wang Yangming's more ambiguous statements—that "there is neither good nor evil in the substance of the mind"—concluded that rules of
good and bad conduct were artificial, not standards that emerged naturally from the mind. Hence, he decided, the student should never force
himself to follow such rules in the process of self-cultivation. To be truly
good, he should simply act directly and naturally, without reflection and
without any intentions to be good, on the inner promptings of his mind.[54]
A later critic summarized Wang Ji's argument in some disgust: "Those
who could believe in *liangzhi* could come and go by themselves, as the
bead travels across the abacus, without need of any control, keeping naturally from waywardness. Thus earnest fidelity and cautious behavior, as
well as all action that flows from the concern for reputation, are to be
considered artificial behavior."[55] Wang Ji's repudiation of moral reason-

---

[51] For a summary of Wang Yangming's thought, see Wei-ming Tu, *Neo-Confucian
Thought in Action: Wang Yang-ming's Youth (1472–1509)* and William Theodore de Bary,
"Individualism and Humanitarianism in Late Ming Thought," pp. 150–157.

[52] Wang Yangming, *Instructions for Practical Living and Other Neo-Confucian Writings
by Wang Yang-ming*, p. 159.

[53] Wang Yangming, *Instructions for Practical Living*, pp. 225–226, 239–240.

[54] Takehiko Okada, "Wang Chi and the Rise of Existentialism," pp. 126–127.

[55] Huang Tsung-hsi, *The Record of Ming Scholars*, p. 116.

ing or self-conscious moral intention was championed by members of the Taizhou school, comprising the most "radical" of Wang Yangming's disciples. Man, they argued, would act perfectly only if intentions to do good or avoid evil did not interfere with the operation of his innate knowlege of the good; he had to "live in the present" (*dangxia*), responding spontaneously to every changing situation.[56]

Wang Gen, the founder of the Taizhou school, chose to emphasize the suggestion in Wang Yangming's philosophy that anyone, not just the man with access to classical learning, could become a sage. A commoner himself, he claimed that the Way was best discovered not in abstruse texts, but in the everyday actions and feelings of "ignorant men and women" (*yufu yufu*).[57] Wang Gen devoted his life to this proposition, traveling about the countryside lecturing to audiences drawn from all the social levels of each community, struggling always to make the Way relevant to the needs of daily life.[58]

The Taizhou school attempted then to expand the audience for the teaching of the Way beyond the rather limited boundaries implicitly imposed in the state-sponsored orthodoxy. Scholars had access to moral cultivation (of a sort) through examination preparation and official service; the Taizhou thinkers hoped to offer entry into the Way to the vast number of people in effect excluded from this system. At the same time they tried to extend the doctrinal inclusivity of the Way, drawing freely on Buddhist and Taoist ideas and texts to support their definitions of the path to moral perfection. Indeed, the concept of spontaneous action espoused by Wang Ji and members of the Taizhou school, whatever its real intellectual source, closely resembled the Chan doctrine of acting "without a purposeful mind" (*wuxin*) and was frequently identified with this "heterodox" doctrine (see chapter 2). In fact, Chan was a major influence on the Taizhou school throughout its history: Zhou Rudeng (1547–1629?), the last great exponent of the school, even asserted the fundamental identity of Confucian and Chan doctrines in his *Orthodox Transmission of the Sages' Learning* (*Shengxue zongzhuan*).[59]

The thinkers of the Taizhou school, as well as many other followers of Wang Yangming, also questioned the traditional definition of the scholar's role in society. Wang Yangming had eventually accepted the conventional scholar's career, had performed brilliantly in the examinations, and served energetically in a variety of official posts. But his students, in many cases put off by the corruption of the bureaucracy and by the severe lim-

[56] Heinrich Busch, "The Tung-lin Academy and Its Political and Philosophical Significance," p. 79.
[57] de Bary, "Individualism and Humanitarianism," p. 168.
[58] Hou Wailu et al., *Zhongguo sixiang tongshi*, vol. 4, part 2, pp. 958–995.
[59] Busch, "The Tung-lin Academy," p. 85.

itations on what could be accomplished in office, turned to other, often somewhat unconventional forms of public service. Wang Gen, as we have seen, devoted himself to popular education. He Xinyin, despite a promising start up the examination ladder, abandoned pursuit of an official career and took up reform of his lineage as a vocation.[60] Yet others were attracted to the career of "knight-errant" (*youxia*) and dedicated themselves to the righting of individual instances of injustice or suffering.[61] Wang Yangming's doctrine of the unity of knowledge and action took on new meaning here: with the new personal and subjective interpretation of knowledge as the individual's *liangzhi*, there inevitably came new and varying interpretations of what appropriate action was.

These men garnered a great deal of attention in their own day largely because of their radical alienation from conventional forms of literati service and from the intellectual requirements of Neo-Confucian orthodoxy. But, though they may have dominated the intellectual debates of the period, they should by no means be taken as representative of late-Ming literati thinking or gentry life. Many members of the gentry resented the "licentious" and relatively free-wheeling lives of some Taizhou associates: witness Li Zhi's (1527–1602) persecution by Macheng gentry alarmed not so much by his philosophical works as by his practice of taking on female students.[62] Yet other literati, probably the majority, were absorbed in personal career concerns, in the struggle to "climb the ladder of the bureaucratic hierarchy and amass wealth," and hence were either ignorant of or indifferent to the issues raised by the Taizhou school.[63]

There were also men who objected quite seriously to the philosophical premises of the school, especially to the alarming principle put forth by Zhou Rudeng that good and evil were absent from human nature as well as from the mind. The Donglin Academy, founded in 1604 by Gu Xiancheng (1550–1612) came, more than any other group, to stand for resistance to the "wild" teachings of the Taizhou school. While the Donglin Academy included a range of thinkers united more by their opposition to imperial autocracy than by a common philosophy, there was intellectual unity within the ranks at least in opposition to the "neither good nor evil" (*wushan wu'e*) doctrine of the Taizhou school.[64] Donglin thinkers feared the loss of moral consensus and political unity that would result if all

[60] Ronald Dimberg, *The Sage and Society: The Life and Thought of Ho Hsin-yin*, pp. 40, 43–47. See also Willard Peterson, *Bitter Gourd*, p. 87.

[61] Peterson, *Bitter Gourd*, pp. 84–94; Dimberg, *The Sage and Society*, pp. 41–42.

[62] Ray Huang, *1587: A Year of No Significance*, pp. 217–221.

[63] Mori, "The Gentry in the Ming," p. 49.

[64] Mizoguchi Yūzō, "Iwayuru Tōrinha jinshi no shisō—zenkindaiki ni okeru Chūgoku shisō no tenkai," pp. 123–126.

literati began to act in the faith that good and evil were open to individual, subjective interpretation. Gao Panlong (1562–1626), Gu's younger associate, attacked the "easy" Taizhou mode of self-cultivation that advocated "living in the present." To achieve enlightenment, he argued, man had to follow an arduous course of study and self-examination involving the investigation of things (*gewu*), the cultivation of perfect mental attentiveness (*jing*), and quiet-sitting (*jingzuo*).[65] The goal of enlightenment was a recognition of the great unity (*datong*) of men and all things, the recognition that all things shared the same substance or cosmic matter (*qi*; also "pneuma"). *Qi* was formed into different things, each with its own *li*, its own law or principle. It was these *li* that constituted the first objects of study; the scholar had to understand them (through the investigation of things, the practice of inner mental attentiveness, and quiet-sitting) before he could comprehend the great unity.[66]

Donglin thinkers were very much caught between the Cheng-Zhu orthodox tradition and the form of Neo-Confucianism developed by Wang Yangming. They were attracted to the relatively vigorous moral training prescribed by the Cheng-Zhu school: the investigation of things was in fact the hallmark of the orthodox mode of self-cultivation.[67] The rules of the Donglin Academy reflected this more traditional view of moral cultivation, for they encouraged the practice of the classic Confucian virtues backed by the authority of the Classics.[68] But the Donglin thinkers departed quite significantly from Zhu Xi's dualistic metaphysics in their understanding of *li* and *qi*. Like most followers of the Wang school, they believed in the monism of *qi* and subordinated *li* (which for Zhu had been the one transcendent moral "Principle" of all things), defining it as the multiple laws that governed the distinctions among all things. As a consequence of this change, human desires, as products of *qi*, could be seen, not as dangerous and precarious forces that might, if indulged, easily lead to evil (as the orthodox interpretation would have it), but as potentially positive feelings, forces that, with proper guidance, might encourage a man to virtuous action. These philosophical changes led them also to a concern, somewhat like that of the Taizhou school, for comprehending and meeting the everyday desires and economic needs of the common people, whose concerns were, the Donglin thinkers argued, almost completely neglected by the late-Ming government.[69]

[65] Busch, "The Tung-lin Academy," pp. 122–129.

[66] For a fuller treatment of the philosophy of the Donglin group, see Mizoguchi, "Iwayuru Tōrinha jinshi," pp. 231–245.

[67] Mizoguchi explains the ambivalent attitudes held by Donglin thinkers to Zhu Xi and Wang Yangming in ibid., pp. 235–245.

[68] Busch, "The Tung-lin Academy," p. 87.

[69] Mizoguchi, "Iwayuru Tōrinha jinshi," pp. 244, passim. See also Peterson, *Bitter Gourd*, pp. 72–73.

The Donglin partisans resembled the Taizhou school in one other respect as well: their willingness to criticize contemporary society and government. In fact, they shared the Taizhou thinkers' profound suspicions of the growing autocracy of the central government, first opposing the efforts of Zhang Juzheng (1525–1582) to strengthen central control over the economy and local society, and then increasingly, toward the end of the sixteenth and through the early seventeenth centuries, protesting the growing influence of eunuchs in government and their abuse of imperial power. Alarmed at the corruption, inefficiency, and arbitrariness of a government led, since the late sixteenth century, by indifferent and/or incompetent rulers, careerist bureaucrats, and eunuch factions, Donglin affiliates were concerned with the very Confucian task of ensuring that good men—that is, their associates and supporters—were in office. Indeed, the eventual success of the Donglin Academy in this task after the fall of the eunuch Wei Zhongxian encouraged the formation of a variety of other societies designed more narrowly to ensure examination success and bureaucratic recruitment for their members. The most famous of these, the Restoration Society or Fu She, succeeded in dominating the networks of bureaucratic recruitment through most of the last decades of the Ming.[70]

But Donglin partisans were not all devoted exclusively to stuffing the ranks of the bureaucracy with "their" men. The leading thinkers of the group were committed to a distinct vision of how society ought to be ruled. Fearful of the growing arbitrariness and absolutism of the imperial government and the greater oppression and exploitation practiced by the large gentry landlords who supported the government, these men argued for a more decentralized distribution of political authority, for a government based on a form of "public consensus" (gonglun). They believed that political power should be shared with local elites—middle and lower-level landlords, literati, and merchants—who were better able than the far-distant emperor or absentee landlords, it was argued, to understand the real material needs and "hidden feelings" of the people.[71]

Many Donglin affiliates acted on these convictions in their own communities, establishing community compacts (xiangyue) for the moral instruction and political regulation of the people, or benevolent societies (tongshan hui) for the provision of aid to the local poor. Both Gao Panlong and Chen Longzheng (1585–1645), a Donglin supporter, were lead-

[70] On the conflict between the political and reformist goals of the Donglin Academy, see Frederic Wakeman, Jr., "The Price of Autonomy: Intellectuals in Ming and Ch'ing Politics." On the Fu She, see William Atwell, "From Education to Politics: The Fu She;" and Inoue Susumu, "Fukusha no gaku." On the differences between the Donglin Academy and the Fu She, see Dennerline, The Chia-ting Loyalists, pp. 23–39, 158–171.

[71] Mizoguchi, "Iwayuru Tōrinha jinshi," p. 203.

ers of just such philanthropic associations.[72] Others led community efforts at land reclamation, flood control, famine relief, or public works construction.[73] Donglin partisans were also the primary supporters of the "equal field, equal service" (*juntian junyi*) reform, which benefited peasants and small or middle-ranking landlords by limiting gentry tax exemptions and allocating corvée service according to amount of land owned.[74] In support of some of the new commercial interests of the late Ming, they also opposed the harsh taxes imposed on mining by the eunuch agents of the Wanli emperor.[75]

In late-Ming society, the Donglin supporters conceived of their task as an all-embracing one, and their practical, "statecraft" (*jingshi zhiyong*) interests touched on almost all levels of the social, political, and economic order, extending from the central government down to village society. Unlike many of the Taizhou school thinkers, the Donglin affiliates seemed, however, to accept more or less conventional methods of political reform. They certainly did not question the validity of traditional social forms, the fundamental structure of the government, or the content of Confucian morality. Their enemies were those who threatened these traditional structures and values, be it corrupt and incompetent powerholders like Wei Zhongxian or Wen Tiren (d. 1638) or the wild and irresponsible scholars of the Taizhou persuasion. The former disrupted political order by selfishly refusing to share power; the latter overturned moral order by denying the authority of fixed standards of right and wrong.

With the change of dynasty, the more conservative philosophical and ethical stance associated previously with the Donglin Academy gained clear ascendancy in the intellectual world. Though there was a movement to reconcile the philosophies of Wang Yangming and Zhu Xi, the Wang Yangming school, particularly the Taizhou branch of it, was fairly thoroughly discredited with the fall of the Ming. The "empty theorizing" and consequent neglect of political service associated with the Taizhou thinkers were cited by leading intellectuals as a cause of Ming dynastic decline.[76] The Cheng-Zhu school slowly regained its earlier popularity. Zhang Lixiang, for example, a much stauncher supporter of Zhu Xi than any of the earlier Donglin partisans, emphasized study of the Classics as

[72] Fuma Susumu, "Dōzenkai shōshi: Chūgoku shakai fukushi shijō ni okeru Minmatsu Shinsho no ichizuke no tame ni," pp. 37–76; and Joanna Handlin, "Benevolent Societies: The Reshaping of Charity During the Late Ming and Early Ch'ing," p. 311.

[73] Mori, "The Gentry in the Ming," pp. 47–51.

[74] Hamashima Atsutoshi, *Mindai Kōnan nōson shakai no kenkyū*, pp. 449–501; Mizoguchi, "Iwayuru Tōrinha jinshi," pp. 207–209.

[75] Mizoguchi, "Iwayuru Tōrinha jinshi," pp. 131–135; and Ray Huang, "The Lung-ch'i and Wan-li Reigns, 1567–1620," pp. 530–531.

[76] Benjamin Elman, *From Philosophy to Philology: Intellectual and Social Aspects of Change in Late Imperial China*, pp. 50–53.

the primary means of "probing principle" (*qiongli*). To return order to a society disrupted by the license of the Taizhou thinkers, he urged the practice of constant reverence and strict adherence to the rules of propriety.[77] Lu Shiyi (1611–1672), another Cheng-Zhu follower, stressed the importance of practical action and urged scholars to apply the fruits of their study in local educational and charitable activities as well as in government service.[78] Now, indeed, statecraft issues and practical studies became the primary focus of the intellectual leaders of the day, particularly those alienated from the Manchu government. While Ming loyalists like Gu Yanwu and Huang Zongxi (1610–1695) were developing programs for the sweeping reform of political and social institutions, other scholars, many of them officials, continued the interests of earlier statecraft adherents and turned their attention to the restoration of local order—the development of the public lecture system, the creation of local schools, and so forth.[79] Thus the early Qing intellectual climate was shaped both by a reaction against the more radical and independent elements of late-Ming thought and the urge to continue the practical moral and statecraft interests of Donglin affiliates and other like-minded scholars.

THE LEDGERS OF MERIT AND DEMERIT

It was in the context of these intense economic, social, political, and intellectual changes that the ledgers of merit and demerit achieved a new, and at first glance somewhat surprising, popularity. As moral diaries that encouraged a rather mechanical view of moral cultivation, the ledgers seemed texts unlikely to attract the serious attention of Chinese literati. And yet in the late Ming they did capture elite interest. Sponsored by some scholar-officials and vilified by others, the ledgers provided a forum for debate over issues crucial to thinkers of the time—the connection between virtue and social status, the proper approach to self-cultivation, and the relationship between men and their fate, to name just the most significant.

The ledgers of merit and demerit underwent a long and complex development before achieving the height of their popularity in the late imperial period. Though the belief in retribution that underlies the ledgers has a very long history in China, extending back to the earliest of the Confucian Classics, a program of merit accumulation did not really begin to develop until around the fourth century A.D. Over the next several centuries, a series of Daoist scriptures and apocryphal Buddhist sutras elaborated the system as a means of attaining immortality or salvation. The most famous

[77] Okada Takehiko, "Chō Yōen to Roku Futei," pp. 1–12.
[78] Ibid., pp. 15–26.
[79] Elman, *From Philosophy to Philology*, pp. 53–55.

and most popular statement of the system, the *Tract of Taishang on Action and Response* (*Taishang ganying pian*), published in the late twelfth century, provided a neat outline of the operation of supernatural retribution. Shortly thereafter, the first extant ledger of merit and demerit was produced: the *Ledger of Merit and Demerit of the Taiwei Immortal* (*Taiwei xianjun gongguoge*) was the first text to assign point values to the good and bad deeds it listed, to suggest, in effect, that man could keep score of his merit points. A handbook of one of the new Daoist sects of the Song (960–1279), the *Ledger* was designed to aid sect members in their quest for immortality and, perhaps more important, to provide them with standards of behavior amid the military upheavals, social disorder, and political chaos resulting from the Jin invasion.

Although the system of merit accumulation, particularly as explained in the *Tract on Action and Response*, received considerable official and imperial attention in the Song and Yuan (1279–1368), it was not really until the sixteenth century that the ledgers of merit and demerit themselves achieved a wide vogue. Then, largely through the efforts of a scholar-official from Zhejiang named Yuan Huang (1533–1606), they gained a popularity among literati that was to last at least through the early twentieth century. Yuan attributed his own successes in life to the accumulation of merit points; in fact, his record of his experience of ledger use played a major role in spreading knowledge of the system to the educated elite in the late sixteenth and seventeenth centuries. Through the seventeenth century a series of new and ever more complex ledgers was produced, attesting to the demand for the texts. These ledgers continued to be republished through the eighteenth and nineteenth centuries (and indeed to this century), though the number of original works declined in the eighteenth century.

This study is an effort to explain the widespread popularity of the ledgers during the Ming-Qing transition period. To what extent do the ledgers reflect elite responses to the socioeconomic changes taking place, particularly in the southeast? Do their prescriptions reveal any shifts in attitudes toward commercialization and the merchant class? What needs did the ledgers, with their focus on earning worldly status rewards, fill in the highly competitive society of the late Ming? In the more ordered and controlled society of the early Qing? What sort of social ideology do the texts express—that is, how do they explain the status hierarchy and define relationships between statuses? Do they make provisions for contemporary changes in the hierarchy? Do they include, for example, prescriptions that recognize the growing social and economic independence of the peasantry? The tenant and bondservant rebellions of the seventeenth century in particular presented a strong challenge to the status system—do the ledgers acknowledge these challenges, and if so, what do they make of them? Do they reflect a willingness to accommodate social change, or a desire to contain and repress it?

The ledgers assume a distinctive understanding of the operation of retribution, one based on a faith in a host of overseer gods and spirits and commonly associated with "heterodox" Buddhist and Daoist doctrines, or, even worse, with popular "superstitions." How did the elite justify their interest in the ledgers of merit and demerit? How did Yuan Huang, the first major literatus advocate of the ledgers in the Ming, himself come to believe in such texts, and how did he explain or justify his belief? Did literati, in adopting beliefs and texts from heterodox and popular traditions, alter them to suit their own purposes, and if so, how? How did ledger-users and authors after Yuan Huang, particularly those of the scholar-official elite, come to accept the ledgers? How did they justify their reliance on such sources? In short, what does the popularity of the ledgers in the late Ming suggest about the distinction frequently made in contemporary scholarship between popular and elite cultures in late imperial China?

Finally, I want to examine the implications ledger use had for the Neo-Confucian process of self-cultivation. What was the scholarly reaction to the conventional prescriptive morality of the ledgers? The texts became popular at a time when many of Wang Yangming's followers were questioning traditional assumptions about the definition of moral action—did their ideas affect the ways in which the ledgers were used? How did the more cautious and conservative Donglin thinkers react to the texts, particularly to their claims for human autonomy and self-control? How is the system of divine retributive justice that is presented in the ledgers reconciled with Neo-Confucian cosmological views? Can the texts be associated with any one school of Neo-Confucian thought? And (returning to the first set of questions) what are the connections between the Neo-Confucian philosophical assumptions of the ledgers and the social ideology the ledgers express?

In sum, in tracing the history of the ledgers of merit and demerit in the sixteenth and seventeenth centuries, I hope both to illuminate major shifts in the late-Ming and early-Qing intellectual climate and to examine the relationship between Neo-Confucian ideology and social change.

CHAPTER ONE

Merit Accumulation in the Early Chinese Tradition

AT THE RELIGIOUS and philosophical heart of the system of merit and demerit lay the belief in a supernatural or cosmic retribution, a belief that has been a fundamental, at times *the* fundamental, belief of Chinese religion since the beginning of recorded history. In the simplest terms, the belief in retribution is the faith that some force—either a supernatural force like heaven or the gods, or an automatic cosmic reaction—inevitably recompensed human behavior in a rational manner: it rewarded certain "good" deeds, be they religious sacrifices, acts of good government, or upright personal conduct, and punished evil ones.

Oracle bones testify that as early as the Shang (1766–1025 B.C.?) men believed in a system of recompense between the king and the gods, including both the ancestors of the ruling lineage and Di, the highest god. In return for the appropriate prayers and sacrifices, these beings were expected to provide anything from the cure of a royal toothache to victory in battle.[1] The Zhou (1025?–256 B.C.) conquerors of the eleventh century also held this faith in the reciprocity between the ruler and the supernatural powers but gave it a moral dimension not present in the Shang: heaven, the new god, bestowed the mandate to rule (*tianming*) on the man who had proven himself capable of ruling virtuously, and he and his descendants held their mandate only as long as they continued to rule virtuously. The king and his ministers were thus squarely responsible for their own political fate: as King Mu of Zhou warned his officials, "You should ever stand in awe of the punishments of heaven. It is not that heaven does not deal impartially with men, but that men ruin themselves."[2]

This view of fate as moral retribution dominates the earliest Zhou texts, including those later incorporated into the Confucian canon. The

[1] David N. Keightley, *Sources of Shang History: The Oracle-Bone Inscriptions of Bronze Age China*, pp. 33–35, 85–87.

[2] James Legge, trans., *The Chinese Classics*, vol. 3, p. 610. This belief in supernatural retribution was mirrored in the human realm in the value of reciprocity or recompense (*bao*) between men. The *Record of Rites* explains this social value as follows: "In the highest antiquity [people] prized [simply conferring] good; in the time next to this, giving and repaying was the thing attended to. And what the rules of propriety value is that reciprocity. If I give a gift and nothing comes in return, that is contrary to propriety; if the thing comes to me, and I give nothing in return, that also is contrary to propriety." See Lien-sheng Yang, "The Concept of *Pao* as a Basis for Social Relationships in China," pp. 291–309.

Classic of History warns, "On the doer of good, heaven sends down all blessings, and on the doer of evil, he sends down all calamities."[3] A constant refrain of the dynastic poems in the *Classic of Songs* is the ruler's need to live up to heaven's moral expectations: "The charge is not easy to keep. / Do not bring ruin on yourselves. / Send forth everywhere the light of your good fame; / Consider what Heaven did to the Yin."[4] The *Conversations from the States (Guoyu)* predicts that a "licentious, lazy, rude, and careless" ruler will suffer the vengeance of supernatural beings: "spirits . . . go to watch his dissoluteness and send down calamity."[5] The Zuo commentary on the *Spring and Autumn Annals* is full of cautionary tales of kings defeated ultimately not by a human enemy, but by their own misdeeds.[6] All these texts assume the existence of a heaven or a group of spirits fully conscious of human actions and vigorously active in their punishment or reward. This is fate acting truly as heaven's command.

Later, Han (202 B.C.–A.D. 220) writers, while still holding to the basic concept of retribution, developed a somewhat different cosmological foundation for the belief. Retribution was not necessarily dependent on a morally conscious and actively judgmental heaven or group of spirits. Rather, the cosmos responded automatically and naturalistically to human actions through the movements of *qi*, the "subtle and pervasive pneuma" that constituted all things.[7] A human deed, as a movement of *qi*, influenced or acted on (*gan*) the *qi* of the cosmos around it, evoking a response (*ying*) exactly appropriate to its own quality and magnitude. *Ganying*, "action and response," later one of the key terms of the system of merit and demerit, referred in the Han to retribution as a cosmological process operating through the intricate system of correspondences that existed between the human and the suprahuman realms.[8] Applied to the

---

[3] Legge, *The Chinese Classics*, vol. 3, p. 198. I have changed the translation slightly. The *Classic of History* is also the source of what is later a key phrase of the system of merit accumulation: *yinzhi*. In its original context, this term refers to the "hidden springs of character" that heaven endows in each man (see ibid., pp. 320, 322); it is later used to mean the secret virtue that a man accumulates in order to improve his fate.

On the concept of *ming* in early China, see T'ang Chün-i, "The T'ien-ming [Heavenly Ordinance] in Pre-Ch'in China," part 1, pp. 195–208; and 2, pp. 29–49.

[4] Arthur Waley, trans., *The Book of Songs*, p. 251 (no. 241).

[5] *Guo yu, Zhou yu*, 1.11b–12a. Reference and translation from Fung Yu-lan, *A History of Chinese Philosophy*, vol. 1, pp. 24–25.

[6] See, for example, Legge, *The Chinese Classics*, vol. 5, p. 540. See other references in Uchiyama Toshihiko, "Kandai no ōhō shisō," pp. 17–20.

[7] John Henderson, *The Development and Decline of Chinese Cosmology*, pp. 26–27.

[8] To my knowledge, the term *ganying* is first used in the commentary on the *xian* hexagram (the "symbol of exerting influence") in the *Classic of Changes*: "*Xian* is here used in the sense of *gan*, meaning mutually influencing. The weak trigram above, and the strong one below; their two influences moving and responding to each other, and thereby forming a union; the repression of the one and the satisfaction of the other; with their relative posi-

political sphere, this doctrine meant that natural disasters or natural benefits were interpreted as cosmic "responses" to specific "actions" or policies of the emperor. Gale-force winds in the summer could be taken as a sign that the ruler or his ministers had violated the rules of propriety; floods in the spring and summer, as a warning about the ruler's failure to listen to his ministers.[9]

Nor was the belief in retribution limited solely to Confucian political theorists. Han seekers of immortality believed that the performance of good deeds was one means of attaining their goal. Adherents of the Huang-Lao cult of immortality in the Eastern Han (25–220), for example, practiced a variety of charitable acts—the feeding of orphans, the repair of roads and bridges, and so forth—in their quest for eternal life.[10] Zhe Xiang, a master of magical arts in the Eastern Han, distributed his family fortune to others, in order to ward off misfortune. "My family has prospered for a long time, and Daoists (Daojia) detest the crime of prosperity," he explained. "In this generation my family will decline, because my sons are not talented. It is said that it is unlucky to lack virtue and have wealth—when a wall is cracked yet tall, its fall will be sudden."[11] Both the followers of the Way of Great Peace (Taiping Dao) and the Way of the Five Pecks of Rice (Wudoumi Dao) believed that illness was a punishment inflicted by demons on wrongdoers; they would be cured only after confessing their misdeeds.[12]

A belief in some form of cosmic retribution was thus at the heart of the earliest indigenous Chinese religious and political visions. This belief was given even greater currency with the introduction of Buddhism to China during the Han. Buddhist doctrine asserted that all the events of a man's

---

tion, where the male is placed below the female—all these things convey the notion of 'a free and successful course' on the fulfillment of the conditions. The advantage will depend on being firm and correct, as in marrying a young lady; then there will be good fortune.

Heaven and earth exert their influences, and there ensue the transformation and production of all things. The sages influence the minds of men, and the result is harmony and peace all under the sky. If we look at the method and issue of those influences, the true character of heaven and earth and of all things can be seen."

Here the mutual influence or "action and response" between weak and strong and female and male is to produce a kind of harmony in courtship; so too the action of heaven and earth produces all things and evokes the response of "harmony and peace all under the sky." See *Zhouyi yinde*, p. 20; translation (with minor changes) from Z. D. Sung, *The Text of the Yi King*, pp. 135–136. See also the explanation in Henderson, *Chinese Cosmology*, pp. 20, 22–28.

[9] These particular examples are from Dong Zhongshu, *Chunqiu fanlu*, 14.64.2a; cited in Joseph Needham, *Science and Civilization in China*, vol. 2, p. 379.

[10] Ying-shih Yü, "Life and Immortality in the Mind of Han China," pp. 103–108.

[11] *Hou Han shu*, vol. 13, j. 82A, pp. 2720–2721. Reference from Henri Maspero, *Taoism and Chinese Religion*, p. 323.

[12] Kubo Noritada, *Dōkyō shi*, pp. 123–124; see *Hou Han shu*, vol. 12, j. 75, p. 2436.

life (as well as of the world at large) were subject to the law of cause and effect (*yinguo* or *ganying*): each event grew out of a specific cause as naturally and inevitably as a particular plant grew from a particular seed. The response or effect was inherent, in embryo form, in the action or cause; no outside agent, no morally sensitive heaven, no movement of pneumas needed intervene in the process. A good action would inevitably produce a good effect, a bad action a bad effect. This relationship extended through the whole series of rebirths a man or creature might experience. Thus an individual's karma—that is, his deeds and intentions—in one life would naturally, through the process of cause and effect (*yinyuan*), determine his status in his next life.[13] While the operation of Buddhist retribution was quite different from that of the action-and-response process or the mandate of heaven, the final message of these concepts was essentially the same: good begets good, evil begets evil.

By the early medieval period, then, the major Chinese schools of belief—Confucianism, the immortality cult, and Buddhism—all shared, whatever their other philosophical or ethical differences, a basic faith in some form of cosmic retribution. Later sixteenth-century authors of the ledgers of merit and demerit were quick to make use of this fact to assert wide-ranging support for their texts; in particular they liked to claim sanction for the belief in the Confucian Classics, notably the *Classic of History*, the *Classic of Songs*, the *Classic of Changes*, and the *Spring and Autumn Annals*. Although there is considerable justice in these claims, the ledgers of merit and demerit in fact assumed a process of retribution quite different in its complexity and religious implications from that found in early Confucianism, or for that matter, in the immortality cult or Buddhism. The ledgers, unlike the texts cited above, set forth an elaborate, rational, and comprehensive method—the method of merit accumulation—for the human manipulation of the process.

Hints that storing up merit might bring long life and good fortune can be found in texts dating from as early as the Han,[14] but there is no evidence for the existence of a numerical method or organized "system" of merit accumulation until the fourth century A.D. Such a system appears, albeit in a rudimentary form, in the *Master Who Embraces Simplicity*

[13] For a fuller treatment of the Buddhist understanding of cause and effect, see Nakamura Hajime, "Inga," pp. 3–53. Nakamura acknowledges (p. 24) that the moral interpretation of causation is the most common: "In everyday conversation, when *inga* is mentioned, most people generally think of *inga hō-ō* (retribution)." For a discussion of the Chinese transformation of the Buddhist concept of retribution, see Paul Varo Martinson, "Pao Order and Redemption: Perspective on Chinese Religion and Society Based on a Study of the Chin P'ing Mei," pp. 121–135.

[14] See, for example, *Han shu*, vol. 7, j. 71, p. 3046, and vol. 8, j. 100A, p. 4208; and Ch'ü T'ung-tsu, *Law and Society in Traditional China*, p. 217.

(*Baopuzi*) of Ge Hong (c. 283–343), where it is simply one of many different techniques designed to aid in the attainment of immortality; 300 merits will make one a "terrestrial" or earthbound immortal; 1,200, a "celestial" immortal, one capable of ascending to heaven. An advocate of "nourishment of life" (*yangsheng*) and himself an aspirant to immortality, Ge also describes a bureaucracy of spirits and astral deities who watched over the human practice of merit accumulation.[15] Thereafter the system of merit accumulation took on a wide variety of forms in the scriptures of certain Daoist and Buddhist sects of the fourth through the sixteenth centuries. Different texts addressed different pantheons of spirits, claimed different purposes for merit accumulation, or developed different standards of reward and punishment. The sects that produced these texts freely borrowed both concepts and gods from one another; Daoist scriptures warned against the consequences of evil karma, and Buddhist sutras included prayers to Daoist spirits.[16] It is thus virtually impossible to associate either the concept or the system of merit accumulation exclusively with any one school or sect; both seem to have entered the generally shared vocabulary of medieval religious thought.

The Basic Principles of Merit Accumulation

The great range in the early versions of the system of merit accumulation notwithstanding, it is possible to detect certain underlying principles generally accepted by almost all, if not all, the advocates of the system.[17]

[15] Wang Ming, *Baopuzi neipian jiaoshi*, pp. 47–48; 114–115.

[16] Very roughly speaking, it is the texts of the Lingbao and Shangqing lines of transmission within the Daoist canon and the aprocryphal Buddhist sutras that contain the most elaborate descriptions of the system of merit and demerit. Recent research has made it clear that there was considerable mutual influence among all these different textual traditions: the Shangqing texts borrow from the Lingbao scriptures, and both incorporate Buddhist doctrines and even popular religious beliefs into their systems. See Michel Strickmann, *Le Taoisme du Mao Chan: Chronique d'une Révélation*, pp. 28–30, 40, 139–144; Isabelle Robinet, *La Révélation du Shangqing dans l'Histoire du Taoisme*, vol. 1, pp. 190–195; and Stephen R. Bokenkamp, "Sources of the Ling-pao Scriptures," pp. 434–444, 477.

The account given here of the development of the merit-demerit system is obviously a highly simplified overview. To my knowledge, no coherent history of the system has been written. The fullest historical treatment is by Yoshioka Yoshitoyo, *Dōkyō to Bukkyō*, vol. 2, pp. 167–227. See also Wolfram Eberhard, *Guilt and Sin in Traditional China*; Sakai, *Chūgoku zensho*, pp. 359–369; Zheng Zhiming, *Zhongguo shanshu yu zongjiao*, pp. 5–61, passim; Strickmann, *Le Taoisme du Mao Chan*; and Michel Soymié, "Notes d'iconographie chinoise: les acolytes de Ti-tsang," part 1, pp. 45–78, and part 2, pp. 141–170.

[17] In summarizing these principles here I am drawing on texts from all different periods and from a wide range of religious and intellectual affiliations, in the hope of providing the reader with some sense of the variety and richness of the expressions of the system of merit accumulation. Throughout this section I rely heavily on the references mentioned in note 16.

Most texts agreed that merit-earning activities had to be done in secret, for if the individual received public praise or remuneration for a deed, he could no longer expect any rewards from the gods—one was never recompensed *twice*. Goodness and evil were seen as qualities subject to enumeration and measurement; every act of good or evil, no matter how small, added to the individual's total. The *Classic of Changes* explains: "If acts of goodness be not accumulated, they are not sufficient to give finish to one's name; if acts of evil be not accumulated, they are not sufficient to destroy one's life. The small man thinks that small acts of goodness are of no benefit, and does not do them; and that small deeds of evil do not harm, and does not abstain from them. Hence his wickedness becomes great until it cannot be covered, and his guilt becomes great until it cannot be pardoned."[18] Retribution was also precisely weighed; rewards and punishments were doled out to match exactly the value of the individual's accumulated merit or demerit. Thus one early Tang Daoist scripture explained that a man who had committed 530 evil deeds could expect his children to be stillborn, while he who had done 720 would be cursed with an even graver misfortune—many daughters, but no sons.[19]

A vast bureaucracy of gods and spirits was needed to oversee this complex process of observing human behavior, to count and measure each individual's deeds, to record them in the heavenly registers, to total up his final score, and to distribute the appropriate rewards and punishments. While the Zhou kings feared the judgment of a rather vaguely defined heaven, believers in the system of merit accumulation suffered the scrutiny of a bewildering (and ever-changing) array of spirits, drawn from both Buddhist and Daoist pantheons. These spirits were everywhere, in heaven, on earth, and even in man—no one could escape their observation. Here retribution was not a spontaneous process unmediated by external agents; rather, rewards and punishments were consciously engineered by an extensive network of interfering gods and spirits.

This relatively sophisticated administration was needed to keep track of all the various factors that entered into the calculation of each man's just recompense. For retribution was not based on the individual's behavior alone. First, it operated very much within the context of the family system. The *Classic of Changes* set this principle forth quite clearly: "The family that accumulates good will have abundant good fortune. The family that accumulates evil will have abundant bad fortune."[20] This meant that the individual carried with him the burden of his ancestors' accumulated merit; he might have to work particularly hard at being good

---

[18] *Zhouyi yinde*, p. 47a; translation from Sung, *Text of the Yi King*, pp. 319–320.

[19] *Yaoxiu keyi jielü chao*, *Daozang* (HY 463), 12.10a–11a. Cited in Maspero, *Taoism and Chinese Religion*, p. 273.

[20] *Zhouyi yinde*, p. 4a; translation from Sung, *Text of the Yi King*, p. 20.

just to overcome a heavy legacy of demerit. Thus one Zhe Hui (fourth century), a follower of the early Mao Shan sect and an aspiring immortal, was warned by the Shangqing Immortals that, because of his father's crimes, he would find it very difficult to earn his goal:

> Zhe Hui's father massacred hundreds of people without pity and seized their property. The spirits of the dead disapprove profoundly. Those whom he injured are always bringing suit and denouncing him before the Heavenly Tribunal (Tiancao); already they are naming Hui [the one now responsible for his father's crimes]. According to the law we should exterminate his whole family. But because Hui has cultivated virtue so assiduously, he alone will get away with his life. But how can there be any security for his descendants? Hui will keep the number of years bestowed on him by heaven, but he is far from achieving immortality.[21]

Naturally, the individual would also want to accumulate as much extra merit as possible to pass on to his descendants, to ensure the continuation and prosperity of the family line.

The calculation of retribution was further complicated by the belief that each man was given a set allotment at birth, a real number (*shu*) representing his lifespan and the general tendencies of his life. While this allotment could be altered (for better or worse) by the man's behavior, it nonetheless affected his life quite significantly—clearly, someone born with an "original fate" (*benming*) of twenty years was going to have to work much harder to live a long time than one with an allotment of sixty. Of course it was important to know the exact sum and constitution of one's allotment; "eight-character" (*bazi*) fortune-telling, based on the eight cyclical characters of the time of birth, became the most popular means of uncovering one's original fate.[22]

Finally, a man might find that his karma from a previous life determined his situation in his current existence. He had no control over this karma—he simply had to accept the inevitable consequences of his past acts. Indeed, the Buddhist term *suming*, used to designate these consequences, quickly took on the meaning of predetermined fate, a fate that the individual had no power to alter.[23] But a man could of course see to it that his current behavior earned him at least a better future rebirth; it might also counteract or modify some of the effects of his previous acts.

All of these contingent factors, then, influenced the disposition of each

---

[21] Strickmann, *Le Taoisme du Mao Chan*, p. 164, citing *Zhengao, Daozang*, HY 1010.8.5b.

[22] See Strickmann, *Le Taoisme du Mao Chan*, pp. 160–161; and Hou Ching-lang, *Monnaies d'offrande et la notion de trésorie dans la religion chinoise*, pp. 106–108, 116–126, 130.

[23] Robinet, *La révélation du Shangqing*, vol. 1, pp. 100–101.

individual's fate in the world. They also went a long way to explain delays in retribution or apparent inequities in the system. It could be observed all too commonly that good men did *not* receive rewards for their deeds, while evil men enjoyed all the blessings of good fortune; reference to one's "original allotment" (*benshu*), the inheritance of merit and demerit, or transmigration could easily explain away these apparent discrepancies.

The final human goal of this system was the attainment of certain spiritual rewards—rebirth in a higher plane of existence for the Buddhists, and immortality (or longevity and good health) for the Daoists. Good behavior, consisting largely of charitable deeds, personal restraint, and, particularly in the Buddhist texts, acts of religious faith like the recitation of sutras, was thus rewarded with spiritual benefits; evil was punished with rebirth in animal or insect form or suffering the tortures of hell. Through the Song at least, the aim of the system was deterrence: the deeds listed were largely evil ones, and the greatest emphasis was placed on the horrible punishments awaiting the man (and his family) who failed to avoid these. Indeed, the system of merit accumulation was often seen as a kind of complement to the human judicial system (the *wangfa*), a means of checking to see that those who deserved punishment really got it through the divine application of the "hidden statutes" (*yinlü*): "He who does what is not good in clear and open view will be seized and punished by men. He who does what is not good in the shadow of darkness will be seized and punished by ghosts."[24]

In its development before the twelfth century, this complex system was tied to the Buddhist and Daoist sects that explicated it. As a result, there developed many different pantheons of supernatural retribution and a great variety in the rules of merit accumulation, usually reflective of differences in sect beliefs. In the late twelfth century, however, two landmark texts were produced, texts that ultimately served as definitive statements of the system. These were the *Tract of Taishang on Action and Response* (c. 1164), a simple yet comprehensive description of merit accumulation and the workings of supernatural retribution, and the *Ledger of Merit and Demerit of the Taiwei Immortal* (1171), the first extant ledger—that is, the first text we have that carried the logic of the system to its natural conclusion by assigning points to the performance of deeds, thereby allowing ledger users to calculate their own store of merit.

Although we do not know how influential these texts were at the time of their production, by the late Ming they had become together the bible of the merit-demerit system. They were seen from that time on as a kit for

---

[24] *Zhuangzi yinde*, p. 63. Translation from Burton Watson, trans., *The Complete Works of Chuang Tzu*, p. 255. On the striking similarities between the ledgers of merit and demerit and the penal codes, see Chün-fang Yü, *The Renewal of Buddhism in China: Chu-hung and the Late Ming Synthesis*, pp. 129–134.

moral cultivation, the *Tract* explaining the workings of the system and the *Ledger* providing a practical guide for its use. As a late seventeenth-century author explained, "The *Tract of Taishang on Action and Response* and the *Ledger of Merit and Demerit of the Taiwei Immortal* are works urging people to accumulate virtue and merit, cultivate themselves, and determine their own fate. The *Tract* points out the great principles of this process; the *Ledger* provides the details for proper behavior, but it is a work that should always be used with the *Tract*."[25] Yet another advocate urged scholars to review the *Tract on Action and Response* every night before using the *Ledger* to fill in their merits and demerits for the day.[26] Both these texts, then, are keys to the understanding of the merit-demerit system in the late Ming and early Qing.

THE *TRACT OF TAISHANG ON ACTION AND RESPONSE*

The *Tract of Taishang on Action and Response*, explicating the "theory" of the system of merit and demerit, is purportedly the record of a speech by Taishang, "the Most High" (the title given the philosopher Laozi in his status as a god). Opening with a quotation from the *Chronicle of Zuo* (*Zuo zhuan*), Taishang asserts that men are ultimately responsible for their own fortunes: " 'Calamity and good fortune do not come through gates, but are summoned only by men themselves.' "[27] He goes on to describe the system of divine recompense, drawn from early Chinese cosmologies and the *Master Who Embraces Simplicity*, that ensures this truth:

> Good and evil are recompensed as inevitably as shadow follows form. Therefore, there are spirits overseeing man's misdeeds (*siguo zhi shen*) in heaven and on earth. According to the gravity of his transgressions, they reduce his lifespan by the appropriate number of hundred-day units (*suan*). After one hundred-day unit is deducted, poverty comes upon the man, he meets with calamity and misery, all men hate him, while happiness and good fortune flee him, and evil stars torment him. When his hundred-day units are all exhausted, he dies.
>
> In heaven there are also the Three Towers (Santai) and the Lord of the North Bushel Star (Beidou shenjun), who record a man's crimes and evil deeds. They reduce his lifespan by twelve-year units (*ji*) or hundred-day units according to this record. Inside a man's body there are the Three Worm Spirits (Sanshi shen) who on every fifty-seventh day of the sixty-day cycle report a man's crimes and transgressions to the Heavenly Tribunal. On the last day of each month, the Kitchen God (Zaoshen) also makes such a report.

[25] "Gongguoge xuyan," in Chen Xigu, *Huizuan gongguoge*, j. *mo*, 21a–b.
[26] *Tongshan lu*, j. *moba*, 1b, cited in Sakai, *Chūgoku zensho*, p. 368.
[27] Legge, *The Chinese Classics*, vol. 5, p. 502.

Whenever a man commits a grave transgression, twelve years are deducted from his lifespan; whenever he commits a small one, one hundred days are deducted. All transgressions, great and small, have an infinite number of causes. He who would seek immortality must first flee these. Then he will be able to enter the true way and avoid the false.[28]

Assuring readers of the omnipresence of supernatural overseers, Taishang gives here only a sketchy account of the bureaucracy in charge of retribution. The Three Towers, a constellation that includes the important Overseer of Fate (Siming) star and the Lord of the North Bushel constellation, are the major (but by no means the only) astral spirits in the central administration of divine recompense.[29] The text emphasizes that there are overseer spirits on earth as well: the Three Worms are spirits actually trapped in a man's body, eagerly awaiting the day when they will be set free by his death. In hopes of hastening their release, they assiduously report all his secret evil deeds and thoughts to the Overseer of Destiny. The Kitchen God supplements these reports with his own observations of the man and his family, made from his central vantage point in the kitchen.[30] Thus man is covered on all sides by a supernatural bureaucracy capable not only of seeing all his actions but also of measuring the relative importance of these actions.

Then follows a brief description of the acts of the good man, consisting for the most part of rather general good deeds and virtuous states of mind: the practice of filial piety and loyalty, compassion for orphans and widows, assistance to the needy, humility, generosity, and so forth. This good man will be rewarded with wealth and success in life; and if he has the dedication to accumulate the necessary number of deeds, he can even

[28] *TSGYP*, *Daozang*, HY 1159.1.1a–21a. For the translation here I have used the standard 30-*juan* text (with Li Shi's commentary and Zheng Qingzhi's poems) in the *Daozang*. I also consulted the following translations: Paul Carus and D. Z. Suzuki, *T'ai-Shang Kan-Ying P'ien*; Michael Coyle, trans., "Book of Rewards and Punishments"; Stanislas Julien, trans., *Le Livre des Récompenses et des Peines*; James Legge, trans., "The Thai Shang Tractate of Actions and Their Retributions"; and James Webster, trans., *The Kan Ying Pien*.

[29] The astronomy ("Tianwen" or "Tianguan") sections of the early dynastic histories contain descriptions of the positions and roles of these and other stars in the bureaucracy of retribution. They are also frequently invoked in the texts of the *Daozang*; for examples, see *Taishang dongxuan lingbao yebao yinyuan jing*, HY 336.4.10a, and 8.4b; *Taishang lingbao zhutian neiyin ziran yuzi*, HY 97.3.22a–b; and *Yuanshi wuliang duren shangpin miaojing tongyi*, HY 89.4.10a–b. Several secondary sources discuss the complex relationships among these different spirits: Inahata Koichirō, "Shimei shinsō no tenkai," pp. 1–15; Oyanagi Shigeta, *Rō-Sō no shisō to Dōkyō*, pp. 340–352; Kubo Noritada, "Kōshin shinkō to Hokuto shinkō," pp. 24–25; Rolf A. Stein, "Religious Taoism and Popular Religion from the Second to Seventh Centuries," pp. 76–77; and Zheng, *Zhongguo shanshu*, pp. 42–47.

[30] For more on the Three Worms, see Kubo Noritada, "Chūgoku no sanshi shinkō to Nihon no kōshin shinkō," pp. 6–12. On the Kitchen God, see Inahata, "Shimei shinsō no tenkai," pp. 2–3, 9–10; and Zheng, *Zhongguo shanshu*, pp. 46, 161–182.

become an immortal: "All men respect him, and the way of heaven protects him. Good fortune and wealth follow him, and all calamities stay away from him. The spirits guard him, and whatever he does meets with success. He can aspire to become an immortal. Those who seek to become heavenly immortals must do 1,300 good deeds. Those who seek to become earthly immortals must do 300."[31]

There follows a much longer section on the misdeeds of the evil man, suggesting that, as in the earlier Daoist and Buddhist scriptures, the gravest concern of the system was deterrence, frightening people away from evil with the threat of punishment. Though the arrangement of these deeds follows no discernible logic, they can be categorized into several different types of deeds. A considerable number deal with the ethics governing the five basic human relationships, first defined in the Confucian canon: "treating one's ruler or parents with secret contempt," "being disrespectful of one's elders and rebelling against those one should serve," "getting angry at one's teachers," "quarreling with members of one's own family," "being unkind and unfaithful to one's wife," "being jealous and suspicious of one's husband,"[32] and so forth. Other relationships are by no means neglected, however; the *Tract* warns, for example, against "deceiving the ignorant," "molesting orphans and oppressing widows," "impeding and obstructing the professions and crafts," "squandering a neighbor's property and causing divisions within his family," "controlling others with charms," "gossiping about a neighbor's misfortune."[33] As in the group of good deeds, several deal with personal self-cultivation—that is, the elimination of the evil intentions, thoughts, and flaws of temperament that may drive a man to wrongdoing: "refusing to correct one's errors," "wishing others to incur loss," "keeping a treacherous heart," "cherishing thoughts of seduction whenever one sees a beautiful woman," "having excessive desires," "being greedy and covetous," and so on.[34] Then certain deeds describe transgressions associated with various professions. Officials are warned not to "cast the laws aside and receive bribes," "throw into disorder the government of the state," "bestow rewards and inflict punishments without justice," "slight and take no account of heaven's people"; merchants not to sell or trade worthless things, alter weights and measures in their own favor, or adulterate their goods; and peasants not to destroy the crops and fields of others.[35] Finally, there are deeds violating certain cultural and religious taboos:

---

[31] *TSGYP*, HY 1159.1.22a–6.5a.

[32] Ibid., 1159.6.14a, 7.1a–2b, 20.1a, 25.2b, 4a, 12a. See also Yü, *Renewal of Buddhism*, pp. 110–112; and Zheng, *Zhongguo shanshu*, pp. 52–59.

[33] *TSGYP*, HY 1159.7.4a, 10.1a, 11.6a, 14.6b–8a, 19.9a, 4a.

[34] Ibid., 1159.8.1a, 13.1a, 16.10b, 18.12a, 24.1a, 14a.

[35] Ibid., 1159.9.1a, 2b, 10.2b, 13.8a, 15.8b, 21.2a, 24.7a–8a, 9a.

jumping over wells and hearths, using hearth fire to burn incense, cooking food with dirty firewood, spitting at the stars, cursing in the direction of the north (the abode of the North Bushel Star), and so on.[36]

Following this long list of evil deeds is a reminder of the inescapable consequences of evil for both the man himself and his whole family:

> For such crimes, the Overseer of Destiny reduces the man's life span by twelve-year or hundred-day units, according to the gravity of the offenses. When a man's hundred-day units are used up, he dies. If when he dies there are still sins left unpunished, the punishment will descend to his children and grandchildren. Whenever a man has cheated others of property, the burden of restitution is reckoned and passed on to his wife and children and all his household, to be made good until death gradually overcomes them all. If they do not actually die, they will meet with flood, fire, robbery, disinheritance, loss of property, illness, and slander, all as restitution for the original misappropriation. Those who have wrongfully put others to death are like soldiers who exchange swords to kill each other. Those who have gained riches improperly are like men who try to satisfy their hunger with rotten meat, or quench their thirst with poisoned wine. They do get some relief, but death comes in the end. Now a mind that tends to good, even if it has not yet become good, will be followed by spirits of good fortune, but a mind that tends to evil, even if it has not yet become evil, will be followed by spirits of disaster.[37]

But then the harsh tone lightens, as Taishang, borrowing (without acknowledgment) from a Buddhist sutra, the *Dhammapada* (*Faju jing*), explains that even a man who has done much evil can attain happiness if he repents and changes his ways: "He who has once done evil things, but then changes, repents, and no longer practices evil, and does all good, can gradually attain good fortune and happiness. This process is called turning calamity into good fortune."[38]

The brief text concludes with a summary of the system of retribution, using the Buddhist division of speech, thought, and action to distinguish the different areas of human behavior subject to considerations of right and wrong: "Therefore, the man of good fortune is virtuous in word, thought, and deed. If he practices these three virtues every day, then in three years heaven will certainly send blessings down to him. The man of evil fortune is evil in word, thought, and deed. If he practices these three evils every day, then in three years heaven will certainly send calamities down to him. How then can he not try to act properly?"[39]

The unknown compiler of this text succeeded admirably in both sim-

[36] Ibid., 1159.27.1a–29.3a.
[37] Ibid., 1159.29.5b–30.6a.
[38] Ibid., 1159.30.7b. See Carus, *T'ai-Shang Kan-Ying P'ien*, p. 79.
[39] *TSGYP*, HY 1159.30.9b. See Yü, *Renewal of Buddhism*, p. 108.

plifying and opening out the system of merit and demerit—certainly in comparison to the somewhat esoteric Daoist and Buddhist scriptures before it—as if for a general lay audience. Much of the *Tract* is in fact drawn from or based very closely on sections of the *Master Who Embraces Simplicity*.[40] But in that work, merit accumulation was simply one of many means of achieving immortality, and in fact is almost lost among Ge Hong's alchemical prescriptions. In the *Tract of Taishang* the merit-demerit system stands on its own: good behavior is the only means to divine reward. Immortality remains the primary goal, but the *Tract* also admits (albeit rather vaguely) the possibility of more immediate and less difficult rewards such as general well-being and wealth.

The cosmology of retribution defined in the *Tract on Action and Response* is also accessible to a general audience; unlike the Daoist and Buddhist scriptures of the early medieval period, it does not bind the system to the gods of a particular sect. A widely known and worshipped god, Taishang, replaces the relatively esoteric scriptures listed in the *Master Who Embraces Simplicity* as the authority behind the system.[41] The other retributive spirits of the *Tract*, both earthly and heavenly, are drawn from a vast nonsectarian pantheon of gods dating back to the Han at the latest. The pantheon of the *Tract* is certainly not the exclusive property of any one of the Three Teachings of Confucianism, Buddhism, and Daoism.

Furthermore, the deeds listed in both sections reflect widely held Chinese values and are applicable to all people, regardless of status or religious belief. Because the text includes several deeds governing filial piety, family relations, and loyalty to the state, some scholars have emphasized the strong Confucian elements in the work. But since these values had by this time been fully incorporated into Daoist and Buddhist scriptures, it might be best to consider them generally accepted "Chinese" moral standards. Similarly, the religious taboos do not commit the reader to any particular doctrine or sect affiliation.

In more direct ways, too, the author has made references to all the major schools of the time. The *Tract* opens with a quotation from the *Chronicle of Zuo*, a classical "Confucian" affirmation of the validity of retribution. But more significant are the Buddhist elements, particularly the quotation from the *Dhammapada* sutra encouraging evil-doers to reform. Here again, the *Tract on Action and Response* has slightly altered the rules of retribution found in its primary source. The *Master Who Embraces Simplicity* harshly ruled that even one small evil deed was enough to cancel out 1,199 good deeds—no mercy was extended to the man who

[40] Yoshioka, *Dōkyō no kenkyū*, pp. 91–104.

[41] Wang Ming, *Baopuzi neipian*, j. 6, p. 114; the texts mentioned are *Yinei jie*, *Zhi Songzi jing*, and *Hetu jiming fu*.

erred. In the *Tract*, however, the gods are more generous; they want men to do good, and are willing to forgive evil as long as the believer truly repents and changes his ways.[42]

It is not at all clear when this brief text (roughly 1,280 characters long) was put in its present form. We first hear of its publication around 1164, when a certain Li Shi (d. c. 1182) "transmitted" (*chuan*) the text, adding an extensive commentary that expanded the modest *Tract* into a thirty-*juan* work, occupying six volumes of the *Daoist Canon*. Li Shi, from Zi-yang county, Sichuan, was originally named Zhiji, but in response to his prayers for the *jinshi* degree, the god Zitong (later Wenchang) instructed him to change his name to Shi. After following this command, he did in fact earn the *jinshi* degree and was ultimately recommended for the posi-tion of Erudite of the National University. Because, his biographer ex-plained, he was unwilling to flatter his superiors, he was ultimately not given this position. Indeed, despite the assistance of several well-placed friends, Li never succeeded in holding a post except for a brief stint as a prefect of Meizhou, Sichuan. He achieved greater renown as a scholar, however, and was noted in particular for his esoteric knowledge and his studies of the *Classic of Changes* and the *Spring and Autumn Annals*.[43]

Li Shi appears to have accepted the *Tract* as a genuine record of instruc-tions sent by Taishang to lead the people away from evil practices. He wrote about the *Tract*:

> The contents of this essay include all items that the Heavenly Offices (Tianfu) established for the punishment and reward of men in the world. People today act for the most part only in pursuit of momentary pleasure; they do not know that after each and every transgression there is punishment. Taishang sent this tract down to the world, because he wanted people of today to know what actions to avoid and what to follow. Recently Zhou Chi spread the teachings of this tract, and he was able to escape the retribution of starvation during famine. Mr. Wang vowed to act according to the deeds in the book, and like-wise extended his lifespan for another fourteen years. From these examples can be seen Taishang's intention of benefiting the people.[44]

There is no solid evidence connecting Li to any of the Daoist or Buddhist sects that transmitted the system of merit accumulation before the twelfth century. But he clearly had a wide knowledge of their scriptures, for in

[42] *TSGYP*, HY 1159.30.7b–8a.

[43] For other views on the authorship of the text, see Sakai, *Chūgoku zensho*, p. 363; and Takao Giken, "Mindai ni taisei saretaro kōkakaku shisō," pp. 18–19. Yoshioka summarizes Li Shi's biography in *Dōkyō no kenkyū*, pp. 78–79. See also Li Shi's autobiography in his *Fangzhou ji*, 10.22b–25b; and the brief biography by Li Xinchuan in *(Jianyan yilai) Chaoye zaji*.

[44] Li Shi, *Leshan lu*, 4.13b–14a; see also 6.2b–3a, 6a–9b.

his notes to the *Tract* he frequently alludes to a god or a method of accounting defined in these scriptures. His references are eclectic—he quotes the Confucian Classics as well as Buddhist and Daoist texts, and he provides many historical and contemporary examples of the workings of retribution.[45]

It is difficult to come to any firm and comprehensive conclusions about the audience for the *Tract on Action and Response* during the Song. Not surprisingly, we have no evidence of widespread use of the text before or during the twelfth century. Some scholars have suggested, however, that the *Tract* was a popular, widely circulating text well before that time, and that Li Shi's version, with his long and scholarly commentary, simply served to give the brief and rather simple tract a form and legitimacy that brought it clearly to the attention of the highly literate elite and ensured the written transmission of the text.[46]

We do have considerable evidence of contemporary literati interest in the *Tract*. Of course Li Shi himself was a member of the educated elite: he held the *jinshi* degree and was a close friend of two consecutive grand councillors, Zhao Xiong (1129–1193) and Wang Huai (1126–1189), and of Hu Jinchen (j.s. 1157, d. 1193), an attendant censor. Zheng Qingzhi (1176–1251), a later commentator on the text, was a noted scholar and high official, twice named grand councillor by the Lizong emperor (r. 1225–1264).[47] No less prestigious a Neo-Confucian scholar and official than Zhen Dexiu (1178–1235) encouraged the distribution of the text. In two different prefaces to the *Tract*, he asserted the validity of the work in Confucian terms: "The world believes that the words 'action and response' (*ganying*) derive just from Daoism and Buddhism. This is not true. The *Classic of History* contains the instruction 'do good and good fortune will be sent down to you,' and the *Classic of Changes* says that accumulating goodness will bring abundant good fortune."[48] He even adduced later Neo-Confucians to support the belief in "action and response": "I have often heard that Yichuan [Cheng Yi] said, 'Whatever moves will cause action and that action must have a response; that response will again cause an action, that action will again have a re-

[45] For examples, see *TSGYP*, HY 1159.25.2b. Li Shi was clearly aware of the teachings of the early Daoist scriptures, and even familiar with the beliefs of the Xu Zhenjun sect, the group that eventually produced the first extant ledger, the *Taiwei xianjun gongguoge*. For Li's references to Xu Zhenjun, see *TSGYP*, HY 1159.1.20a, and *Leshan lu*, 4.10a–b; for his description of Lingbao cosmology, see *Fangzhou ji*, 9.4b.

[46] Yoshioka, *Dōkyō no kenkyū*, pp. 70, 78; see also Oyanagi, *Rō-Sō no shisō*, p. 368.

[47] Yoshioka, *Dōkyō no kenkyū*, p. 90; Herbert Franke, ed., *Sung Biographies*, vol. 1, pp. 156–163.

[48] Zhen Dexiu, "*Ganying pian*," *Xishan xiansheng Zhen Wenzhong Gong wenji*, j. 35, p. 549; reference from Yoshioka, *Dōkyō no kenkyū*, p. 83.

sponse.' "[49] Although Zhen had reservations about the usefulness of the *Tract on Action and Response* to scholars, he believed that it could be an aid in the instruction of the people. Even Song Lizong seems to have shared Zhen's sense of the educational value of the work: so pleased was he with it that, at a cost of one million cash, he commissioned craftsmen to print the text for distribution throughout the empire.[50]

Of course it is impossible to know with any certainty how profoundly and sincerely these scholar-officials and the Lizong emperor believed in the system of merit accumulation. There are, however, many reasons (other than that of personal belief) why the *Tract on Action and Response* might have been attractive to them. Sanctioned by the gods themselves, its prescriptions supported the maintenance of social harmony and stability: a believer was to follow the traditional virtues associated with his or her place in society, as son, husband, wife, student, teacher, official, merchant, or simply good subject. Eschewing the esoteric and expensive alchemical recipes of the *Master Who Embraces Simplicity* and allusions to the special deities of particular and often exclusive Daoist and Buddhist sects, it simplified merit accumulation and made it accessible to a broader audience. No wonder, then, that it became the major vehicle for the spread of the system of merit and demerit.

The *Ledger of Merit and Demerit of the Taiwei Immortal*

The *Ledger of Merit and Demerit of the Taiwei Immortal*, later to become the companion text to the *Tract on Action and Response*, appeared less than a decade after the *Tract*. While the *Tract* set forth the basic principles of the system, the *Ledger* provided precise guidelines for the actual practice of merit accumulation. Indeed, it is the first extant text that explains precisely how men could keep their own moral accounts. Like the *Tract*, the *Ledger* was presented as a work sent down from heaven to correct the misdeeds and relieve the sufferings of the people. Unlike the *Tract*, however, the *Ledger* can be linked to a particular Daoist sect, and even to a particular stage in sect history.

The *Ledger* is a product of a sect founded in the late fourth century in Xinjian county, Jiangxi, to worship Xu Sun (239–292/374?). The sect literature records many different versions of Xu's life, and he was honored for his performance in a variety of roles—Confucian official, dragon-slayer, practitioner of Daoist magical arts, and immortal. As prefect of Jingyang county (Sichuan) under the Jin (266–316), he won the affection of the people through just and compassionate government. Ac-

[49] Zhen Dexiu, "*Ganying pian xu*," *Xishan xiansheng Zhen Wenzhong Gong wenji*, j. 27, p. 423.

[50] Yoshioka, *Dōkyō no kenkyū*, pp. 81–82.

cording to the sect literature, "he protected the people from the rapacity of government clerks and other 'mean people' " and "taught them loyalty and filial piety, compassion and benevolence, forbearance and restraint, diligence and frugality."[51] At the same time he practiced his Daoist arts to aid them: he used cinnabar to change roof tiles into gold so that the people could pay their taxes, and he cast charms to save the people from epidemics. He also rescued them from evil demons, in particular from a series of dragon-like monsters who demanded worship and expensive rites of propitiation. After the fall of the Jin he gave up his official career to wander about and perfect his magical arts. In 374, well over one hundred years old, he was visited by two immortals who informed him that, because in his previous life he had avoided the crimes of killing and of neglecting his ancestors, and because in his present life he had earned much merit by casting charms, curing illnesses, punishing evil, and so forth, he would be granted immortality. He then ascended to heaven, along with forty-two assorted family members and disciples. A temple was erected to the "True Lord Xu" (Xu Zhenjun) at the place of his apotheosis, Mt. Xiaoyao in Xinjian county, Jiangxi. The temple, later named the Yulong Wanshou Gong, became the sect headquarters.[52]

The sect that formed around the worship of Xu Zhenjun, like most Daoist sects of the period, took immortality as its primary spiritual goal. Following the example of Xu Sun himself, the sect prescribed an eclectic mixture of practices—the observance of the rules of filial piety as well as the use of charms—to achieve this goal. By the late Tang and Song the Xu Zhenjun sect had gained quite a following and had even garnered support from at least two emperors. The Zhenzong emperor (r. 998–1022) gave the name "Jade Beneficence" (Yulong) to the central temple of the sect in 1010, and over a century later, in 1112, the Huizong emperor (r. 1101–1125) conferred the title "Perfected Lord of Supernatural Feats and Miraculous Deliverance" ("Shengong miaoji zhenjun") on Xu Sun. Apparently Huizong was particularly impressed with the legends describing Xu Sun's success in destroying demon worship; determined to stop the spread of the "perverse shrines" (yinci) that he believed were undermin-

---

[51] Akizuki Kan'ei, *Chūgoku kinsei Dōkyō no keisei*, p. 90. On the authorship of the *Taiwei xianjun gongguoge*, see pp. 197–199, 210–216; for a discussion of the sect literature and the scriptural tradition it was derived from, see pp. 239, 241–243. I rely on Akizuki for almost all of the following information on the Xu Zhenjun sect and the Jingming Zhongxiao Dao.

[52] "Jingming daoshi Jingyang Xu Zhenjun zhuan," *Jingming Zhongxiao quanshu*, *Daozang*, HY 1102.1.1b–2a, 8b–9b. See Akizuki, *Chūgoku kinsei Dōkyō*, pp. 76–83, 90–92, for a partial translation of Xu's biography; and Judith Boltz, *A Survey of Taoist Literature, Tenth to Seventeenth Centuries*, pp. 70–78.

ing national security, the emperor hoped to enlist the aid of Xu Sun as a kind of dynastic guardian.[53]

Over the course of the twelfth and thirteenth centuries, however, the doctrines and eventually the whole nature of the sect changed rather significantly, in such a way as to intensify its role in the struggle for national survival. It was during this period that the *Ledger* was produced. Pressure for change came in part from the worsening political situation. In the 1120s, southern China became a battleground between Jin troops and the Song army. Enemy troops crossed the Yangzi River in 1129, in pursuit of the Gaozong emperor (r. 1127–1162), and managed to take Hangzhou and Ningbo before they were finally turned back in 1131. Though Xinjian county, the center of the Xu Zhenjun sect, was not at the heart of the worst fighting, it did suffer a few incursions of Jin troops. Soldiers once attempted to burn down the sect headquarters, the Yulong Wanshou Gong, and were reportedly prevented only by miraculous jets of water that spontaneously sprayed out from the columns and rafters and put out the fire.[54]

In 1129, disturbed by the sufferings of the people at the hands of both the Jin and the Song armies, the leader of the sect, He Zhengong, appealed to Xu Zhenjun to provide some relief for his followers. Three years later Xu, as he had promised He, sent down the "Lingbao Jingming secret methods" and the "teaching of loyalty and filial piety, of humility and self-restraint." It is not at all clear what the "Lingbao Jingming secret methods" were—perhaps new charms or other magical techniques for self-protection and the cultivation of immortality. The second gift seems to refer to instruction in values that would help sect followers weather the horrors of war.[55] The emphasis on loyalty, while not at all inconsistent with Xu Zhenjun's own teachings as a virtuous official, in particular reflects a new concern for national unity and strength natural at a time when China was being invaded by "barbarians."[56] Sect leaders were now

[53] Akizuki, *Chūgoku kinsei Dōkyō*, pp. 117, 206; and Boltz, *Taoist Literature*, p. 72.

[54] "Xu Zhenjun zhuan," *Xiuzhen shishu*, Daozang, HY 263.34.5a–b; reference from Akizuki, *Chūgoku kinsei Dōkyō*, pp. 202–203.

[55] "Xu," *Lingbao jingming xinxiu jiulaoshen yinfumo mifa*, Daozang, HY 562.1a–b; see also "Xishan yinshi Yuzhen Liu xiansheng zhuan," *Jingming Zhongxiao quanshu*, HY 1102.1.19b–20a. Both references from Akizuki, *Chūgoku kinsei Dōkyō*, p. 121; see also the discussion on pp. 120–126, 204–210.

[56] "Loyalty" here may also mean a personal kind of loyalty to one's own mind, or, more simply, truthfulness (*cheng*). This was a common Neo-Confucian interpretation, and certainly this is the meaning the term came to have in sect writings in the Yuan, after the sect had changed to the Jingming Zhongxiao Dao. But Akizuki argues persuasively that here, in the Song, it at least also had the meaning of loyalty to the emperor or the state. Provisions in the *Taiwei xianjun gongguoge* urging that certain deeds be done "for the sake of the

interested in developing means, both moral and magical, of easing the social disorder of the time.

The *Ledger* was very much a part of this shift in sect concerns. Although the fiercest fighting ceased in 1131, the Xinjian area was by no means free of trouble: in 1162, fighting between the Jin and the Southern Song erupted again over the issue of tribute payment.[57] The *Ledger*, produced ten years later, was interpreted by sect members as another effort by the spirits to aid them through the disorder of the day. Like the *Tract on Action and Response* and many other Daoist scriptures before it, it was purportedly transmitted by a god to a passive human recorder. This man, You Xuanzi, a Daoist master living in the Huizhen Hall of the Yulong Wanshou Gong, explains in his preface how the text came to be written:

> In 1171, on the second day of the second month of spring, around midnight, I dreamt that I traveled to Zifu palace [located near the North Bushel constellation], and during the court rites there, received the ledger of merit and demerit from the Immortal Taiwei. I was ordered to transmit it to other men of faith. Suddenly, I awoke from the dream. As I tried to recall the items of merit and demerit, they gradually became clearer in my mind. I put on clothing, sat up properly, and reflected on what had happened. I realized that this exalted immortal had descended in spirit from heaven to me. I dared not be lax or careless in carrying out his commission, so I straightened my clothing and adjusted my cap, prepared my inkstone and some good paper, took up my pen, and wrote all the merits and demerits down. In less than an hour it was all done, without my thinking about it or having to focus my attention on the text.

He then describes the technical aspects of ledger use:

> The merit ledger has thirty-six items, the demerit ledger thirty-nine. Each is divided into four sections, with the numbers for the merits and demerits clearly attached. Those who would practice the true way should write out the days and months of the year, and record under them their merits and demerits. Each month and then each year a comparison of merits and demerits should be compiled, so that the user can know himself the total number of his merits and demerits, and can make these totals agree with those recorded in heaven.[58]

In the body of the text, Taiwei elaborates on proper ledger use, encouraging people to keep the ledger by their beds, so that they would remember to record the merits and demerits accumulated throughout the day before they went to sleep. He warns against trying to exaggerate merits and conceal demerits, and explains that merits and demerits might cancel

---

country" tend to bear out Akizuki's point. See his *Chūgoku kinsei Dōkyō*, pp. 157–158, 181–184, 207–298; see also Boltz, *Taoist Literature*, pp. 76–77.

[57] Akizuki, *Chūgoku kinsei Dōkyō*, p. 209.

[58] *Taiwei xianjun gongguoge*, Daozang, HY 186, "Xu," 1b.

each other out. That is the great virtue of the ledger system, Taiwei points out—one can clearly see one's total in a single figure, and thus "know one's own punishment or prosperity, and need not ask about good or ill fortune."[59]

Master You also explains the psychological and ultimately moral effects that this daily use of the ledger would have:

> Usually, when at the end of the day a man has finished recording his merits, he will feel easy; when he has finished recording his demerits, he will feel troubled. These feelings force the sensitive man to recognize the causes of transgressions and good fortune, and the sources of good and evil. If he is aware of these, then he can reduce the number of his failings by half. If he is really careful, he can avoid them altogether. Act according to these rules, move away from evil and closer to good, sincerely follow the true precepts, and you will not be far from achieving immortality.

Despite the obvious Daoist flavor of the text—the "authorship" by the Taiwei immortal and the statement of immortality as *the* goal of ledger use—You makes a strong point, at the beginning of the preface, of highlighting what he considers the equally solid Confucian legitimacy of the *Ledger*:

> The *Classic of Changes* says: "The family that accumulates good will have abundant good fortune. The family that accumulates evil will have abundant bad fortune." The Daoist rules say that if a man accumulates good, heaven will reward him with good fortune; if he does evil, then heaven will punish him with bad fortune. Therefore, the teachings of the Confucians and the Daoists are as one. In ancient times, sages, men of virtue, and distinguished Daoist masters all wrote commandments and instructions for men to use in disciplining their internal thoughts, purifying their minds, regulating their conduct, and controlling their external behavior, so as to aid them in performing meritorious works.[60]

This claim for dual Daoist and Confucian legitimacy is perfectly consistent, of course, with the eclectic practices of Xu Zhenjun himself and the eclectic teachings of his sect.

The *Ledger* is remarkable because it is the first true ledger we have—it offers man a much greater control over the system of merit and demerit and thus over his own fate than any previous texts had. As You assures the reader, "the user can know himself the total number of his merits and demerits, and can make these totals agree with those recorded in heaven."[61] But the text also introduces a slightly more sophisticated explanation of the moral value of merit-demerit calculation than is found in other scriptures. Keeping a ledger is now supposed to help a man to order

[59] *Taiwei xianjun gongguoge,* HY 186.1a–b.
[60] *Taiwei xianjun gongguoge,* HY 186, "Xu," 2a, 1a–b.
[61] Ibid., 1b.

and purify his mind and to recognize the inner sources of his transgressions. Once these "internal thoughts" are properly disciplined, then he will be able to control his external behavior and do good deeds.

The shift here within the merit-demerit system to a greater emphasis on internal cultivation coincided with a broader intellectual interest, new in the Song, in the spiritual cultivation of the self. Contemporary alchemical practices reflect a roughly comparable development away from "external alchemy" (*waidan*), which relied heavily on the consumption of elixirs and pills and on other physical techniques for the achievement of immortality, to "internal alchemy" (*neidan*), which interpreted alchemical medicines to be, not external substances, but forces within the body that could be activated and manipulated through meditation. Hence the major advocates of internal alchemy, the followers of the Quanzhen sect and the Jindan Dao (the Way of the Golden Elixir), both popular in the twelfth and thirteenth centuries, believed that the cultivation of powers within the self was the most effective means to immortality.[62] Even more obvious was the shift that took place within Neo-Confucian philosophy away from the classic Confucian focus on political service to a new emphasis on the process of internal moral cultivation. Drawing on the work of several Northern Song thinkers, Zhu Xi, the great synthesizer of Neo-Confucianism, made individual moral perfection the keystone of his new philosophical program. For Zhu, this process of self-cultivation relied as much on the development of certain states of mind—truthfulness (*cheng*) and inner mental attentiveness (*jing*)—as on the investigation of things—the Classics, historical events, contemporary affairs, and human relationships—outside the mind.[63] In its emphasis on the need for internal reflection in the performance of good deeds and accumulation of merit points, the *Ledger* then participated in one of the major general intellectual trends of its time.

The deeds listed in the ledger itself reflect both the mixed heritage of the Xu Zhenjun sect and the new shift in its concerns. Many of the items reveal the Taoist orientation of the sect: "Using charms or acupuncture to cure one person of a severe illness—ten merits, of a slight illness—five merits (if payment is received from the family of the patient, there is no merit)," "transmitting a charm, a method, a medicine, or a technique for the preservation of life, and so forth—five merits per occasion (one merit if one receives payments)," "for each 100 cash spent on repairing the images of the sages, altars, temple pennants, ornamented vessels, tables,

---

[62] See Holmes Welch, *Taoism: The Parting of the Way*, pp. 131–132; Isabelle Robinet, "Original Contributions of *Neidan* to Taoism and Chinese Thought," pp. 297–307.

[63] Akizuki discusses the relationship between Confucianism and the doctrines of the Xu Zhenjun sect and the Jingming Zhongxiao Dao in "Jōmeidōkyōgaku kanken—Ju, Bu, Dō sankyō kankei o chūshin ni—," pp. 20–35.

chairs, and any contributions—one merit; for each string of cash—ten merits (sharing in a contribution of 100 cash for the repair or purchase of things—half a merit; sharing in a string of cash—five merits, or count one merit for each set of ten things or incidents)." Activities that increase sect membership are highly valued—instructing a new member is worth thirty merits, and printing and distributing the scriptures to others earns ten merits for each chapter (*juan*; up to 1,000 characters) of a minor work, twenty merits for each chapter of a major work.[64]

These "Daoist" deeds are intermixed with other prescriptions in support of "Confucian" or other, more widely accepted values. Failing to venerate one's elders, teachers, or parents brings thirty demerits, and "teaching others that to be immodest, unfilial, undutiful, inhumane, unvirtuous, and uncompassionate are not worth demerits" earns one demerit per occasion. More positively, venerating an ancestor is worth ten merits per person. The new importance of loyalty as a sect doctrine is incorporated into several prescriptions: "Morning and evening burn incense [and vow to] regulate your conduct for the sake of the country and for the sake of the people (*weiguo weimin*)—two merits," "make sacrifices for the sake of the country, the people, your ancestors, orphaned spirits, and your family, praying that they be free of calamities and harm—one merit per portion," and "reciting one chapter of a major scripture for the sake of the country, for the sake of the people, and for the sake of your ancestors, orphans, and orphaned spirits—six merits."[65]

Finally there are several deeds focusing on philanthropic activities, acts that relieve the sufferings of the people. People are urged to pay for the burial of the dead (fifty merits per corpse), to aid widowers, widows, orphans, and the poor (one merit per one hundred cash), to feed the hungry (one merit per meal), to give shelter to the cold and homeless (one merit per night), to contribute one hundred cash to the construction of ferries, bridges, and fords (one merit per hundred cash), and so forth.[66]

The *Ledger*, as a list of specific guidelines, provided sect members with a clearcut technique for salvation during a time when hopes of long life, much less immortality, must have seemed rather dim. And the actual deeds prescribed, without referring to any specific source of disorder, do reveal a concern with easing social distress and ensuring national survival. But what real use was made of this ledger? Unfortunately, no explicit reference is made by title to the *Ledger of Merit and Demerit of the Taiwei Immortal* in other sect writings. Another sect scripture, however, written between 1112 and 1297, does allude to the use of "Jingming reg-

[64] *Taiwei xianjun gongguoge*, HY 186.1b–2a, 4a–b, 3b, 4a.
[65] Ibid., 186.10b–11a, 4b–5a.
[66] Ibid., 186.2b–3a. See also Zheng, *Zhongguo shanshu*, pp. 65–69.

isters for recording merits and demerits" ("Jingming ji gongguobu"), confirmation at least that the sect members did use ledgers, if not necessarily the *Ledger* itself.[67] The successor sect to the Xu Zhenjun group, the Jingming Zhongxiao Dao (Loyal and Filial Way of the Pure and Perspicacious), founded in 1297, also appears to have incorporated ledger use into its program for salvation. One of its scriptures urges the sect members not to forget "the daily record" of deeds, and another praises this record as a tool for moral self-purification.[68] Ledger keeping remained part of sect practices through the Yuan and Ming.[69]

The leaders of the Xu Zhenjun sect and the Jingming Zhongxiao Dao were certainly not alone in recognizing the needs of the people for both spiritual assurance and practical guidelines to behavior in the twelfth century. Indeed, the production of the *Ledger* and the use of ledgers within both sects are part of a larger religious trend, the creation of a "new Daoism" in the Southern Song. Reacting against the esoteric and relatively inaccessible scriptures and rituals of the older, elitist Mao Shan and Tianshi sects, several new sects developed doctrines and practices that tried to meet the real moral, religious, and to some degree social needs of a people oppressed by war, famine, and banditry. Without abandoning their claims to cure through ritual and magical techniques, these sects—the Taiyi, Zhenda, and Quanzhen, as well as the Xu Zhenjun (and the Jingming Zhongxiao Dao)—borrowed freely from Buddhism and Confucianism to broaden the applicability of their doctrines. Now they could appeal to a wider audience of lay people, not just to those willing and able to devote themselves to Daoist arts.[70]

Certainly the *Ledger of Merit and Demerit*, with its inclusion of generally applicable good and evil deeds along with specific sect practices, attests to this concern on the part of the sect leaders. One of the distinguishing features of both the Xu Zhenjun sect and the Jingming Zhongxiao Dao was their faith that salvation was possible for peasants as well as for emperors, officials, and aristocrats; the sect scriptures singled out no one status group as more likely to attain immortality than another. Nor was either sect rigidly parochial in the dissemination of its beliefs; efforts were made to extend the benefits of their teachings to people outside the sect.[71]

---

[67] *Lingbao jingming yuanxing qianshi*, *Daozang*, HY 619.10a; reference from Akizuki, *Chūgoku kinsei Dōkyō*, pp. 199–202.

[68] *Taishang lingbao jingming feixian duren jingfa*, *Daozang*, HY 563.1.18b; *Taishang lingbao jingming rudao pin*, *Daozang*, HY 557.1b; see also Akizuki, *Chūgoku kinsei Dōkyō*, pp. 141–164, 179–194, 200–201.

[69] Akizuki, *Chūgoku kinsei Dōkyō*, pp. 199–202, 256–260.

[70] Ibid., pp. 247–250. For more on these sects, see Kubo, *Dōkyō shi*, pp. 288–336; and Chen Yuan, *Nan Songchu Hebei xin Daojiao kao*.

[71] Akizuki, *Chūgoku kinsei Dōkyō*, pp. 247, 260n.1.

But it is difficult to determine whether either sect succeeded in attracting a wide popular audience. As in the case of the *Tract on Action and Response*, the only solid evidence we have attests to considerable interest and some knowledge of the Xu Zhenjun and the Jingming Zhongxiao Dao on the part, not of peasants and commoners, but of officials and emperors. It by no means enjoyed praise from all scholar-officials: Zhu Xi, for example, attacked the Xu Sun sect as "perverse" (because it encouraged the intermingling of men and women) and lamented the degree to which people were deluded by its rituals.[72] But others actually considered the sect a vehicle for the transmission of the essential values of Confucianism to the people. Thus one supporter, the famous reformer Wang Anshi (1021–1086), argued that Confucians could praise the sect teachings in good conscience because of their very Confucian goal of relieving the sufferings of the people.[73] Twenty-six Song scholars, including such prominent figures as Zhen Dexiu, Huang Tingjian (1045–1105), and Hong Mai (1123–1202), wrote commemorative essays for the sect temple.[74] One later supporter, Zhao Shiyan (fl. early fourteenth century), a vice-censor-in-chief under the Yuan and apparently a sincere believer in the curative powers of the sect charms, praised the sect for transmitting the essential values of early Confucianism to the people:

> The duty of subjects is loyalty, the duty of sons is filial piety. To conform to the three rules [governing the relationships between ruler and minister, father and son, and husband and wife] and the five constants [benevolence, righteousness, propriety, wisdom, and trustworthiness] is to follow the way of loyalty and filial piety. The way of Yao and Shun taught filial and fraternal piety, and the way of Confucius taught loyalty and reciprocity. Thus the essentials of the highest virtue of the Way lie in the Jingming Dao. When living in this world, the honorable Xu Sun did not devote himself only to rushing into the void and making "pure talk"; but, pained that the Way was growing ever more distant from men, he founded a simple and enlightened way for the preservation of the "human way" (*rendao*). He drew on models from the commonplace world to teach the people, and used very simple language to explain the lofty Way. His must be considered a glorious achievement.[75]

[72] Zhu Xi, *Zhuzi yulei*, vol. 7, j. 106, p. 2646. Cited in Akizuki, *Chūgoku kinsei Dōkyō*, pp. 130–131.

[73] Wang Anshi, "Zhongjian Jingyang ciji," *Xiaoyao shan Wanshou gongzhi*, 15.6b–7b; cited in Akizuki, *Chūgoku kinsei Dōkyō*, pp. 126–127.

[74] Akizuki, *Chūgoku kinsei Dōkyō*, pp. 119, 126, 139n.3.

[75] *Jingming Zhongxiao quanshu*, HY 1102, "Xu," 1b–2a; reference from Akizuki, *Chūgoku kinsei Dōkyō*, p. 150. Xu's expression of concern about the growing distance between men and the Way is probably an allusion to *Zhongyong*, chapter 13. See Legge, *The Chinese Classics*, vol. 1, p. 393.

Thus both the *Tract on Action and Response* and the doctrines of the Xu Zhenjun sect (and later the Jingming Zhongxiao Dao) received at least some support from the scholar-official elite. Judged from their own writings, the motives for this support varied considerably: some appeared to believe genuinely in the *Tract on Action and Response* and the Xu Zhenjun sect teachings, and all seem to have been impressed with the potential usefulness of the text and the sect in the transmission of "Confucian" values supportive of social stability.

THE SYSTEM OF MERIT AND DEMERIT AND THE CONFUCIAN VIEW OF FATE

There were, of course, many thinkers who repudiated the view of retribution and fate—indeed, the whole religious system—set forth in the *Tract on Action and Response* and the *Ledger of Merit and Demerit*. It should be apparent by now that there was no single, clearcut way of defining the concepts of fate and supernatural retribution in the Chinese tradition; we are confronted rather with a remarkable range of interpretations and beliefs. For the Shang kings, retribution was recompense, a repayment for offerings and sacrifices made to the royal ancestors. For the authors of the early Confucian Classics, moral retribution operated at heaven's command. Han Confucians favored the concept of a naturalistic retribution powered by the automatic process of "action and response" between cosmological correspondences, a far cry from the bureaucratic supernatural retribution envisioned in the *Tract* and the *Ledger*. For Buddhist philosophers, retribution was a natural, unmediated outgrowth of an individual's deeds.

But there were thinkers, too, who repudiated the very idea of supernatural retribution, be it overseen by a morally conscious heaven, moved by cosmic pneumas, or managed by divine bureaucrats. For these men, fate was random and arbitrary, a force completely beyond human control. Wang Chong (27–97?), perhaps the most determined advocate of the fatalist position, explained, "Man's nature does not correspond to his destiny (*ming*): his disposition may be good, but his destiny unlucky, or his disposition bad, and his fate lucky. Good and bad actions are the result of natural disposition; happiness and misfortune, good and bad luck are destiny."[76] Other thinkers attempted to work a compromise between the different views of fate. For example, the doctrine of "three fates" (*sanming*), popular in the Han, held that a man's life was governed by "longevity fate" (*shouming*), a fixed figure representing his lifespan; "concomitant fate" (*suiming*), operating like retribution to reward or punish

---

[76] Wang Ch'ung, *Lun-heng: Philosophical Essays of Wang Ch'ung*, vol. 1, p. 226.

his behavior; and "accidental fate" (*zaoming*), the kind of arbitrary force Wang Chong believed in.[77]

Though these various views of retribution and fate might have originated in very different religious and intellectual contexts, the terms used to express them came to be used almost interchangeably. Thus *ganying* might refer to the naturalistic movement of cosmic pneumas that results in retribution, but it might also, as in the title of the *Tract of Taishang on Action and Response*, stand for the bureaucratic administration of retribution by anthropomorphic gods and spirits. Certainly, by the twelfth century at the latest, *ganying* and *yinguo* (and *yinguo baoying*) were used interchangeably in some contexts: in both Daoist and Buddhist scriptures they were used to refer to supernatural retribution, though each might also retain its original sense in sophisticated philosophical works. *Ming*, however, is the term that took on the widest range of meanings. It might refer both to the original, predetermined fate a person received at birth, at heaven's arbitrary command, as it were, and to the mandate to govern conferred by heaven on rulers who earned it through their own virtuous achievements. Here *ming*, rather like the English word "fate," includes two potentially contradictory notions: a set, unchangeable destiny (as in the Han concept of "accidental fate") and the success or failure earned through personal moral effort (as in the *tianming* of the Zhou rulers or the immortality "fated" for virtuous followers of the Huang-Lao sect). Thus, while Wang Chong concluded that "Fate is inescapable" (*ming ze buke mian*), Ge Hong stated, with equal conviction and lexical accuracy, "My fate rests with me, not with heaven" (*wo ming zai wo, buzai tian*).[78]

The early Confucian school provided yet another, somewhat subtler understanding of *ming*, one that ultimately presented the greatest challenge to the conception of fate and supernatural retribution found in the merit-demerit system. As supporters of the merit-demerit system were quick to point out, the very earliest Classics—the *Classic of Songs*, the *Classic of Changes*, the *Classic of History*, the *Spring and Autumn Annals* and its commentaries, and the *Record of Rites*—all expressed faith in a form of supernatural retribution. But with Confucius (551–479 B.C.) and Mencius (fourth century B.C.) there was a distinct shift in the interpretation of fate, based on a somewhat different understanding of heaven's relation to man. This shift resulted in a retreat from the concept of supernatural retribution, and an assertion of man's responsibility to do good for its own sake.

To be sure, Confucius never explicitly denied that heaven rewarded

---

[77] Tjoe Som Tjan, trans., *Po Hu T'ung: The Comprehensive Discussions in the White Tiger Hall*, vol. 2, pp. 572–573.

[78] Wang Ming, *Baopuzi neipian*, j. 16, p. 262; citation from Robinet, *La Révélation du Shangqing*, vol. 1, p. 100.

good and punished evil. Indeed, at some points—as when he suggested that good conduct was better than prayer as a defense against premature death—he appears to take the position that man could move heaven through virtuous behavior. But elsewhere he asserted that the circumstances of a man's life were beyond his control: "Life and death depend on fate (*ming*); wealth and honor rest with heaven." Ultimately, Confucius seems to have taken the position that man should worry about improving his conduct, without considering heaven's response to his actions: "Devote yourself earnestly to the duties due to men, and respect spiritual beings, but keep them at a distance" is his definition of wise action.[79]

Mencius made this view much more explicit, largely by refining the Confucian definition of fate. Fate for him referred not simply to what is decreed by heaven; it signified the implicit moral "command" heaven directs toward each man both by endowing him with a morally perfectible nature and by imposing certain external limitations on him. The external circumstances of a man's life—his lifespan, his rank and wealth—are all decreed by heaven, but the good man sees these circumstances not as arbitrary limitations on his actions, but as guides to a course of moral conduct. While man cannot determine or control external forces, he can control his responses to them, simply because he does have control over his morally perfectible nature. If he cultivates this nature and perfects himself, so that he responds appropriately to all external conditions, then he has fulfilled his "proper fate" (*zhengming*): "Though nothing happens that is not due to fate, one accepts willingly only what is one's proper fate. That is why he who understands fate does not stand under a wall on the verge of collapse. He who dies after having done his best in following the Way dies according to his proper fate. It is never anyone's proper fate to die in fetters."[80] As the contemporary scholar T'ang Chün-i has explained, "any circumstances we encounter may reveal to us what we ought to do; it is up to us to handle the circumstances in accord with our duty."[81]

Mencius states quite clearly that man should not expect to receive physical and material—external—rewards for good behavior. Interestingly, he never denies absolutely the operation of some form of supernatural retribution, simply the moral validity of human expectation of reward or punishment. A man should concern himself not with what he believes he deserves, but what he can do to nurture the goodness "within himself,"

[79] *Lunyu yinde*, 7.35 (pp. 13–14); 12.5 (p. 22); 6.22 (p. 11). Translations from D. C. Lau, trans., *Confucius: The Analects*, pp. 113, 84.

[80] *Mengzi yinde*, 7a.1–3 (pp. 50–51); translation from D. C. Lau, trans., *Mencius*, p. 182.

[81] T'ang Chün-i, "The Heavenly Ordinance [T'ien-ming] in Pre-Ch'in China," vol. 2, pp. 35, 31–37; and Tang Junyi, *Zhongguo zhexue yuanlun: Daolun pian*, pp. 500–612.

his moral nature: "Seek and you will get it; let go and you will lose it. If this is the case, then seeking is of use to getting and what is sought is within yourself. But if there is a proper way to seek it and whether you get it or not depends on fate, then seeking is of no use to getting and what is sought lies outside yourself." Thus, in his most famous statement on fate, Mencius concludes that a man who understands fate does virtue for its own sake, accepting without complaint whatever material and physical circumstances heaven has decreed for him—accepting them indeed as the very terms guiding his moral path: "For a man to give full realization to his heart is for him to understand his own nature, and a man who knows his own nature will know heaven. By retaining his heart and nurturing his nature he is serving heaven. Whether he is going to die young or to live to a ripe old age makes no difference to his steadfastness of purpose. It is through awaiting whatever is to befall him with a perfected character that he stands firm on his proper destiny."[82] Elaborating on Confucius, then, Mencius believed that an individual "stood on" or fulfilled his fate—*liming*—through self-cultivation.

This interpretation was to become the basis of the orthodox Neo-Confucian understanding of man's relationship to fate—that is, it became the interpretation established as standard in the civil service examinations in 1313. Zhu Xi, to a considerable degree the author of this orthodoxy, reaffirmed Mencius's ideas in his commentary on the text. Man, he explains, "stands on his proper fate" when he "fulfills what heaven has given him," his morally perfectible human nature. Good and bad fortune "comes without being caused," contrary to what the Buddhists claim; this is true both for the good man who does his best to follow the way and the wicked man who ignores it. Zhu Xi approvingly quotes Zhao Qi's (d. 201) analysis of Mencius's distinction between internal and external seeking: "It says that benevolence is from the self. Wealth and honor rest with heaven; you cannot seek them, so follow what you are fond of [i.e., benevolence]."[83]

Zhu also incorporated the Mencian view of fate into his own philosophical system, as set forth in the *Categorized Conversations of Master Zhu* (*Zhuzi yulei*). *Ming* here was interpreted in terms of principle (*li*) and pneuma (*qi*), the "psychophysical stuff" that forms the physical endowment of things. In terms of principle, *ming* refers to man's perfectible nature, the principle that heaven endowed in him; though the terms are different, this is essentially the same as Mencius's "proper fate," the fate that an individual could choose to fulfill or deny. But in terms of pneuma, *ming* means both the external circumstances of one's life—wealth, pov-

---

[82] *Mengzi yinde*, 7a.1 and 3 (pp. 50–51), translation from Lau, *Mencius*, pp. 182–183.
[83] *Mengzi*, 7.1b, 2a, in Zhu Xi, *Sishu jizhu*.

erty, and so forth—and the physical endowment of *qi* that determines a man's moral quality and intelligence at birth. The first is fixed, as in Mencius, but the second is potentially alterable: if the individual cultivates the principle within him, he may succeed in purifying his endowment of *qi* and achieving sagehood. Though the ontological underpinning of Zhu's view of fate is more complex than Mencius's, the final message is essentially the same: the good man ignores the fixed dictates of external fate while working to fulfill his heaven-endowed moral principle, his "proper fate."[84] He certainly does not engage in the careful calculation of good deeds in expectation of heavenly reward that is encouraged in the *Ledger of Merit and Demerit of the Taiwei Immortal.*

Since Zhu Xi's philosophy and interpretation of the Classics became the basis of the civil service examination system, his views on the issue of fate naturally exerted a widespread if not necessarily profound influence on literati. Even Wang Yangming, the great challenger of the Cheng-Zhu school, agreed with Zhu Xi on this point. He interpreted Mencius's explanation of fate much as Zhu Xi did, and he spoke quite firmly against doing good in the hopes of personal gain: "A man of benevolence conforms to the requirements of righteousness without seeking profit, and understands the Way without calculating merit. When once he has the intention of calculating gain, then even if he conforms to the requirements of righteousness and understands the Way, it is nothing but vainglory and profit."[85] Clearly, not all Chinese scholars, indeed not all officials, held to this Mencian interpretation of fate. But we can be certain that the vast majority of examination candidates were at least taught to believe that man should concern himself only with the perfection of his character while awaiting whatever changes in fortune heaven decreed for him.

These two very different views of fate—that of the mature merit-demerit system and that of classical Confucianism and orthodox Neo-Confucianism—naturally imply very different views of man's place in the cosmos. Both assume a moral universe, but the resemblance stops at that point. For the Confucian, heaven is a transcendent moral order or Way not immediately accessible to human knowledge or control. Though heaven has endowed each man with a good nature, it is not beyond that point really very intimately involved with the lives of men; men themselves decide to become good and then must struggle to learn the will of heaven. For believers in the supernatural retribution of the merit-demerit system, however, man is subject to a vast bureaucracy of gods and spirits (heaven

---

[84] Qian Mu, *Zhuzi xinxue'an*, vol. 1, pp. 480–522.

[85] Wang Yangming, *Instructions for Practical Learning*, p. 14; see also Wang Yangming, *The Philosophical Letters of Wang Yang-ming*, p. 36.

virtually disappears here), coterminous with and patterned after the human bureaucracy. The celestial bureaucracy is obsessively concerned with the affairs of men, examining their tiniest acts and innermost thoughts for hints of evil. This close surveillance is necessary to the maintenance of some degree of moral order in the system of merit and demerit. The authors of the system do not seem to share Mencius's faith that men are born with goodness in them and need only cultivate this original endowment in order to become perfectly good. Rather, in the spirit of Mozi (fl. late fifth century B.C.) and the Legalists, they hold the view that men need constant schooling—the hope of reward and the even more important threat of punishment—to make them behave properly. Men have, in fact, to be hounded into goodness. Certainly, the texts of the system, with their long lists of evils to be avoided, their descriptions of the horrible punishments that followed on evil, their stress on the omnipresence and omniscience of the spirits watching out for human misdeeds, and their precise accounts of the bookkeeping methods used to ensure that *all* deeds are recorded, suggest a pervasive sense of man's predisposition to evil.

Strictly speaking, then, the universe of the merit-demerit system was a rather threatening one for fallible human beings. There was, the texts assure us, no place for man to hide from divine justice. But there were certain beliefs about the real operation of the system that tended to reduce this sense of ever-impending judgment and to suggest even that divine justice might be open to human manipulation. The perception of the gods as divine bureaucrats very much like human bureaucrats made their behavior more understandable and more accessible to human influence. Man was on intimate, even familiar terms with the supernatural, what with the Three Worm Spirits living in his body, the Kitchen God resident in his home, and constellations of overseer stars hovering over his head. Furthermore, despite assurances of impartiality in the scriptures, it seemed that the celestial bureaucracy was just as susceptible to bribery, peculation, and simple error as the human. Stories abound in Chinese fiction of men who were able to bribe or trick the officials of hell into changing their registers of good and bad deeds. A Dunhuang text dating from the late Tang, for example, describes the negotiations that accompany the Tang emperor Taizong's (r. 627–649) descent to hell after his sudden death. Protesting that he is not ready to die, he demands that the registrar of hell, a certain Cui Ziyou, change his record and restore him to life. After rejecting several offers of money, Cui finally accepts the offer of a high-ranking official post in return for an additional ten years of life for the emperor.[86] Such accounts must have made it difficult for men to

[86] The whole story is translated in Arthur Waley, *Ballads and Songs from Tun-huang,* pp.

stand completely in awe of divine justice. When ledgers of merit and demerit began to be produced in the Song, the operation of retributive justice was further demystified—the gods, desirous of helping men to do
good, actually gave them the rules of the moral order, telling them how
many points each deed was worth. Far from "keeping the spirits at a distance," as Confucius had advised, the practitioners of merit accumulation
assumed constant and close contact with the gods.

So, too, the understanding of what goodness itself is and how it is cultivated is quite different in the two systems of belief. For Confucius, Mencius, and Zhu Xi, goodness was a coherent quality achieved after constant
self-cultivation and careful action. When one had achieved goodness, one
was able to follow the will of heaven as one's own will, without hesita-
tions or second thoughts—one had integrated the rules of the moral order
fully into one's own character. For users of the ledgers of merit and demerit, however, goodness was an aggregation of specific good deeds, including acts of faith. One became good simply by doing more good than
bad deeds and, if convenient, as many high-value good deeds as possible.
It is true that the preface to the *Ledger of Merit and Demerit of the Taiwei
Immortal* hints that merit accumulation was a discipline that would lead
to coherent, full-rounded goodness, but there is nothing in the system
itself to ensure this result or prevent a mechanical application of the
method. The precise values assigned the various deeds, coupled with the
concept of mutual merit-demerit cancellation, rather easily encouraged a
primitive form of moral practice. Certain good deeds—urging others to
do good or giving to the poor, for example—do not require rigorous internal cultivation or, for that matter, much real goodness. And why
couldn't saving the lives of one hundred ants (worth a merit each) cancel
out the murder of a human being (worth 100 demerits)? Doubtless this
kind of thinking would have shocked the originators of the system, but
until the sixteenth century little was written to discourage such an interpretation.

Indeed, at first glance it might seem that the system of merit and demerit offered man an extraordinary degree of control over his life. Confucians had allowed human control only over the individual's internal
moral improvement; and fatalists like Wang Chong denied even this limited area of control. By the Song, however, some believers in merit accumulation were beginning to argue that many aspects of a man's life—his
life span, his family's prosperity, and his spiritual condition—could be
improved through the performance of good deeds. But ultimately the system of merit and demerit, by virtue of the very complexity of its rules and

165–174. Soymié discusses this story and other examples in "Notes d'iconographie chinoise," part 2, pp. 147–170; see also part 1, pp. 72–73.

the loopholes in its organization and operation, actually suggests that there were severe and not fully knowable limits to a man's mastery of his fate. The individual's own behavior was by no means the only measure of his fate—at least three other factors had to be worked into the calculation: his original allotment, his inheritance of merit and demerit, and his own karma. Thus even after the individual was able to make a full record of his own deeds, there was no guarantee that he would benefit immediately or at all from them, since he had no influence over his original allotment, his family history, or his performance in a previous life. By the same token, he was not necessarily responsible for his bad fortune.[87]

Furthermore, the confusion and corruptibility of the bureaucratic system made it even harder for a man to be sure that he had real control over his fate. The multitude of spirits concerned with overseeing human behavior and the variety of methods used to record human acts, though they might have impressed man with the thoroughness of the system, must also have made him suspicious of its accuracy. If the spirits were susceptible to bribery, they must surely have been capable of committing clerical errors, easy to make but possibly fatal to the hapless victim.[88] To be sure, the merit-demerit system, even with all its complexities, still encouraged good behavior: bureaucratic lapses were perceived to be exceptions rather than the rule; and a man could always hope to improve his own fate, and could count on being able to improve his next life or the fate of his descendants. But the system, at least in its pre-sixteenth-century expression, by no means offered a failsafe method for reward.

On the other hand, while Mencius and the Neo-Confucians restricted the arena of human control, they allowed the individual full control within it. Each man had the potential to be perfectly good, to be someone who acted properly in any situation. He could not determine or change the external circumstances that put him to the test—for example, he could not arrange to develop his virtue amid wealth rather than poverty—but his course of action within the conditions imposed upon him was free. He was then fully responsible for his acts, unable to blame either a checkered family past or karmic retribution or even a careless celestial scribe for a "death in fetters."

Perhaps because of the very limits it placed on human control and re-

[87] Tachibana Shiraki suggests that these difficulties led to a kind of fatalism on the part of the Chinese, a fatalism that in turn encouraged a reluctance to change among all classes, and a pervasive selfishness among the ruling classes. (See *Dōkyō to shinwa densetsu—Chūgoku no minken shinkō—*, pp. 138–140, 161–162.) But one could argue just as easily that the belief that a man could to some degree control his own fate through his behavior would lead to an optimism about one's chances in life. See Stevan Harrell, "The Concept of Fate in Chinese Folk Ideology."

[88] See also Soymié, "Notes d'iconographie chinoise," part 1, p. 72.

sponsibility, the system of merit and demerit provided an almost airtight ideology, a perfectly consistent explanation for most social phenomena. Confucian thinkers, in contrast, could not really explain why some men, even wicked men, might be wealthy and others, including good men, might be poor, except by rather vague references to heaven's arbitrary decree, or, more subversively, to the moral corruption of the existing order, in which good men were not rewarded by the ruler. The system of merit and demerit could explain everything much more neatly by invoking the concepts of transmigration or inherited merit and demerit. All those gods and spirits, with their records and complex methods of accounting, had calculated each man's moral balance and thus his just deserts down to the half-merit point. They saw to it that the social order, the material world, was perfectly just—was, indeed, a reflection of the internal moral order: with the exception of a few victims (or beneficiaries) of bureaucratic corruption and inefficiency, everyone got in this life what a sensitive and timeless system of cosmic justice had determined he deserved.

Thus the principles and implications of the system of merit accumulation set it clearly apart from the classic Confucian and orthodox Neo-Confucian understanding of man's relationship to fate. In the Song the contradiction between the two systems was not fully explored; in the Ming, however, it was brought to a head when an elite believer in merit accumulation tried to reconcile the Confucian practice of virtue for its own sake with the "heterodox" keeping of a ledger of merit and demerit.

CHAPTER TWO

Merit Accumulation for Status Advancement

IT WAS NOT until four centuries after the appearance of the *Ledger of Merit and Demerit of the Taiwei Immortal* that the system of merit-demerit calculation began to attract widespread notice among Chinese literati. This "morality book movement" began in the sixteenth century, reaching its peak in the seventeenth and eighteenth centuries.[1] While the forces behind the revival of interest in the morality books and ledgers were many and complex, linked to the great social, economic, and intellectual changes of the period, one man in particular did come to be closely associated with the new popularity of the texts: Yuan Huang, a scholar-official from Jiashan county, Zhejiang. Yuan was well able to speak for the ledger system, for he attributed his own considerable success in life to his practice of merit accumulation. His autobiographical essay, "Determining Your Own Fate" ("Liming pian"), one of the major vehicles for the transmission of the ledger system in the late Ming, was written with all the conviction of a well-satisfied convert: in it Yuan claimed that his success in the examinations and even the birth of his first son were the result of ledger use.

"Determining Your Own Fate" certainly appears to have been a persuasive text, for within a century of its publication, at least ten new ledgers were produced. One disgruntled observer complained that they had become even more popular than the Classics among contemporary scholars.[2] Throughout the seventeenth century, and even into the twentieth century, the ledgers were closely associated with Yuan Huang. Many later ledgers and morality books reproduced "Determining Your Own Fate" along with the *Tract on Action and Response* and the *Ledger of Merit and Demerit of the Taiwei Immortal,* the two "classics" of the system, as the basic guides to merit accumulation. Admirers and critics alike associated Yuan Huang with the ledgers, and even casual references to the texts in literary collections and gazetteers commonly linked them to Yuan Huang.

This is not to say that Yuan Huang was entirely responsible for rescuing the system of merit and demerit from obscurity. Knowledge of the system never lapsed completely between the twelfth and sixteenth centu-

---

[1] Sakai Tadao, "Chūgokushijō no shomin kyōiku to zensho undō," pp. 295–296.

[2] These new ledgers are discussed in chapters 4 and 5. Zhang Lixiang, *Yangyuan xiansheng quanji,* 5.10b (p. 115).

ries. The *Tract on Action and Response* remained a popular text, reprinted under imperial auspices, and drawing the attention of at least one new commentator.[3] In the early Ming, the Hungwu emperor (r. 1368–1398) sponsored an extensive campaign of morality-book publication. Most of the texts produced as part of this campaign suggested that divine as well as imperial punishments could be expected for any violation of their prescriptions.[4] It is even possible that new ledgers were written during these four centuries: the *Ledger of Merit and Demerit of the Ten Precepts (Shijie gongguoge)* and the *Ledger of Merit and Demerit for Awakening the World (Jingshi gongguoge)* have been tentatively dated to the Yuan period.[5]

Moreover, from the fifteenth century on, literati were more and more attracted to forms of self-cultivation and education that were in certain ways similar to the ledger approach. These scholars wrote confessional essays in which they described their misdeeds or kept checklists of evil acts and attitudes to avoid.[6] Beyond the narrow limits of literati self-correction, moral list-making was used both to train young students and to regulate the behavior of commoners in community compacts. Lü Kun (1536–1618), in his *Community Compact (Xiangjia yue)*, employed a ledger-like list of good and bad deeds divided into categories of "large good," "small good," "large evil," and "small evil"; in certain circumstances an evil-doer could pay a fine to the community to have his wrong pardoned.[7]

Literati of the sixteenth century also read and used ledgers of merit and demerit. Luo Rufang (1515–1588), though noted primarily as a disciple of Wang Yangming, had in his youth been a follower of the Jingming Zhongxiao Dao, and had kept a ledger of merit and demerit in accordance with the regulations of that Daoist sect.[8] Interest in the texts was by no means limited to Neo-Confucians: Yunqi Zhuhong (1535–1615), the great Pure Land master, read the *Ledger of Merit and Demerit of the Taiwei Immortal* as a young man and admired it so much that he had it

[3] In the late Yuan the text was reorganized and reprinted by Chen Jian, with the title *Taishang ganying ling pian tushuo* (1324).

[4] Sakai, *Chūgoku zensho*, pp. 7–41.

[5] These texts are reprinted in the *Daocang jiyao, Zhangji,* 3.1a–81b. Robert Van Gulick discusses them briefly in *Sexual Life in Ancient China,* pp. 246–250.

[6] For a discussion of these works, see Pei-yi Wu, "Self-Examination and Confession of Sins in Traditional China," pp. 22–34; Handlin, *Action in Late Ming Thought,* pp. 186–212. For an example of this kind of record, see Lü Kun's "Xingxin ji," in *Quwei zhai wenji,* 3.26b–32b, *Lüzi yishu.*

[7] Lü Kun, *Xiangjia yue,* in *Shizheng lu,* 5.23a–25a, 27b–33a, *Lüzi yishu.*

[8] Akizuki, *Chūgoku kinsei Dōkyō,* pp. 175–176. See also Handlin, *Action in Late Ming Thought,* p. 194. Wang Ji, Gao Panlong, and Tu Long (1542–1605) were apparently also familiar with the teachings of the Jingming Zhongxiao Dao.

reprinted and distributed free of charge. As an old man he turned back to this text, revising it considerably and publishing it as the *Record of Self-Knowledge* (*Zizhi lu*, 1606).[9] Indeed, Yuan Huang himself was converted to the system of merit accumulation by a Chan monk, Yungu (1500–1575?; m. Fahui), who was able to supply him with a new ledger, one quite different from the *Ledger of the Taiwei Immortal*.

Thus the system of merit accumulation and even the ledger form itself were hardly unknown in the sixteenth century. Contemporary scholars and officials seem to have valued the form now as a tool, not only for the education of the common people in values supportive of social order, but also for their own personal moral improvement. The late sixteenth century in particular was a time when changes in the economy and in social relations were undermining the traditional role of the literati: the new power and influence of merchants and the greater economic independence of most of the different ranks of agricultural laborers from gentry control created a sense of social and moral confusion. In a culture dominated by a belief in the interpenetration of the social and moral orders, widespread and easily observable changes in social relationships naturally inspired a sense of moral unease or doubt among those who were accustomed to think of themselves as caretakers of a sacred tradition. Furthermore, Wang Yangming's direct challenge to the orthodox interpretation of this tradition exacerbated the sense of insecurity and anxiety, even among those who accepted Wang's ideas. In this context, it is easy to see how texts providing precise outlines for behavior would be attractive to literati whose self-perceived task was to see that the great truths of the culture, specifically those to be found in the Confucian Classics, were expressed in the concrete actions of everyday life.

Nonetheless there were still considerable limits to literati interest in the texts. Confucian scholars were uneasy about the "heterodox" Buddhist and Daoist origins of the ledgers and were quick to repudiate the idea implicit in the system of merit accumulation that one could expect personal benefits in return for good deeds. In their own private self-cultivation, most scholars were careful to keep lists of demerits only, lest their thoughts turn to profit seeking. Luo Rufang eventually repudiated ledger keeping and destroyed his own ledger out of just this fear. Others disliked the piecemeal approach to self-cultivation the ledger method embodied. Zou Yuanbiao (1551–1624), Yang Dongming (1548–1624), and Feng Congwu (1556–1627?) warned their friend Lü Kun against it, arguing that it could never lead to the cultivation of a full and coherent under-

[9] Yunqi Zhuhong, "*Zizhi lu xu,*" *Zizhi lu*, 1a, in *Yunqi fahui*. See Chün-fang Yü, *Renewal of Buddhism*, pp. 101–137, 233–259, for an analysis and translation of Zhuhong's ledger.

standing of goodness.[10] Even in applying their checklists to public education, literati emphasized the proscriptive value of the form, minimizing the notion that good deeds would earn rewards. Lü Kun explicitly warned members of his community compact that deeds done to seek good fortune from the gods could not count as good deeds.[11] However much the intellectual and moral climate of the sixteenth century might have appeared receptive to the ledger form, then, Confucian scholars before Yuan Huang were for the most part reluctant to take up the full ledger-of-merit-and-demerit form, with all its dangerous moral and "heterodox" religious implications. Thus it is not surprising that the two open supporters of the ledger system before Yuan Huang were Buddhist monks—the above-mentioned Yunqi Zhuhong and Yungu.

What was different about Yuan Huang? A *jinshi* degree-holder and official, he shared an education in Neo-Confucian principles with contemporary literati. Why was he able to embrace the ledger system with unambiguous enthusiasm while his contemporaries hesitated over its un-Confucian elements? More to the point, what was it about Yuan Huang's treatment of the ledger system that made it so widely popular? What social and moral conditions made his system attractive to contemporary literati?

THE YUAN FAMILY TRADITION

Yuan Huang's own life appears at first glance to have been unexceptional. From a well-to-do landowning family in Jiashan county, Zhejiang, he was the first of the family to participate in the civil service examinations. After five failures, he finally passed the examination for the *jinshi* degree in 1586. He was appointed district magistrate of Baodi county, Northern Zhili, in 1588, and in 1593 he was promoted to the post of secretary of the Board of War. Sent to Korea as a special military councilor, he was forced to leave this post before completing a full year of service to answer charges of misconduct in office. After his impeachment he returned home to write and look after the family estates until his death at the age of 74.[12]

But a closer examination of the Yuan family tradition and of Yuan Huang's own particular place in the family line reveals habits of learning and extraordinary pressures to succeed that made Yuan Huang's background in fact rather out of the ordinary. They go a long way toward explaining his susceptibility to the system of merit accumulation.

In the late fourteenth century the Yuans appeared to be a family des-

[10] Handlin, *Action in Late Ming Thought*, pp. 189–190, 200.
[11] Lü Kun, *Xiangjia yue*, in *Shizheng lu*, 5.23b, *Lüzi yishu*.
[12] For fuller biographical information on Yuan Huang himself, see Okuzaki, *Chūgoku kyōshin jinushi*, pp. 129–206; and L. Carrington Goodrich and Chaoying Fang, eds., *Dictionary of Ming Biography*, vol. 2, pp. 1632–1635.

tined for success. Owners of roughly four thousand *mu* of land in the village of Taozhuang, Jiashan county, they were one of the prominent families of the area. Yuan Shun, the family patriarch, was known locally as a scholar of the Six Classics (i.e., the *Classic of Changes*, the *Classic of Songs*, the *Classic of History*, the *Spring and Autumn Annals*, the *Record of Rites*, and the *Rites of Zhou*). As a member of a society for the practice of righteousness and propriety, founded by local literati, he practiced a method of moral cultivation similar to that presented in the ledgers of merit and demerit: with other Jiashan literati, he formed a society for the practice of righteousness and propriety. Each member was required to keep a daily record of his conduct, a report of which had to be submitted to the other members every month. Status within the society was determined not by seniority, but by the relative quantity and difficulty of each member's good deeds: "Consequently, all were resolute in the performance of good deeds, as if they were racing toward righteousness."[13]

Shun's vigorous pursuit of virtue had an unfortunate effect on the family's fortunes, however. He sided loyally with the forces resisting Zhu Di's (1360–1424) usurpation of the throne in 1399, and on the accession of the new emperor in 1402, he and his family had to flee for their lives. Abandoning the Yuan home in Jiashan, they settled in Wujiang county, across the border in Southern Zhili. Since they had lost most of their property in their flight from Jiashan, they had to find some other source of livelihood. Official service was of course closed to them; Yuan Shun's political indiscretion had caused his family members to be barred from participation in the civil service examinations.[14] They chose to follow the profession of medicine, which had become one of the most popular and respectable career options for scholars unable to compete for office.[15] Yuan Hao explained this choice as one made largely for moral reasons:

Scholars, peasants, artisans, and merchants are the four categories of people. My family cannot compete in the examinations, my descendants probably do not have the ability to farm, and neither crafts nor mercantile activity can be

[13] Yuan Hao, *YSCS*, 1.1b. The edition used here, from the Naikaku Bunko, is the late-Ming version edited by Hao's great-grandson, Yuan Huang. Okuzaki Hiroshi translates portions of the first two essays of the *Yuanshi jiaxun*, "Jia'nan pian" and "Minzhi pian," in *Chūgoku kyōshin jinushi*, pp. 72–78.

[14] To qualify to take an examination, a candidate had to give the names of his father, grandfather, and great-grandfather; he was excluded from competition if any of these men had been criminals. Yuan Shun, as a "rebel," fell into this category. Yuan Hao was still, three-quarters of a century after the fact, worried about the possibility of punishment for Yuan Shun's actions; he urged the family to wait until the fourth generation after Yuan Shun (Yuan Huang's generation) before planning to participate in the examination system. *YSCS*, 1.31a–b. See Okuzaki, *Chūgoku kyōshin jinushi*, pp. 82–86.

[15] Robert Hymes, "Not Quite Gentlemen? Doctors in Sung and Yuan," pp. 44, 52, 57–65; and Angela Ki Che Leung, "Organized Medicine in Ming-Qing China: State and Private Medical Institutions in the Lower Yangzi Region," pp. 151–153.

considered dependable as a means of raising a family. But we cannot be without a plan. In ancient times Deng Yu had thirteen sons, and he taught them each to master a profession, as the best way of being a model for the world. Today, in selecting a technique from among the professions, only medicine is close to benevolence. In practicing it, one can save life and raise a family, one can spread kindness and save many lives.[16]

Yuan Shun's son Hao (1414–1494), his grandson Xiang (1448–1503), and his great-grandson Ren (1479–1546) were all physicians, and even Yuan Huang studied medicine for a time.

The *Yuan Family Instructions* (*Yuanshi jiaxun*), written by Yuan Hao and published around 1479, reflects the family struggle to come to terms, intellectually and socially, with the abrupt change in family fortunes. Following his father's instructions, Hao repeatedly urged his sons to give up all thoughts of fame and high rank, and to devote themselves to the humble and upright conduct expected of "good commoners" (*liangmin*). For Yuan Hao, the simple precepts contained in Ming Taizu's *Placard of Public Instruction* (*Jiaomin bangwen*) defined the behavior of a good commoner: "Emperor Taizu's *Placard of Public Instruction* says, 'Filially obey your mother and father, respect your elders and superiors, be at peace with your neighbors, instruct your sons and grandsons each to be at peace in a livelihood, do not do wrong.' These define the duty of a commoner. If you fulfill these regulations, and vigorously follow them, you can emulate the worthies, you can imitate the sages, and you can achieve heavenly greatness."[17] Particularly important was the practice of humility—as commoners now, the Yuans were to be especially modest and tolerant in their dealings with others, accepting even unjustified insults without demure. Fearing that the family still might not escape the harsh punishment meted out to other opponents of the Yongle emperor, Hao thus advocated a conservative and self-protective family strategy: the Yuans should stay out of trouble with their neighbors and the authorities by being modest and law-abiding subjects, quietly biding their time and rebuilding the family economy until the time came, four or five generations hence, for them to compete in the civil service examinations.[18]

Not surprisingly, the sudden decline in the family fortunes encouraged among the Yuans a somewhat fatalistic view of life. Quoting from Yuan Cai's (fl. 1140–1195) *Precepts for Social Life* (*Yuanshi shifan*), Hao explained that wealth and social status were fixed arbitrarily by heaven and bore no relationship to an individual's conduct: "Personal conduct and changes in social standing are two separate matters; there is no basis for

[16] Yuan Hao, YSCS, 1.26b.
[17] Ibid., 1.23b.
[18] See Sakai, *Chūgoku zensho*, pp. 351–352.

thinking that proper conduct will lead naturally to glory and honor and improper conduct to misery and frustration. If such were the case, Confucius and Yan Yuan would have been prime ministers, and throughout history there never would have been an inferior man occupying a top post."[19]

Certainly, this fatalistic view would explain why the Yuan family suffered for Shun's courageous and upright practice of one of the cardinal Chinese virtues, loyalty to the rightful ruler. Destined not to acquire official rank, the Yuans, like all men who truly understood the workings of fate, should simply continue to devote themselves to moral action for its own sake:

> Since my family no longer seeks official position, we have cut off thoughts of glory and high status, and hold fast to propriety of conduct. It is on the basis of this precept that we should act: our speech must be pure and our conduct true; we should study and illuminate the Way, and discipline ourselves and aid others, always without the slightest expectation of reward. Without seeking any worldly success, we must study and cultivate the proper moral standards, so that we can become good commoners, so that we can be free of shame. Do not think of glory and rank. Now, fame and achievements are fixed from birth. Ignorant men, without much understanding, wildly rush about, trying to get ahead. But those who gain by rushing about are no more than one or two, while those who do not gain number in the millions. If we take all the people in the world, and only one or two are successful in this way, then most gain nothing, even though they work hard and exert all their energy until death. Without understanding this principle, others succeed by rushing about, but it is only because of their fixed lot that they succeed. If success had been their fate, then even if they hadn't rushed about, in the end, perhaps after some delays, they would have succeeded anyway. Therefore, if you have lofty vision and insight, you can escape the limitations of the concept of causality, attribute events to random fate, and remain at peace with yourself, without grief, pleasure, or resentment.[20]

Here Yuan Hao was prescribing a very Confucian response to the family plight. The gentleman, Mencius argued, "awaits whatever is to befall him with a perfected character"; just so, the Yuans were to devote themselves to study and disciplined conduct, accepting whatever fate had in store for them, "without the slightest expectation of reward."

But alongside this Mencian vision of the "good" life, Hao also preserved the apparently contradictory notion that the accumulation of se-

---

[19] Yuan Hao, YSCS, 1.30b (see also 1.30a); translation from Patricia Ebrey, *Family and Property in Sung China: Yuan Ts'ai's Precepts for Social Life*, pp. 233, 235–236.
[20] Yuan Hao, YSCS, 1.31b–32a.

cret merit over generations would eventually improve the family fortunes. For in the very same essay in which he propounded fatalism and urged his family to do good "always without the slightest expectation of reward," he also made the following calculation: "Over sixty years ago I gave up my studies for the examinations and took up the calling of medicine. Even though I cannot have been free of faults, I have had compassion for the poor, have rescued the distressed, and have thereby accumulated an incalculable store of secret merit. My descendants should preserve it from generation to generation."[21] As soon as possible, in the fourth generation after Yuan Shun, family members entered the examination system, assuming that by then this store of merit would influence the outcome. Yuan Ren, Huang's father, explained: "For several generations my family has accumulated merit without taking the examinations. How could my descendants not be successful in them?"[22] When Yuan Huang later asserted that examination success depended not on the candidate's own ability, but on his ancestors' store of merit, he was clearly referring to this traditional family belief.[23]

The Yuans' faith in two apparently conflicting views of fate is echoed in and perhaps even explained by their ambivalence toward the relationship between Confucian morality and the civil service examination system. Exclusion from the examination system, roughly equivalent to exclusion from the highest ranks of society, was a great blow to the Yuans, as it would have been to any prosperous and ambitious family. The Yuans chose to take comfort in the fact that freedom from examination competition allowed them to practice Confucian virtue in an atmosphere untainted by careerism and worldly ambition. Yuan Hao repeatedly castigated contemporary officials for their ambition and lack of real learning and dedication to the emperor: "As for officials of ancient times, when they were studying, their wills were completely on [the good of] the empire and the nation; as for today's officials, when they are studying, their wills seek only their own individual glory. Their use of their minds is very different, and therefore their service is likewise different. True and upright, superior men do not discuss becoming officials."[24] In contrast, one often found the greatest loyalty and the truest virtue among commoners. If the Yuans carefully fulfilled the duties of the commoner outlined in the

---

[21] Ibid., 1.27a.

[22] Yuan Zhong, *Tingwei zalu*, 2.15.

[23] Yuan Huang, *LMP*, 9a. He wrote: "Generally speaking, those who pass the examinations do so because of the store of merit accumulated by their forebearers. Today, young men who pass smugly and self-importantly take the credit for themselves, without reflecting on the difficulty their ancestors had over the generations in building up [merit] for the examinations."

[24] Yuan Hao, *YSCS*, 1.33b–34a.

Placard, after all, they could "emulate the worthies, imitate the sages, and even achieve heavenly greatness."[25] The Yuans, then, were able to interpret their exclusion from civil service as a benefit: whatever its disadvantages, it allowed them to practice real Confucian virtues with undivided minds.

Of course, reentry into examination competition was nonetheless a clear goal for the family, for as soon as it was legally possible, the Yuans started preparing. Yet even then they did not lose the sense that study for the examinations could have a corrupting influence. Yuan Ren thus warned his sons (including Yuan Huang) to beware of losing their long-cultivated moral purity in the process of seeking examination success:

> There are three ranks of scholars: those who set their wills on virtue form the highest, those who set their wills on worthy reputation form the middle rank, and those who set their wills on wealth and high status form the lowest. These days, young men vary in their natural endowments, but their parents, teachers, and friends hope that they will all attain wealth and high status. If these young men are fortunate enough to succeed in the examinations, [they do not think] beyond wealth and high status—they no longer know what worthy reputation is. How much less do they think of virtue!
>
> My grandfather raised my father to be an outstanding and accomplished scholar; likewise my father raised me not to be ignorant. None of us studied for the examinations, but learned the essence of the Five Classics and the ancients. Now in raising you brothers, and in beginning to teach you to prepare for the examinations, I too do not want you to look vainly toward wealth and high status. The loyal service of Yi Yin and the Duke of Zhou and the writings of Confucius and Mencius are all appropriate objects of study for young men. The attainment of high status rests in heaven; the cultivation of virtue rests in oneself. Do not throw away what is in yourself, nor force that which rests only with heaven.[26]

Yuan Ren was by no means alone in expressing doubts about the moral validity of the examinations. Many more famous thinkers of the late Ming and early Qing, including Fang Yizhi (1611–1671), Huang Zongxi, and Gu Yanwu, criticized the way in which competition for the wealth and status of office tended to corrupt the integrity of examination candidates.[27] In the end, Yuan Ren was clearly ambivalent about the system: he could not help taking advantage of the opportunity to train his sons to take the examinations, but in the midst of their preparation he also could

---

[25] Ibid., 1.23b.

[26] Yuan Zhong, *Tingwei zalu*, 1.4; cited also in Sakai, *Chūgoku zensho*, p. 328.

[27] Peterson, *Bitter Gourd*, pp. 52–63; and Paul Ropp, *Dissent in Early Modern China*, pp. 93–101.

not help reminding them that since worldly success is arbitrarily determined, they should never neglect the honest cultivation of virtue.

The Yuans interpreted their own history as a dogged effort to preserve pure Confucian standards during troubled times. Yuan Hao praised his father for upholding the highest Confucian standards of loyalty in his opposition to a usurper, and considered his brother, exiled in punishment for his father's acts, a hero who needed to feel no shame "before the moral laws."[28] As a sign of his own sentiments, Hao included an essay commemorating the reign of the Jianwen emperor (r. 1398–1402), the victim of Zhu Di's usurpation, in the *Family Instructions*. He also justified the choice of medicine as the family profession in Confucian moral terms: medicine would encourage the Yuans to practice benevolence. The Yuans were careful also to continue their study of the Confucian canon, even though they could not participate in the examinations.

This freedom from participation in the examinations allowed family members to depart somewhat from the orthodox approach to the canon. The Yuans tended to prefer the Five or Six Classics to the Four Books (the *Analects, Mencius, Greater Learning*, and *Doctrine of the Mean*), the texts at the heart of examination preparation in the fifteenth and sixteenth centuries.[29] Furthermore, the Yuans never associated themselves with any particular tradition of classical interpretation. Yuan Ren, in his commentaries on the Classics, made his antagonism to the orthodox Neo-Confucian interpretations very clear. The editors of the *Annotated General Catalogue of the Siku quanshu (Siku quanshu zongmu tiyao)*, commenting on his *Inquiries into the Classic of Songs (Maoshi huowen)*, complained that he "slandered" Zhu Xi by comparing his reading of the *Songs* to "a blind man's passing his hands over an elephant [in a vain attempt to figure out what it was]," and an essay of his on the *Classic of History* was likewise dismissed as "deliberately heterodox."[30] In fact Ren repudiated not only the Cheng-Zhu interpretation, the "orthodox" reading required in the civil service examinations, but also that of the Wang Yangming school. Though a friend of Wang Yangming, Wang Gen, and Wang Ji, he maintained that the family tradition was more faithful to

[28] Yuan Hao, *YSCS*, 1.25a.

[29] All of the essays and commentaries on the Classics in the *Yuanshi congshu* are on the Five Classics. Yuan Huang was the first of the family to write on the Four Books; he wrote the *Yuan Xiansheng Sishu xun'er sushuo* and the *Liaofan Yuan Xiansheng Sishu shanzheng jianshuyi* (both in the Naikaku Bunko). See Okuzaki, *Chūgoku kyōshin jinushi*, pp. 232, 237–239, 245–246.

[30] The comment on the *Maoshi huowen* makes use of a Buddhist phrase describing the delusions of the unenlightened man, who believes that the things of the world are real. *Siku quanshu zongmu*, 17.10a and 12.18a; cited in Okuzaki, *Chūgoku kyōshin jinushi*, p. 238n.19, and p. 214.

Confucian moral truth than either the "commonplace" (*su*) teachings of Zhu Xi or the "empty" (*xu*) doctrines of Wang Yangming.[31]

Maintaining their independence from the two major schools of Neo-Confucianism, the Yuans borrowed freely from other non-Confucian religious and intellectual traditions. As physicians, the Yuans were well trained in methods of cure usually associated with Daoist teachings. Yuan Hao, in the rules for the practice of medicine he passed down to his sons, associated medicine not only with the "Way of benevolence," but also with the "Way of immortality." He urged physicians to study the "gate of the mysterious" (*xuanmen*), the "gate of the mysterious female" (*xuanpin zhi men*), and the proper methods for preserving one's *yang* cosmic matter (*yangqi*), as these techniques would all be useful in treating diseases not curable through the prescription of conventional herbal medicines and acupuncture.[32] Yuan Ren, Hao's grandson, wrote several essays on the movements of cosmic pneuma (*qi*) and offered advice on the manipulation of these movements for the extension of life.[33] As Yuan Hao himself admitted, the Yuans tended to use these techniques for purposes other than the attainment of immortality, but they nonetheless bespeak considerable familiarity with Daoist learning, particularly that of the Jindan or Inner Alchemy school.[34] Furthermore, the Yuans were interested in techniques of prognostication also commonly linked to Daoist practices. Both Yuan Hao and Yuan Ren studied Shao Yong's *Supreme Principles that Rule the World* (*Huangji jingshi*), an elaborate numerological analysis of the past and prediction of the future based largely on a process of division by the number four.[35] Thus the Yuan family scholarly tradition included a fairly broad knowledge of so-called Daoist techniques of inner alchemy and prognostication as well as thorough study of the Confucian Classics.

Buddhism, the other great "heterodox" religion, also entered into the Yuan family beliefs, although its role was rather small in the generations before Yuan Huang. Yuan Hao made several favorable references to Buddhism in his prescriptions for study in the *Family Instructions*, urging at

---

[31] Yuan Zhong, *Tingwei zalu*, 1.4. For a discussion of the Yuan family scholarly tradition, see Okuzaki, *Chūgoku kyōshin jinushi*, pp. 212–220. On Yuan Ren's relationship with Wang Yangming and his followers, see Wang Ji, "Yuan Canpo xiaozhuan," in *YSCS*, 11.1b–2a.

[32] Yuan Hao, *YSCS*, 1.28a–b.

[33] Yuan Ren, "Yunqi zonglun" and "Wuyun lun," in *YSCS*, 10.53a–56b.

[34] Sakai, *Chūgoku zensho*, pp. 334–336.

[35] Yuan Ren, "Ji Xianzu Juchuan yishi," in *YSCS*, 10.50b. See Sakai, *Chūgoku zensho*, pp. 334–337. On Shao Yong and the *Huangji jingshi*, see Michael D. Freeman, "From Adept to Worthy: The Philosophical Career of Shao Yung," pp. 481–482; and Anne D. Birdwhistell, *Transition to Neo-Confucianism: Shao Yung on Knowledge and Symbols of Reality*, pp. 14–15, 46–48, and passim.

one point that his sons use the four types of practice (*gongfu*) of the Buddhists in their moral cultivation.[36] In his last instructions to his sons, Yuan Ren included an injunction to respect the Three Treasures (*sanbao*)—that is, the Buddha, the Buddhist laws, and the Buddhist monastic orders. His wife, Yuan Huang's mother, was noted for her Buddhist piety and charitable deeds.[37]

This mixed intellectual and religious tradition heavily influenced Yuan Huang's own thinking. He certainly shared his father's hostility to the orthodox Cheng-Zhu readings of the Confucian Classics, for in his own commentary to the Four Books he made it clear that he included Zhu Xi's interpretations only for the sake of readers interested in examination preparation.[38] While he was much more sympathetic to the Wang Yangming school in his readings of the Classics and in his understanding of merit accumulation, he remained very much an independent thinker, leaning toward the Taizhou school perhaps, but ultimately the author of a quite distinctive system of thought.

There is no doubt that his inheritance of the family knowledge of Daoist medical and prognosticatory techniques also played a role, albeit a minor one, in this system of thought. Although he repudiated the cruder forms of fatalism, Yuan himself was skilled in certain methods of prognostication. While serving in Korea he is said to have practiced "watching for the ethers" (*wangqi*), trying to predict the success of the Chinese expedition through an analysis of atmospheric forces.[39] After his retirement he dabbled in methods of attaining immortality, searching for herbs that might endow eternal life or practicing the techniques of the Jindan school.[40]

But Buddhism became perhaps the dominant influence on Yuan Huang's personal beliefs. His mother's piety made a deep impression on him as a boy, and his later conversion to the merit-demerit system by a Chan monk must have strengthened his faith. Peng Shaosheng (1740–1796), who included Yuan Huang in his *Biographies of Lay Monks* (*Jushi zhuan*), described Yuan's life in retirement, "reciting sutras and incantations and practicing Chan meditation," and praised his disciplined adherence to the Buddhist Dharma and his ambition to save others from the

[36] Yuan Hao, *YSCS*, 2.6b; see also 2.3b–4a, 5a, 8a, 11a, 15b–16a.

[37] Yuan Zhong, *Tingwei zalu*, 2.9, 15–16, 18. See Okuzaki, *Chūgoku kyōshin jinushi*, p. 211, on the Yuan family interest in Buddhism.

[38] Yuan Huang, *Liaofan xiansheng sishu shanzheng jianshuyi, Fanli*, 1b–4a. Reference from Liu Ts'un-yan, "Yuan Huang and His 'Four Admonitions,' " p. 126.

[39] Goodrich, *Ming Biography*, vol. 2, p. 1633; see also Derk Bodde, "The Chinese Cosmic Magic Known as Watching for the Ethers," pp. 351–372.

[40] Peng Shaosheng, *Jushi zhuan*, 45.3b–4a.

evils of the "five kaṣāya periods of decay" (*wuzhuo*).[41] Yuan Huang was also an active supporter of Buddhist institutions. He regularly made contributions to monasteries and temples in the Jiashan and Wujiang areas and was one of the initial organizers of the project to publish the Jiaxing Tripitaka, later completed under the sponsorship of Zibo Zhenke (1544–1604) and Guan Zhidao (1536–1608). In an essay explaining his interest in this project, he suggested that examination candidates be tested on the Buddhist sutras as well as the Confucian Classics, a clear indication of the high esteem in which he held Buddhist doctrine.[42] And Yuan's use of a ledger of merit and demerit was grounded in worship of the Buddha and other Buddhist deities; he continued to rely on the advice of monks in his lifelong dedication to the system. At the very least, Yuan had the lay commitment to Buddhist doctrines and practices common to so many of his contemporaries.

Yuan, then, inherited from the family tradition a kind of religious and intellectual inclusivity. This is not to say that he did not discriminate between doctrines: witness his doubts about Zhu Xi's commentaries and his repudiation of an easy fatalism. But he was perfectly willing to accept practices and principles from any teaching or school, as long as they were consistent with his own understanding of the universe. No text reveals more clearly his willingness to draw freely on any and all teachings than his *Guide to Praying for an Heir* (*Qisi zhenquan*), a manual of advice for the production of sons published in 1591. Drawing most heavily on allusions to the Classics, the first two sections of this work urge moral reform—the correction of faults and the accumulation of good. But by far the greater bulk of the text, sections three through ten, outline methods derived from the Jindan school of inner alchemy, accepted medical practice, and popular Buddhist prayers. The aspiring father is urged to "concentrate his essence" (*jujing*), "nourish his *qi*" (*yangqi*), and "establish his spirit" (*cunshen*) through breathing exercises. Designed originally to lead a practitioner to immortality, these methods were commonly put to the more mundane physical end Yuan assigns them here, the conception of a son. Yuan also gives advice on the various stages of pregnancy and the cure of illnesses associated with pregnancy, advice presumably gleaned from his knowledge of the family medical practice. Buddhist principles are introduced to support some of the Daoist techniques: thus Yuan asserts that the Chan concept of meditation (*zhiguan*) is the essence of "establishing the spirit," and he quotes the *Flower Garland Sutra* (*Huayan jing*), Tiantai doctrines, as well as the *Classic of Cinnabar* (*Dan*

---

[41] Ibid., 45.3b. The five kaṣāya periods of decay begin twenty thousand years before the end of the kalpa of "existing and abiding" (*ju*).

[42] Sakai, *Chūgoku zensho*, pp. 339–341. See also Liu, "Yuan Huang and His 'Four Admonitions,' " p. 115.

jing) in support of that method. Finally, Yuan closes his manual with a section listing the incantations or mantras—all of them Buddhist—necessary to the successful completion of the process: an incantation to Guanyin ("Baiyi Guanyin jingzhou"), one to the goddess Zhunti, commonly associated with Guanyin ("Zhunti zhou"), and a dhāraṇī or spell for "following one's mind" (*suixin tuoluoni*). He also outlines the various methods for "fixing" (*shouchi*) the incantation, to ensure that it be efficacious.[43] A true heir to a very mixed family tradition, Yuan Huang freely mixed Jindan techniques, Buddhist doctrines of a variety of sectarian orientations, from Chan and Tiantai to the esoteric school, along with "Confucian" classical allusions in the development of his own methods of spiritual and physical cultivation.

During the 130 years between the family disgrace and Yuan Huang's birth, while the Yuans developed their reputation as physicians, their independent interpretations of the Classics, and their interest in Daoism and Buddhism, they gradually regained economic security and some social status as well. Okuzaki Hiroshi calculates that by the late fifteenth or early sixteenth century, the Yuan medical practice and pharmacy were flourishing, and that the family was once again on a sound financial footing. They were certainly successful in forging marriage alliances with important local families; the Yuans intermarried with the Xu of Wujiang, the Zhu of Pinghu, and the Shen and Qian of Jiashan, all wealthy and prominent families.[44] Yuan Ren, Huang's father, in addition to achieving some distinction as a physician, was friendly with several leading thinkers of the sixteenth century, as well as with influential local families. Indicative of his stature in the Jiashan community is the fact that he was chosen as a "venerable elder" at the local wine-drinking ceremony.[45]

Thus Yuan Huang was born into a family on the fringes of the highest socioeconomic status. By the early sixteenth century, they were wealthy and well-connected enough to associate with the local gentry of Jiashan and Wujiang, but they lacked the civil service degrees that would ensure them entry into the elite status of scholar-officials. Intellectually they were also on the fringes of the major schools of the day. Scholars of the Confucian Classics, they asserted their independence from the state-approved readings of these texts. Though more sympathetic to the approach of the

---

[43] Yuan Huang, *Qisi zhenquan*, pp. 16–17, 25–27; Sakai, *Chūgoku zensho*, pp. 342–344.

[44] Okuzaki, *Chūgoku kyōshin jinushi*, pp. 68–69, 109–114.

[45] Liu Ts'un-yan, "Yuan Huang and His 'Four Admonitions,' " p. 109. Okuzaki, *Chūgoku kyōshin jinushi*, p. 114. Yuan Ren, as mentioned earlier, had studied with Wang Yangming, and was a friend of Wang Ji. The Yuan family had some contact with the families of the distinguished official and scholar Chen Longzheng, and the grand secretary Qian Shisheng (1575–1652).

Wang Yangming school, they ultimately maintained the superiority of their own distinctive interpretations, ones often influenced by Taoist and Buddhist beliefs. In short, the family tradition of scholarship did not require any rigid adherence to a single school, but rather encouraged eclectic borrowings from a variety of beliefs and texts.

Yuan Huang was born just at a time when the ambition of the family for worldly success (without loss of moral purity) flowered. Of the first generation eligible to take the examinations, the burden of restoring family status was his. It was additionally his responsibility to adapt the richly eclectic, morally demanding Yuan-family tradition to new worldly expectations, to make it function in the most challenging calling for true Confucians—that of government service. To a considerable extent, the method of merit accumulation enabled Yuan to perform this task.

YUAN HUANG'S CONVERSION: "DETERMINING YOUR OWN FATE"

The story of Yuan's conversion to ledger use, told in his essay "Determining Your Own Fate," reveals something of the tension between the Yuan family intellectual and moral tradition and pressures to succeed in worldly terms. Eager to take advantage of the family's renewed eligibility for the civil service examinations, Yuan started studying at an early age. But the death of his father interrupted his studies, and his mother urged him to return to the study of medicine, the hereditary family profession. Her reasons echo the claims that Yuan Hao made for medicine in the *Family Instructions*: "Then you can both preserve your own health and bring relief to others. And it was your father's wish that you earn a name for yourself by practicing some profession."[46]

Following the example of his great-grandfather, Yuan Huang then gave up preparing for the examinations and took up the study of medicine

[46] Yuan Huang, *LMP*, 1a. Hereafter I indicate the page numbers of the Chinese text in brackets at the end of each quotation. Ages are given in *sui*.

On its first publication in 1601, the "Liming pian" appeared, without its later title, with three brief "appended notes" (*fulu*) as the *Xingshen lu*. This essay, virtually unchanged and now named "Yuan Liaofan xiansheng Liming pian," was published in 1607 with two other essays on merit accumulation ("Kedi quanping yinde" and "Qianxu lizhong") under the title *Liming pian*. Later versions of the essay have appeared with some of Yuan's other writings on the merit-demerit system in collections entitled *Xunzi yan*, *Yinzhi lu*, and *Liaofan sixun*. See Okuzaki, *Chūgoku kyōshin jinushi*, pp. 249–254.

A partial translation of the "Liming pian" can be found in Liu, "Yuan Huang and His 'Four Admonitions,'" pp. 112–113. Okuzaki has also translated parts of the text; see his *Chūgoku kyōshin jinushi*, pp. 137–140, 147. I consulted both of these translations. For translations and discussions of other essays on merit accumulation attributed to Yuan Huang, see Nishizawa Karō, *Inshitsu roku no kenkyū*; and Ishikawa Umejirō, *Inshitsu roku*. Many different vernacular versions of Yuan's essays have been published in the twentieth century; *Liaofan sixun baihua jieshi* (1962) by Huang Zhihai is just one example.

instead. In the course of a visit to the Ciyun monastery in Beijing, he happened to meet a fortune-teller named Kong, who claimed to have traveled all the way from Yunnan in search of Yuan. Kong explained that it was his duty to pass on to Yuan, as to a disciple, the method of prognostication derived from Shao Yong's *Supreme Principles that Rule the World*. Demanding to know why Yuan was not studying for the examinations, Kong predicted that he would earn *shengyuan* status in the following year. Yuan Huang then took Kong home with him and introduced him to his mother; the Yuans tested his powers by asking him to make certain prognostications. When these turned out to be accurate, Yuan and his mother decided to trust Kong, and Yuan again took up his studies for the examinations.[47] Perhaps the long tradition of family study of the *Supreme Principles*, from which Kong drew his prognosticatory technique, helped to persuade Yuan and his mother of Kong's reliability.

Kong then calculated all the major events of Yuan's life, telling him when he would pass each of the examinations, in what place each time, what offices he would hold, and when he would retire. Two of these predictions distressed Yuan—that he would die relatively young, at age 53, and much worse, that he would die without an heir.

The first of Kong's predictions did come true: in 1550 Yuan passed the qualifying examination for *shengyuan* status in ninth place, just as Kong had said. Yuan was particularly impressed by one of the more complex of Kong's calculations:

> From this time on, whenever I took an examination, my rank, whether high or low, never deviated from Kong's predictions. The only exception seemed to be his calculation that after I had consumed 91 piculs, 5 bushels of rice as a stipend student, I would take the position of tribute student. For when I had received only a little more than 70 piculs, the prefectural director of education, Mr. Tu, endorsed my petition to fill a vacancy as a tribute student, and I began to doubt the accuracy of Kong's predictions. But in the end the petition was rejected by the acting director of education, Mr. Yang.[48]
>
> In 1567, however, the prefectural director of education Yin Qiuming saw me writing essays in the examination hall, and he commented sadly, "These five essays are equal to any five memorials submitted to the throne. How can I allow a scholar of such wide and penetrating knowledge to grow old in the study?" Then he approved my petition to fill a vacancy for tribute-student status. By that time I had actually received 91 piculs, 5 bushels of rice, including the amount that I had been given before. Because of this experience, I believed even

---

[47] Yuan Huang, *LMP*, 1a. Kong says that he is transmitting "Huangji shu zhengchuan" to Yuan; Sakai suggests that this is the title of a prognosticatory handbook based on Shao Yong's work. See *Chūgoku zensho*, p. 334.

[48] See Liu, "Yuan Huang and His 'Four Admonitions,' " p. 112, for another translation.

more that success and failure were fated, and that the timing of events was appointed, so I placidly ceased to strive for success. [1a–2a]

Here Yuan Huang's conclusion is perfectly in accord with the fatalistic vision propounded by his great-grandfather Yuan Hao.

But Yuan Huang's placid acceptance of what was fated for him was rudely shattered in the course of a visit to the Qixia monastery near Nanjing. Yungu, a Chan master he met there while practicing meditation, challenged his belief in fatalism:

Before entering the Directorate of Education, I paid a visit to the Chan master Yungu at the Qixia monastery. We sat together in one room for three days and nights, without sleeping. Yungu, inquiring [about my calmness], said, "The reason that men ordinarily cannot become sages is that they confuse themselves with deluded thoughts. You have sat with me for three days, and you have not had a single deluded thought."

I explained, "My future has been calculated by Mr. Kong. Glory and disgrace, life and death all have fixed allotments; even if I wanted to have deluded thoughts, there would be no place for them."

Yungu laughed and said, "I considered you an exceptional man, yet you are really just an ordinary fellow." When I asked why, he explained, "In the end a man's mind is bound by the forces of *yin* and *yang*, so how can there be no allotment (*shu*)?[49] But only the ordinary man has a fixed lot in life. The exceptionally good man is certainly not constrained by his lot; nor is the exceptionally bad man constrained by his. For the past twenty years you have never moved a hair's breadth because of Kong's predictions—how can you be anything but an ordinary fellow?"

I asked, "Then I can escape my lot?" He replied, "A man determines his fate (*ming*) himself, and secures good fortune himself—this is what the *Classic of Songs* and the *Classic of History* say, and it is a brilliant teaching. Our Buddhist scriptures say that if you seek a good reputation, you will receive it; if you seek wealth, you will receive it; if you seek sons and daughters, you will receive them; if you seek long life, you will receive it. Now speaking falsely is a great prohibition among Buddhists—how could all these Buddhas and bodhisattvas lie and trick people?" [2a–3a]

Yungu here presented the view of fate that Yuan Huang would eventually take up: each man was allotted a destiny at birth, but through vigorous action, either good or evil, he could change this allotment.[50]

[49] *Shu* is translated "allotment" or "fixed lot" to distinguish it from *ming*, "fate" or "destiny." *Shu* refers to the allotment or measure of fate given each man at birth; it can be discovered through different systems of calculation, such as the one Kong practiced on Yuan Huang.

[50] This point is explained very clearly in an exemplary story Yuan told in another essay

Yungu, like Yuan Huang himself from Jiashan county, was one of the pioneers of the effort to revive interest in Buddhist, specifically Chan, doctrines among literati of the Jiangnan area. As his more famous student and biographer Hanshan Deqing (1546–1623) explained, "When the Great Law was in darkness, he zealously proclaimed the Way, and made others understand that it deals with lofty matters."[51] He had considerable success among scholar-officials around Nanjing; he persuaded Lu Guangzu (1521–1597), a prominent official, to help him restore the Qixia monastery on Mt. She. Lu remained one of his most faithful lay disciples, bringing other officials such as Wu Meiquan, a minister of personnel; Zheng Danquan, a minister of justice; and his own brother to hear Yungu's teachings. Though devoted primarily to Chan meditation of the sort he practiced with Yuan Huang, Yungu was well versed in other Buddhist teachings as well, and quite willing to draw on any or all of these to stimulate literati interest in his religion. The nature of his argument to Yuan Huang suggests, too, that he was interested in broadening the base of support for his teachings to include Confucian sources as well. Before even mentioning Buddhist scriptures, he cited two Confucian Classics, the *Classic of History* and the *Classic of Songs*, as evidence that man could change his own fate. This use of Confucian allusions to legitimize Buddhist principles was a common technique of late Ming Buddhist leaders eager to recruit believers from among literati.[52]

But Yuan Huang demanded a more challenging proof from Yungu: the reconciliation of the belief that man could decide his own material fate and Mencius's classic denial of the idea that man could achieve external rewards for virtuous behavior. Yuan first alluded to Mencius's statement: " 'Seek and you will get it; let go and you will lose it. If this is the case, then seeking is of use to getting, and what is sought is within yourself. But if there is a proper way to seek it and whether you get it or not de-

---

on merit accumulation, "Kedi quanping yinde," in *LMP*, 13a. Here, the official Tu Kangxi, after proposing a measure that would aid men unjustly accused of crimes, was visited by a god who explained that he would be rewarded for this good deed through the alteration of his fate: " 'You were fated to have no sons, but now because your proposal for the reduction of punishments was exactly in accord with the mind of heaven, Shangdi will grant you three sons, all of whom are destined to wear purple robes and gold belts [i.e., to become officials].' "

[51] Hanshan Deqing, *Hanshan dashi mengyou ji*, 30.18 (p. 1558).

[52] Yungu worshipped Guanyin throughout his life and was well versed in the beliefs of the Weixin and Jingtu sects. An authority on Huayan also, he taught the doctrines of the four dharma realms and the fundamental unity of all things to two other distinguished students, Lu Pingchuan and Xu Sian. Hanshan Deqing, *Hanshan dashi mengyou ji*, 30.10–18 (pp. 1550–1558). See also Okuzaki, *Chūgoku kyōshin jinushi*, pp. 142–144; and Yü, *Renewal of Buddhism*, pp. 96–97, 228.

pends on destiny, then seeking is of no use to getting, and what is sought lies outside yourself.' " Then he continued the argument himself:

"One can strive hard to be virtuous, good, and righteous, but how can one be sure of securing good reputation, wealth, and rank?"

Yungu explained, "Mencius's statement is correct, but you have misunderstood it. The Sixth Patriarch [Huineng, 638–713] said, 'The field for all blessings is simply the mind.' If your desire arises from the mind, there is no goal you cannot achieve. If you seek within yourself, you will attain not only virtue, goodness, and righteousness, but also a good reputation, wealth, and high status: you gain both internal and external benefits. This kind of seeking will be efficacious. If you do not turn within and examine yourself, but merely chase after things from the outside, then your search follows a fixed path, and you will receive what was fated for you: you will lose both internal and external benefits. Therefore this kind of seeking is useless." [3a–b]

The basic idea here, that the mind is the source of all good fortune, is consistent with what is known of Yungu's beliefs. Holding that the mind was the source of all things in the universe, Yungu believed that the enlightenment of the mind was the foundation of spiritual study (*dawu weixin* or *wuxin weizhu*). The mind then *alone* was the ground for establishing one's fate (*weixin liming*). If man ignored his mind as the source of all things and simply pursued things outside of it, then he would be unsuccessful in his search.[53]

In claiming Huineng's and Mencius's support for this view, Yungu was misquoting the former and certainly straying from the orthodox interpretation of the latter. Huineng stated that merit, not blessings, was created from the mind; indeed, he made a point of distinguishing merit, a spiritual achievement, from material blessings or good fortune.[54] Mencius, at least according to the orthodox interpretation current at the time, certainly

[53] Hanshan Deqing, *Hanshan dashi mengyou ji*, 30.9–12 (pp. 1549–1551); cited also in Okuzaki, *Chūgoku kyōshin jinushi*, p. 143.

[54] Merit means something quite different for Huineng; it is not points earned from good deeds, but seeing into the Dharma nature. In fact, Huineng did not consider the kind of merit accumulation advocated by Yungu to be a valid means to enlightenment. He explained: "Building temples, giving alms and making offerings are simply means of seeking blessings (*fu*). One cannot make blessings into merit (*gongde*). Merit is in the Dharmakāya (*fashen*), not in the field of blessings. There is merit in the Dharma nature (*foxing*); seeing your nature is *gong*, straightforward mind is *de*. See the Buddha nature within you; outwardly practice reverence. If you make light of men and do not cut off your ego, then you have no merit. If your own nature is deluded, the Dharma body has no merit. If you constantly think of virtuous practice and keep a straightforward mind, then *de* will not be held lightly, and practice will always be reverent. The cultivation of your body is *gong*; the cultivation of your mind is *de*. Merit is created in the mind; blessings and merit are different." Translation based on Philip B. Yampolsky, *The Platform Sutra of the Sixth Patriarch*, p. 156.

was not suggesting that external benefits would be earned through internal cultivation; rather, he was asserting that the only kind of destiny a man could be sure of controlling was his moral destiny. But Yungu chose to read this passage as support for his assertion that the mind is the source of material benefits as well as moral perfection, and Yuan Huang was apparently willing to accept this interpretation.

Yungu then encouraged Yuan Huang to examine his behavior, to see if he did really deserve success on moral grounds:

> Then he asked what Kong had calculated for my future. After I had told him, he asked, "Do you think that you deserve to pass the examinations? Or that you deserve to have a son?"
>
> I reflected for a while and replied, "I do not deserve either. The sort of man who passes the examinations possesses signs (*xiang*) of good fortune. My good fortune is slight; moreover, I have not been able to build up merit or accumulate good deeds to increase my good fortune. And I have no patience with troublesome affairs, and am not tolerant of other people. At times I use my abilities and intelligence to override others. Or I believe things too easily, and speak carelessly. All these characteristics are signs of my lack of good fortune—how could it be right for me to pass the examinations?
>
> The dirtiest soil produces the most crops, while the purest water never contains fish. I favor purity—that is the first reason I shouldn't have a son. A peaceful disposition can nourish all things. But I am easily angered—that is the second reason I shouldn't have a son. Love is the source of production and reproduction, and continence is the root of childlessness. I am always concerned about my own reputation, and cannot put aside my own interests to help others—this is the third reason I shouldn't have a son. I talk too much, and thus dissipate my substance (*qi*)—this is the fourth reason I shouldn't have a son. I like to drink, and so wear down my mental energy—this is the fifth reason I shouldn't have a son. I like to sit up all night, and I do not know how to preserve my inborn virtue and nurture my spirit—this is the sixth reason I shouldn't have a son. My other faults and evils are so many that I cannot enumerate them all. [3b–4a]

Yuan read his physiognomical "signs" as symbols of his moral inadequacies. They reflected his failure to cultivate his inborn virtue, and thus explained his lack of good fortune.

Yungu followed this confession with a spirited speech reasserting the validity of the belief in supernatural retribution and urging Yuan to start a new life, one not bound by a passive acceptance of destiny. Again, he used quotations from the early Confucian Classics, here the *Classic of History* and the *Classic of Changes*, to support his point.

Yungu said, "How can this principle—that those who succeed are those who deserve to succeed—apply to the examinations alone? Those who deserve a thousand taels worth of property are surely people who have a thousand taels. Those who deserve one hundred taels worth of property are surely people who have one hundred taels. Those who should starve to death are surely people who do starve to death. Heaven bestows favors simply according to a man's own quality. When did it ever add the slightest bit more than he deserves?

"Now, when it comes to having a son, if you have one hundred generations worth of virtue you will surely have one hundred generations of descendants to preserve it. If you have ten generations worth of virtue you will surely have ten generations of descendants to preserve it. If you have two or three generations worth of virtue you will surely have two or three generations of descendants to preserve it. If your line is cut off without descendants, your virtue is extremely slight.

"You already know your faults, and you should do your best from now on to correct all the characteristics that have kept you from passing the examinations and fathering a son. You must do your best to build up virtue. You must do your best to be tolerant. You must do your best to be compassionate. You must do your best to conserve your mental energy. It will be as if the 'you' of the past died yesterday, as if the 'you' of the future has just been born today. In this way you are a man in whom moral principle has been revitalized, and a man of moral principle can model himself on heaven.

"The 'Taijia' chapter of the *Classic of History* says, 'Calamities sent by heaven may be avoided, but from calamities brought on by oneself there is no escape.'[55] Master Kong's prediction that you would not pass the examination for the *juren* degree is a prediction of a calamity sent by heaven; you can still avoid it. If you now extend the inborn goodness of your nature, exert yourself to do good deeds, and accumulate a large store of hidden virtue, this is good fortune you are making yourself. How can you not take advantage of it? The *Classic of Changes* tells the superior man to pursue good fortune and avoid calamity. But if you say that fate is fixed, how can good fortune be pursued and calamities avoided? In the first section of the *Classic of Changes* it is written: 'The family that accumulates goodness is sure to have superabundant happiness. The family that accumulates evil is sure to have superabundant misfortune.'[56] Do you believe that this is possible?" [4a–5a]

Attracted by the hope of moral regeneration and material reward offered by Yungu and apparently sanctioned by the Confucian Classics, Yuan Huang took Yungu as his teacher.

Yungu then initiated Yuan Huang into the ritual, involving confession,

[55] Legge, *The Chinese Classics*, vol. 3, p. 207.
[56] *Zhouyi yinde*, 2 (p. 4); and Z. D. Sung, *The Text of the Yi King*, p. 20.

a pledge to the Buddha, and an appeal to a bodhisattva, that accompanied the proper use of the ledgers:

> Then I confessed all my past sins before the Buddha. I wrote a petition, seeking first to pass the examination for the *juren* degree, and pledging to perform three thousand good deeds to repay the goodness of heaven and my ancestors if this petition were granted. Yungu took out a ledger of merit and demerit and showed me how to register there what I did that day—if good, then to record the merits, and if bad, to subtract the demerits. Then he taught me to chant an incantation to Zhunti, in the hope that my petition be granted. [5a]

The appeal to Zhunti serves as a reminder of the complex antecedents of the merit-demerit system, for Zhunti, though perhaps most commonly associated with Guanyin, appears as a god or goddess in the Daoist as well as the Buddhist pantheon.[57] Consistently depicted in each of these teachings as an agent of supernatural retribution, Zhunti is an appropriate object of Yuan Huang's prayers for reward.

But a simple appeal to Zhunti was not enough; when making his appeal and performing good deeds, Yuan had to have a pure mind, one free of ambition for reward. Using a Daoist metaphor, Yungu described the proper method:

> He explained to me, "A Daoist writer of charms once told me, 'If you do not know how to draw charms, then the spirits will laugh at you. There is a secret tradition: it is simply to have a mind unmoved by intentions (*budong nian*). When you grasp your brush to write a charm, first release all entanglements with worldly things from your mind, and do not let one speck [i.e., any conscious thought] arise in your mind. From the point where your mind is unmoved (*cong ci niantou budong chu*) draw the first dot. This is called establishing a foundation from chaos (*hundun kaiji*). Then from this beginning complete the charm in one movement of the brush, still without any conscious thought.

---

[57] Maspero, *Taoism and Chinese Religion*, p. 157. Originally a Hindu goddess, Durgā or Marīci, Zhunti became in Chinese Buddhism one of the manifestations of Avalokiteśvara (Guanyin), the bodhisattva who vowed to aid mankind to salvation before entering nirvana him- or herself. Daoist sects appropriated Zhunti into their pantheon and, adapting her Buddhist function to their own ends, made her Doumu, the Mother of the Constellation of the Southern Bushel, assigned to watch over human destinies. Keeper of the registers of life and death, she was worshipped by those who hoped to extend their lifespan or ward off illness. Zhunti appeared, in male form, as a major figure in the late sixteenth-century novel, *Fengshen yanyi* (*Investiture of the Gods*), a legendary account of how good King Wu of Zhou, with considerable assistance from the gods, defeated evil King Zhou of Shang in the eleventh century B.C. There Zhunti's Buddhist and Daoist natures were merged in the character of a warrior who descended from the Buddhist Western Paradise to aid the Daoist god Yuanshi Tianzun in his efforts to protect the Zhou mandate of heaven. See P. K. Whitaker, "A Buddhist Spell," pp. 15–16, 18–19; Xu Zhonglin (attrib.), *Fengshen yanyi*, vol. 2, pp. 676–685; and Henry Doré, *Researches into Chinese Superstitions*, vol. 3, pp. 304–311.

If you do it this way, then the charm will be effective.' All supplications to heaven for the determination of your own fate must be made from a mind free of conscious thought and free of reflection (*wusi wulü*) in order to evoke a response." [5a–b]

The concept that Yungu is describing here—that of action with an unmoved mind or a mind free of intentions—was by this time a fairly familiar one in Chinese thought. Yungu suggests that it is drawn from Daoist teachings, but it might also be possible to claim an early Confucian antecedent: the term *budong nian* is reminiscent of Mencius's *budong xin*, the "unperturbed mind" free of considerations of success and failure required by a man of courage.[58] Elaborating on Mencius's use of the term, Song Neo-Confucians defined this unperturbed mind as a mind that is "responsive to man's moral impulses and yet is also conscious of the total natural order or process which defines his sphere of moral action."[59] With it, a man is able to act selflessly, for he has then " 'no mind' . . . of his own, but sees and acts toward all things with the mind of Heaven and earth."[60]

But this concept is also closely associated with the Chan Buddhist school, where it was used to describe the state in which one achieved sudden enlightenment. Indeed, Huineng claimed that this doctrine of "no thought" or "no mind" (*wunian* or *wuxin*) was his central teaching. It defined the state in which the Chan practitioner would be "unfettered"— that is, seeing all things, but free of attachment to them: "even though you are in the midst of the six dusts [i.e., sight, sound, smell, taste, touch, and idea], you do not stand apart from them, yet are not stained by them, and are free to come and go." At this point, one will "penetrate into all things thoroughly, and will see the realm of the Buddha."[61] This concept of no-thought, be it Confucian or Buddhist in origin, exerted a great influence on Wang Yangming's followers, particularly Wang Ji and the members of the Taizhou school. They, too, believed that man should act spontaneously, with a mind free of intentions either to do good or to avoid evil. Indeed, Yungu's language here echoes some of Wang Ji's writings; Wang too speaks of enlightenment as "establishing one's foundation in the midst of chaos" (*hundun ligen*) in order to achieve a state of "consciousness without consciousness" (*wujiao zhi jiao*).[62] By the late Ming,

[58] *Mengzi yinde*, 2a.2 (pp. 10–11). See Legge, *The Chinese Classics*, vol. 1, pp. 185–187.

[59] William Theodore de Bary, "Neo-Confucian Cultivation and the Seventeenth-Century 'Enlightenment,' " pp. 169–170.

[60] Ibid., pp. 151–152.

[61] Yampolsky, *Platform Sutra*, p. 153. For a fuller explanation of the Chan use of the concept of no-thought, see Yun-hua Jan, "A Comparative Study of 'No-Thought' ('Wu-Nien') in Some Indian and Chinese Buddhist Texts," pp. 43–49.

[62] Wang Ji, *Wang Longxi xiansheng quanji*, 4.11b. See Okada, "Wang Chi and Existentialism," p. 130.

then, the idea that true goodness or spiritual enlightenment was dependent on the cultivation of a mind unmoved by calculation had become common currency, shared by Neo-Confucians, Chan practitioners, and Daoist charm-writers alike.

Yungu, a Chan master himself, was certainly fully aware of the Chan antecedents of the concept of "no-thought." But, interestingly, in continuing his exposition of the mind unmoved by conscious thought, he did not explicitly cite Chan support for this concept. As befits a monk trying to convert a Neo-Confucian literatus, he chose rather to cite Mencius's discussion of the "undivided mind" a man needs to fulfill his moral nature and "stand firm on his proper destiny (*liming*)." Mencius had explained: "For a man to give full realization to his heart is for him to understand his own nature, and a man who knows his own nature will know heaven. By retaining his heart and nurturing his nature he is serving heaven. Whether he is going to die young or to live to a ripe old age makes no difference to his steadfastness of purpose. It is through awaiting whatever is to befall him with a perfected character that he stands firm on his proper destiny."[63]

Yungu picks up the last phrase here, "*liming*,"[64] which Mencius, according to the orthodox Neo-Confucian view, uses to express the gentleman's perfect fulfillment of his moral nature, his "proper destiny," and interprets it to mean "establishing" or "deciding" one's material as well as moral fate. He explains:

> When Mencius discusses learning how to decide one's fate (*liming zhi xue*), he first said, "[For the man who knows heaven,] there is no distinction between early death and long life." Now early death and long life are opposites, but when the mind is unmoved, what is early death? What is long life? And so too, only after you see no distinction between abundance and deficiency can you determine your fate in regard to poverty or wealth. Only after you see no distinction between failure and success can you determine your own fate in regard to life or death. Only after you see no distinction between early death and long life can you determine your own fate in regard to life or death. Men, as creatures born into the world, consider only early death and long life to be important, so I speak of early death and long life, but all favorable and unfavorable circumstances are included in this argument.

[63] *Mengzi yinde*, 7a.1 (p. 50); translation from Lau, *Mencius*, p. 182.

[64] *Liming* had also been incorporated into a Buddhist phrase, *anxin* (or *-shen*) *liming*, referring to the state in which the unmoved mind, cut off from all things, rests at peace in the place heaven decrees for it. Given his argument about the unmoved mind, Yungu probably had this Buddhist reference (drawn in part from the *Mencius* itself) in mind when he labeled his teaching "*liming zhi xue*." See Okuzaki, *Chūgoku kyōshin jinushi*, pp. 509–511n.287.

As for "awaiting whatever is to befall you with a perfected character,"[65] this is the same thing as accumulating merit and praying to heaven. When Mencius speaks of cultivation, it means that if a person has faults and evils, they should be controlled and eradicated. When he speaks of awaiting whatever befalls you, it means that even your slightest desires and even your slightest expectations for the future should be cut off. When you have reached this point, when the tiniest speck will not move your mind, then without leaving the realm of desires, right away you can create your condition at birth [i.e., your inborn goodness]. This, then, is true learning. [5b–6a]

Here Yungu has invested his allusion to *Mencius* with a new, quite unconventional meaning, one, indeed, that is just the opposite of the orthodox interpretation of the passage quoted. Mencius is now adduced to support the belief that man has almost complete control over his fate, external and internal, as long as he can do good with an "unmoved mind."

In teaching Yuan Huang how to cultivate an unmoved mind, however, Yungu turned to Chan vocabulary and a distinctly Buddhist practice, the recitation of incantations to Zhunti: " 'You cannot yet[66] be without a mind (*wuxin*), but you can continue the incantation to Zhunti without interruption. And if you hold to this practice zealously, then when holding to it, you will not be holding to it, and when not holding to it, you will be holding to it [i.e., it will soon become your natural state]. When you reach the point where your mind is not moved, then it will be effective' " [6a]. With this final injunction to preserve an unmoved mind in the act of merit accumulation, Yungu ends his instruction. The rest of the essay describes Yuan Huang's efforts to act on Yungu's teachings.

For Yuan Huang, the conversion to merit accumulation signified a profound transformation in his way of life. As a symbol of his new resolution to rise above the "ways of ordinary men" and decide his own fate, he changed his *hao* from Xuehai, "studying the sea and thereby reaching it," to Liaofan, "putting an end to ordinariness."[67] Indeed, it appears that Yuan did to some extent become a new person. His conviction that he was master of his fate made him much more anxious about his moral performance and his relationship to the gods, but gave him a new self-confidence in the face of other men. He recorded his psychological transformation as follows: "From this point on I was anxious all day. I felt different from the way I had before. Previously I had discharged my duties

[65] *Mengzi yinde*, 7a.1 (p. 50); translation from Lau, *Mencius*, p. 182.

[66] The text here is corrupt. Following later editions, I have read the first *dan* as *wei*; see "Liming zhi xue," in *Mingren zizhuan wenchao*, p. 206.

[67] Yuan Huang, LMP, 6a. Yuan's original *zi*, Xuehai, was taken from a passage in Yang Xiong's (53 B.C.–A.D. 18) *Fayan*: "The hundred rivers study the sea and thereby reach it; the hills study the mountains, but do not reach them. Therefore evil is limited." (See *Yangzi fayan*, 1.4b–5a.)

only very lackadaisically, but now I was always apprehensive and fearful about my situation. When I was alone in my own courtyard, I was constantly afraid of offending the spirits of heaven and earth. When I met people who hated and slandered me, I could calmly tolerate them" [6a–b].

In 1570, Yuan did pass the qualifying examination for the *juren* degree. His place in the ranks of successful candidates was higher than what the fortune-teller Kong had predicted; and when, contrary to Kong's prognostications, Yuan did earn the *juren* degree, he felt confirmed in his choice of the merit-demerit system over fatalism.[68]

In using his ledger of merit and demerit, Yuan quite sincerely accepted Yungu's point that purity of mind was a prerequisite for merit accumulation. Despite his success, he lamented the difficulty of sustaining this purity in action:

> But when I performed righteous deeds I was still not sincere, and when I examined my conduct I found many errors. Sometimes, though I saw what was right, I did not act on it courageously.[69] Or, although I did help other people, at heart I often doubted [my motives in doing so]. Or, although I exerted myself to do good, I transgressed in speech. Or, although I resolved to do good when sober, I then relaxed my resolution when drunk. These faults cancelled out my merits, and days frequently passed empty of merits. From the time I made the pledge in 1569, over ten years had passed until, in 1579, I finally completed the three thousand good deeds. [6b]

Here and in the previous passage, Yuan has developed a habit of constant self-examination and moral anxiety very like the "inner mental attentiveness" that all Neo-Confucians were to manifest in their daily lives.[70] Late Ming thinkers in particular seem to have taken this quality seriously; Yuan's description above of a nagging sense of his moral weakness in the smallest acts of life is reminiscent of many of the "self-strictures" or confessional essays popular at the time.[71] It is at least evidence that he took the moral implications of the ledger system very seriously: merit accumulation was not just a means of earning material rewards, but also a legitimate form of moral cultivation.

His fulfillment of his first pledge for the *juren* degree was marked with a Buddhist ritual and the formulation of another appeal to the Buddha, one that was, as before, almost immediately answered:

[68] Yuan Huang, "Liming pian," in *LMP*, 6b.

[69] *Lunyu yinde*, 2.24 (p. 4): "To see what is right and not to do it is want of courage" (Legge, *The Chinese Classics*, vol. 1, p. 154).

[70] See A. C. Graham, *Two Chinese Philosophers*, pp. 67–73.

[71] See Wu, "Self-Examination," pp. 5–6, 16–38.

I had just gone to Guanzhong with Li Jian'an,[72] and I had not yet transferred the merit I had earned from my deeds.[73] In 1580 I returned south, and for the first time I asked Xingkong, Huikong, and all the other monks of the Dongta Chan temple [in Xiushui county, close to the Yuan ancestral home in Jiashan county] to transfer the merit [for the benefit of another]. Then, in seeking a son I set up an altar to the Buddha, and again promised to perform three thousand good deeds. In 1581 my son Tianqi was born. [6b–7a]

The Buddha having again answered his prayer, Yuan devoted himself to fulfilling his own pledge to perform three thousand good deeds. He explains the mechanics of this process to his children:

> As soon as I performed a good deed, I would record it with a brush. Your mother could not write, so each time she performed a deed, she would use a goose quill to stamp a vermilion circle on the calendar. We might give relief to the poor, or buy fish and shellfish and set them free. One day there were as many as ten-odd circles on the calendar. By the eighth month of 1583, the three thousand had been filled in. Again I asked Xingkong and the other monks to come to our house to transfer the merit. [7a]

Here merit accumulation was very much a family concern. Yuan and his wife added their individual merit points to a shared account. While Yuan was the active agent for the account—he had opened it in the first place and was the direct beneficiary of the supernatural rewards—the family as a whole stood to gain from his good fortune.

The kinds of deeds described here were simple acts of charity and the release of living things, a practice usually associated with Buddhism, but by this time widely practiced by non-Buddhists as well. Yuan also told how official duties could play a part in merit accumulation. He explained how he earned his *jinshi* degree and an official post:

> On the thirteenth day of the ninth month I set up an altar to Buddha, seeking the *jinshi* degree, and pledged to perform ten thousand good deeds for it. I passed the examination in 1586 and was appointed magistrate of Baodi.
>
> [In Baodi] I took an empty ledger and entitled it *Governing My Mind* (*Zhixin pian*). Early in the mornings when I rose to sit in court, servants brought the

---

[72] For another translation, see Liu Ts'un-yan, "Yuan Huang and His 'Four Admonitions,' " p. 114.

[73] *Huixiang* (Pariṇāmanā), literally "to turn toward," is the Buddhist practice of transferral of merit. A man could have the merit he had accumulated himself transferred to the merit-store of another (or simply to that of all people); this type (*zhongsheng huixiang*) would advance him toward the status of a bodhisattva. Or he could "turn from reality to the ideal" (*huishi xiangli*) and turn his merit to the goal of attaining nirvana himself (*puti huixiang*). Thus, in a variety of ways, the individual could increase his merit through this ceremony of merit-transferral. See Liu Ts'un-yan, "Yuan Huang and His 'Four Admonitions,' " p. 115; Okuzaki, *Chūgoku kyōshin jinushi*, p. 145.

book to the yamen guards and placed it on the bench at which cases were heard, so that I could record whatever I did, good or evil, in minute detail. Then in the evenings I set a table up in the courtyard, and, following the example of Zhao Yuedao,[74] I burned incense and reported my actions to heaven.

Your mother, seeing that few deeds had been performed, frowned and said, "Before, when we were at home, we helped each other in doing good deeds, so that the three thousand could be completed. Now you have vowed to do ten thousand, but there are no good deeds that can be done in the yamen. When will you be able to complete them all?"

That night it happened that a god appeared to me in a dream. When I told him that it was difficult to complete the good deeds, he said, "By simply reducing the land tax you can with one stroke complete all of the ten thousand deeds." Now in Baodi the tax for each *mu* of cultivated land was 2 *fen*, 3 *li*, 7 *hao*. My plan was to reduce the rate to 1 *fen*, 4 *li*, 6 *hao*. But at heart I was a little doubtful that this would really work.

Just at that time, the Chan master Huanyu from Mt. Wutai[75] came to Baodi. I told him about my dream and asked whether it was right to believe such a thing. He replied, "With a sincere mind, even one deed can be worth ten thousand good ones. Moreover, if you reduce the tax rate for the whole district, then won't ten thousand people enjoy good fortune?" I donated my salary to provide a vegetarian feast for the monks of Mt. Wutai, and to have the merit of the ten thousand deeds transferred. [7a–b]

As this case indicates, Yuan Huang took Yungu's instruction very much to heart. His nightly ritual of confession and his concern over the validity of the dream indicate that Yuan understood the importance of reverence to heaven and purity of intention in the effective accumulation of merit.

The passage also points up the very mixed antecedents of the system of merit and demerit practiced by Yuan Huang. His use of the *Ledger* was rooted in Buddhist ritual (the prayers to Buddha and the transferral of merit), and he relied heavily on Buddhist monks to guide his interpretation of the system. But his quest for moral perfection and his anxiety about mental purity were also perfectly compatible with Neo-Confucian goals in self-cultivation. Furthermore, he was quite willing to follow the dictates of the system in his actions as an official, providing a nice example of how a "heterodox" practice could influence the conduct of officials in theory devoted to the defense of orthodoxy. Long before Yuan Huang's

[74] Zhao Bian (994–1070), a censor noted for his moral rectitude and integrity, every evening recounted to heaven his actions during the day, a practice designed to ensure that he never did anything he would be ashamed to mention in his report.

[75] Huanyu (m. Faben), was a disciple of Zibo Zhenke (1544–1604), one of the leaders of the Buddhist revival of the late Ming. Zhenke was also a friend of Yuan Huang; he collaborated with Yuan and Huanyu on the plans for the printing of the Jiaxing Tripitaka. Liu Ts'un-yan, "Yuan Huang and His 'Four Admonitions,'" p. 115.

time it had been common for officials to practice leniency in sentencing criminals—giving light punishments or avoiding the death sentence—in order to build up merit for themselves.[76] In Yuan's case, however, this principle was applied with considerably broader effect to the determination of tax rates.

This one case points up, too, how Yuan's belief in merit accumulation encouraged him to fulfill as much as possible the Confucian model of the official whose goal was to "promote profit for the people" and "nurture their virtuous minds." From the very beginning of his term in Baodi, Yuan seems to have thought of his service there as a kind of contract with the gods. On arrival he made a compact with the city god, promising a series of achievements in return for the god's favor: "to improve local customs by valuing frugality," "to be lenient in imposing punishments in order to spare those who are unaware that they have violated the law," "in the collection of taxes and service levies, not only to be lenient about monies imposed in excess of the quota, but also to think of means of evening out the burden and decreasing the amount of the quota," "not only to use punishments to force people to check their evil acts, but also to think of ways of nurturing their virtuous minds and making them modest and humble in their daily lives," "in the assignment of corvée labor, not only to assist the people in their labor, but also to think of means for the re-apportionment of the service, so that the people may enjoy eternal benefit," and so forth.[77]

Two years later, when Baodi suffered a drought, Yuan wrote a prayer for rain to "Shangdi and the many spirits" in which he blamed his failures as an official for the drought. Using the confessional form he later employed in "Determining Your Own Fate," he listed a series of intended reforms that he had not completed. For example: "I thought to relieve the annoyance and suffering caused by the corvée services imposed under the *lijia* system—the supply and care of horses and other miscellaneous services—but I have not yet adjusted the rules, and now, after the levying of rotating labor service, it will be very difficult to adopt new rules," or, "I wanted to emulate the instruction of the *Classic of Changes* 'to take from those above to benefit those below,' in particular to administer taxes in this spirit, but my private affairs impinged on public matters and I feared punishment, and thus could not complete my plans for leniency." At the end of this document he asked that he, not the people, be punished and promised to serve them more effectively in the future, if only the spirits would "soon send down the sweet rain, and change the drought into a

---

[76] Zhu Xi, for example, complained that certain officials of his day routinely reduced criminal sentences one degree in order to earn rewards from the gods. Zhu Xi, *Zhu Wengong zhengxun*, 2–3; cited in Tung-tsu Ch'ü, *Law and Society in Traditional China*, p. 218.

[77] Yuan Huang, *Lianghang zhai wenji*, 13.1a–2a.

good harvest."[78] Yuan also used the system to encourage moral behavior among the people: a Baodi gazetteer from the Qianlong era notes that, as magistrate, he "exhorted criminals to reform, using the doctrine of supernatural retribution for good and evil (*shan'e baoying zhi shuo*)."[79]

It is easy to see the influence of the merit-demerit system at work here, in the faith in supernatural retribution, in the need to give an exact accounting of deeds and policies, and in the belief in the power of self-examination and the confession of error. The system operated to encourage Yuan to take on the responsibilities of the model paternalistic Confucian official whose only thought was to aid the common people. This is not to say that belief in supernatural retribution effectively made him a better official, for it is not clear how many of Yuan's promises, including his attempt to lower the land tax rate, were actually fulfilled.[80] But it did certainly make him highly conscious of what his duties were supposed to be. Yuan did not seem to share the cynicism about the value of official service expressed by so many of his contemporaries, particularly those of the Wang Yangming school. His faith that specific human actions did inspire precise supernatural responses validated the whole process of official preparation and service.

At the close of his essay, Yuan once again repudiated fatalism and, quoting from the *Classic of History*, restated his faith in the ability of man to decide his own fate. He enjoined his son Tianqi (m. Yan, 1581–1627, j.s. 1625) to continue his efforts at merit accumulation:

> Mr. Kong had predicted that I would die at the age of 53. I have never yet prayed for long life, but this year, without ever having had a serious illness, I am 68. The *Classic of History* says, "It is difficult to rely on heaven—its appointments are not constant," and, "Heaven's appointments are not constant."[81] Both these statements are true. Now I understand that what is called good or bad fortune is what a man seeks himself. *This* is the teaching of the sages and worthies; saying that good and bad fortune is fated by heaven is vulgar talk.
>
> Your fate is still unknown. Even if your fate should be glorious, always be dissatisfied with your achievements. Even if it should be favorable, always be doubtful. Even if you have enough food and clothing, always be anxious about poverty and distress. Even if your scholarship is relatively refined, be fearful of vulgarity.
>
> Reflect on the past and praise the goodness of your ancestors; reflect on what

---

[78] Ibid., 13.2b–4b. For the reference to the *Classic of Changes*, see *Zhouyi yinde*, p. 25, no. 41.

[79] *Baodi xianzhi*, 11.11a–b; cited in Okuzaki, *Chūgoku kyōshin jinushi*, p. 184.

[80] Okuzaki, *Chūgoku kyōshin jinushi*, pp. 151–158.

[81] Translations from Legge, *The Chinese Classics*, vol. 3, pp. 213–214, 397.

is near at hand and conceal your father's errors. Reflect on what is above and repay the grace of the state; reflect on what is below and create good fortune for your family. Reflect on what is outside you and save others from distress; reflect on what is within you and defend yourself against depravity. Every day know your errors. Every day correct your faults. Each day you do not know your errors is a day you have been complacent in thinking yourself right. Each day you have no errors that can be corrected is a day when no progress is made. There are many clear-sighted and talented people in the world, and the only reason goodness is not more intensely cultivated and this instruction not more widely practiced rests in the one word "indolence"—because of this fault people put off correcting their faults throughout their lives.

The doctrine of determining one's own fate that I learned from the Chan master Yungu is the most brilliant, the most profound, the most accurate, and the most proper principle. Explore it fully, exert yourself to practice it, and do not waste your life. [7b–8b]

Yuan Huang, in this final celebration of the system of merit and demerit, stressed the constant moral pressures it exerts, even on those whose rank is high and prosperity seemingly assured. He might have been thinking of his own situation here: he achieved scholar-official status, but he was dismissed from his office in the Ministry of War in 1593 after the failure of a Chinese expedition sent to Korea to expel Japanese invaders. This experience by no means shook his faith in the system; apparently it simply made him even more sensitive to the value of humility and of constant self-surveillance.[82] Merit accumulation, fully sanctioned (in Yuan's own mind at least) by the Confucian sages and worthies, remained for him the means of realizing one's full potential, both morally and materially; to neglect it was to "waste your life."

YUNGU'S REINTERPRETATION OF THE LEDGERS OF MERIT AND DEMERIT

Yungu's system of merit accumulation clearly differed from the system as it existed in the twelfth century and before—Yungu (or perhaps a series of unknown predecessors) significantly altered the basic terms of ledger use. Most strikingly, he shifted the goals of the system away from the attainment of distant spiritual rewards like immortality or a superior reincarnation to the achievement of this-worldly material rewards like official appointment and the birth of sons. It was the promise of immediate worldly gain that attracted Yuan Huang; despite his faith in Buddhism and his knowledge of Daoist techniques, he never prayed for either rebirth in the Western Paradise or immortality.

[82] Sakai, *Chūgoku zensho*, pp. 347–348. For an account of Yuan's service in Korea and his impeachment, see Okuzaki, *Chūgoku kyōshin jinushi*, pp. 160–175.

Yungu also minimized the Buddhist and Daoist elements of the earlier system, particularly those requiring belief in a bureaucracy of gods. To be sure, Yuan Huang's merit accumulation still rested on belief in supernatural retribution and assumed the operation of retribution as described in the first chapter. But compared to the pre-Ming descriptions of the system, "Determining Your Own Fate" radically deemphasized the role of the gods in the system of merit and demerit. Nowhere is there a description of the elaborate pantheon that appeared in the *Tract of Taishang on Action and Response*—only the Buddha, Zhunti, and a nameless god are mentioned. Nor is there any suggestion, as in the *Ledger of Merit and Demerit of the Taiwei Immortal*, that the ledger itself is of divine authorship; nor are there any of the detailed explanations of the elaborate systems of record-keeping employed by the celestial bureaucracy in keeping track of human conduct. The emphasis has shifted away from divine control of retribution through a long series of generations or reincarnations to man's control of his fate in the here and now. The keyword now is *liming*, the human determination of fate, rather than *baoying* or *ganying*, the naturalistic or cosmological operation of retribution.

In other ways, too, the system has been secularized or "humanized." The deeds of Yungu's ledger include some religious prescriptions, but these tend to be somewhat vaguely stated, only rarely implying allegiance to a specific teaching. This fact immediately sets Yungu's ledger apart from the *Ledger of Merit and Demerit of the Taiwei Immortal*, and from the Buddhist and other Daoist scriptures before it. The majority of deeds in Yungu's ledger are generally applicable acts of charity or personal moral discipline.[83] Thus, without undermining the essential support of the system in the belief in supernatural retribution, and without explicitly repudiating any of the principles of the earlier system, Yungu detached the program for merit accumulation from its earlier ties to certain popular religious sects and gave it a much broader appeal.

Yungu also created a somewhat more sophisticated method for the accumulation of merit in his new emphasis on the intense mental discipline—the "unmoved mind"—required for successful ledger use. You Xuanzi, the transmitter of the *Ledger of Merit and Demerit of the Taiwei Immortal*, referred once, very briefly, to the desirability of "purifying the mind" in the self-cultivation process, but for Yungu, mental purity, the absence of intention, had become an absolute prerequisite for effective merit accumulation. It was the principle that gave the system its moral

---

[83] See Cynthia J. Brokaw, "Yuan Huang (1533–1606) and the Ledgers of Merit and Demerit," pp. 192–195, for a translation. This ledger, purportedly given to Yuan Huang by Yungu, was not, to my knowledge, published until after Yuan Huang's death, in the Wanli-era collection *Baicheng*. The ledger appeared there together with the "Liming pian" under the title *Xunzi yan*. See Sakai, *Chūgoku zensho*, pp. 344–347, for an analysis of the text.

legitimacy; that, for Yungu at least, rescued it from the charge of encouraging selfish profit seeking, for a mind empty of calculation could not be bent on profit.

It is easy to link Yungu's emphasis on the mind empty of thought to his own Chan training—the idea of "no-thought," after all, was one of the central doctrines of the Chan sect. But, as we have seen, Yungu himself did not refer, except very obliquely, to this possible source; rather, he provided a Confucian authority for his explanation of the concept. Indeed, throughout his argument, Yungu made a concerted effort to provide Confucian justifications for the system of merit and demerit. He drew most frequently on the Confucian Classics to substantiate his points: he quoted the *Classic of History* four times, *Mencius* three, and the *Classic of Songs* and the *Classic of Changes* once each—nine citations in all, compared to only two from Buddhist sayings and one reference to a Daoist practice. *Mencius* in particular became the major prop of the system; even the phrase *"liming"* is from that Classic.[84]

As we know from his biography, Yungu was noted for his success in converting "Confucian" scholar-officials to Buddhism; certainly, the technique he used with Yuan Huang, the use of Confucian Classics to make Buddhist points, was one of his most effective methods. It was particularly important that he drew on *Mencius* in his discussion of fate, since that Classic set the foundation for the orthodox Neo-Confucian understanding of the subject. Trying to convert a scholar at least ostensibly committed to the Neo-Confucian curriculum, Yungu had to be able to reconcile the passage from *Mencius* with the system of merit accumulation.

But, as we have seen, Yungu's argument rested precariously on an idiosyncratic reading of the *Mencius*. He certainly took passages from the text out of context, interpreting Mencius's "undivided mind" as a prerequisite for successful merit accumulation and thus material reward; rather, it is (at least according to the orthodox reading) the state in which the good man, indifferent to his material well-being, fulfills his moral potential. Indeed, Yungu's goal of earning good fortune was an end not worthy of the Confucian moral man, or, for that matter, of the serious Chan prac-

---

[84] Although Yungu did not refer to later Confucians, his argument is not inconsistent with certain Neo-Confucian principles. Zhu Xi argued that a man could distinguish good and evil only if he held his mind in a state of equilibrium, "before the unfolding of pleasure, anger, grief, and joy," when it was one with the principle of heaven. Wang Yangming, too, taught that a man with a mind "aroused by desires and blocked by selfishness, torn by conflicts between ambition for profit and fear of loss, rent by struggles between anger and resentment," will stop at no evil; in order to return to his original state of perfect goodness, he had to rid his mind of such thoughts. See Zhu Xi, *(Yuzuan) Zhuzi quanshu*, 2.2a; and Wang Yangming, *Yangming quanshu*, 26.1b–2a.

titioner. In fact, it is difficult to accept Yungu's method of merit accumulation even in its own terms, regardless of his unusual interpretation of Confucian authorities: how can a man do good and keep track of his merits with a mind untainted by thoughts of profit? The very keeping of a ledger in Yuan Huang's system already suggests a keen interest in one's own material as well as moral progress. As later Confucian critics of the ledgers were quick to point out, Yungu's system encouraged mental purity and good behavior as a means to personal profit—but in the strictest Confucian moral terms, selfishly motivated good behavior cannot be good.

In his enthusiastic conversion to ledger use, Yuan Huang ignored the weaknesses in Yungu's argument. Doubtless the Yuan family tradition facilitated this conversion. His familiarity with popular Buddhist and Daoist beliefs probably made Huang more comfortable with the "heterodox" elements of the merit-demerit system, and the rather unconventional Yuan family tradition in classical scholarship made it easier for him to accept Yungu's interpretation of Mencius. But perhaps the most powerful influence on Yuan was the new worldly rewards—examination degrees, sons, and even wealth—that Yungu set for merit accumulation.

Of these, Yuan focused on examination degrees and a son. Kong's prediction that he would not have an heir would naturally have been of great concern to him, but the desire to succeed in the civil service examinations, given his family history, must have been equally strong.[85] For generations the Yuans had worked to accumulate secret merit in preparation for the great day when they would once again be able to participate safely in the civil service examinations: the pressure on Yuan Huang to succeed and thereby return the family to its previous exalted status must have been overwhelming. His position as an outsider, particularly one from a family that had avoided conventional Confucian studies, would have made him anxious about his ability to succeed in a highly competitive system that emphasized conformity to an intellectual orthodoxy. The merit-demerit system as reinterpreted by Yungu offered him a program for success; moreover, one purportedly based on classic Confucian principles.

Furthermore, the system provided him with a way of explaining the idea of success in morally acceptable terms. The Yuans, as explained earlier, had developed ambivalent feelings about the examination system: it was clearly the path to high status and power, but it was just as likely to lead to moral corruption as well. Yuan Huang's own father had warned him quite strongly about the latter pitfall; and contemporary criticism of the examinations could only have served to reinforce this warning. But the merit-demerit system, by assuring Yuan Huang that his worldly suc-

[85] See Sakai, *Chūgoku zensho*, p. 333.

cess, far from being achieved at the cost of moral decline, would actually be founded on his and his family's moral purity, relieved him of anxiety about betraying his family's moral trust. After generations of rationalizing status decline as an opportunity for moral improvement, the Yuan family needed now a moral justification for worldly success. The merit-demerit system provided just such a justification, in suggesting that their advance to gentry status reflected their advance toward moral perfection.

YUAN HUANG'S INTERPRETATION OF THE LEDGER SYSTEM

The focus of "Determining Your Own Fate" is Yungu's reinterpretation of the merit-demerit system and the conversion of Yuan Huang. After this conversion, Yuan went on to write several other essays that elaborate on the new, allegedly Confucian elements Yungu tried to incorporate into the system. Four essays in particular—"Correcting Faults" ("Gaiguo"), "Accumulating Goodness" ("Jishan"), "Success in the Examinations Depends Entirely on Secret Virtue" ("Kedi quanping yinde"), and "Profiting from Humility" ("Quanxu lizhong")—allow us to reconstruct Yuan's understanding of the relationship between Confucian moral cultivation and merit accumulation.

The first two essays, "Correcting Faults" and "Accumulating Goodness," form part of Yuan's Guide to Praying for an Heir; together they describe how to earn an heir through merit accumulation. The next two, "Success in the Examinations Depends Entirely on Secret Virtue" (in certain passages identical to "Accumulating Goodness") and "Profiting from Humility," were published with "Determining Your Own Fate" over fifteen years later, in 1607, under the title Determining Your Own Fate.[86] All of these essays help us to flesh out Yuan's understanding of merit accumulation, and they all provide useful examples of what Yuan perceived to be the successful operation of the system.

In these works, Yuan broke the process of merit accumulation down into two consecutive stages: the correction of faults and the accumulation of virtue. The first step in the stage of fault correction is the development of a sense of shame (chixin). Quoting Mencius's comment, "Great is the use of shame to man," Yuan explained that shame, the feeling that tells a man when he has done wrong, leads a man to knowledge of his faults.[87] After that discovery, he has to cultivate an apprehensive mind (weixin), a belief in the omniscience of the spirits and a fear of their retribution: "Heaven and earth surround us, and the spirits are difficult to deceive.

---

[86] Okuzaki, Chūgoku kyōshin jinushi, pp. 249–252.

[87] Yuan Huang, Qisi zhenquan, p. 2. Further references to this work are indicated in the text by page numbers in brackets. The passage from Mencius is in Mengzi yinde, 7a.7 (p. 51); translation from Lau, Mencius, p. 183.

Even if a man transgresses in secret, heaven, earth, and the spirits can see his actions as if they were reflected in a mirror. . . . Even though he covers his actions with the greatest secrecy, and disguises them very cleverly, his innermost feelings will ultimately be revealed. In the end it is difficult for a man to fool himself, and if other people can see through his deception as well, then it is not worth one cash. How can one not be trembling with fear?" Finally, he has to have a courageous mind (*yongxin*)—that is, the courage and energy to take on the endless task of fault-correction [p. 2]. Only after these three states of mind have been achieved can a man start the self-correction process.

Yuan Huang then outlined three different methods of fault-correction. First, one's behavior could be changed to conform to externally imposed standards (*cong shishang gaiguo*): "If a man one day kills living things, and the next day is forbidden to do so, or if he one day loses his temper, and the next is forbidden to lose it—these are cases of the faults in one's behavior being changed." In this method of "driving faults away by force," one simply obeyed specific prohibitions, without necessarily understanding the reason for them or feeling the justice of them. Yuan acknowledged that this method, which was both difficult and inefficient, did not treat the source of the problem but simply some of its manifestations; though evil might have been "destroyed in the east, it lived in the west" [p. 3].

Much better was to change faults in accord with principle (*cong lishang gaiguo*)—that is, by understanding the principle underlying rules of conduct and deciding oneself, without any outside pressure, not to commit them. Yuan Huang provided one example of the reasoning this method required:

If previously you frequently got angry at others, you must think, "Each man has his deficiencies, and I should sympathize with them. If a man acts in a way that contravenes principle, what has it to do with me? Really, there is nothing that I can get angry about." And think, "Under heaven there isn't a hero who is truly satisfied with himself, nor is there a teaching that urges us to censure others. A man's actions do not always measure up to his intentions, his virtue is never fully cultivated, nor his feelings fully perfected. If I am always examining myself, then when I am slandered, it is grounds for "grinding and finishing jade" [i.e., for self-cultivation].[88] I should gladly receive slander, as a gift—how can I get angry at it?"

If you do not get angry when you hear slander, then even if the slander blazes like a fire that beclouds heaven, it is really like a fire set in emptiness—in the end it will burn itself out. But if you get angry when you hear slander, even if

[88] For the interpretation of "grinding and finishing," see Legge, *The Chinese Classics*, vol. 1, p. 363.

you cleverly exert yourself to dispute it, it will be like the spring silkworms making their cocoons—you will bind yourself up. Anger is not only useless, but also harmful. All the other different kinds of faults and evils should be thought of according to this principle. Once this principle is clear, faults will disappear of themselves. [p. 3]

Here, rather than blindly obeying a specific prohibition, a man had to think through the reasoning behind that prohibition until he fully understood the moral and psychological advantages of it. Comprehending the principle behind the rule, Yuan explained, would make it much easier to follow.

Though this method was clearly superior to the first, Yuan argued that the third method, "correcting faults in the mind" (*cong xinshang gaiguo*), was the best of all. The most efficient way of getting rid of error was to purify the ground in which it arose: the mind. Yuan explained:

What does "correcting faults in the mind" mean? Error has a thousand sources, but it is simply in the mind that they are all created. When my mind is not moved, how can error be produced in it? A scholar who loves sex or fame, or who is covetous or quick to anger, need not investigate all these various faults category by category. But he should devote his whole mind to the good, and then proper thoughts will frequently appear, and the previous evil thoughts will naturally not arise to pollute his mind, just as when the sun is in the heavens, evil spirits disappear and hide. This is the true transmission of the way to be discriminating and undivided.[89] Error is created in the mind; so too it is corrected in the mind. In cutting down a diseased tree, one cuts right at its roots—why would one need to kill each branch one by one or to pluck off each leaf one by one? [p. 3]

Correcting faults by understanding principle required a laborious working through of the rationale behind a prohibition. Correcting faults in the mind was much more efficient, for, by purifying the source of error, a man could rid himself of all his faults in one stroke.

Yuan believed that this last method was the most effective, but he acknowledged that certain people might find the others congenial:

Generally the best method of correcting faults is to regulate the mind until it is pure and at peace. Only then if your mind moves will you be aware of it, and if you are aware of it, you are without it. If you cannot yet use this method, then you must understand the principle behind your faults, in order to trace them back to their source. If you cannot yet use this method either, then you must destroy your faults according to external standards. If you use the superior method in conjunction with the inferior, it cannot be considered a futile

[89] See Legge, *The Chinese Classics*, vol. 3, pp. 61–62.

method. But if you use only the inferior method and forget the superior, that is stupid. [p.3]

"Purifying the mind" was essential to fault correction; "understanding principle" and obeying external regulations in daily behavior had only limited efficacy and were best used as supplements to the first technique.

After correcting his faults, a man could then move on to accumulate merit. In "Accumulating Goodness" (and again in "Success in the Examinations"), Yuan provided ten general categories of virtuous behavior as a guide: doing good as an example for others; having a loving and reverent state of mind; helping people to perform good deeds; teaching people to do good; saving others from danger and distress; benefiting the people through the repair of public works; making good fortune for others by giving them material aid; upholding the Buddhist laws; respecting and obeying one's elders (a prescription that included proper service to the ruler); and sympathizing with the fate of all living creatures [p. 8]. The ledger purportedly given to Yuan Huang by Yungu was consistent with these general prescriptions. The emphasis in the ledger, as in the list of categories, was on charitable acts and assistance to others: curing illness, saving lives, raising orphans, teaching virtuous behavior, repairing public works, giving aid to the poor, and so forth. The actions rewarded in the case studies given in "Accumulating Goodness" and "Success in the Examinations" also conformed to this type of behavior.

But the simple performance of good deeds was not enough. Even more than Yungu, Yuan Huang stressed that continual moral anxiety and absolute mental purity were prerequisites for the successful performance of good deeds, and that merit accrued only if good was done with a mind empty of considerations of profit. In developing this point, particularly in the essay "Accumulating Goodness," Yuan Huang defines a relatively sophisticated morality of merit accumulation. He makes a distinction between eight different qualities of goodness: true or false, straight or crooked, hidden or open, right or wrong, bent or upright, partial or full, large or small, and difficult or easy [p. 5]. Some of these distinctions had already appeared in the earlier system of merit and demerit: there, only hidden or secret virtue was rewarded, and larger or "heavier" goods were rewarded with appropriately larger rewards. Most of the other distinctions Yuan Huang makes, however, center around the questions of purpose, purity of mind, and effect—matters for the most part only tangentially mentioned in the earlier texts of the system.[90]

Yuan argues that a good deed "counts" only if it benefits others, if it is a "public" (gong) good. Even acts that superficially appear wrong may be considered virtuous if they contribute to a large public good, while ap-

[90] See, for example, Wang Ming, *Baopuzi neipian*, p. 115.

parently good behavior is not meritorious if done for selfish purposes. Speaking through a Buddhist monk, he explains: "If it benefits others it is good, if it benefits oneself it is evil. If it benefits others, then beating a man and cursing a man are both good. If it benefits oneself, then showing courtesy to a man and reverencing a man are both evil. Therefore, goodness done to profit others is public; if it is public, then it is true. If done to profit oneself, then it is selfish (*si*); if it is selfish, then it is false. So, too, what is rooted in the mind is true; what is outside is false. And he who acts without intention (*wuwei er wei*) is true; he who acts with the intention [of earning benefits for himself] is false." Yuan then contrasts the respectful and cautious type of scholar, the sort universally praised and eagerly employed, to the "wild" and idealistic type, the sort frequently viewed as dangerous and irresponsible. The former, interested in preserving his own reputation, is often ineffectual in office. His goodness is "crooked," and though all the county may praise him, he is no better in the end than Confucius's "thief of virtue." It is the "wild" and sincere scholar, whose virtue is "straight," who really deserves employment [p. 6].

Absence of intention and mental purity are so important that they may affect the value of certain apparently "large" or "small" goods. Thus, as the following story illustrates, an impure mind might reduce the moral value of even the most munificent of good deeds:

Once a woman went to a temple. She wanted to make a donation, but, being poor, she had only two cash. She gave them to the temple anyway. The head monk then heard her confession himself.

Later she entered the imperial palace, and gained wealth and high status. Taking several thousand pieces of silver, she returned and donated it all to the same temple. But the head monk simply ordered another monk to transfer the merit from this deed. The woman then asked, "Before, when I contributed two cash, you heard my confession yourself. Now, I have contributed several thousand silver pieces, but you do not transfer the merit yourself. Why is that?"

The monk replied, "Before, although your material goods were few, you gave with a true mind. If I had not heard your confession myself, it would not have been enough to recompense your goodness. Now, even though your material goods are many, in giving of them your mind is not as zealous as it was. It is sufficient to appoint someone else to hear your confession."[91] [p. 7]

Because of the difference in the woman's attitude, her contribution of only two cash was a "full" goodness, but her contribution of several thousand silver pieces merely a "partial" goodness. The woman allowed

[91] I consulted the translation of this story in Liu Ts'un-yan, "Yuan Huang and His 'Four Admonitions,'" pp. 116–117.

her newfound wealth and high status to go to her head, and, with the loss of her original purity and humility, her good deed lost much of its merit value. Another of Yuan's essays, "Profiting from Humility," is devoted entirely to stories of men who succeeded in the civil service examinations because they had cultivated a humble and modest state of mind.[92]

Yuan Huang even suggests that a man should be responsible for the larger repercussions of his deeds, for their long-term effects as well as their immediate impact. An official who is lenient to a criminal may be releasing him to commit other crimes. There is then something "bent" in his goodness—the evil result cancels out the good intention. The man who desires to accumulate merit must carefully think through all the implications of his deeds; his goodness is "true" only if it succeeds in changing the lives of others for the better. Here Yuan Huang relies on two moral judgments purportedly made by Confucius himself to illustrate his point:

> According to the laws of Lu, anyone from Lu who ransomed a man or a woman being held hostage by a feudal lord would receive a reward from the government. Zigong ransomed a man, but did not accept the reward. When Confucius heard of this, he criticized Zigong, saying, ". . . Now, through their actions, the sages changed customs and transformed popular habits, thereby extending their teachings to all the people. They did not act simply to suit themselves. Today there are few wealthy people in Lu, and many poor. If accepting a reward is considered impure, how will the people ransom each other? From now on, no one will ever again ransom anyone from the feudal lords."

Zigong, in refusing a reward for his good deed, appeared to be acting virtuously. But what he really did, Confucius points out, was to set a standard of behavior so high as to ensure that none would follow his example. Ashamed to accept a reward where another had nobly refused one, yet requiring an incentive to do good, no one, particularly among the impoverished population of Lu, would bother to help rescue captives from the feudal lords. Zigong chose to parade his own inaccessible virtue before the people rather than set an example of reasonable and realistic goodness. Yuan contrasts this case to that of Zilu:

> Zilu saved a man from drowning, and the man repaid him with an ox. Zilu accepted it. Confucius was pleased, saying, "Today in Lu there are many cases of men rescued from drowning. One sees it commonly."
>
> In the common view, Zigong's refusal of the reward was virtuous, and Zilu's acceptance of the ox was base. But Confucius blamed and praised according to the context.

[92] Yuan, *LMP*, 21a–24a.

Zilu behaved in a way that at first glance seemed greedy. Yet in accepting a reward for his good deed, he was in effect ensuring that others, hopeful of reward also, would be eager to perform the same deed. Here only Confucius had the far-reaching moral vision to see beyond the deed to its larger effects, to see that Zigong's "selfless" deed in fact hurt the people of Lu, while Zilu's "selfish" act in fact benefited them. Yuan suggests here that a ledger user has to be sensitive to the long-range impact of his deeds. He warns:

> To know a man's goodness, do not consider his current actions, but consider the spread of corrupt practices. Do not consider one time, but all time. Do not consider one person, but the whole world. Even if his current action is good, if its effect harms people, then what seems good is really not good. Even if his current action is not good, if its effect aids the people, then what is not good really is good. But this is just one part. There are other considerations, like the righteousness of unrighteousness, the propriety of impropriety, the trustworthiness of untrustworthiness, the compassion of hardheartedness—all should be distinguished. [pp. 6–7]

Yuan's criteria for meritorious action, then, were quite demanding: one had to act with a mind pure of selfish calculation, purely for the good of others, and, much more difficult, one had to have the vision to work out the final effects of one's actions.

Throughout his discussion of proper moral action, Yuan consistently called into question the validity of absolute moral values as well as the accuracy of conventional moral judgments. Goodness, in his mind, was contextually defined, dependent more on the judgment of the actor and his calculation of the greater effects of his deeds than on strict adherence to a fixed definition of righteousness, propriety, and so forth. Certainly, standards set by other people could not be accepted as accurate guides to genuine goodness; other people simply did not have the transcendent knowledge required to decide what was good and what was not. "The spirits of heaven and earth reward good and punish wickedness in accord with the sages' sense of right and wrong," he explains, "but their judgments are not in accord with those of the common world" [p. 6]. Of course, this point also explained what people saw as lapses in the distribution of rewards and punishments: since men in general had no real understanding of how moral judgments should be made, they had no right to question the workings of retribution.

But this idea had important repercussions for real meritorious moral practice as well. He who wishes to accumulate merit, Yuan warned, cannot rely on popular judgment, on the "ears and eyes of the world." He must depend rather on his own inner moral sense: "He can only follow the hidden tendencies to good at the source of the mind (*xinyuan yinwei chu*), silently cleansing away error, silently making lists (*jiandian*)" [p. 6]. Despite (and rather puzzling in light of) his reliance on a ledger of explicitly defined prescriptions, then, Yuan believed that effective moral action involved a highly disciplined, sensitive, and ultimately independent interpretation of stated values. Like many of Wang Yangming's followers, Yuan argued here that man should act only on the goodness he finds within himself—this is, indeed, genuine goodness, the only type recognized by the sages and the spirits.

Yuan's system as ideally described in "Accumulating Goodness" is rather intimidating in the demands it puts on the individual to achieve the highest degree of mental discipline. But at the same time that Yuan made his system morally challenging, he also made it accessible to all socioeconomic groups. Since purity of mind and an internally cultivated moral vision were all that was needed to do good effectively, a poor man could accumulate merit just as easily as a rich one. This is the message of the story of Zhang Weiyan, included in the essay "Profiting from Humility." A fine scholar from Jiangyin county, Jiangsu, Zhang went confidently to take the provincial examinations in Nanjing in 1594. When he did not pass, he cursed the examination officials in a fury. A Daoist priest took him aside and told him that only he was to blame for his failure: "I have heard that when writing essays it is most important to have a peaceful spirit and a calm mind. Just now I heard you cursing the examination officials, and your mind was not at all calm. How can your essays have been good?" Zhang asked how he might change, and the Daoist urged him to do good deeds and build up his store of secret merit, so that the gods would reward him with the desired examination degree. When Zhang protested that he was too poor to do good deeds, the Daoist replied, "Good deeds and secret merit are all created from the mind. If you always keep your mind in a state of virtue, then you will gain countless merits. It is like the business of becoming modest—you don't have to spend any money at all to achieve it."[93]

Thus, with a pure mind, "one cash can dissipate a thousand kalpas of crime." But, "if a man does not forget his mind [i.e., if he is conscious of his goodness], then even if he distributes 200,000 taels of pure silver, his good fortune will not be complete" [p. 8]. This is not to say that a wealthy man could not earn merit through the expenditure of money. Indeed, in his ledger Yuan lists several deeds requiring expenditure; one merit is awarded for each one thousand cash spent. (Presumably this merit is earned only if the deeds are done with a completely pure mind.) But at points Yuan does seem to suggest that the poor had an advantage over the wealthy in merit accumulation: since it is more difficult for them to

[93] Yuan Huang, *LMP*, 22b–23a.

do good, particularly good that involves expenditure of time or money, the spirits reward them more heavily than they would the wealthy for small acts of goodness. Certainly, the story of the female temple-donor, quoted above, tends to support this point: the wealthy, both because good deeds are relatively easy for them and because they are more likely to be corrupted by their wealth and status, have to work harder to earn real merit.

Yet, however much Yuan stressed the importance of mental purity and moral self-discipline in merit accumulation, he never lost sight of the this-worldly practical goal of his system: status advancement through success in the examinations and appointment to official posts for either the individual ledger user or his descendants. Wealth, though mentioned by Yungu as a possible reward, did not figure prominently in Yuan's interpretation, except as an inevitable side effect of official appointment. In the stories in the essay "Accumulating Goodness," in which the birth of sons was supposed to be the goal of merit accumulation, most of the moral heroes were rewarded not simply with sons, but with sons who later earned examination degrees and became distinguished officials. Furthermore, the language of his writings—a classical Chinese not easily accessible to nonliterati—suggests that he was addressing most directly a rather limited audience of educated men and aspiring officials.

The case studies Yuan provides in "Accumulating Goodness," "Profiting from Humility," and "Success in the Examinations" indicate, too, that he saw the ledgers as practical guides largely for men desirous of entering the official elite. His examples emphasize the immediate applicability of his system to their goal. Rather than drawing on stories of great, but remote, historical figures to illustrate the efficacy of merit accumulation, Yuan described the experiences of his contemporaries, including rather obscure men from his own native place who never achieved nationwide fame, as well as highly successful scholars and officials such as Ding Bin (j.s. 1571, d. 1633) and Feng Mengzhen (1546–1605).[94]

---

[94] Some of the examples are of Yuan Huang's own friends or acquaintances: Ding Bin, like Yuan from Jiashan, traveled with Yuan to take the metropolitan examination in 1571; Feng Mengzhen (z. Kaizhi), also from Jiashan, hosted Yuan in Beijing in 1577; Xia Jiansuo, from Jiashan, was a friend whom Yuan later visited while serving in Beijing in 1592; Bao Ping, from Jiaxing prefecture, married into a branch of Yuan's family and was a close friend of Yuan's father; Zhi Li served as a clerk in Jiashan and was a contemporary of Yuan's grandfather. Finally, Tu Kangxi, from Jiaxing prefecture, was the grandfather of Tu Shufang, a *jinshi* of 1577, the man who memorialized the emperor to pardon the Jianwen martyrs and their descendants. There is no evidence that Yuan Huang knew Tu Shufang, but he had reason to be grateful to him, for it was his act that finally freed the Yuan family from any onus attached to their past involvement in the resistance movement against Zhu Di. Yuan certainly used many cases of men not known to have any connection to him or his family (though most of these were from Zhejiang or Jiangsu provinces). But the important

Many were at the bottom of the examination route: *shengyuan*, often working as tutors, clerks, and other yamen functionaries, who, though from families without a tradition of official service, had the basic education necessary to begin examination study. All of them received the same kinds of rewards—that is, success in the examinations and high official placement, or the birth of sons who won these distinctions to their vicarious glory. The story of Yang Zicheng nicely illustrates the pattern:

> Yang Zicheng, from Yin county, Zhejiang, started out as a county clerk. His heart was set on benevolence and generosity, and he was law-abiding and fair. The county magistrate at that time was severe and harsh. On one occasion he had a prisoner beaten until the blood gushed out of him, and yet his anger was still not appeased. Yang knelt before him and asked that the prisoner be released. The magistrate said, "If I tolerate this man's violation of the law and his repudiation of what is right, then how can I get angry at anyone else's crimes?" Zicheng kowtowed and replied, [quoting from the *Analects*,] " 'Those in authority have lost the Way and the common people have, for long, been rootless. If you succeed in extracting the truth from them, do not be pleased at your own ability but have compassion on them.' If one cannot even be pleased, then how much less suitable is anger?"[95] Thereupon the magistrate controlled his anger.
>
> Zicheng's family was poor, yet he never accepted presents of food. Whenever he met a prisoner who lacked provisions, he used all possible means to aid him. One day there were several new prisoners waiting to be fed. His family was also short of rice, and if he gave some to these prisoners then his family would have nothing to eat. Yet if he thought of his own family, then the prisoners would have nothing. He discussed the problem with his wife, and she asked, "Where are these prisoners from?" He replied, "They are from Hangzhou. Along the road they have suffered from hunger, and their faces are a pale and greenish color." Thereupon his wife took all their rice and cooked gruel to feed the prisoners.
>
> Later two sons were born to them. The elder was named Shouchen and the younger Shouzhi. The former served as the vice-minister of the Beijing Board of Personnel, the latter as the vice-minister of the Nanjing Board. Zicheng's elder grandson was vice-minister of the Board of Punishments, and the younger was a surveillance commissioner in Sichuan. They were all famous officials.[96]

The deeds Yuan describes in his exemplary stories were for the most part of a general moral nature, not requiring membership in a particular sect

---

point here is that he tended to draw on immediate, contemporary examples of upward mobility through merit accumulation, rather than on distant historical proofs. See *Liming pian* and *Qisi zhenquan*, passim.

[95] *Lunyu yinde*, 19.19 (p. 40); translation from Lau, *Mencius*, p. 155.

[96] Yuan Huang, *LMP*, 9b–10a. On the Yang family, see *Mingshi*, vol. 16, j. 184, pp. 4875–4878; and Brokaw, "Yuan Huang," p. 185n.140.

or adherence to a certain philosophical school—in short, acts appropriate to all men. His heroes might assiduously cultivate a particular virtue (frequently humility), contribute to the upkeep of a temple or the repair of a religious image, or simply perform a variety of charitable deeds—feeding prisoners, rescuing the poor from cold and starvation, saving victims of flood, and so forth. Though many of these deeds did require monetary outlay or some economic sacrifice, Yuan continued to insist that there was no absolute need for a man to spend money to accumulate merit.[97] His message here was that, with education and a real devotion to virtue, anyone could achieve success in the examination system for himself and/or his descendants.

Yungu and Yuan Huang significantly reshaped the merit and demerit system to express concerns and aspirations very different from those of the twelfth-century *Tract on Action and Response* and *Ledger of Merit and Demerit of the Taiwei Immortal*. By shifting the focus of the ledgers from religious and other-worldly goals to secular and this-worldly ones, they transformed the basic nature of the system. Man now had a much firmer and more immediate control over his fate—he need not wait until his next life or the end of this one to enjoy the fruits of virtue. While the *Tract* and the *Ledger of the Taiwei Immortal* offered longevity and immortality as primary rewards, Yungu and Yuan Huang promised the material reward of status advancement through success in the examinations. The deeds prescribed in their system also reflect this shift: largely moral acts of a secular nature, they did not commit the ledger user to any particular religious affiliation or set of religious acts. To be sure, merit accumulation remained for Yungu and Yuan Huang a program founded in certain religious beliefs, for it still depended entirely on the belief in supernatural retribution. Yuan Huang himself practiced the system in the context of religious belief—he made his appeals for rewards to the Buddha, repeatedly sought the advice and assistance of Buddhist monks, and nightly reported his conduct to heaven. But, in contrast to the earlier pre-Ming system of merit and demerit, the emphasis was no longer on man's dependence on this supernatural system, but on his power over it, on his ability to decide his own fate in this world. Merit accumulation was now first and foremost a way for the individual to master his destiny, not for the gods to deter men from evil.

At the same time that they stressed human control of fate, both Yungu and Yuan Huang gave the merit-demerit system a greater moral sophistication. Man might now be able to decide his own fate, but with this power came a heavier moral responsibility. Yuan Huang in particular in-

[97] Yuan Huang, *LMP*, 14a–15a, 17b.

terpreted merit accumulation as a practice requiring great mental discipline. A ledger user had to develop the same constant attentiveness to the moral details of his daily actions that Zhu Xi demanded of the serious scholar. In terms that could be appealing to both Chan Buddhists and Neo-Confucians (most particularly those of the Wang Yangming school), Yuan also emphasized the need to do good with a mind free of calculation and selfish thoughts. And in language reminiscent of Wang Yangming, Wang Ji, and the Taizhou thinkers, he repudiated worldly moral judgments and urged men to follow the springs of goodness in their own minds. No longer could mechanical merit accumulation—the sort of automatic cancellation of a large evil with many insignificant acts of goodness allowed (though certainly not encouraged) in the *Ledger of the Taiwei Immortal*—be considered efficacious. In fact, a ledger user needed an unusually sensitive moral vision to accumulate merit that would actually yield rewards.[98]

Yuan Huang and Yungu also changed the form of argumentation in their presentation of the merit-demerit system. "Determining Your Own Fate" in particular is very much a polemic, as if its authors realized the need to convince their audience of the validity of merit accumulation. The twelfth-century *Tract on Action and Response* and the *Ledger of the Taiwei Immortal* urged people to do good; "Determining Your Own Fate" has first to establish the truth of its premises, a challenge apparently not felt by either Li Shi or You Xuanzi, both of whom seem to have been confident of the divine authorship of the texts they transmitted. "Determining Your Own Fate" attempts to meet this need by adducing the authority of each of the three teachings in support of the system of merit accumulation—hence the freedom with which Yungu moved back and forth among Confucian, Buddhist, and Daoist citations and illustrations. But there is an obvious emphasis within this argument. Daoism was by far the weakest partner, garnering only one explicit allusion. References to the Buddhist tradition were much more plentiful, even predominating in Yuan Huang's description of the rituals tied to ledger use.

In explicating the principles behind the system of merit and demerit, however, Yungu and Yuan Huang alluded only briefly to Buddhist sources. Rather, it is from Confucianism that both men drew real legitimation for the ledger system. *Mencius*, one of the basic texts of Neo-Confucianism, provided (in Yungu's and Yuan Huang's idiosyncratic reading of it) the most important "proof" that man could control his own fate—"*liming*," the slogan of the new ledger system, was taken from

[98] This point remains a standard part of most later ledgers, usually incorporated into stories of busy good-doers who fail to receive rewards because their deeds were done with an impure mind, one full of selfish intentions. Chün-fang Yü gives an example of one of the more famous of these stories in *Renewal of Buddhism*, pp. 113–114.

Mencius. But Yungu and Yuan Huang also freely drew on the *Classic of Songs,* the *Classic of Changes,* and the *Spring and Autumn Annals* for evidence of supernatural retribution. Indeed, they never relied on a Buddhist or Daoist allusion when a Confucian one would do—or sometimes even when it would not do. Although Yuan Huang never explicitly referred to a Confucian thinker later than Mencius, his description of the mental attitude required in merit accumulation is perfectly compatible with certain principles of a Neo-Confucian program of self-cultivation.

Thus the system of merit and demerit developed by Yungu and Yuan Huang is really a "Confucianized" version of a system originally associated principally with Buddhism and Daoism.[99] The Buddhist bones of the system still show through the rather thin Confucian skin stretched over them; but Yungu and Yuan Huang were nonetheless able to argue with some justice that theirs was a system enjoying the backing of several Confucian Classics. Even the most redoubtable Confucian scholar could now feel safe using a ledger of merit and demerit—or so Yungu and Yuan Huang wanted their readers to believe.

However unconventional Yungu's and Yuan Huang's claims about the philosophical sources of merit accumulation may have been, their ledger system itself was quite conventional, even conservative, in its definition of literati success and status advancement. For Yuan in particular, passage of the examinations (and the consequent appointment to office) appeared as the primary legitimate goal of ledger use; commercial success or wealth, despite its increased respectability in the sixteenth century, was never treated as a serious aim. At a time when the examination system was being roundly criticized for its failure to produce truly virtuous men, Yuan Huang, by associating the achievement of degree status with moral improvement, was defending the system and the officials it produced. Against those who attacked competition in the examinations as a barrier to the achievement of Confucian sagehood, Yuan Huang was asserting rather that the former simply reflected the latter. As he explained in the title of one of his essays, "Success in the Examinations Depends Entirely on Secret Virtue."

The merit-demerit system also provided a convincing moral explanation of examination success and failure. We know from contemporary

[99] The troubled term "syncretic" is often applied to Yungu's and Yuan Huang's work, and indeed to the whole tradition of ledger publication in the late Ming and early Qing. It is undoubtedly true, as I have said in the text, that Yungu, Yuan Huang, and later ledger authors drew freely on principles, practices, and stories from each of the Three Teachings to support the system of merit accumulation. But their effort seems more eclectic than syncretic, as they made no attempt to integrate the principles and practices they borrowed into a comprehensive and systematic philosophy. See Shimizu Taiji, "Mindai ni okeru shūkyō yūgō to kōkakaku," and Sakai, *Chūgoku zensho,* pp. 226–317.

complaints about the repeated failure of well-known scholars that the
decisions of the examination graders often seemed arbitrary. Once its basic premises were accepted, the system of merit and demerit gave perfectly
logical reasons for surprising results. The unsuccessful candidate could
have inherited a burden of demerit from his ancestors, or he could have
sinned grievously in his previous life and only now have received his punishment. Or perhaps he had simply not been sincere in his performance
of good deeds. Yuan Huang often favored this last option in his writings:
since only heaven and the spirits could know what went on in a man's
mind, he explained, only they could tell if his intentions were pure. By
attributing failure to a lack of sincerity or mental discipline on the part of
the candidate, Yuan Huang was providing a very Neo-Confucian explanation for failure, one that reinforced the moral legitmacy of the examinations. The apparent injustices of the system were signs not of grader
prejudice or bad government, but of the inexorable dedication of heaven
and the gods, even over considerable periods of time, to the reward of the
virtuous and the punishment of the wicked.

Yuan Huang read the merit-demerit system, then, as a reaffirmation of
the existing social hierarchy: he deserved his own high status because of
his (and, more important, his family's) earnest performance of good
deeds. Belief in merit accumulation allowed him to accept without much
question the moral justice of the social hierarchy—though he conceded
that there were good men among the common people, he nonetheless asserted as a general rule the natural moral ascendancy of scholars (as men
of higher status and thus of greater virtue) over the common people.[100]

Yet implicit in Yuan's view of the system of merit and demerit is an
essentially dynamic vision of society. The social order was linked to the
always changing moral behavior of individuals, and hence it too was dynamic, always changing. The order was hierarchical, to be sure, but it was
not static. According to the principles Yuan set forth, anyone, of almost
any status, could get ahead or, more realistically, ensure that his descendants got ahead, if he was assiduous, sincere, and patient enough in the
performance of good deeds. Though Yuan himself illustrated his system
with examples drawn largely from those of literati status, it was logically
applicable to any member of any status in Chinese society. By justifying
and championing the vigorous pursuit of good fortune within the established hierarchy, Yuan's version of the ledger system encouraged upward
social mobility at the same time that it reaffirmed the validity of the existing status structure. Moreover, it helped to explain the sudden social
changes of the late Ming, and to assure readers that these changes, nec-

[100] Yuan Huang, *Lianghang zhai wenji*, 10.4a–6a; cited in Okuzaki, *Chūgoku kyōshin
jinushi*, pp. 105–106; see also 461–475.

essary to the perfect alignment of moral and social realities, were ultimately not threatening to the social order, but essential to its authentic
preservation.

It is easy to see why the message of Yuan's system was such a popular
one in the late Ming. At a time of political weakness, increased economic
opportunities, and social upheaval—when much in life seemed out of human control—Yuan's claim that man could direct his own fate must have
been comforting, particularly since he also supplied quite specific instructions as to how such an effect was to be achieved. In the absence of assured political leadership and ethical consensus, Yuan's ledger offered
precise, divinely sanctioned guidelines for behavior for those puzzled,
amidst the moral debates of the period, as to what exactly proper conduct
was. For those desirous of getting ahead during a time of economic opportunity and social uncertainty and unrest, it offered a method of ensuring success in the examinations, or at least a way of bolstering their
chances of success. Furthermore, the deeds of the ledgers could even be
seen as aids to success in an elite social status: since the ledgers presumably explained how the existing elite had "made it," their prescriptions
could be interpreted as rules for elite behavior. Thus the ledgers helped
their users not only accumulate merit, but also train for what they hoped
would be their future social standing.[101]

Finally, by asserting a special Confucian validity for the system of merit
accumulation, Yungu and Yuan Huang gave it an air of legitimacy important to men concerned about finding a place for themselves in a civil
service system founded on mastery of the Neo-Confucian orthodoxy.
And, as the system drew on Neo-Confucian principles of self-cultivation,
status advancement was made to go hand-in-hand with moral improvement, supposedly the highest goal of the true Confucian scholar. It was
now, Yungu and Yuan Huang claimed, "all right," even in Confucian
terms, to practice merit accumulation.

[101] For similar interpretations, see Kristin Yü Greenblatt, "Chu-hung and Lay Buddhism
in the Late Ming," and Rawski, "Economic and Social Foundations," pp. 15–16, 28–29.

CHAPTER THREE

The Debate over Supernatural Retribution and Merit Accumulation

YUNGU and Yuan Huang were quite successful in their efforts to persuade their peers of the legitimacy of merit accumulation. Contemporary observers assure us that their *Ledger of Merit and Demerit* was indeed popular among scholars studying for the examinations. Zhang Lixiang, the late Ming social critic, complained that examination candidates studied it as seriously as they did the Four Books, the Five Classics, and Zhu Xi's *Reflections on Things at Hand* (*Jinsi lu*), the fundamental texts of examination study: "It is Yuan Huang's *Ledger of Merit and Demerit* that serves as the sacred text for today's scholars," he lamented.[1] But use of the texts was by no means limited to struggling students. Distinguished literati and officials of the late Ming used Yuan's work also. Zhou Rudeng, one of the leaders of the Taizhou school and a successful official (his highest appointment was vice-administrative commissioner of Yunnan), was converted to ledger use after a long debate with Yuan Huang. Tao Wangling (b. 1562; j.s. 1589), a Hanlin academician and Taizhou affiliate, and his brother Shiling both used ledgers; Wangling's disciple, Qin Hongyou, followed their example.[2] Lu Shiyi, though he later repudiated the ledger system, did use Yuan Huang's ledger as a young man; he also wrote his own ledger, *Investigating Things and Extending Knowledge* (*Gezhi pian*).[3]

Other ledger-like texts and morality books enjoyed a considerable vogue in this period as well. At least ten new ledgers have survived from the century after Yuan's death in 1606, and the titles of many others appeared in contemporary writings.[4] It was also during this period that active interest in the *Tract of Taishang on Action and Response* was revived; although the text was clearly well known before the late Ming, a flood of new editions, often with new annotations, appeared in the sixteenth and seventeenth centuries, and even well into the eighteenth cen-

---

[1] Zhang Lixiang, *Yangyuan xiansheng quanji*, 5.10b–11a; reference from Okuzaki, *Chūgoku kyōshin jinushi*, pp. 421–422.

[2] Dong Yang, "Liuzi nianpu," *LZQS*, 40.50a (vol. 6, p. 3585).

[3] For Lu's use of the ledgers, see Ling Xiqi, "Zundao xiansheng nianpu," 4b–6a; and Lu Shiyi, *Futing xiansheng wenchao*, 3.20b. References from Sakai, *Chūgoku zensho*, p. 389.

[4] See, for example, Chen Zhixi, "Caiyong gujin shumu," *Quanjie quanshu*, *ce* 1; and Sakai, *Chūgoku zensho*, p. 382.

tury.[5] Thinkers as disparate as Yang Qiyuan (1547–1599), a Taizhou affiliate and friend of Yuan Huang; Gao Panlong, a cofounder of the Donglin Academy and enemy of the Taizhou school; Tu Long, the dramatist and aspiring immortal; Tao Wangling; and Yuan Huang himself wrote prefaces to new editions of the *Tract*.[6] The work remained popular through the early Qing at least. Continuing a tradition established by Emperor Lizong of the Song, both the Shunzhi (r. 1644–1661) and the Yongzheng (r. 1723–1735) emperors sponsored publication of the *Tract*.[7] Hui Dong (1697–1758), the distinguished *kaozheng* scholar, published his own annotated edition of the text—done of course in *kaozheng* style—as an appeal to the gods to cure his mother's illness.[8]

This is not to suggest that the concept of supernatural retribution and the idea that man could decide his own fate in Yuan Huang's terms were placidly accepted by all late Ming thinkers. On the contrary, even many of the scholars who used ledgers or sponsored morality-book publication expressed some ambivalence about the method of merit accumulation and its moral and social implications, and tried to modify the method to ease their doubts. Yuan Huang's "Determining Your Own Fate"—although it earned several articulate defenders—also aroused the antago-

[5] I exclude from this list versions of the *Taishang ganying pian* included in other morality books; nor do I include new editions clearly named in other sources but no longer extant. For example, Zhang Xuecheng wrote an afterword to the text, but although his essay survives in the *Zhangshi yishu*, 29.12b–14a (pp. 721–722), the text does not. (See David S. Nivison, *The Life and Thought of Chang Hsüeh-ch'eng*, pp. 94, 235–238.) I know of the following versions published between the late Ming and the nineteenth century: *Taishang ganying pian jingzhuan* (1604); *Taishang ganying jingzhuan jiyao* (edited by Liu Mengzhen in the Ming but published in the Qing); *Tianxia diyizhong haoshu* (edited by He Shengxiu and Cao Delin, 1655); *Taishang ganying pian* (edited by Xu Xingzhi, 1664); *Taishang ganying pian tongjie* (edited by Wang Menglan, 1664); *Taishang ganying pian shuyan* (1667); *Taishang ganying pian xinzhu* (edited by Wang Jiazhen, 1676); *Taishang ganying pian tushuo* (edited by Ma Jun, published in 1694); *Taishang ganying pian jijie* (edited by Wang Daoquan, published in 1758); *Taishang ganying pian zhujiang zheng'an huibian* (Qing); *Taishang baofu* (edited by Huang Zhengyuan, Qing edition); *Taishang ganying pian jizhu* (edited by Tao Ningzuo, published in 1734); *Taishang ganying pian zhuzheng hebian* (edited by Wang Nizhen, published in 1843); *Taishang ganying pian zhu* (edited by Wang Yantang, published in the Qing); and *Taishang ganying pian zhu* (edited by Hui Dong, published in the Qing).

[6] Gao Panlong, *Gaozi yishu*, 9a.43a–45a; Tu Long, *Hongbao ji*, 42.15a–17a; Yuan Huang, *Lianghang zhai wenji*, 5.1a–2a. Tao Wangling's preface was written for the 1604 edition of the *Tract* in the Naikaku Bunko. See Sakai, *Chūgoku zensho*, pp. 251–257. For a general discussion of the literati audience for the ledgers and other morality books, see Sakai Tadao, "Minmatsu Shinsho no shakai ni okeru taishūteki dokushojin to zensho. seigen."

[7] Yü, *Renewal of Buddhism*, pp. 102–103; Sakai, *Chūgoku zensho*, p. 257.

[8] Hui Dong, "Xu," 1a–b (p. 5649), *Taishang ganying pian zhu*. Zhang Xuecheng and Yu Yue (1821–1906) are two other distinguished scholars who wrote prefaces to the text. See Yü, *Renewal of Buddhism*, pp. 102–103.

nism of many influential scholar-officials, so that by the end of the seventeenth century Yuan Huang was routinely linked with the notorious Li Zhi as an example of the type of irresponsible and "depraved" literatus responsible for the fall of the Ming.

The controversy over Yuan Huang's *Ledger* and other morality books is, in the end, simply an expression of a larger intellectual preoccupation with the issues of retribution and human control, issues increasingly seen in the sixteenth and seventeenth centuries as relevant to the definition of both moral self-cultivation and elite status and responsibility. Self-cultivation, the process whereby the individual perfected himself morally, fully recovering the pure goodness within him, was the goal of all right-thinking Neo-Confucian scholars. The morally perfected scholar, then, was expected to take on a leading role in society, to "bring peace to the world," to put this larger goal in its most ambitious terms. Yuan Huang, as we have seen, accepted the conventional route—an official post in the national bureaucracy—to this goal. But as the central government became more corrupt and bureaucratic service more dangerous in the course of the seventeenth century, serious thinkers searched for ways of reinterpreting the responsibilities associated with elite status. This is not to say that they necessarily rejected or devalued official service; they simply developed other areas and techniques through which elites might try to "bring peace to the world," even if the world referred simply to their own individual communities. In the very late Ming both the moral and the sociopolitical foundations of elite status thus became matters of heated debate, particularly between members of the Taizhou school and the more conservative thinkers associated with the Donglin Academy.

Yuan Huang's *Ledger* never became the center of this debate—indeed, some of the contributors to the discussion in the seventeenth century made no mention of Yuan Huang or his work by name. But the popularity of Yuan's *Ledger*, and the obvious appeal of his bold assertion that man could control his own fate—both moral and material—did serve to sharpen the terms of the debate over self-cultivation and social status. For Yuan's interpretation of the ledger system forced thinkers to confront certain questions about fate and the process of moral learning, and about their relationship to the larger social order: How much control did man have over his destiny? Could he actually expect the concrete material rewards promised by Yungu and Yuan Huang? Would adherence to the specific rules listed in the ledgers make a man truly good, and thus give him the control he desired? Could a serious Neo-Confucian hope to profit materially, as Yuan Huang suggested he could, from good deeds? If heaven did indeed reward the good and punish the evil, how did the mechanism of retribution operate? How might belief in retribution influence the social order, particularly accepted definitions of status? What were the consequences of the belief, not just for the ambitious individual, but for the whole community?

THE ADVOCATES OF "DETERMINING YOUR OWN FATE": THE TAIZHOU SCHOOL

By and large the most enthusiastic supporters of Yuan Huang's ledger system were members of the Wang Yangming school, particularly the Taizhou branch. Yuan Huang himself claimed to be an adherent of the Wang school, and he did follow some of Wang's ideas in his reading of the Classics.[9] His own personal contacts were closest to members of the "wilder" branches of the school. He studied with Wang Ji and Taizhou affiliate Luo Rufang (himself a one-time ledger user), and remained friends with two of Luo's disciples, Zhou Rudeng and Yang Qiyuan, both of whom he converted to ledger use.[10]

This association between Yuan and the Wang Yangming school is borne out, too, in certain aspects of Yuan's system of merit accumulation. In asserting that man could control his own fate by cultivating the spontaneous goodness in his mind, Yuan was building on a principle at the center of Wang Yangming's teachings. Wang had insisted that "the highest good is inherent in one's own mind"—as long as one followed this innate knowledge of good, then one's moral choices in life would naturally be correct. "If one's innate knowledge is clear," Wang explained, "it will be all right either to try to obtain truth through personal realization in a quiet place or to discover it through training and polishing in the actual affairs of life."[11] The self was the source now of moral and intellectual judgment; even Confucius might be found lacking if measured against the reasoning of one's innate knowledge: "If words are examined in the mind and found to be wrong, although they have come from the mouth of Confucius, I dare not accept them as correct. How much less those from people inferior to Confucius! If words are examined in the mind and found to be correct, although they have come from the mouth

---

[9] Yuan Huang, "Keji fuli," *Lunyu*, 2.6a, in *Liaofan Yuan xiansheng sishu shanzheng jianshuyi*. Here Yuan made it clear, too, that he did not himself agree with Zhu Xi's commentaries on the Classics; he explains that although he included Zhu Xi's interpretations to aid the examination candidate, he supplemented these readings with others from more recent scholars, lest "our candidates suffer by having even less material for study, their standards be lowered, and in a general sense the atmosphere of study and the prospects of the nation be hurt" ("Fanli," 1b–4a). Translation (with some changes) from Liu, "Yuan Huang and His 'Four Admonitions,' " p. 126.

[10] Wang Ji, "Yuan Canbo xiaozhuan," YSCS, 11.1b–2a.

[11] Translation from Wang Yangming, *Instructions for Practical Living*, p. 217.

of ordinary people, I dare not regard them as wrong. How much less those of Confucius!"[12]

Wang Gen, the founder of the Taizhou school, attributed even greater power to the individual. It was a mistake, he argued, to measure oneself by the ways of the world; rather, each man, with his innate knowledge of the good, should think of himself as the measure or standard, and the world as the object of measurement: "The individual is a measure, and the world, states, and families are each a square. Adjust the measure to know whether the square is straight. . . . Certainly do not seek the measure in the square."[13] Here Wang introduces a precept—that a man should "create his own fate" (zaoming)—that sounds very close to Yuan Huang's injunction to man to "determine his own fate." In adjusting the world to his own measure, Wang argued, a man might have to struggle against the heavenly command (tianming) and "create his own fate," his own role in society, against or despite his material conditions. Thus Confucius, though fated by heaven never to gain any political power himself, used other means to see that his Way was made known in the world.[14] Here Wang was arguing very much against the common injunction that man "accept his place" in life; everyone should, if necessary, fight against the material conditions of his life to fulfill the dictates of his innate knowledge. Wang Gen himself, who abandoned a career as a merchant to study and teach his version of the Way, might well be taken as a model for men who wished to "create their own fate." His practice of lecturing on the Way to "ignorant men and women" as he traveled about the Chinese countryside suggests that he took quite seriously the idea that anyone could struggle against his or her lot in life, rise against fate, and change it, even to the point of becoming a sage.

Wang Gen's concept of "creating one's own fate" is ultimately different from Yuan Huang's notion of "determining one's own fate," for Wang envisioned his process as one of struggle for moral achievements (not material gain) against what heaven had fated: "He who creates his own fate is struggling with heaven."[15] For Yuan, in contrast, heaven and the gods actually encouraged men to seek material as well as moral goals in deciding their own fate; they would adjust material fate in response to human actions. Yuan Huang had, if anything, simply extended the principle so that in his system its scope was broader, and the process, now encouraged by heaven and the gods, much easier. Wang encouraged men to ignore

[12] Ibid., p. 159.

[13] Wang Gen, Wang Xinzhai quanji, 2.3a–b; translation in part from Carson Chang, The Development of Neo-Confucian Thought, vol. 2, p. 117.

[14] Wang Gen, Wang Xinzhai quanji, 2.9a–b; see also 5.14b–15b.

[15] Ibid. On Wang Gen's understanding of fate, see Shimada Kenji, Chūgoku ni okeru kindai shii no zasetsu, pp. 110–112, and Okuzaki, Chūgoku kyōshin jinushi, pp. 455–457.

material barriers and seize charge of their moral fate; Yuan stated that they could do both at the same time—indeed, they had to do both at the same time because the two were inextricably linked.

Yuan's method of managing one's own fate implied a much more dynamic vision of social mobility, for as each person improved his moral state, he was inevitably, whether he liked it or not, also advancing his social standing. A similar vision was implied, in slightly different terms, in the views of another Wang Yangming follower, He Xinyin. Rejecting the conventional idea that the individual should placidly accept his position in life, He argued that a man had what amounted to a moral responsibility to master the next highest status position in society: "One should avoid the lower status and master the higher status. How could one avoid the higher and master the lower, not aspiring to the higher and growing accustomed to the lower? If you are a peasant or artisan, yet aspire to the status of merchant, then you can enter into the aims of merchants. If you are a merchant, yet aspire to the status of scholar, you can enter into the aims of scholars. If you are a scholar, and yet aspire to the status of sage or worthy, you can enter into the aims of sages and worthies." He Xinyin goes on to urge the benefits of aspiration to higher status: even if a man has not fully "mastered" the terms of a new, higher status, he is still better off than he had been in his previous lower status. Thus a peasant aspiring to merchant status had an advantage over a peasant with no such ambition, just as a scholar aspiring to be a sage had an advantage over one who was content to remain a simple scholar. Finally, He asserted that the individual's place in the status system was dependent on his own actions: "Transcending the status of peasant and artisan to become a merchant, or transcending the status of merchant to become a scholar is a matter of human transcendence and human action."[16] He does not emphasize the moral nature of the hierarchy (though it is implicit in the assumption that at the very top is the status of sage); otherwise, he asserts very much what Yuan Huang does: man can and should decide his own fate.

For Yuan, He Xinyin, and even Wang Gen, there is a common faith in man's ability to control at least the events of his own life through the cultivation of his innate goodness, the "pattern" within his mind. Thus Taizhou adherents were attracted to Yuan's method of self-cultivation in large part because of the power it gave the human mind to create the moral and material circumstances of life. One enthusiastic advocate praised Yuan's *Determining Your Own Fate* for just this reason: "the work records the sayings of Yungu, that fortune and misfortune come from the self, and that the creative force is in one's own mind—these pronouncements would not have been possible without penetrating in-

[16] Liang Ruyuan (He Xinyin), *He Xinyin ji*, j. 3, pp. 53–54.

sight. One cannot say that it is not a great conveyance [to enlightenment; *dasheng*]."[17] Certainly, Yuan's emphasis in *Determining Your Own Fate* on mental purity, on the necessity of acting without intention, must also have strengthened the attraction his work had for Taizhou scholars, for it matched, at least superficially, the doctrine held by these thinkers that action should be spontaneous, uncontaminated by any hint of conscious purpose or moral reasoning. Furthermore, these men were likely to be more open than other conservative scholars to the references within Yuan's system: as men avowedly attracted to both Buddhist and Daoist doctrines, they were not put off by the eclectic and heterodox sources of the ledger. Indeed, one of the attractions for them must have been Yuan's "reconciliation" of Mencius's understanding of fate, the Chan doctrine of no-thought, and Daoist and Buddhist beliefs in supernatural retribution.[18]

But in another way the Taizhou school endorsement of the ledger system might seem at first glance rather startling. The Taizhou school is generally associated with the view that prescriptions of right and wrong were artificial constructs tending, if anything, to give a false sense of goodness. Since they arose from relative moral judgments, they "created" evil: "filial piety is known only where there is unfilial feeling, and the genuinely filial know nothing of unfilial feeling."[19] The mind was the source of moral truth, and since there was neither good nor evil in the substance of the mind, adherence to moral standards imposed from the outside should have no place in the self-cultivation process. The individual was free to—indeed, he ought to—follow spontaneously the impulses of his transcendent mind. But Yuan Huang's whole program of cultivation was based on adherence to externally imposed rules of conduct—what was a ledger of merit and demerit but a list of such rules? And, in his practice of the system, Yuan Huang, was certainly self-conscious about his moral progress; it was hardly a spontaneous realization of his innate knowledge of the good. How could any of the Taizhou thinkers sympathize with the

---

[17] Zhou Rudeng, *Dongyue zhengxue lu*, 7.19a–20a. For another translation of this passage, see Liu, "Yuan Huang and His 'Four Admonitions,' " pp. 121–122. See also Sakai Tadao, "Yōmeigaku to Mindai no zensho," pp. 353–363.

[18] Another Taizhou affiliate interested in merit accumulation was Guan Zhidao. Attracted also to Buddhism and Daoism, Guan clearly shared Yuan's faith in supernatural retribution; he believed that his family's fortunes depended on a legacy of secret merit (*yinzhi*) passed from generation to generation. Yuan and Guan worked together on plans for the publication of the Jiaxing Tripitaka, but we do not know whether Yuan ever discussed his belief in the ledgers with Guan. See Guan, *Cong xianwei suyi*, 5.1a–10a; and Araki Kengo, *Minmatsu shūkyō shisō kenkyu—Ken Tōmei no shōgai to sono shisō—*, pp. 30–31, 41–42, 286. For the attitudes of members of the Wang Yangming school, see Sakai, "Yōmeigaku to Mindai no zensho," pp. 343–353.

[19] Huang Zongxi, *Mingru xue'an*, 7, "Taizhou," 5, p. 69.

kind of moral anxiety and constant self-examination Yuan Huang sub-jected himself to in "Determining Your Own Fate"?

Indeed, Zhou Rudeng, the most articulate defender of the Taizhou po-sition in the late sixteenth century, at one point in his career clearly stated his opposition to the very principles at the heart of the ledger system. In the course of the famous nine-point debate between Zhou and Xu Fuyuan (1535–1604), a more cautious follower of Wang Yangming, in the late 1590s, Xu challenged Zhou to explain how men could act without moral standards to follow. There were real distinctions between right and wrong, Xu claimed, and these had to be observed in personal conduct: "The sage teaches people to do good and avoid evil. In ruling the empire, he must reward good and punish evil. The Way of heaven is likewise to bless the good and send calamity on the wicked. 'The family that accu-mulates good will have abundant good fortune. The family that accu-mulates evil will have abundant misfortune.' No one has ever been able to contradict this [truth]. But you say now that 'there is neither good nor evil [in the substance of the mind]'—then what will people avoid and what will people follow?" This passage could well be a defense of ledger use. Zhou replied first with a demonstration of the essential artificiality and relativity of moral judgments. Then he commented on Xu's belief in using the doctrine of reward and punishment to teach proper behavior: "Rewarding the good and punishing evil are both expedients, [ways to 'make the people follow a path'].[20] The doctrine of 'abundant good for-tune and abundant misfortune' resembles the basic principle of the Chan Buddhists and is not incompatible with the doctrine of cause and effect (*yinguo*). But if we use this doctrine to discuss the emptiness of reality, then we will understand reality superficially. 'What to avoid' and 'what to follow'—these two phrases will become the great ills of scholarship. We should not use them."[21] Zhou made just the argument one would expect of a Taizhou purist: one might use the doctrine of retribution as an expedient means of leading the people, but a real scholar knew that it was an artificial creation, just as human standards of right and wrong were artificial structures. For a true understanding of the emptiness of reality, one had to avoid thinking in terms of "ought" and "ought not."

Given this straightforward opposition to the use of moral rules to guide conduct, how can we explain the success of Yuan's ledger among follow-

[20] An allusion to *Lunyu*, 8.9 (10): "The people may be made to follow a path of action, but they may not be made to understand it." See Legge, *The Chinese Classics*, vol. 1, p. 211.

[21] This debate is recorded in Huang Zongxi, *Mingru xue'an*, 7, "Taizhou," 5, pp. 68–69. For a discussion of the inconsistency of Zhou's stand and a partial translation of the debate, see Liu Ts'un-yan, "Yuan Huang and His 'Four Admonitions,'" pp. 119–122. Wu Pei-yi presents a rather different picture of the Taizhou interest in retribution and merit calculation in "Self-Examination," pp. 16–19, 37–38.

ers of the Taizhou school? Interestingly, it is Zhou Rudeng himself who provided at least a partial explanation, for within a decade of the debate quoted above, he had converted to use of a ledger. After first resisting the idea of merit accumulation, he decided to keep his own ledger, the *Record of Daily Knowledge* (*Rizhi lu*), as the result of a night-long conversation with Yuan Huang himself. Thereafter he was one of the most enthusiastic advocates of ledger use—he tried to persuade his friends to keep ledgers,[22] and he contributed a laudatory preface to the 1607 edition of *Determining Your Own Fate*. It is here that, in a dialogue with a friend, he explained his change of heart:

> In 1601, during the twelfth month, when the snow was deep, a friend brought me a copy of Yuan Liaofan's [Huang's] own account of the good deeds he had done in his life. In consequence of the great number of these, he received an increased life span. He circulated this work within his household, in order to instruct his sons.
>
> My friend asked, "Should this text be published?" I replied, "It will be of great benefit to people, and should be published right away." He said, "You speak of the doctrine that there is neither good nor evil in the substance of the mind. What does Yuan's work have to do with this doctrine [*dasheng*, literally, "great conveyance"]?" I replied, "There being no goodness in the substance of the mind means that the mind does not grasp goodness. Goodness is not absent. One is never aware of each grain of rice when eating, but does that mean that one is not eating rice? One is never aware of each thread of silk when wearing clothing, but does that mean that one is not wearing silk?" . . .
>
> My friend said, "Can one seek what one wishes through prayer?" I said, "As long as one understands, then things are not blocked. If one doesn't understand, then even if one seeks virtue, benevolence, and righteousness, one's mind is still grasping [goodness—i.e., it is still blocked]. If one understands, then one can seek good fortune, long life, and descendants, and achieve them all."[23]

Zhou still claimed here that the substance of the mind was without good or evil; the shift in his stance came with his evaluation of the usefulness of moral standards. He argued that, though the mind was not conscious of goodness, acts deriving from the mind might be separated one from the other and labeled "good" or "bad," just as eating might be conceptualized as eating an accumulation of separate grains of rice, or wearing clothing as wearing an arrangement of separate threads of silk. Thus, though the separate grains of rice and the separate threads of silk actually did exist, one was not conscious, in the act of eating or wearing, of their separate existence. So too with doing good. Absolute goodness in action

[22] Zhou Rudeng, *Dongyue zhengxue lu*, 7.20b–21a.
[23] Ibid., 7.19a–20a.

could be achieved only if the actor was unconscious of "doing good": "The good done by good men has no measure of goodness, and is goodness without intention."[24] But this absolute goodness was nonetheless expressed in separate acts of goodness, much like those listed in the ledgers of merit and demerit. Or, to turn this proposition around and put it in Yuan Huang's own terms, specific acts of goodness were efficacious—that is, they "counted"—only if done in a state of mind unconscious of or not "grasping" of their worth in separate merit points.

It is the notion that real goodness was achieved only in a state of "no thought," with a mind that was not "grasping" at goodness, that Zhou Rudeng and Yuan Huang held in common here. As we have seen, it was a concept that had long been popular among members of the Taizhou school and other followers of Wang Yangming, such as Wang Ji. And it appears to have been this shared notion that allowed Zhou to accept ledger use: it was all right to follow moral rules as long as you were not holding to them out of a misguided belief in their absolute rightness or wrongness, as long as you did not lose sight of the "whole" goodness of which they were simply imperfect and fragmentary representations. In this way adherence to explicit standards of right and wrong could be incorporated into Taizhou notions of self-cultivation.

It must be admitted, however, that neither Yuan's nor Zhou's attempt to reconcile ledger use and a mind devoid of moral intentions was completely convincing in either philosophical or psychological terms. How could one use a ledger without some consciousness of good performed, if not in the commission of the specific deed itself, at least in the very self-conscious act of remembering, measuring, and recording the deed? If deeds done in this context did not constitute true goodness, why did either Yuan Huang or Zhou Rudeng bother with a ledger?

The answer may lie in part in the extraordinary moral pressures their expanded sense of human control created for the individual. If the belief that a man could create his own moral and material fate gave the individual a power and a freedom he had not possessed before, it imposed as well a crushing responsibility. Critics were quick to attack the "easiness" of the Taizhou moral program; their argument was that by freeing man from conventional moral standards and encouraging him to follow the dictates of his innate knowledge, it made self-indulgence a substitute for serious moral cultivation. But one could argue equally persuasively that for the man serious about attaining sagehood, the Taizhou method presented a much deeper personal challenge: the would-be sage had both to define for himself and then to follow, perhaps in the face of public criticism, the "true" moral rules within his mind. It is no wonder, then, that

[24] Huang Zongxi, *Mingru xue'an*, 7, "Taizhou," 5, p. 72.

Taizhou followers might embrace a method like Yuan Huang's—one that asserted the moral primacy of the "unmoved" mind at the same time that it encouraged adherence to stated moral rules.

For Tao Wangling, a disciple of Zhou and the author of a ledger himself, there was no question but that the ledgers, as lists of specific injunctions, provided a discipline needed for the process of self-cultivation. He defended the "measuring" mentality that defined the moral system of the ledgers: "When calculations are correct, then increase and decrease can be examined. When laws and edicts are clear, then promotion and demotion are not confused. When a curriculum of study is established, then there is a schedule for studying and resting. If there is none, then it makes no difference if one is diligent or lazy, it makes no difference if one is high or low, for there is no reference for judging excess or insufficiency."[25] The ledgers, he continued, by setting up standards for measurement, allowed one to judge one's progress and assess the size of the task before one—a small accumulation of merit and a large total of demerit, for example, should spur one on to move earnest efforts at self-cultivation.

Like Yuan Huang, Tao invoked the frightening power of the spirits as a sanction for the system: "In this world there is such a thing as open merit and secret demerit for the people; there is no such thing as open merit and secret demerit for the spirits. Every night I write down my [points], burning incense and working without companions, alone, surrounded on all sides by a horde of ghosts and spirits watching me."[26] Here, in a sense, we have come full circle, for with Tao's comments we have a recapitulation of Xu Fuyuan's position in defense of absolute moral standards, as stated in his debate with Zhou Rudeng: moral measurements, what Zhou once dismissed as relative judgments of good and evil, were necessary in the actual practice of self-cultivation. Furthermore, the specter of supernatural retribution was not simply an expedient means of making the people obey, but a force felt through the presence of "hordes" of ever-watchful spirits. The Taizhou thinkers, perhaps as a very consequence of the great claims they made for the independence and creative moral power of the individual, were as oppressed by fears of evil and as attracted to external moral guidelines as were their more conservative contemporaries.

The complex Taizhou response to the ledgers reveals a profound ambivalence within the school about the issue of human control. Eager to believe with Yuan Huang that man could, with the proper mental discipline, order his own material and moral fate, they were nonetheless aware

[25] Tao Wangling, *Gongguoge lun*, pp. 1–2. This manuscript version lists Tao Wangling as the author. Sakai Tadao, however, attributes it to Shiling, Wangling's less famous brother, who was also a follower of Zhou Rudeng. See *Chūgoku zensho*, p. 257.

[26] Tao Wangling, *Gongguoge lun*, pp. 1–2.

(as was, of course, Yuan Huang himself) of the intellectual, moral, and social difficulties involved in making one's own way in the world. The value of Yuan's ledger system was that it promised the individual an unprecedented degree of control over his own life, while at the same time providing him with a method of attaining moral certainty. Worldly success signified moral progress; thus the successful man need not suffer doubts about the dictates of his innate goodness. The clear rules of right and wrong set forth in the ledgers offered unambiguous guidelines to those who needed these dictates supported or reinforced, and the prescriptive nature of these rules was softened and even undercut by Yungu's and Yuan Huang's assertion that they could be effectively followed only with a mind free of moral intention. In short, the ledgers, as interpreted by Yuan Huang, allowed the Taizhou thinkers to have their cake and eat it too: they could claim human moral autonomy and control over fate at the same time that they could ensure that their actions were good.

CRITICS OF YUAN HUANG AND THE LEDGERS OF MERIT AND DEMERIT

The more conservative Confucian scholars of the seventeenth century did not share the Taizhou school's enthusiasm for Yuan Huang's ledger system. Yuan's critics as a group had much broader intellectual affiliations than his supporters did: they included followers of Wang Yangming who repudiated the extremists of the Taizhou group, associates of the Donglin Academy, thinkers who placed themselves between Wang Yangming and Zhu Xi, and men who hoped to revive the "pure" Cheng-Zhu school of Neo-Confucianism. Their objections to Yuan Huang's ledger system were similarly wide ranging.

Perhaps the most common charge brought against the system was that it was "heterodox," a Buddhist and Daoist method masquerading as Confucian. Gao Panlong attacked the Buddhist belief in ghosts and spirits that underlay the system of merit and demerit,[27] while Liu Zongzhou (1578–1645) contemptuously equated Yuan's view of fate with Daoist theories of "emptiness" (*xu*) and Buddhist doctrines of "nothingness" (*wu*): "They are as different from our Confucian understanding of what is right and wrong as heaven from earth." Liu repudiated the possibility of any reconciliation of Buddhism and Confucian doctrines like the one Yuan suggests: "Yuan Huang is a student of Confucianism, but he truly believes in Buddhist causality, and has taken his whole life to illustrate the Buddhist law. But it is not true that life follows Buddhist doctrine. He has transmitted the *Ledger* as an aid to salvation, but this act has strongly

---

[27] Gao Panlong, *Gaozi yishu*, 9a.23b–24a.

affected the understanding of the true Way."[28] The mix of Buddhist (and Daoist) and Confucian beliefs in Yuan's *Ledger* was enough to invalidate the whole system for Liu Zongzhou.

Members of the orthodox Neo-Confucian school based on Cheng-Zhu philosophy were particularly disturbed by the "heterodox" elements of the ledger system. Lu Shiyi, perhaps the leading defender of the orthodoxy in his time, had as a young man used Yuan's ledger and had even written a ledger of his own. But he turned against the system, urging his disciples not to use it, on the grounds that it "mixed Confucianism and Buddhism" and thus confused scholars.[29] Zhang Lixiang, a stern advocate of a return to the stricter moral standards upheld in Zhu Xi's teaching, attacked Yuan Huang for much the same reason: "Today, Yuan Huang and Li Zhi mix Buddhism and Daoism with scholarship [i.e., with Confucianism]. The source of this problem is a misunderstanding of the Way of the sages. Now disasters and wild beasts [i.e., the belief in retribution] dominate the methods of self-cultivation employed by men."[30]

Another sure sign of Zhang's enmity here is his association of Yuan Huang with Li Zhi, the most notorious of the late Ming "free-thinkers." For Zhang, a bitter enemy of even the milder forms of Wang Yangming's thought, Li, in his indifference to official service, his attraction to Buddhism, and—most strikingly—his repudiation of established Confucian moral standards, demonstrated the horrible dangers of Wang Yangming's philosophy. Through the late seventeenth century Yuan and Li continued to be stuck together as symbols of late Ming intellectual corruption. In his history of the Ming, Zha Jizuo (1601–1676) paired Yuan and Li, indicting them for their perversion of the sages' teaching.[31] As late as 1747, the author of the Wujiang county gazetteer identified Yuan Huang and Li Zhi as men whose teachings had flourished in the late Ming to the detriment of the "true" Confucian way.[32]

Much of the criticism of Yuan Huang derived from fears of the so-called heterodox tendencies of many late-Ming thinkers. The scholars quoted above were trying to purify the Confucian tradition, to identify the true Way, to recover it from the tangle of Buddhist, Daoist, and Taizhou ideas under which it had been buried in the sixteenth and early seventeenth centuries. This "true" orthodoxy had to be vigilantly protected from the danger of any new "heterodox" entanglements. When Yuan Yan (1581–1627), Huang's son, petitioned the Wujiang authorities

---

[28] Liu Zongzhou, "Zixu," 1a, *Renpu*, in *LZQS*, j. 1 (vol. 1, p. 159).

[29] Lu Shiyi, *Lun Xuechou da*, 4.20a–b, in *Lu Futing xiansheng yishu*.

[30] Zhang Lixiang, *Yangyuan xiansheng quanji*, vol. 1, p. 473. Reference from Okuzaki, *Chūgoku kyōshin jinushi*, p. 421.

[31] Zha Jizuo, *Liezhuan*, 18.6, *Zuiwei lu*, pp. 67–68.

[32] *Wujiang xianzhi*, 57.20b; cited in Okuzaki, *Chūgoku kyōshin jinushi*, p. 133.

to erect a shrine to his father as a "local man of virtue," the educational intendant angrily denied what he called the "polluted" request, one that would have had him "establish heterodox theories, transgress against the Way, turn on the Classics, plunder scholarship, and pervert the true teaching." More and more as the century wore on, "the true teaching" came to be explicitly identified with the Cheng-Zhu tradition. The scholar Li Le (j.s. 1568) argued that Yuan should indeed be excluded from the ranks of orthodoxy because he did not follow Zhu Xi's *Categorized Conversations* in his reading of the Four Books, and thus failed to understand principle correctly.[33]

Naturally, scholars were also worried about the effect the ledger system might have on Confucian education and hence on the purity of the official elite. As we have seen, Zhang Lixiang, a devoted teacher, lamented the popularity of the ledgers, claiming that students of his day viewed Yuan's *Ledger* as a text as sacred as the standard works of the Neo-Confucian curriculum. By suggesting that heterodox beliefs might help students pass the civil service examinations, the *Ledger* threatened the stability and the authority of the Confucian Classics, the real backbone of Neo-Confucian orthodoxy. After all, it was only after the text became popular among literati that conservative scholars began to take it as a serious threat. A naive and "superstituous" belief in supernatural retribution was fine for the people, but once literati embraced it, it became a serious danger undermining the supposed moral purity and homogeneity of the ruling elite. Thus the attack on Yuan Huang and his ledger system must be seen as part of an effort by a growing number of seventeenth-century thinkers to recover and protect Confucian orthodoxy, and, by extension, to ensure the training of scholars able to bring moral order to the empire.

But critics of the ledgers were not simply concerned with keeping Confucian tenets pure of heterodox defilement. Many were also disturbed by the faults of the system as a method of moral practice. Liu Zongzhou argued that the merit-demerit system could not be a true one because it rested on a division of good and evil into large and small—it suggested that moral behavior could be measured and counted off in points. This assumption contravened principle itself, since principle was not something that could be fragmented or measured: "to divide faults by number is to break up principle; there is no large or small, many or few [in principle]."[34]

But the largest concern seems to have been with the damaging psychological effects that ledger use would have on the correction of faults and the cultivation of real, "whole" goodness. In several letters warning

[33] *Wujiang xianzhi*, 57.21a–22a.
[34] Liu Zhongzhou, *LZQS*, 19.13b (vol. 3, p. 1330).

against ledger use, Liu launched a particularly thorough attack on the various "tricks" ledger use might play on even the most dedicated of scholars. Recording good deeds for merits encouraged, he argued, a kind of moral pride in the ledger user—there was a danger that in his pleasure over his moral achievements he would neglect the correction of faults. If he used his meritorious deeds to cancel out his faults, as the ledgers required, the latter were covered or concealed; in that way he would never really get rid of them. Or if the faults listed in the ledger happened not to include all of his own particular faults, then he might miss out on complete fault-correction—he might not even be aware of what all his faults were.[35]

Furthermore, the ledgers allowed a man to mark down simply his demerit totals—he did not need to record the circumstances or the content of each bad deed. As a result, the "root" of the evil could not be examined, and thus the hopes of his being able to change it diminished. Liu feared, too, that the act of writing down one's demerit points might become a substitute for actually changing them—the ledger user was lulled into thinking that he was working at fault correction when all he had really done was record his demerits. Finally, Liu argued that the whole ledger system dealt in irrelevancies—that is, it encouraged a man to focus on the details of his behavior when he should have been thinking of larger moral issues: "In their normal cultivation of righteousness, it is fundamentally the highest righteousness that gentlemen should know; they seek their innate knowledge of the good and rest in that. They certainly do not delight in correcting irrelevant matters."[36]

Wang Fuzhi (1619–1692), a later critic of the system, complained of much the same set of problems. Wang worried that a ledger user might be led to believe erroneously that the accumulation of quite small and separate acts of goodness would result in large rewards. The doctrine of secret merit, which was "circulating popularly again," suggested that "if you save a bunch of insects or distribute a basket of beans, then you can expect limitless profit." He used the case of Wang He of the Eastern Han to expose the dangers of such a belief. Wang prided himself on all the merits he had accumulated by releasing prisoners, whether guilty or innocent, from punishment. He became arrogant about his "goodness," believing that his posterity would flourish because of his actions. But the automatic release of criminals was in violation of both the law and the

---

[35] Ibid., 19.13b–14b (vol. 3, pp. 1330–1332); see also Dong Yang, "Liuzi nianpu," *LZQS*, 40.49a–50b (vol. 6, pp. 3583–3585).

[36] Liu Zongzhou, *LZQS*, 19.13b–14b (vol. 3, pp. 1330–1332); see also 40.49a–50b (vol. 6, pp. 3583–3585). Interestingly, the Taizhou thinker Lin Chun (1498–1541) gave up ledger use for the first reason Liu mentioned here—that it gave one a false impression of moral reform. See Wu, "Self-Examination," p. 38.

duty of officials, so instead of building up merit for his family, he was in fact setting them up for disaster. Final proof of the fact that he was not genuinely good, despite his performance of what in the ledgers were considered good deeds, was his support of the usurper Wang Mang. Wang He was branded a rebel by historians, and his lineage destroyed—a fitting end, Wang Fuzhi suggested, for a man who believed that goodness consisted of misguided and mechanical acts of "compassion."[37]

Thus these men, though disturbed by the heterodox sources of the ledgers, were also unwilling to accept the arithmetical moral practice of the ledgers. Not only did it contravene the coherence of the true principles of the universe, it also encouraged only a fragmented, piecemeal reform of "irrelevancies." Even worse, it might trick its users into believing they were correcting their faults and practicing virtue when in fact they were simply evading the real, serious issues of self-cultivation. Such a system could not lead to coherent and genuine goodness, but only to the shallow, deluded, and ultimately destructive "goodness" of men like Wang He.

But perhaps the gravest flaw of the ledgers in the eyes of Yuan Huang's critics was the fact that they encouraged good deeds for the sake of personal profit. Confucian moralists were by no means the only ones to see moral contradiction in the system. Li Yu (1611–1680?), the irreverent dramatist and short-story writer, was the most entertaining commentator on the ironies of the system of merit accumulation; he wrote several plays and short stories satirizing the mechanical and often amoral (or even immoral) "good" behavior resulting from a literal application of the arithmetical morality of the ledgers. In one of these, a childless merchant appealed to the Buddha for a son and was told that one would be born to him if he contributed a stipulated amount of money to a Buddhist temple. The merchant, reluctant to part with such a large sum, gave only a portion of the amount requested. A child was born to him, but it was a hermaphrodite. Only as the merchant handed over the full contribution in slow stages was the child gradually transformed into a male.[38] Unlike Liu Zongzhou and Wang Fuzhi, Li Yu was not angry over the moral abuses associated with merit accumulation; he was simply amused by the hypocrisy of an ethical system that put a price tag on goodness, that made charity into a kind of currency for the purchase of a son.

Concern over this kind of moral profit-seeking was expressed in more

[37] Wang Fuzhi, *Du Tongjian lun*, vol. 3, pp. 80–81.
[38] Li Yu, "Bian nü wei er pusa qiao," in *Li Yu quanji*, vol. 13, 1a–15a (pp. 5577–5625). See Shizue Matsuda, "Li Yu: His Life and Moral Philosophy as Reflected in His Fiction," pp. 89–91, for an attempt to identify this story as an allusion to Yuan Huang's own. For Li Yu's other satires on the idea of merit accumulation, see *Li Yu quanji*, vol. 12, 1a–16b (pp. 5231–5262), particularly 16b (p. 5262) where the *Taishang ganying pian* is quoted, and vol. 14 (pp. 6051–6131). I am grateful to Diane Perushek for these references.

serious terms in the writings of contemporary thinkers. Scholars had long been worried about what they perceived as a kind of "commercialization" of morality among their contemporaries. Feng Congwu, an opponent of the Wang Yangming school and admirer of Gu Xiancheng, felt the need to write an essay emphasizing the distinctions between the path of goodness, followed by the legendary emperor Shun and the sages, leading inevitably to great cultural achievements; and the path of profit, taken by Robber Zhi and other wicked men, leading to notoriety and disgrace.[39] Gu Xiancheng, quoting the *Analects*, reminded his followers that the man who singlemindedly pursued benevolence treated wealth, poverty, high and low rank, confusion, and danger—all the contingencies of life—as one. He would neither seek out nor avoid wealth or poverty, for his mind was fixed solely on proper behavior.[40] Gao Panlong devoted a whole lecture to the Donglin Academy to the same passage and the same message.[41] Liu Zongzhou, criticizing scholars who studied simply for the sake of the examinations and officials who served merely in order to enrich their families, warned against the search for "external" material goals: "The greatest stimulus to today's scholars is the search after externals. This represents a chronic illness. . . . Everyone is from birth naturally immersed in the [things of the] world, and caught up with external things, going back and forth among them. All of one's energies are expended on externals. If students want to follow the Way, they should take the energies they devote to seeking after externals, and [use them] to cultivate themselves."[42] Lü Liuliang (1629–1683), like his friend Zhang Lixiang a critic of Wang Yangming and an advocate of orthodox Neo-Confucianism, denied that there could ever be an advantage to seeking profit by any means: "It is not that, if you seek it, you will necessarily not get it, but simply that getting is not the result of seeking. . . . There is no connection between [seeking and getting]."[43] Even Li Zhi, so often attacked by more conservative thinkers as a cause of late Ming moral decline, lamented the dominance of market values in the formation of human relationships.[44] Yuan Huang's claim that goodness and profit were indissolubly linked, were in a sense reflections of each other, would have served simply to increase the fears of these men.

[39] Feng Congwu, "Shanli tushuo," 8.4à–8a. See Handlin, *Action in Late Ming Thought*, p. 130.

[40] Gu Xiancheng, *Dangxia yi*, 2a–b, in *Gu Duanwen gong yishu, ce* 9.

[41] Gao Panlong, *Gaozi yishu*, 4.4a–5b.

[42] Liu Zongzhou, *LZQS*, 8.17b (vol. 1, p. 492). I consulted the translation in Chang, *The Development of Neo-Confucian Thought*, vol. 2, pp. 176–177.

[43] Lü Liuliang, *Lü Wancun xiansheng sishu jiangyi*, 42.1b; and T. S. Fisher, "Accommodation and Loyalism: The Life of Lü Liu-liang (1629–1683)," part III, pp. 8–9.

[44] Li Zhi, *Xu fen shu*, pp. 78–79. Reference from Handlin, *Action in Late Ming Thought*, pp. 130–131.

Certainly, it is this aspect of the system of merit and demerit that aroused the greatest fears among the more conservative of contemporary observers. The grand secretary Zhu Guozhen (1557–1632) lamented the popularity of the system even among men who ought to have known better, "men of learning":

> Today men do good always in expectation of reward. There is even a theory that a thousand good deeds will be rewarded with a thousand [pieces of silver], and ten thousand good deeds rewarded with ten thousand pieces. I think that this idea was created for ignorant villagers. Men of learning should know that man only concerns himself with his own affairs, and does good for its own sake, not in expectation of reward. Take the man who saved the ants or the man who returned the belt. These two acted directly from the dictates of their minds, just as the man who saved the child from falling into a well in *Mencius* had. If they had had a reward in mind, the spirits would not have rewarded them.[45]

Liu Zongzhou more directly blamed Yuan Huang for encouraging this kind of false moral consciousness. In his preface to his own guide to self-cultivation, the *Manual for Man* (*Renpu*), written in part as a response to Yuan's *Ledger*, Liu explained his concern over the false motives for good behavior advocated by Yuan Huang:

> A friend once showed me the *Ledger of Merit and Demerit* of Yuan [Huang]. I read it, and doubted its worth. [Huang] himself says that he received it from Yungu. [He claimed that] all the changes and cases of retribution in his life were derived from [his use of the *Ledger*], and that merit and demerit decidedly never fail to fulfill their promise [of recompense]. I consider this belief to be of great harm to the Way. Confucius said, "The Way is not distant from men; when men consider the Way as something far from them, it is not the Way." Those who speak of the Way these days distance it high above men, immersing it in emptiness; they believe that they are speaking of human nature, but it is not really human nature. They distance it far below man, deriving profit from it; they believe that they are speaking of fate, but it is not really fate. If it is not human nature and if it is not fate, then it is not man; thus, what they consider to be the Way is distant from man. These two errors are the same in basic nature, but they diverge in name as they are manifested.
>
> It is the idea of profit (*gongli*) that deludes men most profoundly. Laozi used emptiness to discuss the Way; the Buddha used nothingness to talk of the Way—both theories are most elevated and ingenious. Even we Confucians cannot compete with them. Their intent is to deal with life and death, . . . but their

[45] Zhu Guozhen, *Yongchuang xiaopin*, 10.10a. I consulted the translation in Yü, *Renewal of Buddhism*, p. 294. The man who returned the belt was Pei Du (d. 838). He was rewarded with a brilliant career for returning a valuable belt to its owner. I could not trace the reference to the man who rescued the ants.

beliefs lead them back to selfishness and profit. Thus Taishang has his *Tract on Action and Response*, and the Buddhists speak much of causality (*yinguo*). It appears that, taking life and death as the objects of their doctrines, they use the concepts of emptiness and nothingness to establish their teachings. They falsely state that meritorious action is actually bound to the passions, heterodoxy, and delusion. Their views are as different from our Confucian understanding of what is right and wrong as heaven from earth. These theories of emptiness and nothingness are really the worst extreme of profit seeking.[46]

The ledgers, Liu asserted in yet another attack, made it easy to fall into the "path of profit"; the man who expected to receive rewards for his actions was "without good and full of evil" (*wushan you'e*). Lu Shiyi, who had studied briefly with Liu, eventually gave up his own ledger-keeping practices for just this reason. Warning his friends and disciples against the ledgers, he explained, "You forget the trap once you have caught the fish; you forget the snare once you have caught the hare"—that is, the ledger user tended to neglect moral cultivation once he got his reward.[47] Thoughts of profit would not, as Yuan Huang's system suggested, spur a man on to good behavior; ultimately they would distract him from the practice of real, coherent goodness.

Both Liu and Lu were reaffirming what is essentially the Mencian position on human strivings: the good man cultivated his goodness regardless of the material circumstances of his life. Interestingly, neither denied that good would necessarily bring material profit, but each insisted that the truly good man did not harbor any hopes of profit as he did good. And for them, despite Yuan Huang's insistence otherwise, it was not possible to practice merit accumulation with a mind free of hopes of material success.

A Rejoinder to Yuan Huang: Liu Zongzhou's *Manual for Man*

Although many scholars rose to attack Yuan Huang's system of merit accumulation, Liu Zongzhou was the only one to construct a coherent program specifically designed to overturn the method of self-cultivation advocated in the ledgers of merit and demerit, to meet the challenge that Yuan's *Ledger* presented, as Liu saw it, to the proper understanding of the Way. According to his biography, Liu wrote the *Manual for Man* in alarm at the growing popularity of Yuan's work and the proliferation of new ledgers based on his system and sanctioned by other literati. Written

[46] Liu Zongzhou, "Zixu," 1a–b, *Renpu, LZQS*, j.1 (vol. 1, pp. 159–160) and 19.13b (vol. 3, p. 1330). The lines that Liu attributes to Confucius are from the *Zhongyong*, chapter 13. See Legge, *The Chinese Classics*, vol. 1, p. 393.

[47] Lu Shiyi, *Lun xuechou da*, 4.20b, in *Lu Futing xiansheng yishu*.

in 1634, the text was to be used as a guide to self-cultivation for members of the "Society for Bearing Witness to Humanity" (Zhengren Hui).[48] Liu's preface is in essence an attack on Yuan's *Ledger*, specifically on its use of Buddhist and Taoist doctrines to sanction moral profit seeking. He explains:

> Because of these errors [in Yuan's work] I was moved specifically by the idea of giving witness to what it is to be human. I wrote the explanation of the "Chart of the Ultimate in Humanity" ("Renji tu") to teach scholars to keep demerit ledgers under six categories of affairs and moral lessons. To speak of faults without speaking of merits is a means of distancing [thoughts of] profit. The general title of the work is *Manual for Man*. In evaluating how to become human, nothing is better than this work. Once a student sincerely knows what it is to be human, he will understand over half of the Way. Then he will gradually attain the position of sage.[49]

Thus Liu does not entirely repudiate the ledger technique—keeping a partial ledger is an aspect of his method of self-cultivation. He simply claims that his method, as described in the *Manual*, will allow a man to fulfill his moral potential and become a sage without falling into the trap contained in Yuan Huang's *Ledger*—that of personal profit making.

Liu's *Manual* opens with the "Chart of the Ultimate in Humanity," a clear statement of Liu's position within the intellectual controversies of the day: "That which has no goodness yet is perfect goodness is the substance of the mind" (*wushan er zhishan xin zhi ti ye*). Liu sides here with Wang Yangming in his belief that the mind is perfect goodness. But he reformulates Wang's famous dictum that there is neither good nor evil in the substance of the mind in such a way that it is impossible to draw from it the dangerous moral conclusions that ruined, in Liu's eyes, Wang Ji and the members of the Taizhou school. For Liu the mind is transcendent and thus in a sense "without goodness"—he even identifies it with the Great Ultimate, the source of all things.[50] But its whole substance is grounded in perfect goodness, and hence some of its manifestations are the moral rules of the universe—for example, the rules governing the five relationships. Liu rhapsodizes on the powers of the mind, and by extension of men themselves, who alone possess minds:

> How great man is! He knows nothing and yet there is nothing he does not know. He can do nothing and yet there is nothing he cannot do. . . . The *Classic*

[48] Dong Yang, "Liuzi nianpu," in *LZQS*, 40a.50a–b (vol. 6, pp. 3585–3586).

[49] Liu Zongzhou, "Zixu," 1b, *Renpu*, *LZQS*, j.1 (vol. 1, p. 160).

[50] Liu Zongzhou, *LZQS*, 1.2a (vol. 1, p. 161). I am very grateful to Thomas Peele for allowing me to consult his translation and analysis of the *Renpu* ("Liu Tsung-chou's *Jen-p'u*").

of Changes says: "In all the processes taking place under heaven, what is there of thinking? What is there of anxious scheming? They all come to the same issue, though by different paths; there is one result, though there might be a hundred anxious schemes. What is there of thinking? What is there of anxious scheming?"[51] The knowledge that knows nothing knows without anxious scheming. The ability that can do nothing is able without study. This is what is called "the good without the good (wushan zhi shan)."

"The superior man preserves it." No good is greater than his. The mass of men "discard it."[52] No transgression is greater than theirs. Good and bad fortune, regret and remorse are simply actions on these. Accumulation of good and accumulation of what is not good are the ways of man and beast respectively. If a man knows that he is not good and reforms, or if he starts from goodness and ends where there is nothing that is not good, his way is the best and his grasp of essentials is blameless. Thereby he fulfills the study of man.[53]

The good man or "gentleman" thus strives to model himself on heavenly processes, to do good unconsciously, naturally, without "anxious scheming." Here Liu is in perfect agreement with Yuan Huang and most other contemporary Neo-Confucians—the only real goodness is goodness done without consciousness of one's goodness.

How is this state to be achieved? Liu explains: " 'The superior man preserves it' simply means to have a mind that does not think or scheme. It is what Master Zhou Dunyi [1017–1073] meant by 'regarding quietude as fundamental and establishing the ultimate of man.'[54] But the best means of returning to goodness lies in the mending of transgressions. This method is different from that of not thinking of either good or evil. That is the learning of the sages."[55] Here Liu firmly distinguishes himself from the thinkers of the Taizhou school: one does not preserve one's innate knowledge of the good and rid oneself of deliberate consciousness of one's goodness simply by "not thinking of either good or evil," but by actively rooting out one's faults and "mending transgressions."

Having established the outline of his method for moral perfection, Liu goes on to discuss the actual practice of self-cultivation. In the second section of the Manual, entitled "Essential Guidelines for Bearing Witness to Humanity" ("Zhengren yaozhi"), Liu introduces a concept taken from the Doctrine of the Mean (Zhongyong): "watchfulness over the solitary self" (shendu), the preservation of the original purity of the mind. Liu describes this state: "At this time, before even one thought has arisen,

---

[51] Zhouyi yinde, Xici 2.3 (p. 46); Sung, The Text of Yi King, p. 316.

[52] Mengzi yinde, 4b.19 (p. 31): "That whereby man differs from the lower animals is but small. The mass of people cast it away, while the superior men preserve it." See Legge, The Chinese Classics, vol. 1, p. 325.

[53] Liu Zongzhou, LZQS, 1.3a (vol. 1, p. 163).

[54] Zhou Dunyi, "Taiji tushuo," Jinsi lu, 1.1a–2a, in Zhuzi yishu.

[55] Liu Zongzhou, LZQS, 1.3b (vol. 1, p. 163).

there is no place where good can be manifested, much less for what is not good to come into being. Where there is only genuineness and no falsity, in a place without sight or sound, there is nothing that will allow self-deception. I, along with it, am totally without self-deception. Thus even though not one good is established there, I know myself, am content in myself, am complete in myself, and have fully reached the ultimate of goodness. The Ultimate of full, utter good is already complete."[56] This state of solitary self-watchfulness is achieved through quiet-sitting and book learning—the very tasks between which Zhu Xi suggested the scholar should divide his day.

This state of watchfulness over the self allows one to discover and restrain the development of error, or, as Liu puts it, "to divine the movement of intention (*nian*) in order to know the stirrings [of action]." How exactly does this work? Liu believes that everything in the universe is *qi* or cosmic pneuma—even principle (*li*), which in Song and orthodox Ming Neo-Confucianism was generally taken to be prior to *qi* is for Liu simply the principle of *qi*. Thus the human mind is composed of cosmic pneuma. But unlike the *qi* of creatures, this *qi* is, in its "solitary substance," perfectly stable. When thoughts arise in the mind, its *qi* moves, fluctuating between movement and quietude; it is in the course of these motions that feelings are manifested. As long as a man's thoughts remain good, these motions will remain in perfect equilibrium: "If a thought is like its origin [i.e., purely good], then the feeling returns to the nature. When there is movement containing nothing that is not good, then movement is also stillness."[57]

But problems arise when one loses control of this equilibrium and allows one of the movements to go either too far or not far enough. Then one's *qi* is disturbed from its perfect balance, and one becomes "attached" to a thought or intention. As this intention becomes stronger and stronger, and one's *qi* more and more lopsided, the imbalance within one's mind will manifest itself as an evil act. "If one happens to become attached to a thought and thereby transgresses, there will be times when this overflows into evil."[58] The results of the "fixation" of one's *qi* in one state is, in other words, a kind of fragmentation of one's consciousness: the false distinction between inner and outer arises in the mind, and one begins, as Liu warns in another essay, to exalt the outer.

The way to prevent this process of transgression is first to learn to recognize the "incipient tendencies" (*ji*) toward the imbalance of *qi* that arise in the mind, and then to control or restrain them, to return the movement

---

[56] Ibid., 1.3b–4a (vol. 1, pp. 164–165).

[57] Ibid., 1.4a (vol. 1, p. 165).

[58] Ibid., 1.4a (vol. 1, p. 165). This sentence does not appear in the earliest edition of the *Renpu* (1634) but is contained in the final version approved by Liu himself.

of pneuma firmly back to its state of equilibrium. Liu explains: "Just at the moment when thoughts move, redouble your awareness [of them], and do not allow them to flow into transgression and become something not good. Just when there is something not good, always recognize it and stop it. Having stopped it, return it to its origin. If [the thought] transgresses this [limit], it will expand outward and you will not succeed in controlling it."[59] Hence the need to be "watchful over the solitary self": it is in that state that one can observe and guard against one's incipient tendencies to evil.

In the next three sections, Liu emphasizes the importance of conduct and external appearance as expressions of one's state of mind. First, one's deportment, including bearing, appearance, speech, and temperament, should always be dignified, to indicate the human potential within one. Second, the principles governing the five relationships (between ruler and minister, father and son, and so forth), as the "Way extending to the world," must be internalized. Third, one then extends in turn the principles of the five relationships "to fill the space between heaven and earth"—that is, to know that "all things are my father and mother, brothers, husband and wife, ruler and minister, and friends." Here Liu accepts without question that the mind in its perfect goodness contains all the rules of proper behavior.[60]

It is here, too, that Liu makes clear his understanding of what it is to decide one's fate, or as he puts it, to "fix" fate (dingming). His first section is entitled "being cautious in one's bearing in order to fix one's fate" (jin-wei yi yi dingming); for him, man fixes his fate simply by fulfilling his moral potential, by expressing in all his actions the perfect moral nature bestowed on him by heaven: "The heaven-conferred nature cannot be seen, but it is seen through deportment, mien, speech, and temperament. Each has its proper pattern. It is this that is called 'nature.' Therefore it is said: 'Dignified bearing is the means by which one fixes one's fate.' "[61] Liu takes the Mencian position here—the only good fortune for the "gentleman" is the perfect actualization of the goodness born in his mind.

Having asserted the validity of absolute moral rules and enjoined man to "fix his fate" by following them, Liu then puts forth his program for attaining sagehood: "changing to the good and correcting transgressions." The student should simply follow the judgments of his original mind as to what is good and what is not good, a task that requires constant self-examination and investigation.[62]

[59] Ibid., 1.4b (vol. 1, p. 166). Translation from Peele, "Liu Tsung-chou's Jen-p'u," pp. 50–51.

[60] Liu Zongzhou, LZQS, 1.5a–6a (vol. 1, pp. 167–169).

[61] Ibid., 1.5b (vol. 1, p. 168); translation from Peele, "Liu Tsung-chou's Jen-p'u," p. 53.

[62] Liu Zongzhou, LZQS, 1.6b–7a (vol. 1, pp. 170–171).

Liu clearly sees "correcting transgressions" as the more arduous of the steps to sagehood, for he devotes the rest of the *Manual* to a discussion of this process. It is here that he incorporates a type of ledger into his method of self-cultivation. He presents six different "ledgers recording transgressions" (*jiguo ge*), each listing a different type of transgression to be recognized, recorded, and, of course, corrected. Each type of transgression corresponds to a stage in the advance of the "stirrings" of the imbalanced *qi* into volitional thought and then action. The first ledger, identifying the very slightest stirrings of evil ("Subtle transgressions ruled by solitary knowing," "Weiguo duzhi zhu zhi") deals with "falsity" or "delusions" (*wang*), the first suggestions of improper goals: "It is desire for profit and fame and attachment to life and death. Its crude expression is liquor, sexual desire, greed, and anger." The second ledger lists "Hidden transgressions ruled by the seven emotions" ("Yinguo qiqing zhu zhi"): excessive joy, hidden anger or resentment, sadness, excessive fearfulness (for example, over gossip and mockery, or over the threat of the unexpected), excessive love for one's wife and children, cruelty to those not related to one or to those of low status, and indulgence in physical desires. The third ledger deals with "Obvious transgressions ruled by [the laws of] the nine deportments" ("Xianguo jiuyong zhu zhi"). "Obvious" because they are expressed in physical attitudes and actions, these are largely postures or expressions that reveal a lack of reverence and caution. Under the "Deportment of mouth," for example, Liu lists "mugging the words of others," talkativeness, and nagging; under "Deportment of disposition," obstinacy, self-indulgence, and laziness.[63]

Fourth, and much more serious, are the "Great transgressions ruled by the order of the five relationships" ("Daguo wulun zhu zhi"). Each of the five relationships is treated—twenty-one examples of how not to act for the father-son relationship, sixteen for the ruler-minister, seven for the husband-wife, nineteen for the elder-younger brother, and sixteen for the friend-friend. Generally these all follow long-established Chinese values, warning against the neglect of hierarchical boundaries. The family relationships follow the values of filial piety, and the ones for friendship urge trust and mutual moral instruction. The rules governing the ruler-minister relationship are interesting in that they seem to reflect Liu's own practice of frequently admonishing the ruler and his own high standards of public service. He warns against:

Serving the ruler in a manner contrary to the Way.
Perpetuating the wickedness of the ruler.
Allowing the ruler to do evil.

[63] Liu Zongzhou, *LZQS*, 1.7b–9a (vol. 1, pp. 172–175).

Obtaining initial advancement to office by cheating the ruler. (By illegitimate inquiries, appointment by lot, worming ahead through personal contacts.)

Gaining promotion through cheating. (Using connections to speed up the process.)

Seeking rapid advancement through connections.

Not loving the people.

Not applying oneself fully to one's office.

Receiving bribes.

Clinging to life at the expense of morality.

Manipulating officials while residing in one's native place.

Putting public affairs off on subordinates.

Being tardy in completing national tasks.

Dodging corvée duty.

Speculating on one's own about imperial commands.

Privately discussing the pros and cons of a family's connection with the government.[64]

If the student does not avoid all the evils arising from the neglect of the five relationships, then he will naturally commit the "Miscellaneous transgressions ruled by the hundred practices" ("Congguo baixing zhu zhi"), listed in the fifth ledger. Liu points out that these ninety-three evils are organized as deeds to avoid when alone ("fantasizing," "loitering," and so forth); excesses in eating, sexual intercourse, and spending on luxuries and entertainments; faults of character; errors in study; and acts that undermine the Way. The faults of character make the longest list and cover a whole range of transgressions harming social or community relations. There are warnings against litigation, vengeance, theft, usury, greed, toadying for advancement, false business practices, oppression of the poor, and cruelty to animals. In the last section of acts that "go against the Way," Liu comes out firmly against heterodox teachings. After having urged men not to "blaspheme and profane spirit-altars," he warns them against certain religious practices:

Consulting geomancers.

Praying to pass civil service examinations.

Staying in Buddhist monasteries.

Paying respects to Buddhist monks.

Copying practices from Daoism.[65]

Finally, the sixth ledger covers "Completed transgressions" ("Chengguo"), which consist of real action on any of the previously described sets

[64] Ibid., 1.9a–10a (vol. 1, pp. 175–177). See Peele, "Liu Tsung-chou's *Jen-p'u*," pp. 62–63, for the section translated here.

[65] Liu Zongzhou, *LZQS*, 1.10a–11a (vol. 1, pp. 177–179).

of incipient transgressions. Liu advises long periods of quiet-sitting and self-criticism to expunge these various completed transgressions. "Subtle evils" (the completion of "Subtle trangressions") may require only two hours of solitary self-watchfulness, while "great evils" take a full day of intensive criticism to correct. This kind of discipline enables the student to return "to reach the ground of reform," the perfect equilibrium and goodness of the mind. Liu ends the series of ledgers on a positive note: "Even if a person commits extreme evil or great crimes, his innately good mind is still in itself not destroyed. It is still the same as the sage's. It is only corrupting habit that ruins things. If one is awakened, this mind glimmers with a small brightness like a flame, the stream will overflow, and one is already a sage."[66]

Liu's six ledgers describe the thoughts and behavior the student is to watch out for, but they do not really define in practical terms the process whereby one becomes aware of these tendencies to evil. After the ledgers, however, he appends a brief essay, "Method for Criticizing Transgressions" ("Songguo fa"), which explains how, through a form of quiet-sitting, one can make oneself aware of all one's tendencies to transgress. Liu even provides detailed instructions for the physical setting of self-criticism:

Place a stick of incense and a bowl of water upon a clean table. Lay out a rush-mat seat below it. Just at dawn assume a reverent attitude and be seated. Cross your legs and join your hands. Hold your breath and rectify your demeanor. While in a dignified and majestic state, inspecting with a bright light, expose your constant malaise. . . .

Then move on and criticize yourself: "You are a seemly man. One day you slipped, fell a thousand yards, became as bird or beast, and fell into all sorts of degeneration. How could you have come to this?"

Answer: "Yes, yes." Additionally project ten eyes and ten hands which together see and all speak words like these. Answer: "Yes, yes." Thereupon the square-inch [that is your mind] is troubled, you have tiny beads of painful sweat, a blush radiates from your cheeks, as if you were on the rack. Having become agitated, you rouse yourself again: "Do not obtain a perfunctory confession." Respond: "No, no." Again project ten eyes and ten hands for confirmation and assistance. Respond again: "No, no."

Thereupon a thread of bright *qi* comes slowly, as if proceeding to the Great Void, and you know that everything preceding was [due to] false causes. If false, then it is not real. Thoroughly real, self-possessed, profound, and pure—welcome it and there is nothing that comes, follow it and there is no place to go. Indeed, this is your original, true face. This is just the right time to persevere along with it. Suddenly a mote of dust arises; blow it away. Persevere again.

[66] Ibid., *LZQS*, 1.11b (vol. 1, p. 180).

Once more a mote of dust rises; blow it away. It will be like this several times. Do not be forgetful, do not try to force help on it. Do not ask what the effect will be. In a flash tidy yourself and rise. Stay shut in your chamber all day.[67]

Like so many of his late Ming contemporaries—indeed, even rather like Yuan Huang himself—Liu believed that a rigorous practice of confession and self-criticism was a prerequisite for the correction of faults and ultimately the attainment of moral perfection.[68] This was the true "learning of Confucius," the way the master himself had achieved the status of sage.

In the *Manual for Man* Liu Zongzhou has clearly acknowledged the validity of a certain type of ledger use; indeed, his "ledgers recording transgressions" are the basis of his program for self-cultivation. But he has just as clearly completely transformed the meaning of the ledgers, purifying them of all the characteristics that angered him in Yuan Huang's system. His ledgers are demerit (or "transgression") ledgers only, so that a student, since he does not record his good deeds, avoids both the Scylla of moral pride and the Charybdis of "covering" his errors with merits. Liu complained that Yuan's ledger allowed a man to mark down points while forgetting the roots of error in the mind; Liu's system, with its elaborate method of self-criticism, which encourages the student to dwell on even the slightest stirrings of error (like sitting in a disrespectful posture, "with the legs spread out") in the mind, can hardly be accused of neglecting the mental sources of evil.[69] And since he does not assign points to his deeds, he avoids the "fragmentation" of principle that he attacked in Yuan Huang's *Ledger*. Nor can Liu's ledgers be said to focus on irrelevancies of conduct, at least as Liu meant the term. Liu orders his "transgressions" into categories and his ledgers into a sequence; the student who uses them in conjunction with Liu's method of self-criticism is following a coherent process of self-cultivation, one that allows the incorporation of smaller acts of restraint or goodness into a whole, pure goodness. One certainly cannot rely on the random commission of various good deeds allowed in the ledgers of merit and demerit.

But most important is the fact that Liu's ledgers do not in any way encourage profit seeking. This, indeed, is his own explanation for using a demerit ledger only—to "distance profit."[70] Though his use of the term "fixing fate" is reminiscent of Yuan Huang's "determining fate," it is

---

[67] Liu Zongzhou, *LZQS*, 1.12a–b (vol. 1, pp. 181–182); translation based on Peele, "Liu Tsung-chou's *Jen-p'u*," pp. 70–71. See also Wu Pei-yi, "Self-Examination," p. 27. The *Manual* concludes with three "Discussions of Correcting Transgressions" ("Gaiguo shuo").

[68] See Wu Pei-yi, "Self-Examination," pp. 16–38.

[69] Liu Zongzhou, *LZQS*, 1.8b (vol. 1, p. 174).

[70] Liu Zongzhou, "Zixu," 1b, *Renpu, LZQS* (vol. 1, p. 160).

clear from the context that Liu is referring simply to each man's ability to fulfill his heaven-endowed moral potential, not to his power to determine his material fate.

It is true that, in emphasizing the primacy of qi and identifying evil as an aberration in the movement of qi, Liu is assuming that human thoughts and actions influenced or "moved" the qi of other things in the universe. Man then could be rewarded or punished for his acts by the "responses" of qi he stimulated. But Liu never carries his argument through to this conclusion. He stops his discussion at the description of the constitution and operation of the human mind, as if obeying Confucius's injunction to devote oneself to the "affairs of men" rather than the workings of the spirits. The moral perfection to be achieved through his system of self-cultivation is the only possible human goal for Liu Zongzhou. For men had been decreed by heaven to embody moral perfection, to be the very foundation of the cosmos; "they are 'created,' not as creatures, but as co-creators for the task of providing necessary assistance in the cosmic transformation of heaven and earth."[71] In the face of this responsibility, the search for material benefit becomes petty-minded and irrelevant. Certainly Liu, whatever he thought of the operation of "action and response," believes that the good man should do good without considering the possibility of reward.

Liu's program for self-realization had to have, in practical terms, a rather limited application. There is nothing in his *Manual* to suggest that he would bar anyone from the process for status reasons, no hint that certain people could never become sages. But it is clear, from the moral self-consciousness and the amount of time and energy required to attempt his program, that the *Manual* would be appropriate largely for a literati audience. The inclusion of a ledger of deeds for officials and the very nature of the general prescriptions, not to mention the fact that the text was designed for a scholarly society, all indicate that Liu was writing for men like himself, scholars and officials. These were the men who had to be perfected morally, to be made sages, for the task of assisting in the "cosmic transformation of heaven and earth" and the more mundane tasks of teaching the people and preserving local order. Liu does not seem to have shared Yuan Huang's dynamic vision of society in either moral or status terms: though there is no statement in the *Manual* that precludes the possibility of a peasant becoming a sage, Liu is not interested in either stating

---

[71] Wei-ming Tu, "Subjectivity in Liu Tsung-chou's Philosophical Anthropology," p. 231. For a thorough study of Liu's ethical philosophy, see Yamamoto Makoto, *Minjidai Jugaku no ronrigakuteki kenkyū*, pp. 722–898.

such a possibility or encouraging such a result. He seems to have assumed that sages would emerge from the ranks of scholar-officials.

The Donglin Partisans: The Neo-Confucian Theory of "Action and Response"

Liu Zongzhou, in his *Manual for Man*, made the most direct and concerted attack on Yuan Huang's system of merit and demerit, reasserting the classic Mencian stand that the true gentleman concentrates on moral improvement without thinking of heaven's response to his actions. Liu seems to have been almost exclusively interested in the minutiae of an intense program of self-cultivation; heaven, much less ghosts and spirits, does not figure in his *Manual*. Other thinkers, often ones closely associated with Liu Zongzhou in the effort to combat the "harmful" effects of Taizhou moral excesses, were much more ambivalent about the belief that a man might be materially rewarded for his good deeds. Several Donglin leaders and partisans—Gu Xiancheng, Gao Panlong, and Chen Longzheng—struggled to develop a "Confucian" theory of action and response that would assure man some control over his fate without falling into the errors of Buddhist or Daoist "superstition." Even some of the sharpest critics of the Wang Yangming school and the most conservative defenders of the Cheng-Zhu school—men like Zhang Lixiang and Lu Shiyi—admitted the principle of retribution while denouncing the ledgers of merit and demerit. This ambivalence (as has been seen, shared to some degree even by Liu Zongzhou himself) is a measure of the appeal of the idea that man could determine his own fate.

In making arguments for a kind of Confucian theory of action and response, these thinkers were able to exploit the ambiguities within the Confucian canon itself on the subject. At the same time they were careful to distinguish their views as sharply as possible from the "corrupt" beliefs of Buddhists and Daoists. Above all else, their system had to be a Confucian one, superior in part because it avoided the moral and intellectual pitfalls of Buddhism and Daoism. Gu Xiancheng, for example, was perfectly willing to acknowledge the principle of causation: "The creation is great. How can we say there is no doctrine of causation?"[72] Gu defended his stand by quoting the texts of the ancient sages—the *Classic of History* and the *Classic of Changes*—to support his claims for the existence of a Confucian belief in retribution. But he went on to define this "true" belief in terms of how it differed from the Buddhist concept of retribution. The basic difference lay in the Confucian and Buddhist definitions of "past and future," he claimed. For the Confucians, "past and future" referred

[72] Gu Xiancheng, *Zhengxing bian*, 5.28a, in *Gu Duanwen Gong yishu*.

to the merit one could inherit from one's ancestors and pass down to one's descendants; for the Buddhists it meant, of course, transmigration, one's karma from a previous life and for a future rebirth.[73] The Buddhist belief, he argued, was first of all simply false: if men had a possibly infinite number of lives, why hadn't the great legendary sages of the past—Fu Xi, Huangdi, Yao, and Shun, not to mention the Buddha himself—returned to bring peace to the world?[74]

But even more serious for Gu was the moral danger involved in accepting the Buddhist view: it suggested, Gu maintained, that men were not really responsible for their acts. Each man in his present life was simply automatically living through a life in a sense predetermined by his behavior in his last life. "If we accept the doctrine of the Buddhists on behavior," he warned, "then every loyal minister, every filial son exists simply to recompense the benefits of his previous life. Every traitorous minister, every treacherous son exists simply to recompense the grievances of his previous life." Hence, in the Buddhist view, a scholar who did wrong and suffered disgrace had not really harmed goodness, for his actions were simply the inevitable, personally uncontrollable effects of deeds done in a previous, now forgotten life. By attributing everything to the workings of transmigration, the Buddhists, Gu argued, absolved men of responsibility for their moral choices: "They deny the spontaneity of the human mind and the human capacity to avoid self-delusion. . . . As a result, moral constants and the principles of human relationships are both forgotten."[75]

On the other hand, according to Gu, the Confucian understanding of causation, although it allowed for the passive inheritance of merit and demerit, preserved the principle of human responsibility. A man chose to do right or wrong, and he and/or his descendants would be rewarded or punished for that choice. His behavior in a life now completely beyond his control (or even his memory) did not predestine him to be either a loyal minister or an unfilial son. Gu was asserting that man did have much greater control over his fate than the Buddhist doctrine of the "three lives" (*sanshi*) of past, present, and future rebirths would allow (at least in his interpretation of it). Of course, Gu Xiancheng limited his discussion to the issue of moral fate—he did not touch on the question of man's control over his material conditions, and in that sense he was quite distant from Yuan Huang. But in his claims for human moral responsibility and control, he was making claims that echoed, in a strictly moral context, Yuan's belief that man could "decide his own fate."[76]

[73] Gu Xiancheng, *Xiaoxin zhai zhaji*, 9.7b–8a, in *Gu Duanwen Gong yishu*.
[74] Gu Xiancheng, *Zhengxing bian*, 5.28a–b, in *Gu Duanwen Gong yishu*.
[75] Gu Xiancheng, *Xiaoxin zhai zhaji*, 9.8b, in *Gu Duanwen Gong yishu*.
[76] Paul Varo Martinson finds a similar consciousness of human moral responsibility set in

Gu's younger associate and a principal leader of the Donglin Academy, Gao Panlong, went far beyond Gu's rather sketchy comments on causation and man's moral responsibility. Like Gu, he rejected the Buddhist belief in causation (*yinguo*), though for slightly different reasons—because it suggested that ghosts and spirits were in charge of retribution and that man could have complete control over heaven's responses with their assistance. Gao complained that this doctrine encouraged people to do good for profit.[77]

But Gao also rejected the fatalistic position that heaven decided moral fate without regard for human behavior; such a belief, he claimed, would make the teachings of the sages irrelevant. Gao explained his own understanding of the operation of action and response:

> Between heaven and earth, action and response (*ganying*) meet like a circle without end to produce distinctions among people and things. Action and response thereby produce ghosts and spirits; it is not the case that ghosts and spirits control action and response. For everyone in the world, each mouthful of food and drink is set beforehand as a response. This is the fate that cannot be changed. For everyone in the world each good and bad deed can be categorized as action. This is the fate created from the individual. To suppose that since action produces a response, people therefore are moving heaven, is wrong. [9a.43b]

He suggests, then, that while man has no control over his physical conditions, over what he eats and drinks, he can control his moral life. Each person could make himself good or bad: "This is the fate created from the individual."

Here Gao seems to be very close to the Mencian view of fate. But as he goes on to explain the cosmic operation of the Confucian view of action and response, he seems to shift his ground somewhat, suggesting that a man can in fact change his "fixed" material fate: "But then is it true that the fate that is already fixed cannot be changed? I say, Why can it not be changed? Allotment (*shu*) is cosmic pneuma (*qi*). *Qi* is principle (*li*). Principle is the mind (*xin*)." Here he explains the psychophysical links between the human mind and each individual's allotment of fate; they mutually influence each other by virtue of the fact that they are all composed of *qi*:

> The transformations of the mind are limitless, and they produce the distinction between good and evil. The greatest evil is to consider having intentions as important (*yi you xin wei da*); the greatest good is to consider the absence of

---

the framework of retributive justice in *Jin Ping Mei*. See his "Pao Order and Redemption," pp. 383–420.

[77] Gao Panlong, *Gaozi yishu*, 9a.44b–45a. In the discussion that follows, page references to this work are given in brackets in the text.

intentions (*wuxin*) to be truthfulness (*cheng*). The evil of having intentions invites calamities. The good of being without a mind moves the spirits. Therefore, the sages valued the action of being without a mind. If it happens that the principles of this action change, *qi* changes. When *qi* changes, allotment changes—all changes are from the transformations of the mind. This is why people consider the fate endowed by heaven to be created by people themselves. [9a.44a]

The mind, then, is capable of producing all kinds of movements and transformations, as well as the distinction between good and evil. This distinction arises when intentions or conscious thoughts take over the mind—they will produce evil. When evil "moves" in the mind, its *qi* also shifts, moving the *qi* outside of it, including that which makes up the allotment or fate of the individual; thus an evil thought will naturally evoke an adjustment in one's allotment. Man can change his allotment for the better if he empties his mind of calculation. For in that state of purity, the purified *qi* or cosmic pneuma in his mind acts on or moves the pneuma that constitutes all things in the universe, including, of course, that which makes up his individual allotment. Thus one's allotment can be changed and improved through a kind of chain reaction moving from the pure *qi* of the intentionless mind through the *qi* of the universe and finally through the *qi* of the individual's own allotment.

Gao comes very close to sharing the assumptions of Yuan Huang's system of merit and demerit. He certainly shares Yuan's view that the only kind of goodness that will move heaven is unself-conscious, a goodness free of expectation of recompense. Like Yuan, he even uses this principle to explain why some apparently good men are never rewarded with good fortune. In his preface to the rules of his local charitable association or "benevolent society" (*tongshan hui*),[78] he records the following exchange with a disciple:

[Chen] Zhixing asked, "If the good are necessarily fortunate, why is it that there are cases where this is not so?" I replied, "Whenever you do virtuous deeds for people, do not expect rewards from them. Moreover, do not, in bestowing on the people that which is not to be recompensed, expect a reward from heaven. If you seek good fortune in doing good, then in doing good, there will be no good fortune. . . . Hence one's doing good is like being thirsty and drinking, being hungry and eating. Drinking and eating—are they also done in expectation of recompense?

The Way is simply two—benevolence and lack of benevolence. Benevolence gives birth to the Way, lack of benevolence destroys the Way. There are tens of thousands of different misfortunes in the world—all destroy the Way. There

---

[78] See Fuma, "Dōzenkai shōshi," pp. 41–76.

are tens of thousands of different types of blessings in the world—all give birth to the Way. Benevolence produces good and [this in turn produces] good fortune, as the shadow follows the form. If your mind has intentions [i.e., if it is seeking good fortune], then it is not benevolent; "unconscious" goodness leads to good fortune. [9.42b–43a]

In a lecture to this society, Gao explicitly established the link between behavior and material circumstance that so preoccupied Yuan Huang: he told the cautionary tale of a community so immersed in bad customs and wickedness that it was entirely destroyed by attacking pirates, agents of heaven's "response" to human evil [12.33b–34a]. Even in more personal documents, Gao expressed a belief in retribution, for in his *Family Instructions* he urged his descendants to accumulate goodness and avoid error as a means of gaining good fortune: "Goodness must be accumulated. Accumulate it today, accumulate it tomorrow. Accumulate little acts of goodness, and accumulate great acts of goodness. One mistaken thought, one mistaken word, or one mistaken deed is the seed of self-destruction and family failure. . . . Watch for error in yourself to seek good fortune; examine yourself to escape bad fortune" [11b.20a].

But in his understanding of the mechanism of action and response, Gao did depart from Yuan Huang.[79] Over and over he emphasized the automatic, naturalistic operation of action and response, in which movements of cosmic pneuma, by a kind of osmosis, transmitted the human "actions" and the heavenly "responses" that recompensed them. Heaven here was somehow both a personalized "knowing" entity and an automatic moral force adjusting without thought to the movements of cosmic pneuma:

There is nothing more important than for man to know heaven, for if he knows heaven, then he will know the inevitability of action and response. When people today speak of heaven, they have in mind the "blue vault above." They do not realize that heaven includes everything from the highest heavens and above to the greatest depths of the earth and below; from our skin and hair and bones and marrow to all within and beyond the six points. Consequently, when we have a good thought, heaven always knows it, and when we have an evil thought, heaven always knows it. Knowing men's good and evil, heaven requites it with good and evil. It does, however, not do so out of vindictiveness. It is a general law that action and response are connected like form and shadow; a good action is followed by a good response, and an evil action is followed by an evil response. Action and response are automatic or natural in their relationship.

[79] There is a passage in Gao Panlong's biography suggesting that he repudiated "the study of deciding one's own fate" (*liming zhi xue*), but he never makes a direct reference to Yuan Huang or the ledgers of merit and demerit. See Hua Yuncheng, "Gao Zhongxian Gong nianpu," 28b.

One might say: If action and response are automatic in their relationship, then why do you speak of heaven? Why do you say that heaven knows everything? The answer is: we speak of heaven because it is automatic and natural; because it is one thing and not two. If one said: there is one thing which acts and another which responds, one would make it two. Only because it is not two is it infallible.[80] [3.26b–27a]

Gone from this system were the actively interventionist gods—the Buddha and Zhunti—of Yuan Huang's experience; ghosts and spirits existed for Gao only as manifestations of *qi* passing on, as it were, the actions of men and the responses of heaven. Ignorant people might claim that it was one's allotment from the gods that decided one's life, but they did not understand that allotment (*qishu*) was actually "formed from the human mind and habits" [12.33b]. Thus Gao meant quite literally that "a man's doing good is automatically seeking good fortune, and his doing evil is automatically seeking bad fortune"; in either case, his *qi* would automatically set in motion the operation of heaven's response. "Therefore there is no good or bad fortune that is not sought in the self" [3.27a–b]. Ironically, despite his attacks on the Buddhists, Gao's understanding of action and response is here not far from the concept of causation found in philosophical Buddhism.

Gao must be distinguished from Yuan Huang in yet another way: in his application of the concept of action and response. Though his understanding would seem to admit a use very like Yuan's own emphasis on the material rewards to be earned from the system, Gao tended to deemphasize this conclusion. He stressed, rather, that men should keep their minds on the pursuit of goodness, "benevolence and righteousness," pure of any calculation of their own wealth or rank [9.42b–43a; 3.27b]. Furthermore, the very few cases he presented to illustrate the operation of action and response were usually warnings against the evil consequences that would inevitably result from evil customs—hence the story of the depraved community overwhelmed by pirates. When the story had a happy ending, it was usually a generalized happiness. When, for example, the *qi* of a county was harmonious, then it would move a cosmic "mass" (*tuan*) of harmonious *qi* to produce rain when it was needed and to ensure a bountiful harvest—in short, to provide for the prosperity of the county as a whole [12.19a–b].[81] Or when he urged his descendants to accumulate goodness, he suggested rather vaguely that this goodness would bring only unspecified "good fortune" or "benefit" to the family at large. Gao eschewed the promises of concrete, individual rewards that characterize

---

[80] Translation from Busch, "The Tung-lin Academy," pp. 131–132.

[81] See also Angela Ki Che Leung, "Organized Medicine in Ming-Qing China: State and Private Medical Institutions in the Lower Yangzi Region," p. 149.

Yuan Huang's interpretation of merit accumulation. As a result, despite the fact that his system could have operated to produce those effects, he avoided the suggestion that immediate personal profit could be gained from good deeds.

Chen Longzheng, another Donglin affiliate, expressed in his writings an even sharper ambivalence about the operation of retribution. He shared Gao Panlong's general understanding of the operation of action and response: since man's actions and words were all *qi*, they "moved" or influenced the *qi* of the universe, creating ghosts and spirits (also made of *qi*) who "responded" automatically to these actions and words. Man was able to "move" *qi* only if his actions and words were perfectly sincere, if they were straight from the mind. Chen explained: "Ghosts and spirits are *qi*. Man's good actions and good words are also *qi*. Every act and word that is good should be enough to move ghosts and spirits. But there are cases in which this is not true. Why? Ghosts and spirits are *qi* and [thus] interpenetrate the human mind. Good acts and words come out of the mind and the spirits interpenetrate them. But if they do not come out of the mind, then the ghosts and spirits see the mind and do not trust this *qi*. This is the meaning of the doctrine that if one is not sincere, then one is not able to communicate with spirits."[82] Like Gao Panlong and even Yuan Huang himself, he argued that good acts were truly good only if done without thoughts of personal gain: goodness was complete only when one neither expected rewards from heaven or man, nor planned to pass one's merit down to one's descendants. Any calculation of profit in the performance of good deeds would lead to evil, for, since there would be no reward for such manipulative "goodness," the man hoping to benefit from it would sink into wicked ways in anger and disappointment over his frustrated expectations [20.33b].

Chen used this understanding of action and response to explain the task of "accumulating goodness" (*jishan*) or "collecting righteousness" (*jiyi*). These two concepts, attributed by Chen to Confucius and Mencius respectively, referred to the day-by-day practice of different acts of goodness or righteousness; for Chen they encapsulated the proper method of self-cultivation. A critic might argue that this method was too scattered and fragmentary, subject to the same flaws as Yuan Huang's ledger system: one was encouraged to pile up different acts, without ever developing a coherent, "whole" moral perfection that would lead to genuinely spontaneous goodness. But Chen explained that as long as all of one's acts were "pleasing to the mind" (that is, sincere), then even though each expressed a different moral principle, they nonetheless "produced the

[82] Chen Longzheng, *Jiting quanshu*, 6.13a. Further references to this work are indicated by bracketed page numbers in the text.

'floodlike *qi*,' building it up without break or fragmentation, everything properly in one piece. How can it be scattered or patched?" Thus, because of the potential interpenetration of the *qi* of all things, even the commission of scattered acts of goodness, as long as they were done in complete sincerity, might be formed into the "floodlike *qi*" that would move the ghosts and spirits [5.9a–b].

But Chen Longzheng was reluctant to conclude that the individual could expect personal material rewards for his goodness. Indeed, on occasion he directly repudiated the suggestion that this might be the case: when his son recovered from a serious illness shortly after Chen had donated to a famine-relief effort, he explicitly denied that his son's cure was a reward for his own generosity [21.21a–b].[83] Like Gao Panlong, he seemed at times to claim simply that the rewards of an individual's virtue were a diffused and widespread good fortune, not a precise material reward for the individual himself: "Now great virtue receives good fortune, [but] it is not the man himself who receives it, nor is it in the forms of emolument, rank, fame, and longevity. . . . If a man does goodness on his own it is said there is virtue in him, [and] he allows the world to get his goodness. This, then, is a sage bringing good fortune to the world" [3.8a–b]. Only Buddhists, Chen remarked contemptuously, believed that a single individual would be rewarded with wealth and rank for his good acts. The sage knew that his "reward" was simply the greater goodness (transmitted through the movements of *qi*) brought to the people: "Do a good deed, and everyone will be pleased with it. Save a person, and everyone will respond to it. It is not necessarily that you yourself will receive [anything as a reward]. Do an evil deed, and everyone will be angry at it. Harm a person and everyone will resent it. It is not necessarily that you yourself will receive [anything as a punishment]. The people are one *qi*, their minds are one spirit. This makes for a great interpenetration" [3.3a]. Here Chen argued that specific good deeds were rewarded only in the most general way: the whole cosmos, all the people, benefited from the good *qi* stirred up by the virtuous behavior of specific individuals, but these individuals themselves were rewarded only in the sense that they too participated in the general good fortune. They could not expect the personally applicable material rewards that Yuan Huang had promised them.

But elsewhere Chen Longzhong seemed to be quite ready to admit that an individual was directly and specifically rewarded for his good deeds, a view clearly in conflict with the position stated above. The conflict within Chen's own thinking emerges most vividly in his lectures to the benevo-

[83] Reference from Handlin, "Benevolent Societies," p. 322.

lent society he formed in his native Jiashan in 1631. Although in these lectures, urging members to contribute to the society charities, he occasionally remarked that one should never expect rewards for doing good [23.13a, 4.23b],[84] he more frequently suggested to his audience that they would in fact be individually as well as collectively rewarded for their charitable activities. He used the concept of retribution to persuade all the different socioeconomic groups in the society to do good, altering the terms of the concept to suit each group. At the top, he warned the "wealthy and high-ranking" not to get so absorbed in money-making and in increasing their own good fortune that they neglected the sufferings of their fellow men. Such men, "thinking that they are every day getting good fortune in the world, do not know that they are every day creating retribution in the world. Why use the very foundations of good fortune to create future retribution?" [24.10b–11a]. Thus these people are urged to be generous to the less fortunate, to a large degree as a means of ensuring the maintenance of their high status: they should use their wealth not only to aid others but also to ward off a decline in their fortunes [24.5b].[85]

People of more moderate means and rank are abjured to think too of their status, though from a somewhat different perspective. They should follow a middle path, neither catering to their superiors, nor taking advantage of their inferiors [24.5b]. Chen promised an array of blessings for those "middle-ranking" people who never cheated or hurt others, who were "good from the inside," "sincere and honest": the ghosts and spirits would protect them, their families would be healthy, the neighborhoods in which they lived would be contented, with jails free of criminals, and so forth. They would be able to afford to teach their sons to read and study, and thus could hope to advance the standing of their family. Those people who were dishonest and self-seeking, and who wasted their time and money in Buddhist and Daoist religious ceremonies, earned the opposite fate: "Retribution (baoying) comes to them, no one has compassion for them, and the ghosts and spirits fail to preserve them" [24.11a–b].

Finally, those of the lowest rank, the poor, received the longest and most detailed lecture on retribution and doing good. Chen expressed his

[84] See Mizoguchi, "Iwayuru Tōrinha jinshi," pp. 162–170; and Handlin, "Benevolent Societies," pp. 320–325.

[85] A slightly different rationale for charitable giving by the wealthy was offered by Yang Dongming, another Donglin affiliate and founder of the Guangren Hui (Society for the Spread of Benevolence). He explained to the members of this society that their wealth was a reflection of their goodness, and charity a means of spreading this goodness: "You are wealthy. This is not just an accident, but is certainly due to the depth and reach of the roots of your goodness. . . . You must propagate your goodness to promote the principle of life." Yang, Shanju gongke, 1.1b; reference from Leung, "Organized Medicine," p. 149.

sympathy for the desperate poverty and misfortune many of these people suffered, but warned them that it would be a mistake to try to correct the situation forcibly, by rising up and seizing wealth from others: "It is difficult to explain the lot appointed by heaven above (*shangtian mingshu*). Relying on human force to change it—this absolutely cannot be done" [24.12a]. At one point, he urged people of low status simply to be contented with their station (*anfen*), carefully avoiding the various "sicknesses" associated with either sullen resignation or bitter resistance to poverty [24.6a–b]. But his final message to these people was that it was possible, over the long run, to change fate through more peaceful internal, moral means:

> But the human mind is most spiritual, truly different from that of all other creatures. Thus the ancients, either through the operation of filial minds or through the charitable acts of true minds, could act on heaven and earth, and move the ghosts and spirits. As *Do Good for Secret Merit* (*Weishan yinzhi*)[86] says, "the evidence that bad fortune can be changed to good is very great." The *Tract of Taishang on Action and Response* opens with the saying, "Calamity and good fortune do not come through gates, but are summoned only by men themselves." Clearly, both texts are referring to the word "fate" (*ming*). If you want to use force to plot a change in what lies outside you, you will surely be unsuccessful. If you have a perfectly fair and perfectly sincere mind, without your knowing it, what lies outside will change of its own. These words are not said only for the sake of the poor, but I feel they have a particular relevance for the poor [24.12a–b].

Here the appeal was adjusted to suit the intellectual and moral sophistication and fastidiousness of each group. The wealthy and high-ranking were treated to a subtle suggestion that a single-minded pursuit of profit and good fortune might bring punishment from heaven. (In the preface to the lectures, written in the classical language for the eyes of the literate, the belief in retribution was supported with an allusion to the *Classic of Songs* [23.14a].) The moderately well-off were exhorted to do good for the benefit of themselves and their communities, both to be rewarded with the protection of the ghosts and spirits. Finally, the poor were subjected to the crudest and most obvious appeal, with a clear assurance that they could change their fate through moral conduct, and an equally clear warning that violent measures would have no effect on their material cir-

---

[86] This ten-*juan* morality book was published in 1419 under the auspices of the Yongle emperor. It contains biographies of 165 historical figures, each of whom was rewarded for virtuous deeds. The emperor ordered that it be distributed to all imperial princes, ministers, the National Academy, and prefectural and county schools, and that it be included, with the *Great Warnings*, among works tested in the civil service examinations. Sakai, *Chūgoku zensho no kenkyū*, pp. 20–21; and *Mingdai chizhuan shukao fuyinde*, p. 37.

cumstances.[87] The message was backed up with the opening line of the *Tract on Action and Response*, by this time a proverbial reference to the belief in supernatural retribution. Despite the difference in form and level of abstraction, the basic message in each case was the same: the individual and his family (and even his community) would benefit materially from the performance of good deeds, while evil would bring nothing but misfortune.

Chen's and Gao's ambivalence about the concept of retribution was shared, rather surprisingly, by one of the most conservative late Ming–early Qing Neo-Confucians, an ardent supporter of the Cheng-Zhu school, Zhang Lixiang. Zhang was, excluding Liu Zongzhou, perhaps the most vociferous critic of Yuan Huang's *Ledger*. Yet in his "Instructions to My Sons" ("Xunzi yu"), he quoted the *Classic of Changes* to urge his descendants to accumulate goodness, to guard the family against bad fortune. "It is not that you want to seek good fortune and happiness from heaven," he explained,

> but in fact [literally, "in terms of constant principle"] blessings and catastrophes, good and bad fortune always come from heaven. The power of accumulating goodness cannot but be feared. The slightest intrigue or suspicion between father and sons and between brothers, the slightest incident between husbands and wives and between mothers and sons in the private quarters—do not say these are not enough to move heaven and earth or to act on the ghosts and spirits. Heaven and earth and the ghosts and spirits are not on the outside; they are simply in our own bodies and hearts. If you are good, then there is a response of harmonious *qi*; if you are not good, there is a response of perverse *qi*.[88]

This is a rather surprising admonition from the man who castigated Yuan Huang for introducing the idea of retribution into the examination curriculum.

All these thinkers, then, despite their protests that wealth and rank were arbitrarily fated and that the individual should never seek good fortune in doing good, in fact did believe in a modified, "Confucian" version of supernatural retribution or action and response. Up to a point they

---

[87] It is interesting that sickness, like low status, another "misfortune," was also treated by late Ming and early Qing philanthropists as a kind of retribution: disease was a punishment for and thus a reflection of immorality. It might symbolize the general moral decay of a community, or the moral turpitude of one specific individual. This belief actually affected the organization of philanthropy; Angela Leung records the example of a dispensary that required all its patients to promise to correct their faults as well as take their medicine, on the grounds that physical ills could not be cured until moral weaknesses were eradicated. Leung, "Organized Medicine," p. 149.

[88] Zhang Lixiang, *Yangyuan xiansheng quanji*, 47.1a–b and 2b–4b.

seem little different from Yuan Huang, particularly in their assurance that the only good that could be recompensed was that done with a pure, uncalculating mind. Where they parted from Yuan Huang was in their understanding of the operation of retribution. Emphasizing the automatic operation of "action and response," these thinkers also emphasized the weight of human responsibility in the creation of a prosperous environment. "Buddhist and Daoist" gods were not in charge of *this* system, and ghosts and spirits figured only as transformations of pneuma through which cosmic responses to human actions were transmitted. Nor was man ever a powerless symbol of transmigration, entrapped in a position determined by a previous existence he could no longer even remember. Man here was to a large extent in charge of the operation—he was not dependent on the compassion of occasionally whimsical gods nor on his own past karma, but on himself. He took more responsibility not only for his own moral behavior (or as Mencius would say, his "proper fate"), but also for the well-being of his immediate community.

In contrast to Yuan Huang, these thinkers also deemphasized the individual personal or "selfish" aspect of merit earning. Although individuals did gain from good deeds in their system, the thrust of the accumulation of goodness was the more diffused benefits to be enjoyed by the family line or the community at large. There is never any suggestion that an individual could tote up points in expectation of an examination degree or other reward "worth" a certain merit total. The implication is that heaven would benefit those who thought first of the public good, not of their own merit account.

The Confucian understanding of action and response was by no means the invention of Gu Xiancheng, Gao Panlong, Chen Longzheng, and Zhang Lixiang. In describing the movements of cosmic pneuma in the process of "action and response," they were drawing on cosmological principles formulated at least as early as the Han, and generally accepted (though with varying degrees of enthusiasm) by Confucian thinkers ever since. These principles lay at the basis of Cheng-Zhu cosmological thinking: even Zhu Xi believed in the existence of ghosts and spirits and in the ability of human actions to "move" natural forces and evoke specific responses.[89] But Gu, Gao, and Chen gave the argument a value and prominence that previous thinkers had not. They were asserting the power of the good man to change, through his influence on the movements of cosmic pneuma, the material circumstances of life around him. And in their

[89] Zhu Xi, *Zhuzi yulei*, 3 ("Guishen").2b–3a (pp. 54–55). It is interesting that just at the time—the late Ming and early Qing—that Donglin thinkers were invoking this process of action and response as a sanction for social action, other Chinese thinkers were beginning to call into question the real operation of the process. See Henderson, *Chinese Cosmology*, pp. 119–173.

focus on the importance of *qi* in the action-response process, they were also advancing one of the major shifts in late imperial Chinese philosophy, the trend among Ming and Qing thinkers to deny Zhu Xi's dualism of principle and *qi*, and to assert the primacy of *qi*.[90]

But these thinkers' articulation of a theory of retribution based on action and response did not emerge simply out of this shift in metaphysical outlook. Nor does this shift help at all to explain the obvious ambivalence many of these thinkers felt about the concept of retribution, particularly its application to material circumstances. Is there any way of explaining their struggles to work out a view of retribution that allows for considerable human control, yet at the same time remains respectably Confucian?

None of these men seems to have felt the specific social and familial pressures to succeed in the examinations that shaped Yuan Huang's thinking about retribution. Most were from families with recent histories of official service, and thus did not have Yuan's very personal reasons for needing to succeed. It is nonetheless interesting that three of them—Gao, Chen, and Zhang—often thought of accumulating goodness in the context of maintaining and improving their family fortunes. At a time when people were keenly aware of the precariousness of elite status, concern for the future of the family line might well have made belief in retribution attractive. But this concern still does not really explain these thinkers' anxiety to justify their distinctively Confucian theory of retribution.

Nor do any of these men seem to have shared either Yuan Huang's or He Xinyin's relatively dynamic social vision. Certainly, they do not use the belief in retribution first and foremost to encourage hopes of upward mobility. Their primary message was not that any man could become a sage (or a *jinshi* degree-holder) through the accumulation of merit, but rather that all men should practice goodness as much out of a fear of retributive punishment as out of an assurance of divine reward. Hence their apparent lack of interest in the precise calculations of merit points that Yuan Huang would have his ledger-users make.

Gu Xiancheng, Gao Panlong, Chen Longzheng, and, to some degree, Zhang Lixiang, seem to have been much more interested in the concept of retribution as both a reason for and a spur to social reform, as a belief that could provide both an ideology for elite action and a sanction for elite status. Assuredly they also saw its usefulness in popular moral instruction—thus both Gao and Chen approved the "superstitious" variety of retribution found in the *Tract on Action and Response* as a means of

---

[90] Yamanoi Yū, "Shushi no shisō ni okeru ki," in *Ki no shisō—Chūgoku ni okeru shizenkan to ningenkan no tenkai—*, pp. 434–435; Yamanoi, *Min Shin shisōshi no kenkyū*; and Ira Kasoff, *The Thought of Chang Tsai (1020–1077)*, pp. 36–53.

teaching the people to do good.[91] But the interesting factor here is their use of the concept, in a suitably "Confucianized" form, to explain the necessity for elite social activism. All these men were associated to varying degrees with the Donglin Academy—Gu and Gao were its most famous leaders, and Chen and Zhang were affiliates, though not formal members—and shared the Donglin commitment to greater local participation in government. The central government, first strenghtened through the reforms of Zhang Juzheng and then corrupted by the growing influence of eunuchs and careerist bureaucrats at court, now exploited the very social groups—the small to middle landlords, the middle-range entrepreneurs, and the peasants—it was supposed to protect, or so the Donglin partisans claimed. Not only ignorant of but also indifferent to the special conditions and needs of different communities, the government devoted its efforts to ruthless and arbitrary extraction of resources from local populations. Large and often absentee landlords, who in better times might have been expected to defend their communities against government depredations, colluded with corrupt officials and other members of the "national elite" for their share of the spoils.[92]

Shocked by the excesses of the autocratic imperial system and the great "bully" gentry landlords (*haochiang*) who supported it, Donglin partisans argued for what one scholar has called a "rural hegemony" comprised largely of local landlords and literati who would administer local affairs in such a way as to fulfill the "hidden feelings" and desires of the common people.[93] In the absence of rational government regulation, it was the responsibility of local elites—men of wealth, high standing, and thus some degree of nonofficial authority within their communities—to maintain order and ensure the welfare of the people. Certainly the Dong-

[91] Gao Panlong, *Gaozi yishu*, 9a.44b–45a.

[92] In general, I have accepted the characterization of the Donglin partisans made by Ono Kazuko and, most fully, by Mizoguchi Yūzō. Though many Donglin affiliates were themselves from large landlord families, in their social, political, and economic attitudes, they sympathized, at least in theory, with the small- to middle-level landlord group (*chūshō jinushi sō*); this was the sector of the rural population they believed should take over leadership roles in their communities, defending the peasantry against the depradations of the government and large, usually absentee, landlords. These Donglin also partisans sympathized with new commercial interests to the extent that they saw these threatened by the arbitrary power of the emperor and his eunuchs. See Mizoguchi, "Iwayuru Tōrinha jinshi no shisō," pp. 134, 178, and passim; and Ono Kazuko, "Tōrinha to sono seiji shisō." Mori Masao also discusses the interest Donglin affiliates (and Chen Longzheng in particular) had in implementing their statecraft ideas in local society, through the establishment of benevolent societies, the organization of famine-relief efforts, and reform of the labor-service system. He emphasizes, however, that these men formed a small minority within the gentry category as a whole, and he characterizes most late–Ming gentry as "careerist" (*shengguan facai*). See "The Gentry in the Late Ming," pp. 48–50.

[93] Mizoguchi, "Iwayuru Tōrinha jinshi," pp. 134, 202–203.

lin partisans saw themselves as champions of such local leadership. Just as most of their positions at court were stands against the growth in central power, so, too, many of their views on rural issues were defenses against what they perceived as the encroachment of the government on local prerogatives. This antagonism against arbitrary central control fueled their opposition to the Wanli emperor's efforts to force collection of taxes on mining ventures in the late sixteenth and early seventeenth centuries, for example. They were equally fearful of abuse of privilege and wealth by large gentry landlords and merchants at the expense of the peasantry and middle-ranking commoner landlords and merchants—hence their advocacy of the equal-field equal-service system, designed to reduce inequities in taxation in the late Ming.[94]

What is interesting here is the degree to which the Donglin thinkers justified their role in local society, and even some of their social and political positions, by means of the concept of cosmic retribution.[95] The wealthy and high-ranking in Chen Longzheng's benevolent society were informed that they had a responsibility to use their riches for the good of the community, particularly the poor (from whom, in a human model of "action and response," they could expect the "response" of gratitude).[96] If they refused to do so, Chen warned that they were simply building up disaster for themselves—that is, they would be punished for their greed with bad fortune. More specifically, he criticized the wealthy who consistently evaded the labor services they owed, thereby ensuring that the poor would have to bear a heavier burden. "How could the Way of heaven and human feeling," he warns, "allow you to be secure in your wealth for long?"[97] The bad fortune promised the unfeeling wealthy might well take the form of popular uprisings; Chen reminded his audience that impoverished peasants, incited by the example of neighbors or by the teachings

---

[94] Ibid., pp. 129–133, 211–212; and Mori, "The Gentry in the Late Ming," p. 51.

[95] See also Mizoguchi, "Iwayuru Tōrinha jinshi," pp. 208–209, 239–241.

An instructive comparison can be made here to the arguments used by officials of the Southern Song to encourage local elites to contribute to famine relief. Robert Hymes points up the "absence of ethical consensus" on the issue of charity in the Song: officials, eager to enlist the assistance of local elites in famine relief, argued as often from utility or self-interest as from moral obligation. Hymes concludes, "The use of such arguments from self-interest may reflect underlying disagreement or uncertainty as to the ethical basis—or more broadly, the basis in general rules of social behavior—of charity in general." (See *Statesmen and Gentlemen: The elite of Fu-Chou, Chiang-Hsi, in Northern and Southern Sung*, pp. 162–163.) By the late Ming, the Donglin thinkers seem to have developed, on the basis of their view of retribution, a consensus about these "general rules of social behavior." Unlike their Song counterparts, they united moral and utilitarian incentives, arguing that public goodness would yield private benefits.

[96] Chen Longzhen, *Jiting quanshu*, 24.1b–2a.

[97] Ibid., 24.4b–5a.

of popular "licentious dramas," could easily become bandits, intent on seizing wealth from those unwilling to use it for charitable purposes.[98]

Scholars have argued quite persuasively that men like Gao and Chen, in their concern with local charity, were working out a moral justification for the new wealth from commercial sources and land investment enjoyed by so many of their status.[99] There was nothing wrong in their eyes, then, with the accumulation of wealth—indeed, it could have moral value, as long as it was devoted to the performance of good deeds. The concept of action and response provided the religious justification for this view: those blessed with good fortune (here wealth) had been rewarded for virtue and hence somehow deserved their status, but to maintain that status and good fortune, it was necessary for them to expend their wealth in the performance of good deeds. Retribution linked to the concept of social recompense became a means of reinforcing the obligation of the wealthy and high-ranking to protect and aid their communities. In a sense it allowed the merging of both selfish, personal goals and public, community aims, for in aiding the poor, the rich were also ensuring their own continued reward from the cosmic action-and-response cycle. This fit perfectly with the Donglin assertion that the selfish (si) interests of local leaders could be identified with the public (gong) needs of their communities.[100]

Thus the action and response form of retribution became the ideological basis of the program for social and political reform urged by Donglin partisans. It was made into a kind of "mandate of heaven" for local landlords and literati, a social ideology for the gentry: their very standing in the community imposed a responsibility on them to serve the interests of the community (often against those of the central government), to fulfill the moral promise reflected in their wealth and status. If they failed in their duties, then by the very workings of the cosmos, misfortune would come upon them. The ruler feared the moral dissatisfaction of heaven and the loss of his empire, through either heaven-inspired natural disasters or popular rebellion; the local gentry feared the influence of their "evil" qi and the loss of their wealth and standing, through either family decline or popular uprising and seizure of their wealth.

Furthermore, retribution provided a comprehensive social ideology, one that could apply to all status groups. In the form of the human value of reciprocity or recompense, it could even regulate relations between them. Thus Chen and other Donglin supporters reminded landlords of the kindness they owed their tenants, whose hard labor supported the landlord class, while tenants and other peasants were admonished to re-

[98] Ibid., 24.18a; see also 24. 4a–b, 13a, 14a.
[99] Handlin, "Benevolent Societies," pp. 330–331.
[100] Mizoguchi, "Iwayuru Tōrinha jinshi," pp. 204–207, 244, 248–250.

turn their landlords' "actions" of charity with the "response" of gratitude—certainly not with acts of rebellion. Reciprocity, an earthly application of retribution, was to express the mutual social and economic dependence of the different status groups of society.

The debate over the moral legitimacy of Yuan Huang's *Ledger of Merit and Demerit* points up several issues of special concern among Chinese intellectuals of the sixteenth and seventeenth centuries: the validity of the prescriptive approach to moral behavior, the need for purity of mind in the performance of good, and the relationship between profit and goodness.

Underlying and linking these smaller points of debate, however, is the tension between a widely held faith in human perfectibility and what one scholar has called a "deep awareness of the human proclivity to evil."[101] All the thinkers discussed here seemed to share, albeit in different ways, a strong belief in the human potential for moral perfection. Yuan Huang and Zhou Rudeng celebrated the "creative power of the human mind" as the agent of moral transformation. Liu's *Manual* rejoices in the ability of man to achieve the "ultimate in humanity." Gao Panlong and Chen Longzheng believed that good men could transform the customs and even the weather of their communities through the purification of their *qi*.

At the same time that they held this faith in human perfectibility and moral control, however, they shared with their contemporaries an apparently pervasive fear of moral failure, a need to watch critically over every act, to weed out faults and establish the pure mental ground required for successful self-cultivation. Thus, though Liu Zongzhou believed in the perfectability of man, he also insisted on the necessity "for each person to engage in a continuous and strenuous moral struggle against evil."[102] The tension between these two points shaped all aspects of the debate over ledger use in the seventeenth century. For Yuan Huang and his Taizhou supporters, the ledgers of merit and demerit dissolved the tension, operating to ward off evil (through the prescriptive morality and point-keeping self-discipline they advocated) and to ensure human control (through merit accumulation). Indeed, Yuan Huang was bold in his assertion of human control: man could expect material benefits as well as moral perfection from merit accumulation. Ledger use thus yielded both profit and goodness.

But for Liu and other, more conservative Confucian scholars, Yuan Huang's *Ledger of Merit and Demerit* exacerbated the tension—it encouraged men to give in to their evil proclivities, their selfish desires for

[101] Wu, "Self-Examination," p. 6.
[102] Tu, "Liu Tsung-chou's Philosophical Anthropology," p. 219.

personal profit, in promising that they could decide their own material fate. For them, Yuan's system contained an internal contradiction, one that guaranteed failure: in encouraging a desire for individual profit, Yuan Huang's method of cultivation violated the perfect purity of mind essential to the performance of real goodness, and instead led man to the evil of selfishness. The prescriptive morality of the ledgers simply encouraged a piecemeal, insincere, and hence ultimately false goodness.

But these critics of Yuan's opportunism were not necessarily united in their own efforts to delineate the boundaries of human control. Liu Zongzhou claimed a much smaller scope for man's mastery of fate—the individual could hope to perfect himself only morally. In the *Manual* he simply avoided discussion of the possibility of any kind of material reward for good deeds—the good man focused exclusively on his own internal cultivation, resolutely avoiding the fragmentation in purpose that would come with a search for external benefits. In Liu's writings the ledger form was carefully subordinated to a strict program of moral cultivation. Thus, in the *Manual*, "ledgers" of demerit alone served simply as tools of moral discipline, not as handbooks to worldly success. Profit and goodness, though not strictly antithetical here—Liu, after all, never flatly denied that virtue was materially rewarded—could never be merged into a single goal, for the thought of profit precluded the attainment of goodness. Liu returned the ledgers to use within what he believed to be a genuinely Confucian system, one that focused on self-cultivation and "kept the spirits at a distance"—that is, one that refused to speculate on man's ability to manipulate heaven.

The Donglin thinkers do not seem to have been as sure as Liu of the rigid limits on human control of fate. While reiterating that one should never do good with the thought of reward in mind, to varying degrees they seemed to believe that the individual's goodness might somehow be rewarded with good fortune.[103] Gu Xiancheng admitted the operation of cause and effect over generations but chose to emphasize the moral responsibility to do good that the system imposed on the individual rather than the material benefits it would yield him. Gao Panlong and Chen Longzheng believed in a cosmology of "action and response" dependent on the movements of cosmic pneuma; in their world, good acts could indeed "move" or cause good effects. Each tended to emphasize good responses that were not specific to the individual actor; their good men transformed local customs and brought prosperity to a whole commu-

---

[103] Concern over this issue did not fade after the seventeenth century. The eighteenth-century scholar Li Fu (1675–1750), for example, made an impressive effort to reconcile the different sides of the debate and defend the usefulness of the ledgers. See Li Fu, *Mutang chugao*, 18.6b–9a and 33.23a–b; and Chin-shing Huang, "The Lu-Wang School in the Ch'ing Dynasty: Li Mu-t'ang," pp. 141–150.

nity. That they might also earn examination degrees or prosperity for themselves and their families was to be considered a secondary effect. Such individual rewards demonstrated, too, that "selfish" (si), personal goals need not conflict with the broader, "public" (gong) good—indeed, they might, if appropriately pursued, contribute to the general good.

The Donglin thinkers' understanding of the retributive process thus reflects a political and social orientation somewhat different from Yuan Huang's. Yuan posits entry into the national bureaucratic elite and official service as the ultimate reward of merit accumulation. The Donglin partisans, disillusioned with (and barred in the early seventeenth century from participation in) a government that, far from ensuring the welfare of the people and maintaining social order, seemed intent on disrupting local economies and encouraging social disintegration, made community order and harmony their primary concern. Thus, in Chen Longzheng's view of the operation of cosmic action and response, local statecraft interests overrode Yuan's focus on status advancement. Retribution now was interpreted to sanction and stimulate private local elite efforts at community management and social reform; such tasks were the special responsibility of the local elites, as beneficiaries of the cosmos-endowed reward of high status. And the action-response process ensured that it was only by working actively for the public good that the elite could hope to fulfill their own personal ambitions.[104]

For the poor, of course, "working for the public good" was a very different process, a much more passive one: they were to accept their lot in life, and above all else, not make trouble, if they hoped to improve their fortunes. For Chen and other Donglin thinkers, then, the belief in supernatural retribution supported a social and political ideology that tended to encourage social stability by requiring the vigorous and benevolent leadership of local elites within their communities and the uncomplaining acquiescence of those of low status. While the Donglin affiliates did accept the basic premise of Yuan Huang's argument—that some force above men rewarded good and punished evil—they applied this belief in a very different political, moral, and social context: in their hands, "action and response" sanctioned the paternalistic regulation of communities by local elites more than it justified individual efforts at rapid status advancement. It was essentially their understanding of the retributive process and its social uses, not Yuan Huang's, that came to dominate the production of ledgers of merit and demerit in the seventeenth and eighteenth centuries.

[104] See Leung, "Organized Medicine," pp. 149–150, 156.

CHAPTER FOUR

Preserving the Social Hierarchy in the Seventeenth and Eighteenth Centuries

FAR FROM turning people away from the ledgers of merit and demerit, the debate over their usefulness and validity seems rather to have stimulated interest in the texts. Certainly literati were more than ever interested in producing them: through the seventeenth century at least ten new ledgers were published after the appearance of Yuan's "Determining Your Own Fate"; in addition to these extant texts, we can find references to many other titles in the writings of the day. This boom in ledger production continued into the early eighteenth century, though by the end of the century very few original texts were being put out.

THE NEW LEDGERS OF MERIT AND DEMERIT

While most of these new ledgers retained the basic form and rationale of the earlier system of merit accumulation, they were conceived in terms ultimately quite different from the ledger of Yungu and Yuan Huang. They were produced in a new context, at a time of considerable social and political upheaval. The *Record for Gaining Good Fortune* (*Diji lu*; preface dated 1631) was completed by Yan Maoyou in 1622, when corruption and factionalism were rife within the bureaucracy; the *Complete Book of Exhortations and Admonitions* (*Quanjie quanshu*; preface dated 1641) was written by Chen Zhixi in 1639, when the Ming was on the verge of collapse. The four other major ledgers of the century all appeared as the new "barbarian" dynasty was consolidating its power—Li Guochang's *Essentials of Self-Cultivation* (*Chongxiu zhiyao*; prefaces dated 1666 and 1667); Hu Rongshi's *Collection of Ledgers of Merit and Demerit* (*Huibian gongguoge*; preface dated 1671); Chen Xigu's *Compendium of Ledgers of Merit and Demerit* (*Huizuan gongguoge*; written between 1671 and 1687); and Xiong Hongbei's *Meritorious Deeds at No Cost* (*Bufeiqian gongdeli*; published late in the century).[1]

[1] In the appendix there is a list of the major extant ledgers and morality books published in this period, most of which are treated in this chapter. For a general discussion of these works and their authorship and dating, see Sakai, *Chūgoku zensho*, pp. 378–403. For ledgers produced in the late eighteenth and nineteenth centuries, a period beyond the scope of this study, see Sakai Tadao, "Kōkakaku no kenkyū," pp. 40–44.

Conditions of authorship also changed for these later seventeenth-century ledgers. The ledgers continued to be written or edited[2] by men with at least some scholarly aspirations, though of wide-ranging social and official success. Yan Maoyou, from Pinghe, Fujian, was clearly an active participant in the political and intellectual life of the seventeenth century. A friend of many Donglin supporters and himself a member of the Restoration Society, he was awarded a special *jinshi* degree in 1634 for his extensive knowledge of the Five Classics, and thereafter he served briefly as a censor.[3] As an outspoken critic of Christianity, he contributed to the *Collection for the Destruction of Vicious Doctrines (Poxie ji)*, written to combat the influence of Father Guilio Aleni (1582–1649) in Fujian province.[4] Chen Xigu (1634–1687) of Yin county, Zhejiang, author of the *Compendium of Ledgers of Merit and Demerit*, was a *jinshi* of 1676 who served as a Hanlin compiler and an educational intendant in Henan before returning home to open his own academy. His friendship with Huang Zongxi and the poet-painter Zheng Liang (j.s. 1688) placed him high in contemporary literati circles.[5] Much less is known of the other authors, however. Li Guochang of Jinxi, Jiangxi, never advanced beyond tribute-student (*gongsheng*) status, despite his reputed devotion to the study of Song Neo-Confucianism and his rather high official contacts.[6] Hu Rongshi (d. 1695), the son of Hu Jiagui, a well-known martyr to the Ming cause, never held any examination degrees and remained at home in Kunshan county, Jiangsu, studying and organizing local charities.[7] Of Chen Zhixi, author of the *Complete Book of Exhortations and Admoni-*

---

[2] Most of the ledgers discussed here seem to have been compilations of references and stories drawn from other morality books or ledgers rather than original productions. For example, Chen Zhixi, author of the *Complete Book of Exhortations and Admonitions*, speaks of his work as that of a compiler: impressed by the virtuous sayings contained in works like the *Record for Gaining Good Fortune*, the *Extension of Benevolence (Guangren)*, the *Reform of Errors (Zuofei)*, and the *Resolution to Do Good (Daojian)*, he excerpted what was most useful from these works, corrected their errors, and updated their stories. The *Complete Book* was the fruit of these efforts. Chen minimized his own contribution here: although he borrowed stories and allusions from other works, the whole conception and arrangement of the work were clearly his. But it is equally clear that by this time the ledgers involved considerable research in other moral texts, for Chen listed no fewer than forty-nine titles in his bibliography of works consulted. See "*Quanjie quanshu* xiaoyin," 2a; and "Caiyong gujin shumu," in *Quanjie quanshu, ce* 1.

[3] *Fujian tongzhi*, 214.25b; see also Sakai Tadao, "Gan Moken no shisō ni tsuite," pp. 261–262.

[4] Jacques Gernet, *China and the Christian Impact: A Conflict of Cultures*, p. 11.

[5] This information is from Huang Zongxi's eulogy to Chen Xigu in *Beizhuan ji*, 44.25a–26b; see also *Yin xianzhi*, 42.1a–2a.

[6] Zhou Lianggong, "Xu," 5a–b, *Chongxiu zhiyao*. Zhou also explains that *Chongxiu zhiyao* was not completed at the time of Li's death, and that the final version was prepared by his son, Yuanxing. See "Xu," 3a–4b.

[7] *Guochao qixian leizheng (chubian)*, 382.45a–47b; and *Suzhou fuzhi*, 95.13a.

tions, nothing is known but that he was from Changzhou, Southern Zhili, and that he failed repeatedly to pass the examinations.[8] Xiong Hongbei remains a completely obscure figure.

These authors were aided by groups of consultants or critics (*canding, jianding*) and financial contributors. While Yuan Huang's *Ledger* and Yunqi Zhuhong's *Record of Self-Knowledge* were individual and to some extent personal works, these new texts tended to be group efforts.[9] Contributors were drawn largely from the local community, though on occasion they might include scholars or officials from other parts of China who had formed friendships with the author, often while serving in his native place. Indeed, sometimes quite distinguished officials and scholars appeared on the roster of a ledger's supporters. The *Record for Gaining Good Fortune* lists Wen Zhenmeng (1574–1636), a Hanlin compiler and senior director of instruction to the Chongzhen emperor; Gu Xichou (j.s. 1619), head of the Ministry of Rites in the Chongzhen era; and Qi Biaojia (1602–1645), a prominent official and Ming loyalist (and student of Liu Zongzhou), to name just a few of the best known.[10] The *Essentials of Self-Cultivation* was compiled with the assistance of several distinguished officials and scholars of the early Qing, including Zhou Lianggong (1612–1672), famous for both his literary talent and his military successes against the rebel Zheng Chenggong (1624–1662), and Yao Shisheng (j.s. 1658), a well-known scholar who placed second in the 1658 examinations for the *jinshi* degree.[11] Many other consultants for the seventeenth-

[8] Chen Zhixi, "Xiaoyin," 2b–3a, *Quanjie quanshu*.

[9] It is difficult to assess how important a role these various "consultants" played in the actual production of the morality books and ledgers. Presumably, some, particularly the more famous, simply lent the prestige of their names in support of the effort, at the most contributing a laudatory preface or a donation toward the publication costs. But it is possible that some participated more directly in the production of the morality books, perhaps helping in the compilation process by lending out useful texts or passing on stories or personal experiences particularly revealing of the operation of retribution.

What interest did all these people have in the publication of the ledgers? Unfortunately, those who simply made financial contributions did not necessarily leave explicit explanations of their motives. On occasion, however, the texts stated the purpose of individual donations: "to cure a mother's illness" or to pass the examinations, and so forth. (See, for example, Zhou Dingchen, "Yinsong xiangshi," in *(Zengding) Jingxin lu*, 1a–4a.) Thus some sponsors were in part interested in earning merit for themselves. Doubtless social pressures to participate in a community project headed by a member of the local elite also played a role in encouraging contributions of funds toward ledger publication.

[10] For other notable supporters of Yan's *Record*, see Sakai, "Gan Moken," pp. 259–262.

[11] Arthur Hummel, ed., *Eminent Chinese of the Ch'ing Period*, pp. 173–174; *Beizhuan ji*, 10.21a–23a and 89.12b–14a. Li compiled his ledger after consulting fourteen different sources, and he was aided by a total of fifty assistants—sixteen consultants and thirty-four "editors." Many of these were officials noted to varying degrees for their efforts to maintain order amid the unsettled conditions of life after the Manchu conquest. Zhou Lianggong, as a rebel-queller, obviously fits into this category; Yao Shisheng, though perhaps best known

century ledgers were local officials or degree-holders, but the largest number were obscure figures who assisted in ledger production apparently in expectation of reward: "to ensure passage of the district examination," as one hopeful contributor explained.[12] Sometimes a whole community might cooperate in ledger publication. For example, the *Ledger of Merit and Demerit for Spreading Goodness (Guangshan pian gongguoge)*, published in Liaoning in the early eighteenth century, lists a restaurant and a religious society along with forty-three other local contributors, including twenty-nine Chinese and Manchu bannermen and one reputed Hanlin academician.[13]

The ledgers of the seventeenth and eighteenth centuries, then, were compiled by authors from all levels of the educated elite, from failed examination candidates to successful scholar-officials, who were "assisted" by groups, sometimes local communities, of consultants and financial

as a scholar and literary man, was also honored for his service as judge in Qiongzhou prefecture (Hainan), particularly for his administration of famine relief and his suppression of a military rebellion there. Qian Guangzhu, another consultant, gained only the *juren* degree (1642), but his skill in scattering bandits in his native place after the fall of the Ming, and perhaps his tact in allowing the credit to go to the official in charge, earned him the attention of the Qing government. He was given a post in the Ministry of Works and sent to Yangzhou, where he managed to expel the "corrupt officials, litigious pettifoggers and mountain bandits" who were disrupting the city. (See *Taicang zhouzhi*, 20.2a.) Several other consultants—Wang Kun (j.s. 1652), Liao Yingzhao (j.s. 1659), Tang Qisheng (j.s. 1659), Wang Younian (j.s. 1659), Zhang Shiren (j.s. 1661), and Su Rulin (j.s. 1652)—were also noted for their skill in local administration, in the settlement of disputes, in ensuring fair tax collection, and in offering relief to the people during periods of economic hardship. Cai Fangbing, son of the loyalist Cai Maode (1586–1644), who died defending Taiyuan, Shanxi, against Li Zicheng, never achieved an official position but was a noted scholar of the Cheng–Zhu school and the author of several political texts. (See *Guochao qixian leizheng [chubian]*, 119.9a, 247.29b–30a, 340.39a–b; *Nanfeng xianzhi*, 25.4b; *Fuzhou fuzhi*, 55.13a–b, 62.5a–b; Hummel, *Eminent Chinese of the Ch'ing Period*, p. 622.) Three others also held official positions: Zheng Xiu (j.s. 1652) became an investigating censor, Gui Hong (j.s. 1655), a secretary in the Ministry of Rites, and You Minggui (j.s. 1658), a prefect for Songjiang prefecture. Most of the other assistants for the collection appear, rather like the contributors to the *Record for Gaining Good Fortune*, to have been residents of Jinxi, Li's native county, or neighboring Linchuan county, at the most distinguished for local service or extraordinary virtue. Gui Shengmai, for example, the author of a preface to the *Essentials of Self-Cultivation*, was noted for his exceptional filial piety; he was awarded a banner in commemoration of his practice of this virtue in 1725. (See *Suzhou fuzhi*, 88.27b.)

[12] "Yinsong xingshi," 1a–4a, in Zhou Dingchen, *(Zengding) Jingxin lu*.

[13] *Kuangshan gongguoge*, the last three folio pages. Or, to give another example, the Kangxi edition of the *Huizuan gongguoge* was funded by members of the Qingpu county community—8 of the 150 names listed in the ledger have brief biographies in the local gazetteer; they are noted either for their extraordinary filial piety and virtue, or for scholarly achievement. See *Qingpu xianzhi*, 29.9a–b (Qu Rangong), 29.15b–16a (Ye Zhiqi), 29.25b–26a (Sun Qi), 30.2a (Shao Shigao), 30.2a–3b (Wang Yuan, j.s. 1688), 30.4a (Sun Hong), 30.6b–7a (Jin Shiqi), and 30.13a (Wu Zhouhong).

sponsors. Though it is impossible to assess fully the social composition of these assistants, they did include well-established and even eminent officials as well as men who left no record but that of their purchase of a few ledger pages.

By and large, these new ledger authors and supporters had intellectual sympathies very different from those of Yuan Huang and his associates. Yan Maoyou, author of the *Record for Gaining Good Fortune*, was himself a member of the Restoration Society, and many of his more famous advisers—Gu Xichou, Wen Zhenmeng, Qi Biaojia, Lin Han (j.s. 1616, d. 1636), Wang Daokun (j.r. 1621), and Wei Chengrun (j.s. 1628)—had been supporters of the Donglin partisans, and hence opponents of the Taizhou school.[14] Most ledger authors and their assistants favored the more orthodox approach to learning and moral cultivation—that is, the approach of the Cheng-Zhu school of Neo-Confucianism. Chen Xigu, for example, author of the *Compendium of Ledgers of Merit and Demerit*, was a devoted follower of Zhu Xi and an ardent investigator of the principles of things. His friend Huang Zongxi reported that even in his last illness he would stay up late reading, to complete his exhaustive study of principle in all its manifestations.[15] Other ledger advocates began to advertise the texts as practical guides to the "extension of knowledge" (*zhizhi*), as translations of the abstract principles of the Classics into concrete rules for everyday use;[16] few authors claimed, as Yuan Huang had, that they were keys to the realization of the individual's innate knowledge of the good. Some ledgers were even modeled on Zhu Xi's program of learning: Hu Rongshi, in his *Collection of Ledgers of Merit and Demerit*, explained, "In using this ledger, people can go from the curriculum of 'lesser learning' (*xiaoxue*) up step by step to the Way of the sages. The order follows Zhu Xi's *Lesser Learning* and *Reflections on Things at Hand* (*Jinsi lu*)."[17]

[14] Sakai, "Gan Moken," pp. 263–266.

[15] *Beizhuan ji*, 44.26a.

[16] Chen Xigu includes a category of deeds for "the extension of knowledge" in his ledger for self-cultivation ("Xiushen ge") in the *Huizuan gongguoge*; see also Xu Ben, "Xu," 1a–b, *Liming gongguoge*.

Perhaps the best example of a ledger devoted to the encouragement of Neo-Confucian self-cultivation is Chen Hu's (1613–1675) *Primer for Sagely Learning (Shengxue rumen shu* or *Shengxue rumen)*, which is organized around the steps of the Neo-Confucian self-cultivation program extracted by Zhu Xi from the *Greater Learning*. The first part, the "Curriculum for Greater Learning" ("Daxue richeng"), for example, is broken down into the following steps: "the extension of knowledge" (*gezhi zhi xue*), "truthfulness" (*chengyi zhi xue*), "the rectification of the mind" (*zhengxin zhi xue*), "self-cultivation" (*xiushen zhi xue*), "aiding the world" (*qijia zhi xue*), and "bringing about peace" (*zhiping zhi xue*). See Chen, *Shengxue rumen shu*, 3b–4a, 19a–27a; and Sakai, *Chūgoku zensho*, pp. 388–389.

[17] Hu Rongshi, "Tiyao," 1b–2a, *Huibian gongguoge*.

It is by no means the case that all these ledger authors were supporters of the Cheng-Zhu

These changes in ledger authorship and production point up a shift in the elite conception of the social implications of the ledgers of merit and demerit. Over the course of the seventeenth and early eighteenth centuries, there was a marked change among those who wrote, edited, and funded the ledgers in the understanding of how the texts might function in society. Just as Yuan Huang had transformed the meaning of the merit-demerit system in the late sixteenth century, so too his successors shifted yet again the social goals of the system. Yuan Huang had urged the aspiring scholar-official to use the ledgers to perfect himself and thus get ahead in the world; the new authors of the seventeenth and eighteenth centuries delivered the same message to the individual ledger-user—they continued to assure him that he could indeed advance his status through merit accumulation. But this message now was part of their larger concern with ensuring social stability, with regulating, even containing, social mobility. Their conception of ledger use reflected an interpretation of retribution and a view of the ideal society much closer to the vision of the Donglin thinkers than to that of Yuan Huang. Thus, while none of these men ever repudiated Yuan Huang—indeed, he continued to be invoked as one of the great moral authorities behind the ledger system[18]—they did nonetheless conceive of the ledgers as fulfilling a social function much broader than that of simply "determining the fate" of the individual user. The texts now became encyclopedias of proper behavior, designed to guide anyone and everyone in the conduct appropriate to his or her place in society. Over the course of the seventeenth century, then, the ledgers became comprehensive blueprints for the reform of a society perceived as disordered and morally corrupt.

---

school. Chen Xigu, author of the *Compendium of Ledgers of Merit and Demerit*, clearly taught the principles of this school in his ledger, but Yan Maoyou announced in his *Record* that he was a follower of Wang Yangming. Many of the authors seemed to want to suggest that their texts were flexible enough to be employed in a variety of different methods. A remarkably wide range of authorities, including members of opposing philosophical schools, might be cited in these later works to support their method of self-cultivation. Li Guochang, for example, quotes Zhu Xi, Lu Xiangshan (1139–1192), Fan Zhongyan, Shao Yong, Chen Xianzhang (1428–1500), Xue Xuan (1389–1464), Wang Yangming, and Wang Gen (among others) in his ledger for the "regulation of the mind." Even ledger authors who did choose to affiliate themselves with one particular school tended to be generous in their reliance on a whole collection of different sources: Chen Xigu, for example, an avowed follower of the Cheng-Zhu school, nonetheless occasionally adduced passages from Wang Yangming to back up his prescriptions for self-cultivation. See Li Guochang, *Chongxiu zhiyao*, j. 10, passim; and Chen Xigu, *Huizuan gongguoge*, 3.15a.

[18] All or part of Yuan Huang's *Liming pian* was frequently included in later ledgers. See Yan Maoyou, *Diji lu*, 8.59a–63a; Chen Zhixi, *Quanjie quanshu*, 2.37a–49a; Chen Xigu, *Huizuan gongguoge*, j. *mo*, 4a–7a; Yan Zheng and Yan Yunlu, *Dangui ji*, 4.24a–42a; and "Quanshan pian," 103a–120a in *Tongshan lu*. Or, if his work was not cited directly, he was quoted as one of the "pioneers" of the system of merit accumulation. See, for example, Tao Ting and Tao Gong, *Guyi hui*, 13.1b–2a; and Li Guochang, *Chongxiu zhiyao*, passim.

Many ledger advocates, in explaining their motives for supporting ledger production, spoke openly of their concern about the disorder of the times and the evil effects it had on the lives and customs of the people, and of their despair at the inadequacy of the central authorities to deal with such disorder. Shen Yunzuo, writing in 1641, just before the fall of the Ming, saw Chen Zhixi's *Complete Book of Exhortations and Admonitions* as a work that would aid in bringing peace to an unsettled society: "In the world today, armies ravage the country, and the people are oppressed. The emperor seeks worthy men as a thirsty man searches for water. Here [Chen Zhixi] has devised broad plans for ruling the world and aiding the people, and he has also established teachings for the cultivation of virtue."[19] Chen himself seemed to share his friend's gloomy view of current affairs, as well as his conviction that private, nonofficial efforts to disseminate morality books and ledgers of merit and demerit might cure contemporary ills. "Alas!" he complained, "These days people's minds are getting worse and worse, all because they do not know these exhortations and admonitions. The best way to rescue people from the decline in mores is to use the way of retribution (*baoying*) to hold back flood and beat back fire."[20]

Gu Xichou, in an undated preface to the *Record for Gaining Good Fortune*, much more explicitly emphasized the connection between the ledgers and social and political reform: "Now our sagely emperor is reforming the various institutions of government; both the court and the people are anxious, fearing only that this effort will fail. . . . But it seems that [his ministers] have not yet been able to arouse the natural goodness in the people. Even if one guides the people with virtue and orders them with ritual, one cannot get results in a day. These methods are not as good as using the doctrine of good and bad fortune to move people, for it is easier to understand. Thus this book should be published without the slightest delay."[21] Here Gu envisioned the morality books as performing almost a political function; in the moral vacuum created by the failure of leadership, these texts could aid the emperor in leading the people to proper behavior. Gu was not far wrong in his recognition of impending crisis: the Ming dynasty was on its last legs by the time the *Record* was published.

Even after the ultimate political disaster, the fall of the dynasty in 1644, ledger supporters continued to bemoan the moral failings of their times and to suggest that morality books might correct some of these. Li Ruding, in his 1666 preface to Li Guochang's *Essentials of Self-Cultivation*, wisely eschewed any specific political criticism but attacked both the ig-

[19] Shen Yunzuo, "*Quanjie quanshu* shu," 5a–b, in Chen Zhixi, *Quanjie quanshu*.
[20] Chen Zhixi, "*Ganying pian zhu* xiaoyin," *Quanjie quanshu*, 1.2a.
[21] Gu Xichou, "*Dijilu* xu," 4b–5a, in Yan Maoyou, *Diji lu*.

norance of contemporary scholars and the corruption of general public morals:

> The book industry is in dire straits these days. The Six Classics, the twenty-one histories, the authorities on the Classics—these are not read. There are even those who cannot say the titles of these works. Of the books that fill the shops, half are plagiarisms and copies of examination themes, all claiming that they were selected by so-and-so or so-and-so who passed the examinations. Superficial and vulgar scholars gather in the shops, as if attracted by barking dogs. If it is said that the essays were well selected, then there is a market for them; if it is said that they were poorly selected, there is no market. This is the way false studies are encouraged.
>
> Even worse than these texts are licentious sayings and love songs, the fictitious "histories," romances, and novels that are published and circulated. Thus, after *Water Margin* (*Shuihu zhuan*) was published, villains frequently gathered in the greenwood, and after *Golden Lotus* (*Jin Ping Mei*) came out, there were nightly elopements from the women's quarters. Such works are the means of instructing thieves and licentious women. . . . They really do great harm to the manners, morals, and minds of the people. The honored [Li Guochang] was sorrowful and hurt at this situation, and thought of a way to correct it by distributing earlier moral works throughout the world.

The ledgers were valuable because they could teach people, particularly young people, the values appropriate to their station in life:

> In urging people today to read [Li's] work, I say to students of the Classics that it affirms the profound writings of the ancient philosophers; it can fill out the limited experience of students and refine their writing style. To children of the common people, it sets forth historical cases in support of retribution, each with clear proof; it can teach filial piety, reverence, and yielding; it can protect people against heterodoxy and affirm sincerity. It would not be necessary to read even one of the reprinted examination essays, and all works instructing thieves and prostitutes could be taken and burned. If we follow this work, there will be no heterodox studies, and the country's customs will not be divided. How can [Li's] work not be magnificent? All that I have said is likewise for the sake of improving the manners, morals, and minds of the people.[22]

Hu Rongshi, author of the *Collection of Ledgers of Merit and Demerit*, like Gu Xichou, saw the ledgers as texts that might aid the ruler in his efforts to educate and civilize the people. Quoting no less an authority on this subject than the emperor Ming Shizong (r. 1521–1567), Hu explained the special value of the morality books: "There is nothing to be ashamed of in these words, for not only do they support the Classics of

[22] Li Ruding, "Xu," 1a–2b, *Chongxiu zhiyao*.

the sages, but they also supplement the civilizing effects of government (*wanghua*)."[23] Xu Ben (j.s. 1718), the editor of the *Ledger of Merit and Demerit for Determining Your Own Fate* (*Liming gongguoge*, prefaces dated 1747 and 1748), even more baldly argued that the ledgers were ways of "forcing people to behave correctly."[24]

The ledger advocates of the seventeenth and eighteenth centuries, then, explicitly emphasized the broad educational value of the texts. While Yuan Huang had offered the individual user a sure-fire way to moral transformation and material success, these men viewed the ledgers rather as means to the moral transformation of society as a whole, as a way of aiding in the general "civilizing" effects of government. Certainly Yuan Huang would never have denied that use of his *Ledger* would also have this generally ameliorative effect, but his focus was openly on individual self-advancement, not societywide reform. And while the ledgers of the seventeenth and eighteenth centuries still encouraged individual moral improvement, just as Yuan Huang had, they now expressed a larger concern: the dissemination of the ledger message to all people, so that the resulting improvement in the behavior of many individuals would end in a collective transformation of social mores, a change in the moral quality of society as a whole, and, perhaps more to the point, the restoration of a stable order.

Along with this reorientation in the conception of ledger usefulness went an important, though subtle, change in the treatment of retribution. Certainly, the idea that man was rewarded for his good deeds and punished for his bad acts was preserved through the later ledgers of merit and demerit; it remained, as before, the foundation of ledger use. And, as before, in the stories recounted to illustrate the system in these texts, rewards were bestowed by a wide variety of spirits on those who did good. *Meritorious Deeds at No Cost* urged its users not to lose faith in retributive justice no matter what the provocation: "Even if you see that the good sometimes suffer bad fortune and you yourself experience poverty, do not let it discourage you from doing good; even if you see bad men prosper, do not lose faith in ultimate recompense."[25]

If we look just at the body of the ledger texts, then, it appears that the later ledger authors held Yuan Huang's zealous commitment to the belief in retribution. But these men did not, in fact, always fully share his enthusiasm for the idea; if we read the prefaces to their ledgers, where they were setting forth their own understanding of ledger use, we find that for the most part they shared the Donglin thinkers' ambivalence about the no-

---

[23] Hu Rongshi, "Tiyao," 5a–b, *Huibian gongguoge*. For more on this ledger, see Sakai, *Chugoku zensho*, p. 386.

[24] Xu Ben, "Xu," 1a–b, *Liming gongguoge*.

[25] Xiong Hongbei, *Bufeiqian gongdeli*, in Chen, *Xunsu yigui*, 4.50b.

tion of divine recompense. Many treated the idea simply as an expedient means of getting people of only mediocre intellectual and moral abilities to behave well. Li Hao, for example, in a preface (dated 1702) to an early eighteenth-century edition of the *Collection of Ledgers of Merit and Demerit*, excuses the use of retribution in the following terms:

> Someone has said, "Good people correct themselves to do what is right, and do not plot their own profit. They understand the Way and do not calculate merits. If they record items in a ledger, by and large one would see that the merit places are few and the demerit places many [i.e., these people are more aware of their faults than their virtues]. But for a man to consider his own merits and demerits clustered together [in such a ledger]—doesn't it stimulate a careless and opportunistic attitude not in accord with the teachings of the sages?" But I say that this is not the case. Throughout the world only the most intelligent people understand the Way. As for men of medium-range intelligence and below, if one does not waken and shock them with great cries and urgent summons, it is not enough to jolt them from deafness and arouse them from blindness. Therefore this book, as soon as it is published, can act as a herald's bell, as a slogan over one's desk, as a boat on a rough sea, as a blow from Buddha's stick.[26]

So, too, Gu Xichou, in the passage from his preface to the *Record for Gaining Good Fortune* quoted above, sees the "doctrine of good and bad fortune" as a convenient and easy way of "moving the people." He makes a point of reassuring the reader that his friend Yan Maoyou, the author of the *Record*, does not himself believe in doing good for reward, but is simply using the idea to "arouse people to pursue [goodness]."[27] Thus these ledger authors, in contrast to Yuan Huang, define different motivations for good behavior, largely on the basis of social standing: the common people do good only for reward, while the morally superior gentleman does good only for its own sake.

But it is not always clear whether these men themselves actually disavowed the belief in retribution itself or simply felt that it was not an appropriate ground of action for "gentlemen," for men of their education and status. Few seemed really to question the validity of the concept itself. Chen Xigu, in his *Compendium of Ledgers of Merit and Demerit*, explained, "When a gentleman does good, he does all that he ought to do and that is all; he does not expect that he will be rewarded by heaven. When he gets rid of evil, he stops doing anything that he should not do and that is all; he does not fear misfortune from the spirits." Unfortunately, "today, there is about one person in the whole world who does

---

[26] Li Hao, "*Huibian gongguoge* xu," 2b–3a, *Huibian gongguoge*.

[27] Gu Xichou, "*Diji lu* xu," 3a–b, *Diji lu*. This disavowal seems a little forced, for Yan Maoyou's own preface to the *Diji lu* is an explication and defense of the principles of retribution, cast very much in Buddhist terms.

good without expecting reward, and who does not do evil without fearing punishment. I know that it is certainly impossible to use such a man as an example for the people. To force them to do good is certainly not possible, and in the end will make those who do good in the world few and those who do not do good many. Then how can one explain the need to do good, using a principle that does not deceive? Lead them with what they desire and frighten them with what they fear—this is the way."[28] Chen did not deny the operation of retribution—it was a "principle that does not deceive" people, and he quoted the *Classic of Changes* and the *Classic of History* in support of the belief. But he adopted an attitude toward retribution typical of most of these ledger authors and preface-writers—true scholars and "gentlemen" did not need rewards and punishments to encourage them to do good and avoid evil, but most people, those of the middle class and lower, did require such a belief as a spur to good behavior. Chen actually carried this claim through the body of his *Compendium* as well: in the section of his ledger devoted to the behavior of scholars, he told no stories of virtue rewarded, in line with his insistence that the superior man do good without thought of profit. Such men, we are led to assume, do not need the assurances of retribution required by lesser men. Ultimately, then, in these texts the promise of rewards for good deeds was justified in a sense as a teaching technique: it motivated people to learn and practice goodness.

In invoking the concept of retribution as a stimulus to moral improvement, the ledger authors were by and large careful to distinguish even their contingent and limited understanding of the concept from what they believed to be the debased Buddhist and Daoist notions of retribution. But they confessed that they were willing to make use of these "superstitious" ideas simply because they were likely to have a wider popular appeal. Like Gao Panlong, many seemed to feel that the true Confucian doctrine of *ganying*, "action and response," was too abstruse for most people; hence one had to rely on stories of "ghosts and spirits to make one's point." Thus Li Ruding defended Li Guochang's use of the Buddhist and Daoist doctrine of retribution in his *Essentials of Self-Cultivation*: "Buddhist doctrines cannot be accepted [as true], but are easy to understand; Daoist doctrines cannot be accepted [as true], but they appeal to the peasants. They certainly have limitless value as means of guiding the masses and the ignorant."[29] So, too, Chen Xigu, who in the preface to his *Compendium* repudiates the Buddhist and Daoist concepts of *yinguo* and *baoying* as "perverted and shallow,"[30] nonetheless relies, in the body of

[28] Chen Xigu, "Xu," 1a–2a, *Huizuan gongguoge*.
[29] Li Ruding, "Xu," 3a–b, *Chongxiu zhiyao*.
[30] Chen Xigu, "Xu," 4b, *Huizuan gongguoge*.

his ledger, on extensive quotations from Buddhist scriptures and Daoist works and on stories describing the operation of karma and the retributive manipulations of a large collection of ghosts and spirits. Yuan Huang was quite willing to accept the Buddhist elements in Yungu's system of merit and demerit, but these ledger authors feel the need to explain the frequent Buddhist and Daoist allusions in their ledgers as concessions to the limits of popular imagination, as yet another aspect of a moral teaching technique. The people would respond to the belief in retribution only if it were tied to cherished Buddhist and Daoist "popular superstitions."

The gentleman, in contrast, needed only the reassurance of the Classics and the great Confucians of the past to be persuaded on the value of the ledgers, or so the new ledger authors suggested. While explaining away the Buddhist and Daoist attachments of the ledgers, they were eager to give the texts new and fuller Confucian sanctions. They began to claim support for ledger use from famous Northern Song Confucians: Fan Zhongyan (989–1052) and Zhang Jun (1097–1164) both, as one author put it, "reverently and sincerely" practiced merit accumulation.[31] More subtly, the whole weight of the historical and philosophical tradition was brought into the texts to justify the message of the ledgers—a wide range of moral authorities was quoted, and the stories told to illustrate ledger prescriptions were now drawn from famous incidents in Chinese history as well as from the contemporary events and personal cases Yuan Huang liked to quote.

But the ledger authors took their claims for Confucian sanction even further than this. Yuan Huang and Yungu relied on quotations from the earliest Classics—the *Classic of Songs*, the *Classic of History*, the *Classic of Changes*, and the *Spring and Autumn Annals*—as well as on a very free reading of *Mencius* to justify their system of merit and demerit. The later ledger authors relied on these same allusions (though most wisely dropped references to the *Mencius* text), but they went one step beyond this argument to compare the ledgers to the Classics, to suggest that the

[31] "Xinlu," 4a, *Riqian chushe*; Chen Zhixi, *Quanjie quanshu*, 2.1b. It is possible that the ledger authors are suggesting a real intellectual affinity here, asserting a link between the concrete ethical and statecraft concerns of the "practical" Neo-Confucians of the Northern Song and the practical moral orientation of the ledgers. It is also possible that the association is the result of confusion about the authorship of both the *Tract of Taishang on Action and Response* and the *Ledger of Merit and Demerit of the Taiwei Immortal*. The former text was attributed to Li Shi, whose *hao* was Changling. Li Changling was the name of the father-in-law of Fan Zhongyan, one of the great "practical" Confucian reformers of the Sung. It was thus easy for later scholars to assume that Fan's father-in-law had produced the work. The author of the *Ledger* had been mistakenly taken to be Zhen Dexiu because Zhen's *hao*, Xishan, forms part of the colophon to the text (referring in this case, however, to a place); Zhen was also associated with the "practical" Neo-Confucianism of the Song. See Yoshioka, *Dōkyō no kenkyū*, pp. 73–80; and Sakai, *Chūgoku zensho*, pp. 366–371.

ledgers offered the same kind of instruction found in the sacred texts of Confucianism. "I see that the contents of this ledger explain many of the subtle meanings and profound statements of the sages and worthies," explained Chen Xigu of his *Compendium*: "it also accords with the doctrines of the Classics and their commentaries. It can serve to uphold the basic human relationships, to rectify men's minds, and to harmonize this generation with the great Way."[32] Zhang Qi, in a preface dated 1671, claimed that the *Collection of Ledgers of Merit and Demerit* would help a reader "understand the principles of the hidden teachings of the Six Classics and of the subtle discussions of all Confucians of the past."[33] Xu Ben, author of the *Ledger of Merit and Demerit for Determining Your Own Fate*, also saw the ledgers as a key to the Classics; they were the "string that connects the scattered cash of all the Classics." More specifically, he compared his own ledger, the *Ledger of Merit and Demerit for Determining Your Own Fate*, to the *Spring and Autumn Annals*: "[My ledger] is closest in essence to the *Spring and Autumn Annals*. The *Annals* is a praise and blame text. [Similarly,] those who use this ledger judge reward and punishment in their own minds; they cannot tolerate self-delusion or unwarranted praise in secret. They dare not deceive themselves."[34] The ledgers, then, as lists of specific good and bad deeds, simply and explicitly stated, were seen as handy guides to the real meaning of the more prescriptive of the Confucian Classics.[35] Just as the *Spring and Autumn Annals* pointed up the moral lessons of history by singling out some figures for praise and others for blame, so too the ledgers, in distinguishing clearly between good and bad behavior and in illustrating these distinctions in stories from history, helped readers to make the appropriate moral choices in their own lives. But the ledgers had the advantage of being more accessible than the Classics: they distilled the moral essence of the Classics into a form appealing not only to scholars but also to those of "middling" abilities.

There were also striking changes in the size and organization of the ledgers from the seventeenth and eighteenth centuries, changes that reflect the authors' new perceptions of ledger function. Over the course of the seventeenth century the ledgers became much longer and much fuller, covering a gradually widening range of human relationships and behavior. Yuan Huang's *Ledger* consisted of a mere hundred deeds, none very fully explained, ordered according to merit-demerit point value. The pre-

---

[32] Chen Xigu, "Xu," 4a–b, *Huizuan gongguoge*.

[33] Zhang Qi, "Xu," 2a, *Huibian gongguoge*.

[34] Xu Ben, "Xu," 1b–2a, *Liming gongguoge*; see also Li Ruding, "Xu," 4a–5a, *Chongxiu zhiyao*.

[35] It is probably no coincidence that these were the very Classics that were becoming popular again among serious scholars in the early Qing. See Pi Xirui, *Jingxue lishi*, pp. 287–297.

scriptions described charitable behavior or personal acts of compassion and self-discipline, with a few deeds of religious devotion. Both the *Record for Gaining Good Fortune* and the *Complete Book of Exhortations and Admonitions* have relatively brief ledgers, but they are embedded in detailed ten- and twelve-*juan* morality books that provide real-life cases and stories illustrative of the types of deeds in the ledgers. The deeds, now arranged topically, include a much fuller range of activities: the *Record*, for example, listed deeds under sections entitled "filial obedience" (*xiaoshun*), "harmony" (*hemu*), "teaching of compassion" (*cijiao*), "leniency to inferiors" (*kuanxia*), "education" (*quanhua*), "charity" (*jiuji*), "exchanges of property" (*xiaocai*), "extravagance and frugality" (*shejian*), "personal conduct" (*xingxing*), "reverence for the sages" (*jingsheng*), and "regulation of the mind" (*cunxin*). Like the *Complete Book*, it also includes a special ledger for officials ("Dangguan gongguoge").[36]

By the late seventeenth century, long ledgers—one over 850 folio pages—began to be published independently, with annotations and illustrative stories incorporated into the ledger form itself. The *Essentials of Self-Cultivation* of Li Guochang is the first of the ledgers to stand on its own in this way, but the largest and most complex of this type is the *Compendium of Ledgers of Merit and Demerit*. Its author, Chen Xigu, wrote it in response to what he felt was a need for a fuller guide to proper conduct:

> The original ledger of the Taiwei Immortal contains only a rough outline of deeds, and its users must extrapolate other deeds from its categories. It has been transmitted over a long period, during which the worthies of earlier times have expanded and edited it, refining its rules so that people could easily follow it. . . . I have researched all the different editions, carefully chosen among them, divided their contents into categories of deeds, and set forth each in detail, so that there are neither omissions nor repetitions. . . . I have added supporting quotations, evidence, notes, and explanations to the text. The development of the ledgers of merit and demerit has reached its greatest achievement with this work.[37]

Chen is quite correct: his is the fullest of all the ledgers surviving from the seventeenth century. Twelve-*juan* long, with two extra chapters of introductory and concluding materials, it is the most comprehensively annotated of all the ledgers. Each deed may be followed by a "general discussion" (*zonglun*), explaining the significance and the order of the deed, an "added note" (*zengzhu*), distinguishing the deed from others like it, an "extension of meaning" (*guangyi*), a fuller discussion of the deed, a "clar-

---

[36] Yan Mayou, *Diji lu*, 8.64a–71a, 4.80a–84b; see Sakai, *Chūgoku zensho*, pp. 378–383.
[37] Chen Xigu, "Fanli," 1a, *Huizuan gongguoge*; cited in Sakai, *Chūgoku zensho*, p. 392.

ification" (faming), providing supporting material from the Classics or other writings, "evidence" (zhengshi), giving real examples of action on the deed, or an "appendix" (fulu), including whatever other comments Chen wished to add.[38] Here the ledger has indeed almost become a Classic, as Zhang Lixiang had bitterly predicted: Chen lavished as much attention on the annotation of his ledger as would normally be reserved for a sacred text or more distinguished work of philosophy. Every effort was made to ensure that the reader understood the importance and the nature of each deed.

Chen, in the organization of his ledger, reveals the same interest in comprehensive coverage shown by Yan Maoyou. His ledger contained a section on household relationships ("Jinlun ge"), further subdivided into deeds for parents, uncles, brothers, wives, children, other relatives, servants, and masters; one on self-cultivation, including categories for "the extension of knowledge," "regulation of the mind," proper behavior, language, sexual desires, property, service to the gods, and the "preservation of good fortune" (xifu); and one on relationships with others ("Yuren ge"), divided among deeds for social intercourse (jiaojie), charity, and education. There follows a series of "special subject" ledgers, for "loving all creatures" ("Aiwu ge"), for craftsmen, for "meritorious deeds costing money" ("Feiqian gongdeli"), for women, and for officials.

Ledger authors after Chen tended to favor compact abridgments of the long ledgers of the late seventeenth century. In the early eighteenth century a somewhat condensed version of the Compendium was published, the Summary of the Ledgers of Merit and Demerit (Gongguoge jiyao; preface dated 1717). Its author, an obscure scholar named Li Shida, explained that though he greatly admired Chen's Compendium, he found it too cumbersome for daily use, and so edited out some of the more esoteric notes.[39] Thirty years later, an even more reduced version, Xu Ben's Ledger of Merit and Demerit for Determining Your Own Fate, was published, again to enhance the usability of the ledger form.[40] Finally, within two decades of Xu Ben's ledger, a Jiang Wenlan produced the Record of Enlightenment (Chenzhong lu; preface dated 1763), a short four-juan morality book and ledger drawing heavily on earlier texts, particularly the Complete Book of Exhortations and Admonitions. In making their abridgments, these authors did not sacrifice the comprehensive coverage offered in the Compendium. Both Li Shida and Xu Ben retained all of Chen's categories and deeds; they simply reduced the explanatory material. Even completely new ledgers reflect this dual concern for both com-

[38] Chen Xigu, "Fanli," 1b–2b, Huizuan gongguoge.
[39] Li Shida, "Xu," 1b–2a, Gongguoge jiyao; see Sakai, Chūgoku zensho, p. 394.
[40] See Sakai, Chūgoku zensho, pp. 394–395.

plete coverage and compactness. The *Ledger of Merit and Demerit of Lord Wenchang* (*Wenchang dijun gongguoge*; preface dated 1724), covers a fuller range of topics than even the *Compendium*, but because it is without annotations or explanations, it could be printed up in a compact and easily usable volume.

But it is a new type of ledger, one organized according to status group, that perhaps most fully reflected these concerns for both comprehensiveness and accessibility. *Meritorious Deeds at No Cost*, written by Xiong Hongbei, listed prescriptions for eleven different status levels within Chinese society: local gentry (*xiangshen*), scholars (*shiren*), peasants (*nongjia*), craftsmen (*baigong*), merchants (*shanggu*), physicians (*yijia*), yamen workers (*gongmen*), women (*funü*), soldiers (*shizu*), Buddhist and Daoist monks (*sengdao*), servants and laborers (*pubei gongyi*), and people in general (*dazhong*).[41] As the title suggests, the book claimed that one did not have to be rich to earn merit. Its message was: anyone and everyone could earn merit, even men unwilling or unable to "buy" merit. Of course Yuan Huang had also made this point in his stories about merit-accumulation; but what in Yuan's work had been a general concept, part of his "theory" of moral action, was now given concrete and practical expression in a more accessible form—*Meritorious Deeds at No Cost* was a compact, easily portable guide to inexpensive or "free" merit-making for just about any status or occupational group in Chinese society. Now the poor peasant or poor scholar who wanted to earn merit had a list of specific deeds to turn to for guidance.

While the scope of the ledger prescriptions was broadened to encompass behavior for all Chinese, so, too, the nature of the rewards promised for good behavior was adapted to suit a much wider variety of circumstances and hopes. Yuan Huang's subjects invariably earned status rewards—that is, examination degrees for themselves and/or their descendants. While success in the examinations remains one of the most popular rewards in the later ledgers, long life, cure of sickness, and rescue from natural disaster became alternative forms of recompense. Generous land-

---

[41] The most accessible version of this work is included in Chen Hongmou's *Xunsu yigui*, 4.43a–51a, in *Wuzhong yigui*.

Bufeiqian gongdeli is the most sophisticated early Qing ledger arranged by social status, but it is neither the first nor the only example of the type. The *Thirty-six Virtues of the Zuibi Tang* (*Zuibi Tang sanshiliu shan*) of Li Erjing (from Jinan, Shandong), also dating from the late seventeenth century, roughly follows conventional social divisions; it lists thirty-six prescriptions each for officials, gentry (*shenhuan*), scholars (*shixing*), merchants (*shanggu*), and peasants (*nongjia*). (It is revealing that merchants are here placed ahead of peasants, a reversal of the idealized order.) *Guangshan pian gongguoge*, written in the early eighteenth century, also includes a ledger organized by status and occupational groups, as does Shi Chengjin's *Chuan jiabao quanji sanji*. See Sakai, "Kōkakaku no kenkyū," pp. 38–39; his *Chūgoku zensho*, p. 397; and Okuzaki, *Chūgoku kyōshin jinushi*, pp. 8–9.

lords might be saved from fatal illnesses by the prayers of their grateful tenants to the local city god, or wealthy gentry who promoted famine relief find themselves living into their nineties. Wealth was still rarely offered as a reward, but there is one case of a merchant who recovered the amount of his contribution to a public works project: the gods did not make him wealthier, but they saw to it that he would not be poorer for his charity.[42] Religious rewards also became popular again. In one case a virtuous servant was elevated to the Western Paradise for his loyal service, and in another a good man was made the god of a mountain for his willingness to help a destitute man preserve his livelihood.[43] Recompense might even come in cosmetic form: one Xi Baisan, afflicted with an unsightly wen, gave two cash to a Daoist beggar (an act worth one merit), and that night his wen disappeared.[44] This greater variety in the types of rewards offered also served to open the ledgers out to a broader audience: those who had neither hope of nor desire for success in the examinations could find some goal more suitable to their station and situation.

Within a few decades of Yuan Huang's death, then, the ledgers of merit and demerit he had done so much to popularize underwent a transformation in sponsorship, form, and meaning. For Yuan the overriding goal of ledger use was worldly advancement for the individual user; moral action was the means to that end. His ledger, organized by point value, and his illustrations of successful merit accumulation served to advertise that a man—theoretically any man—could determine his own fate in this world through moral effort.

The ledger advocates of the seventeenth and early eighteenth centuries were much less concerned with the advancement of the individual ledger user; they were worried, rather, about the stability of the social order as a whole. The popular disturbances of the seventeenth century, ranging from relatively small-scale tenant and bondservant uprisings to large peasant rebellions, demonstrated quite brutally the fragility of the old order. Certainly, it had become impossible now to cherish the belief that the various parts of Chinese society, harmonized by relationships of mutual dependence and reciprocity between statuses, cohered into a stable and secure whole. Agricultural workers, in demanding contracts that recognized their growing economic influence, were in essence refusing to accept the paternalistic landowner-cultivator relationship that went with this vision. At the same time they were demanding new powers and contractual rights far beyond those previously associated with their local social (and in some cases, legal) status. To make matters worse, through most of the

---

[42] Chen Xigu, *Huizuan gongguoge*, 7.25a.
[43] Ibid., 7.25a–b.
[44] Ibid., 7.4a.

seventeenth century China lacked an effective central political authority—scholar-officials and local elites could not really rely on the government to restore order. Through the establishment of local benevolent societies and schools, the organization of community compacts and relief efforts, and, of course, the publication of morality books, these men took private action to do what had been considered the responsibility of the government. It is revealing that in the early Ming, morality-book production was largely under imperial auspices;[45] by the seventeenth century, most new morality books and ledgers were privately compiled and published.

Anxious over the demands of a society clearly pluralistic or "fragmented," as they would have put it, in its religious beliefs, moral values, and social ambitions, the ledger authors of the seventeenth century hoped to recreate the moral and social coherence they believed had at one time— in the early Ming—actually existed in Chinese society. The greater complexity of their ledgers—the definition of different motivations for good behavior and the proliferation of moral, social, and occupational categories, wider-ranging intellectual references, and more varied rewards— reflects a desire to recreate a coherent and unified order. These texts offered something for everyone. They would help restore order first by stating the different rules that applied to different social places, and then by defining the values of reciprocity and mutual dependence that, by mediating status relationships, stabilized the social hierarchy, securely glueing its different levels together. Thus the acknowledgment of some degree of pluralism would, paradoxically, encourage the final integration of the separate parts into a stronger, more stable order.

In sum, for the ledger advocates of the seventeenth and eighteenth centuries, maintenance of the social order was the major concern. Their ledgers, to be sure, outlined the same general system as Yuan Huang's work did. But in treating the doctrine of retribution not as an article of faith but as an expedient technique for luring the populace to goodness, they betrayed an uneasiness with the "ungentlemanly" opportunism of Yuan's Ledger—they suggested that they could uphold such a doctrine only if it contributed to a greater good, the moral education of the people. Without radically altering Yuan Huang's program of merit accumulation, they nonetheless shifted the focus of his system away from individual advance to the creation of a stable social and moral order. For Yuan this was certainly a desired effect of ledger use, but it was not its primary purpose; the ledger was first and foremost a guide for aspiring officials. The later ledger authors, however, saw this individual goal of status advance as simply a step to the achievement of their grander aim, the reform of cus-

[45] See Sakai, *Chūgoku zensho*, pp. 8–27.

tom and the regulation and coordination of the whole social order. If each individual followed the guidelines appropriate to his station to be found in the new, more comprehensive ledgers, then—whether he achieved his goal or not—all would be right with the world.

THE SOCIAL VISION OF THE LEDGERS OF MERIT AND DEMERIT

The major concern of the authors of the ledgers of merit and demerit of the seventeenth and eighteenth centuries was, then, the articulation and explication of rules of behavior for the moral education of all members of Chinese society. These ledgers express a comprehensive social vision, a program for social order supposedly derived by their authors from the profound meaning of the Classics.

This social order is presented as a creation or natural reflection of the moral order, the Way. The concept of retribution ensures that everyone will get what he deserves sooner or later; thus each person's place in society is simply a consequence of his moral stature. This view is of course implicit in Yuan Huang's system of merit and demerit as well. But Yuan chose to emphasize the other side of the belief in retribution—that is, the side that encourages self-advancement and material benefit. "The pursuit of good fortune and avoidance of bad depends on the individual," he proclaimed.[46] To be sure, Yuan accepted the hierarchical structure of Chinese society, but he saw it as a dynamic hierarchy. Only the individual's moral capacity limited his opportunities for movement up the scale of statuses. Like He Xinyin, he urged people on to the active "pursuit" of advancement. In his system, social ambition, because it could only be realized through moral improvement, was unquestionably both desirable and good. Although the ledgers of the seventeenth and eighteenth centuries also rested on this same principle of retribution—status rewards were still offered for good behavior—the emphasis on the social message of retribution has shifted. The point is that the social order literally *as it is* mirrors divine moral evaluation. Retribution does not as much encourage advance now as affirm the status quo. The gods put each person where he belongs, and will reward not the person who attempts to "transcend" this place, but the one who happily accepts it, cheerfully performing the duties appropriate to it.

These new ledger authors were concerned primarily with defining the types of behavior that would help in the preservation of the status quo. The individual ledger user might still hope to advance in status by using the ledgers, for these ledgers did indeed contain stories much like those in Yuan Huang's essays, demonstrating that such rewards were inevitable.

[46] Yuan Huang, *LMP*, 23b.

But from the broader perspective of the ledger authors, these demonstrations were a convenient means of getting "petty" men—that is, those unwilling to do good without the promise of reward—to act as they ought within their social place. These ledger authors looked beyond the issue of individual success or failure to the preservation of a finely balanced hierarchy in which everyone kept to his place or at most advanced very slowly, over generations, up the social scale. Stability was valued over change; change, when it occurred, had to be contained and regulated as carefully as possible.

Replacing Yuan's emphasis on advancement was a new effort to persuade ledger users to "rest in their status" (*anfen*) or "take pleasure in the fate bestowed by heaven" (*letian anming*).[47] Chen Zhixi, in his *Complete Book of Exhortations and Admonitions*, published just before the fall of the Ming, warned his readers against any attempts to change their livelihood or their residences—even travel here was seen as a potential evil, inviting thievery, fornication, fire, and so forth.[48] He included in his work a vernacular gloss on the Six Maxims by the unknown Li Changke that forcefully presented the case for accepting one's lot in life (and incidentally undermined the whole concept of retribution on which the *Complete Book* was based):

> "Be at ease with the constants—this is good fortune. Keep your place throughout your life." These words are perfect. One often sees men who have made a great deal of money running into all sorts of dangers and catastrophes—their situation is not as good as that of a petty merchant who contents himself with peace and stability. Often men who have ambitious and wild thoughts seek to move beyond their station—their situation is not as good as that of craftsmen or peasants who are pleased with their place over the long term. Thus the ancients say, "The myriad affairs of life do not originate in the plans of men; a life is all arranged by fate." If your fate (*mingyun*) is good, you need not seek to advance yourself, and if your fate is not good, you waste your effort in seeking advancement. Even if you chance to be lucky, in the end your ingenuity will fail, and, though you look high, you will fall low. The ghosts and spirits will forget you, and you will end up ruined. Therefore a man must follow his own livelihood, and rest his mind in that.[49]

Where Yuan assured man that he could change his own fate, Li suggests that he is at the mercy of his fate. And where Yuan urged the energetic "pursuit" of good fortune, Li warns that "you waste your effort in seeking advancement." Here, then, one gets ahead by not trying to get ahead.

---

[47] Li Guochang, *Chongxiu zhiyao*, 1.30a.
[48] Chen Zhixi, *Quanjie quanshu*, 4.38a–b.
[49] Li Changke, "Shengyu liuyan jie," in Chen Zhixi, *Quanjie quanshu*, 3.28a–29a.

Nor, Li argues, should people make the mistake of thinking that high status is necessarily desirable: "How do you know that employment at court is not difficult to accept? Those who are officials have their own 'official' problems, even more severe than those of you ordinary people (*nimen baixing*)." Other occupations are perfectly acceptable—not everyone should aim at officialdom:

> Outside of the scholarly profession, nothing is so good as farming. . . . Plant mulberry in the garden and cotton in the fields, and you have clothing. Raise fish in ponds and cattle at home, grow vegetables in your garden, and you have food. When there is flood or famine, plant more and harvest less—you can still make a living. Never setting eyes on a government office, never setting foot in a city market—you are a prime minister of the mountains, an immortal in this world. This is the best life. Why would you want to be an official? Even if your family has no land, you can rent several *mu* . . . and diligently plow and plant them. When done, you give several pints of rice in rent to the landlord. Even though you eat vegetables and plain food, it is still tastier than the rich food of the wealthy. Even though you wear coarse clothing, it is still warmer than the thin brocades of the wealthy. Furthermore, your wife is not arrogant and extravagant, and your sons and grandsons are not idle and licentious. There really are many advantages to farming.[50]

Li Guochang, author of the *Essentials of Self-Cultivation*, tries to explain away the conundrum presented in the passages above: how can one reconcile the belief in "establishing one's own fate" at the heart of the merit-accumulation system with the injunction to accept placidly one's appointed lot? In the section of his ledger devoted to this latter injunction, Li writes: "Now teaching that one enjoys moral rectitude by taking pleasure in heaven's command is the sages' doctrine of true destiny (*yun*). . . . Those who are at ease with their fate do not try to change it, but in truth can decide their own fate themselves, fulfilling the goodness in their minds, cultivating themselves, even developing the strength to view premature death and long life as one, awaiting fate without speaking of it and spontaneously developing a creative mind."[51] Here we have come full circle, back to Mencius's claim that for the gentleman only moral fate is controllable. These ledger authors preserve the notion of retribution, but it is used as a rationale now, not for status advancement, but for status containment. "Preserving simplicity and fulfilling the rules," as Li urges in another section,[52] man should trust in heaven without seeking to better his station. The process of retribution ensured that the social hierarchy

---

[50] Li Changke, "Ge an shengli," in ibid., 3.29a–b.
[51] Li Guochang, *Chongxiu zhiyao*, 1.40a–b.
[52] Ibid., 1.40a.

was a morally founded order, and thus these ledger authors concluded that movement within the hierarchy ought to be restricted as much as possible.

The Place of Servants

This concern with limiting social mobility emerges most vividly in the ledgers' and morality books' treatment of people in lower status positions and their relationship to their superiors. Servants received marked attention in the ledgers of the seventeenth and eighteenth centuries; some ledgers contained whole sections on the behavior of this group, and all devoted considerable space to the rules governing the servant-master relationship. The high incidence of bondservant rebellion and the number of legal conflicts involving servants in the period suggest that this relationship was a particularly sensitive one. Ledger writings on the place of servants thus provide a good case study of elite prescriptions for easing one of the major points of tension within the late Ming and early Qing social hierarchy.

Chen Xigu, in his ledger on "Servants' service to their masters" ("Jiapu shi jiazhu"), sets forth the highly ambivalent attitude representative of most ledger authors on the place and function of servants:

> To be a servant is still to be a man. It is a temporary status. What is there to be ashamed of? But often servants assume that their low status means that there is no principle by which they can gain prosperity or rank, and they do not take themselves seriously. This attitude reflects an ignorance of the principle of retribution (*guobao*). Do not believe that it will have no effect on lowly status. Inquire into the minds of men: who does not want longevity and plan how to extend his life? Who does not want to live in peace and good health?
>
> If you accept this ledger, first you must serve your master with all sincerity. Then you must deal with others with the utmost sincerity. If all servants—those who are parents, siblings, wives, and daughters—set their wills and move their minds so that in every word and act (for no action is insignificant), they follow the ledger without interruption, then they will be rewarded with what they desire, and even with what they have not dared to desire, with things outside their expectations. Heaven's recompense never fails.[53]

Chen makes it quite clear in the opening sentence that servants are in a fairly bad way—they must be reassured of their own humanity. But he moves on to encourage them to good behavior by "leading them with what they desire" (as he put it in his preface)—the hope of recompense in

---

[53] Chen Xigu, *Huizuan gongguoge*, 2.88b. Further references to this work are given in the text as page numbers in brackets.

the form of prosperity or higher rank. The belief in retribution is invoked to explain the potential fluidity of the status system: a servant is a man like others; he wants what others want and, by dint of virtuous behavior, ought to be able to get what he wants. Certainly, he should never refuse to take his moral potential seriously—this would be to disavow the possibility of status advance. But the definition of proper behavior here is first and foremost sincere service to his master. A servant, then, can move beyond his status only after fulfilling the very principle of servitude to the utmost, only after he has become the perfect servant. Without by any means denying the possibility of upward mobility for servants—indeed, by emphasizing that possibility—Chen encourages servants to give their masters devoted service.

A story appended to this introductory comment more colorfully illustrates these points. At the same time, it reminds the reader that servitude, the lowest state in the social hierarchy, was a morally "deserved" position. Wu Mao, a servant of Wu Liufang of Jingyang, Southern Zhili, was a very virtuous man. When, at the fall of the Ming, rebel troops invaded the area, he stayed behind to guard the household property while the Wu family fled. He was killed by the rebels, wounded seven times before he finally died. He then appeared to his brother in a dream and explained that his karma was such that he would have been reborn seven times as a pig to expiate his store of previous evil deeds. But in his status as a servant he was so virtuous that he was freed from the wheel of transmigration altogether (the seven wounds representing his seven rebirths) and transported directly to the Western Paradise. Thereafter, the Wu family set up an image of him and sacrificed to it. Chen Xigu comments:

> According to the Buddhist scriptures, for a man to be a servant, he must not have cultivated himself in a previous existence. It is the same for all men—[if they do not act properly,] they find themselves in lowly positions. . . . Now, people in the world agree that though Wu followed the proper precepts and was active in virtue, he brought calamity on himself [through his sins in a previous life]. . . . In the end he was killed by bandits. People use this reasoning as a pretext for their unwillingness to do good. But who knows how deep Wu's previous transgressions were, or how generous his recompense? How would the world have known the circumstances of his death? Fortunately he explained it all clearly to his brother, and revealed himself to his master, telling the world so that his story could be known, and so that all those unfortunate enough to be born into lowly positions could bestir themselves to action. [2.90a–b]

Chen is assuring his audience, then, that the social hierarchy is morally based: despite superficial evidence that virtue is not rewarded, cosmic moral justice is always quite precisely preserved, so precisely, in fact, that

Wu's seven reincarnations all had to be disposed of before he could go to his just reward.

Yet having made it clear that there is a moral justification for each servant's low status, Chen goes on to assert that servants can in fact be good. "Who is to say there are no sages or virtuous men among servants? I wish that people would not treat servants lightly, and that servants would not throw themselves away" [2.89b]. Clearly, the possibility of a virtuous servant is one that Chen finds surprising and somewhat confusing: in his ledger for masters, a master is heavily penalized (300 demerits out of a possible but rare 1,000) for "treating a servant who is virtuous in conduct and talented in study as a servant," a provision that in itself suggests that virtue and the state of servitude were considered mutually exclusive [2.79b]. But he does make some effort to understand and explain the difficulty of goodness for those in servile positions, as in the following comment:

> Master and servants are the ruler and ministers of a family. But from ancient times to the present, loyal ministers have been many and righteous servants few. How can we say, though, that there are no servants who love righteousness? Now a ruler's treatment of a minister glorifies his whole household and enriches his family. It is unceasing grace, and it should be generously repaid [through the minister's service to his ruler]. As for servants, they only receive several pieces of silver in payment for their own persons, and then they sink into a lowly status—their feelings already at that stage are to be pitied. How much more so after they take up service! They work bitterly hard, yet no one sympathizes with their plight; they fall ill, yet no one knows of their state.
>
> What distinguishes the master-servant from the ruler-minister relationship is the fact that in the former the feelings are those between strangers. Even those who are naturally disposed to be good—how can they follow through on their thoughts of gratitude and recompense to their masters? Even though they want to accumulate virtue and seek good fortune, how do they know whether the master will sympathize with them or not? . . . But if they serve an unkind master, it will be easier for them to increase their good fortune. After suffering for a short time, they receive good fortune later. Men of determination will certainly find it to their advantage to control themselves before an unkind master.[54] [2.89a–b]

All these passages reveal quite vividly the contradictions within this view of the moral potential of servants. Servants occupy a lowly status, one that supposedly reflects some moral failing on their part, and one that certainly dooms them to physical distress. To make matters worse, the servant is a "stranger," with no bonds of kinship to bind him to the affec-

[54] See also Hosono, "Minmatsu Shinsho Kōnan," p. 16.

tions of his master. For these reasons it is a matter of some surprise if a servant acts virtuously. But it *is* possible, and the servant struggling to do good despite a cruel master is comforted with the information that the harshness of his struggle increases the value of his own good behavior, so that he can expect quicker or better rewards than a servant with a kind and compassionate master. In any event, the servant must obey his master and remain firmly loyal to his master's interests, however he is treated; otherwise, Chen warns, he will receive no rewards from the gods.

Not surprisingly, the specific prescriptions Chen lists for servants to follow in the accumulation of merit are overwhelmingly concerned with the preservation of household harmony and the authority of the master within the household. Only four (of forty-nine) items prescribe behavior that could be interpreted as potentially disruptive of household unity; all these urge the servant to encourage his master to do good, or to admonish him against wrongdoing. In the latter case, twenty demerit points are deducted for not trying to correct a master's faults, but even in that case the servant is absolved of any demerit at all "if the master has a harsh personality, and you do not speak out of fear of him." Another eight prescriptions encourage harmony among servants: a servant is not to give particularly difficult tasks to other servants (ten demerits for the transgression, one merit for avoiding it), he is not to spread stories about fellow servants (ten demerits), he is not to harbor resentment against more successful servants (one demerit or merit), he is to aid other servants in illness or difficulty (one merit or demerit), and he is to conceal another servant's petty faults from the master (one merit) [2.91a–94a].

The other thirty-seven items all deal with the preservation of harmony between master and servant, largely through prescriptions for the subservience of servants. One thousand merits are awarded a servant who follows this prescription: "Be thoroughly respectful and affectionate. To the end of your life do not have one thought of deceit. Perform your duties as efficiently as possible." For helping to perpetuate the control of the master's direct line of descent, two thousand merits are the reward: "If you help the young master establish himself in the family and are never unfaithful to him, double the merit" [2.92b]. Stories of servants who practice this kind of loyalty are popular in other ledgers as well; Li Guochang tells several stories of servants who rescued their late master's orphaned sons from poverty or from the plots of their relatives, and who were thus rewarded with official titles (usually posthumous) or illustrious descendants.[55] Again, the servant is encouraged to act with an almost sacrificial loyalty to his master, with the promise that he or his descendants will be rewarded with advancement out of servant status.

[55] Li Guochang, *Chongxiu zhiyao*, 6.13a–16a. See also *Riqian chushe*, 18a.

In other, more specific items, Chen Xigu urges servants to act so as to acknowledge and protect the master's authority both at home and in the community. Within the household, the servant is urged to "be polite and gracious to the master. Follow his desires in carrying out his orders. Then he will always be pleased" (one merit per day, and ten extra merits if this behavior is continued through one month). These basic prescriptions are repeated in different forms throughout the ledger: the servant is to "serve his master with his whole heart, without deceiving or cheating him" (fifty merits per year), to "be respectful to the young master" (one hundred merits), to admonish other servants who ignore the master's orders (one merit per incident and one demerit for not performing this service), to be "respectful and observant of decorum" to relatives of the master (one hundred merits), and to care for the grave of a deceased master (five merits). In the demerit section, servants are warned against "amusing themselves, even when they have no work, in a way that arouses their master's resentment" (one demerit), against "not paying close attention to the master's instructions" (one demerit), against deceiving the young master (one demerit per incident), against using crude language before the master (one demerit), against speaking rudely to the master (three demerits), against inciting other servants to acts of disloyalty (ten demerits per incident), against enticing the young master to self-indulgence and ruin (one hundred demerits), and against "sowing discord among family members by spreading stories that are half-true, half-false" (three hundred demerits) [2.93a].

In accord with the idea that the servant cursed with a cruel master should do nothing but bear the situation patiently, comforting himself with the knowledge that he is accumulating more merit because of the greater wrongs he must endure, the ledger urges compliance with even an unjust master: "If your master beats, gets angry at you, and curses you, and your service is harsh and bitter, do not cherish resentment in your mind (for each incident, ten merits; in extremely difficult and unbearable situations, if you are not resentful, add five times the merit)." Some acknowledgment of the difficulty of this prescription is offered in the demerit section, where the negative version of the item is given relatively low value in terms of demerits assigned: "If you do not willingly serve your master, but do so with a mind divided from his wants, for each word or thought of resentment, one demerit. Even if your master is harsh and difficult to serve, avoid dissatisfaction and thoughts of running away." Servants are also urged to protect the master's authority within the community: they are warned against discussing their master's affairs outside the household (fifty demerits) or his faults (one hundred merits for not discussing these), and encouraged to protect his reputation (one merit) [2.93a].

These prescriptions dictate the proper behavior of the servant toward the master, the acts that reflect the attitude appropriate to an obedient, "good" servant. They are designed first to preserve the authority of the master and the subservience of the servant above all else (in that a servant is supposed to remain faithful even to a cruel tyrant). They bolster the harmony of the household by prescribing rules for servant behavior that will ensure harmony both among the group of servants and among the household members (the power of servants to disrupt family harmony is acknowledged in the rule against spreading gossip). Finally, they encourage servant loyalty to the master and his household vis-à-vis the rest of the community.

In these prescriptions is also reflected a fear of servants' gaining power or wealth inappropriate to their station, whether doing so hurts their masters' authority or not. While identification with the fate of the master and his household is encouraged, servants are urged "not to use the master's authority to oppress others" (twenty merits a year), and not to "swindle others for the master's sake" (one demerit per two hundred cash) [2.92,94a]. These are clearly warnings against bondservant manipulation of their masters' power to claim wealth and privileges for themselves, not uncommon practices among the "brazen bondservants" so feared by late Ming and early Qing social critics.[56] Chen is also aware of the possibility of economic reversals—that the bondservant may at some time become wealthier than his master—and he emphasizes the obligations the servant still has to the master. He is responsible for providing for a master's burial (fifty merits), for care of the master's grave (five merits), and for charities to a poor master (one merit per one hundred cash). Plotting against a master who is losing his authority deserves one hundred demerits. Finally, the greatest number of demerits (one thousand) goes to the servant who, on becoming wealthy himself, does not aid his master in poverty [2.92b].[57] A servant apparently never escapes his moral status as a servant, no matter what happens to his economic status.

Other morality-book authors take an even tougher stand on the issue of a servant's economic condition. For Chen Zhixi, author of the *Complete Book of Exhortations and Admonitions*, servants are not supposed to be wealthy at all. He recounts the following cautionary tale:

A bondservant of the Ji family of Songling was near death. He had property of three thousand pieces of silver and a son of just ten; his master was Ji Chunyuan. The servant called his master and wanted to present him with half his property, asking that the master use it to care for his soon-to-be-orphaned son.

[56] McDermott, "Bondservants in the T'ai-hu Basin," pp. 693–698.
[57] For a story of a servant who does support his impoverished master, see Chen Zhixi, *Quanjie quanshu*, 8.49a–51a.

The master said, "I accept this money, without accepting your designation of how it should be spent. For you are a man of low status (*xiaren*)—how could you have achieved such wealth without having done something to hurt others? Since the wealth you have accumulated exceeds your status, you have lost years from your life span. How can you benefit your descendants? It is best to use half your money to create virtue for your son." The servant wept in gratitude and then died. The master spent half the servant's money doing all kinds of good deeds. He hired a famous teacher and had his own son and the servant's son study together. Afterward, both sons passed the examination in the same year.

Alas! That servant certainly was extraordinarily clever, but his master was worthy to an even greater degree. How could the recompense [*ying*, "response"] of the sons' passing the examinations in the same year have been accidental?[58]

The servant was being punished with a premature death for an accumulation of wealth not suited to his lowly place, and hence assuredly achieved through corrupt and immoral means. The demerits he had accumulated threatened his descendants also, and it was only by donating the money to the performance of good deeds that he could redeem and improve his family's fortunes. The servant had really committed two types of evil: the wicked practices he used to accumulate his money, and beyond that, the presumption of trying to advance himself beyond his status by means outside of and inimical to his master's control. Economic advancement was not the proper way to self-improvement for servants; it was rather the performance of good deeds that would ensure success along the elite-dominated ladder of advance. "Petty men who wish to accumulate wealth, day and night make plots to do so, and they expend all their efforts to reach this goal," Chen warns. "It is best if their masters pressure them to do good instead."[59]

It is not necessarily bad, however, for a servant to be capable in money matters, as long as his talents are devoted to the enrichment of his master's family. Chen Xigu presents A Ji, servant to the Xu family of Chun'an, Zhejiang, as the correct economic model for the servant to follow. Left after the death of his master to care for the widow and her daughters, A Ji carefully invested their meager property in the lacquer trade, and managed to so enrich the family as to earn handsome dowries for the daughters, education for the sons-in-law, and provision for the family after his death. Chen marvels at A Ji's virtue: "Ji was a rustic man, enfeebled with age, not at all familiar with the ideas of the *Classic of Songs* and the *Record of Rites*, [but] with a mind roused to kindness. He was willing to exhaust all his energies working . . . for the sake of others,

[58] Chen Zhixi, *Quanjie quanshu*, 5.33b. Okuzaki, *Chūgoku kyōshin jinushi*, p. 464.
[59] Chen Zhixi, *Quanjie quanshu*, 5.33b.

forgetting himself right up to his death. . . . How could even a member of the gentry, a scholar, one who understands principle and acts on right-eousness, do better than this?"[60] A Ji, in contrast to the servant of the Ji household, behaved like a real "gentleman" because he accumulated wealth for the benefit of his family, not for his own personal aggrandize-ment.

The nature of the service ethic advocated in these morality books is clearest in one exemplary tale common to several of the books, a story that presents the servant-protagonist with a moral dilemma (rather rare in the ledgers), a choice between two moral values, loyalty to his master and honesty. Chen Zhixi appears to have been the first to use this story:

Two wealthy families of Kunshan county were feuding. One had fields that had just been planted. The other secretly called his servant, a certain Zhou, gave him several pecks of deccan-grass seed, rewarded him with wine and food, and ordered him to scatter the seeds of the weed over the fields of the other family that night. The servant thought of all the labor the other family had expended to plant their fields, and how hopefully they were looking forward to their har-vest. How could he bear to harm them? But it was his master's order; further-more, if he refused to do it, then all that would happen was that another servant would be told to do the harm. So he pretended to acquiesce in the plan, but secretly boiled the seed. That night his master watched from a distance, and saw that he scattered the seed on the fields. Later, when the seeds did not grow, the master was very surprised that the plan had not worked, but he did not suspect that the servant had followed his own plan.

Afterward, the servant had a son who passed the examinations. The master's son suddenly went mad, and a spirit spoke through him, saying, "Because of what a certain servant did on a certain night during a certain month in a certain year, heaven has given him a son of high rank; because of what a certain master did on a certain night of a certain month and a certain year, heaven has pun-ished him by cutting off his family line." The other family members looked at each other in puzzlement, not understanding the meaning of this statement; only the master and the servant nodded to each other in comprehension.[61]

This story might at first glance seem to contain a status-disruptive rather than a status-confirming message: the servant is rewarded for an act in subversion of his master's authority. But this act of subversion is put into a context that changes its final meaning, for the servant defies his master in a way that still confirms his status as a servant in the larger

[60] Chen Xigu, Huizuan gongguoge, 2.90b–91a. This story also appears in Li Guochang, Chongxiu zhiyao, 6.15a–16a. It seems to have been based on a true story; see Tong, "Col-lective Violence in a Premodern Society," p. 210.

[61] Chen Zhixi, Quanjie quanshu, 6.30a–b. This story is cited and discussed in Okuzaki, Chūgoku kyōshin jinushi, pp. 466–467.

social order. He does, after all, obey the letter of his master's command; there is no open defiance of a superior's authority or even any attempt at gentle moral suasion from the servant. He is a good man in large part because he remains a good servant. The master here is evil because he deviates from the ethical terms of his position as a landowner and master, and the servant is virtuous because he does a good deed *without* trying to move beyond the limits of his status as a servant. Indeed, when forty years later Chen Xigu used roughly the same story in his ledger for servants, he explicitly drew out this interpretation:

> If [Zhou] had not deceived his master, and had brought himself to perform the task his master set, he would have damaged his nature to an unspeakable degree. If he had refused to do the deed, then there would have been other men to do it. Thus he accomplished all the merit he could have. . . . This servant did two things faultlessly: outside the household, he did not violate principle; inside the household, he did not violate his master's orders. Serving a master as [Zhou] did accords with [proper] feelings; his behavior exactly fulfills the demands of propriety and righteousness. After his death he was honored and placed among the ranks of the gentry (*jinshen*). And yet it is said in the world that to be a servant is to be without glory or rank.[62]

Thus it is not the servant's place to defy or expose his master. The gods are introduced to make that final moral judgment and to impose punishment, and they assure the ledger user that the existing status order is based on moral principles, indeed is constantly being adjusted to match moral truth. Just as Li Guochang had promised, the gods reward men who know their place.

The prescriptions for servants in these ledgers all reflect the authors' fears of status upheaval, not surprising at a time when some bondservants were in fact accumulating wealth for themselves, abusing or challenging their masters' authority, and in some cases, rising up to kill and steal from their masters. Even Chen Zhixi, writing just before the outbreak of bondservant rebellions in the 1640s and '50s, seems to have been very aware of these dangers. He recounts the story of a man unwilling to fulfill his corvée obligations because he fears his servants will seize his property in his absence.[63] The ledger authors were anxious about the breakdown of what they perceived as an ideal, harmonious master-servant relationship based in part on the loyalty and submission of servants. If only servants could be taught again to keep their place, to restrain their ambition for wealth and higher status, to devote themselves to the welfare of their mas-

---

[62] Chen Xigu, *Huizuan gongguoge*, 2.90a.
[63] Chen Zhixi, *Quanjie quanshu*, 7.66b–67b; cited in Okuzaki Hiroshi, "Chūgoku Mindai no ikikata—zensho ni arawareta ichisokumen—," pp. 43–44.

ters—in short, to serve them loyally and obediently—then the old, "good" order might be restored.

The Responsibilities of the Elite: Scholars, Officials, and Local Gentry

Ledger authors by no means limit their instructions to members of low social status, however. Certainly the ledger provisions and stories encourage behavior that would tend to keep servants "at peace in their place" (while constantly working for future social advance). But it is impossible to read the ledgers as texts designed simply to that end, for they do present a whole social vision, one that emphasizes the duties and status obligations of holders of high status—scholars, officials, and local gentry—as well. As befits texts designed to reinforce a stable social hierarchy, they are concerned with relationships between statuses, the points at which they interlock from both directions, not simply with the containment of one particular group.

It is clear that, in the minds of the ledger authors, the educated elite were to play the dominant role in maintaining this interlocking social hierarchy. The ledgers of the seventeenth and eighteenth centuries reflect views on this point very close to those of the Donglin thinkers treated in the last chapter: members of the elite had to justify their high status by accepting considerable responsibility for the welfare of their communities. The ledgers in a sense carried the ideas of Chen Longzheng about elite responsibility to their logical conclusion, explaining the retributive basis of elite status, and then specifying in some detail how members of the elite should act on their nonfamilial responsibilities—to their tenants, their servants, and the poorer members of their local communities.

Yan Maoyou, in the *Record for Gaining Good Fortune*, is, for example, preoccupied with the services that scholars, officials, and gentry can perform: half of his morality book is an "official mirror" (*guanjian*), explaining the rewards for the virtuous in office, and half a "public mirror" (*gongjian*), devoted to more generally applicable moral advice, but still directed primarily at the elite. Under a section entitled "Recompense for the Virtuous Conduct of Gentry at Home" ("Xiangshen jiazhu yixing zhi bao"), he announces that the local gentry, even more than scholars, are the major force in the education of the people: "Local gentry are the hope of the country. Doing good while dwelling at home, they can influence their county, they can sweep their neighborhood [clean], they can nourish the backward. Their ability to transform others is one hundred times that of scholars (*shiren*)."[64] These deeds of transformation may consist of relatively small and scattered acts of moral example: Ning Lixiang, one of

---

[64] Yan Maoyou, *Diji lu*, 4.56a; cited in Sakai, *Chūgoku zensho*, p. 81.

Yan Maoyou's cases, instructed the residents of an unspecified locality in Liaodong, where he had fled in the wake of rebellion, to care for their oxen properly, to learn to yield to one another in drawing water from the one local well, and to follow the proper classical forms in offering sacrifices. He was rewarded for these transformations in customs with longevity and the offer of an official post.[65]

Chen Zhixi, in his *Complete Book*, is much more aggressive in asserting elite obligations to society. Wealthy and powerful men who have compassion for the poor, he suggests, are not simply acting kindly; they are fulfilling a social duty sanctioned by the cosmos:

> Heaven and earth are the great parents. All beings produced between heaven and earth, all beings within the seas are brothers. The world has never had parents who can bear to see their children in want; thus it is not possible that heaven and earth would not be compassionate toward the difficulties of their people, whether a child or a man, whether wealthy or poor. If a man is wealthy and willing to give away his excess, considering wealth to be insignificant, then his parents must be very happy. When he meets others in disaster, and in the same spirit sympathizes with them, aids and supports them, then his parents must be even happier. . . . The virtue of having compassion for the poor and contributing to the needy, regardless of the human response, is certainly what heaven and earth love. The bitterness of hoarding wealth and ignoring the sufferings of others, regardless of human resentment, is certainly what heaven and earth hate.[66]

Chen was quite upset by the failure of contemporary gentry to accept the duties inextricably bound to their place in society. Such negligence, he warned, would have the inevitable consequence of undermining the good fortune that had assured them gentry status in the first place. "Recently, in times of flood and drought," he complains, "gentry members with large stores of grain have been hoping daily that rice prices would rise precipitously. They refuse to aid even their closest relatives and friends. Therefore I have written an imaginary 'Reply of the Gods to a Request for Rain' ":

> "We see down below that men of wealth do not aid the poor, those of high rank do not aid the lowly; even worse, kin do not aid kin. Who is not suffering from the drought? Yet we see that the mass of poor people have difficulty seeking aid from the wealthy, the lowly have difficulty seeking aid from those of high rank, and even worse, kin have difficulty seeking help from kin. Who will answer the cries for help? Even when people of the same status make the requests, many are not answered. You are no fewer than ten thousand *li* away from heaven;

[65] Yan Mayou, *Diji lu*, 4.59a–60b.
[66] Chen Zhixi, *Quanjie quanshu*, 5.20b–21a.

how can you look then to us for a response? Rather, you should look inside yourselves, and constantly think of aiding others. If you rain on other people, then we will rain on you as well."

Chen follows this speech with another imaginary divine lecture, "Response to Those Seeking Longevity":

"How could heaven select those of high rank on the basis of personal preference? The masses of lowly people have no one to support them; we have commissioned you to support them. How could heaven select who is to be wealthy on the basis of personal generosity? The masses of the poor have no one to aid them; we have given you the responsibility to aid them. When disasters strike, you have the power to keep people alive, but you do not have the virtue to want to sustain life. Now, do you want Shangdi to sustain your lives? Then you must seek inside yourself, and constantly think of aiding others. If you give long life to the people, then we will give long life to you."[67]

The gentry are playfully reminded here that their status depends on their virtue: high status and good fortune may reflect virtue, but it is virtue accumulated in the past—the maintenance of high status and good fortune requires continuing virtue. Retribution may operate to justify the low status of servants, but it also serves to arouse the elite to a sense of its moral and social responsibilities. Here we see the concept of elite social responsibility suggested by some of the Donglin thinkers worked out in all its details. Gao Panlong and Chen Longzheng warned that by the natural cosmic process of retribution, wealthy gentry would be punished if they did not care for their dependents and contribute to community welfare. Chen Zhixi, through the mouth of his imaginary god, states a much blunter quid pro quo policy: either the gentry live up to their social responsibilities or they can expect no mercy or help from the gods. And just as his concerns about bondservant recalcitrance were based on observation of real tensions in the master-servant relationship, so too his anxiety about gentry failure to fulfill their traditional responsibilities was founded in an awareness of growing gentry alienation from rural society, resulting from the growth of commercial opportunities and the increase in absentee and rentier landlordism. At such a time it was particularly important that gentry be reminded of their responsibilities—indeed, that they be made to feel that their very position depended on fulfilling these responsibilities.

It is clear, too, from Chen's work that random good deeds or acts of purely personal restraint were not really enough to complete the obligations of the gentry. The elite was seen as having responsibilities to the people that paralleled heaven's responsibilities to all men. They were, in

[67] Chen Zhixi, *Quanjie quanshu*, 5.21a–b; Okuzaki, *Chūgoku kyōshin jinushi*, pp. 469–470.

short, charged with overseeing the welfare of the people, or more precisely, their tenants, their servants, and poorer members of the community at large.

Chen gives some idea of the responsibilities gentry owed their tenants
in the following account of a model landlord:

> Lu Pingquan [m. Shusheng, 1509–1605] of Yunjian [Songjiang] loved to do
> good deeds throughout his life. He treated his tenants particularly generously.
> Often he admonished his descendants about their laborers and servants: "The
> peasants labor bitterly through the four seasons until they gather in the harvest
> in the fall. It is impossible not to sympathize deeply with them. When you col-
> lect rent, do not use the large measure. When checking the luster of the rice, be
> a little lenient. When there are floods or droughts, give generously from your
> own supplies, and do not hold the peasants responsible for repaying the
> amount. In the winter, to avoid shortages, give them rice. When tenants are
> involved in court cases, or when they have severe illnesses, you must do as much
> as you can to save them. Reduce their rice payments when they reach the age
> of fifty. If they achieve any honors, then increase the exemption. From the time
> they are sixty on, for each grandchild, increase their exemption from the pay-
> ment of rice rent." Therefore all of Lu's tenants, all households, had enough
> food and clothing.
>
> When Lu was ninety-five he became ill and was close to death several times.
> His relatives and friends all went to pray at a temple. An old friend suddenly
> burst into the scripture room, saying that he had seen over a hundred old peas-
> ants prostrating themselves before the altar, praying that Lu be preserved.[68]

As a result of these appeals, the city god petitioned heaven for a reprieve.
An emissary from heaven agreed to extend Lu's life one twelve-year unit
because of his "compassion for peasants and his over forty years of sowing virtue." Chen adds an editorial comment:

> Peasants work hard to the end of their lives, without time for leisure. Together
> with their families they labor, and there is no one in their families who has
> peace. If there chances to be flood or drought, they exhaust all their strength to
> no avail. . . . Thus it is best that high-ranking and wealthy families have the
> greatest compassion for tenants. Do they not exhaust all their strength to nour-
> ish us, and bear great suffering for us?
>
> Wang Wensu every summer went with his servants to the fields, to see the
> hard labor of his tenants. Shen Wending, whenever winter came, had boundless
> compassion for the peasants. Zhu Shangbao of Jingyang wept when he heard
> of the death of any of his tenants, and tried to aid their families. Ding Qinghui

---

[68] Chen Zhixi, *Quanjie quanshu*, 5.28a–b; Okuzaki, *Chūgoku kyōshin jinushi*, p. 468.
This story is also told in Chen Xigu, *Huizuan gongguoge*, 5.25b–26a. See *Mingshi*, j. 216,
no. 104, vol. 19, pp. 5694–5696, for a biography of Lu.

[m. Bin] treated his tenants as a father his sons. There was none who was not enriched in his service. These four men continued the tradition of generosity established by Lu Pingquan, and for this reason they all attained long life.[69]

Here is an acknowledgment of the sufferings of tenants (and servants) and of the dependence of the elite, the "high-ranking and wealthy" families, on the hard labor of the peasantry. The terms of this dependence are not called into question—Chen never suggests that there is anything unjust or wrong with the relationship itself, as long as landlords fulfill their duties. Allusion to the hardships of peasants is used as moral pressure on the elite to treat their dependents kindly, a pressure backed by the claim of divine sanction. Landlords and masters should be kind to their tenants and servants because they can expect worldly rewards from the gods for this kindness, and, it is hinted, because they are in fact dependent on peasant labor.

Later, in the 1680s, Chen Xigu emphasized this latter point; in his *Compendium* he quotes the admonition of a Zhu Chinsan to landlords: "If you allow your tenants to take pleasure in their labor, then the fields will be fertile, the rents not deficient, and in normal years rent collection will not require much effort. . . . If, on the contrary, you oppress your tenants, without making the slightest compromises, the tenants will be exhausted and the fields will therefore decline. Those who produce a great deal will be burdened with fields without tenants to work them. Thus how can you not think of ways to be compassionate and supportive?" [5.23a][70] Thus it is very much in the landlords' own interests to take care of their tenants. They can thereby not only earn divinely apportioned rewards like long life, but also ensure their own continued prosperity: a contented tenant is a hard-working and loyal tenant. The relationship here is governed by discretionary rules, dependent on the paternalistic grace (and good sense, both Chens suggest) of the landlord, rather than by any contractual regulations or laws protecting the tenant. Here again the ledger authors are responding to a real change in social and economic relationships—the greater economic power of tenants and their greater willingness to challenge landlord authority or simply desert their landlords—by trying to reassert a vision of what landlord-tenant relations had been in the past: a harmonious, paternalistic relationship based on "mutual support and mutual nurturance." Their sense of anxiety, even panic, about the increasing difficulty of holding tenant loyalty is revealed nicely in their awareness of landlord dependence on tenant labor. The balance is tipped here: early sixteenth-century writers like Xu Jie emphasized mutual dependence, while both authors here stress the reliance of landlords

[69] Chen Zhixi, *Quanjie quanshu*, 5.28b–29a; Okuzaki, *Chūgoku kyōshin jinushi*, p. 468.
[70] See also Okuzaki, "Chūgoku Mindai no ikikata," pp. 30–31.

on tenants. If landlords do not treat their tenants well, they will lose them—a consequence dictated in the vision of the ledgers not only by contemporary economic realities, but also by the moral requirements of a world ordered by the principle of retribution, both human and divine.

The ledgers also devoted considerable space to the duties masters owed their bondservants, an indication of the anxieties many felt over the tensions within this important relationship in the very late Ming and early Qing. Chen Xigu's *Compendium* contains the most detailed ledger for masters, suggesting the broadest range of responsibilities for that status. A master was first responsible for the proper selection of servants and the careful limitation of their power. He protected the purity and correctness of the status order by making sure that no one who did not "deserve" to be a servant became one: he had to investigate carefully a servant's background to be sure that he or she had not come from a good family, and was thus unsuitable for bondservant status. One hundred demerits were earned by the man who, on learning that he had received such a person from a "good, old family" as a servant, refused to return him. Several other items dealt with the need for care in this regard: accepting a servant without checking his antecedents was worth twenty demerits, and inquiring about a servant's family background earned three merits. Under this last item there was a story of a district magistrate, Zhong Lijin, who one day came across a newly purchased maid weeping over her chores. She explained that her father had at one time been magistrate of the district. On the death of her parents, she was passed to the household of a clerk, who then sold her to Zhong. "I saw your honor taking care of official business and thought of how my ancestors would lament the decline of my family." Zhong verified her story, released her from service, and arranged her marriage to the son of a locally prominent family. Zhong then dreamt that a god promised him long life and illustrious descendants, and, sure enough, he lived to the age of 96 and all of his sons became officials [2.75a–b]. Such was the reward of a man who righted misalignments in the social hierarchy.

Similarly, masters are given responsibility for seeing that servants do not take on more power than they should by abusing their masters' authority. Li Guochang, in his *Essentials of Self-Cultivation*, shares this fear of servants' abusing their masters' authority; he devotes a whole section to the "restraint of servants," largely urging masters to keep few servants and to regulate those few carefully.[71] For Chen Xigu, however, the best way to solve this problem is through the careful selection of servants, so here, too, the investigation of the servant's background becomes an important precaution. Failure to check the servant's previous position, re-

---

[71] Li Guochang, *Chongxiu zhiyao*, 6.3a–4b.

sulting in the employment of trouble-makers and sycophants, is worth one hundred demerits; accepting cruel and violent men as servants and accepting runaway servants who have been disloyal to their previous masters are both worth thirty demerits. Officials are urged not to take on simply anyone who offers himself as a servant (thirty merits), an injunction doubtless designed to prevent the common practice of men commending themselves to officials to avoid taxes and take advantage of association with official wealth and privilege. Indeed, Chen suggests that great families of rank make it a family rule not to employ strong or clever servants, ones capable of either tricking the family or abusing the family's power to enrich themselves (one hundred merits). Finally, there is one definite injunction against allowing servants who, relying on their master's power to protect them, create disturbances or commit crimes (twenty demerits, or if a crime is committed, the master is penalized the number of demerits associated with it) [2.79b–80a, 77a, 78b, 81b–82a]. These rules all suggest a recognition of a common late-Ming phenomenon—the tendency for ambitious bondservants to manipulate their masters' authority to gain power and wealth for themselves. In the *Compendium* the master is held largely responsible for curbing the ambitions and power of his servants.

But the primary emphasis within the section of instructions for masters is on the necessity for masters to treat their servants with kindness and sympathy, very much as they were to treat their tenants. The introduction to this ledger emphasizes that compassion, a rational principle of reprimand, and a sense of fairness should govern the master's behavior to his servants:

> The Buddha Sūjata said, "There are five obligations all people have to their servants. The first is to learn whether they are hungry, thirsty, cold, or hot before compelling them to work. The second is to see that they are cared for when they are ill. The third is not to flog them brutally; you should find the truth in a case of wrongdoing, and only then decide responsibility. If you have a right to be angry, be angry; if you don't, instruct them on how to correct their faults. Fourth, if they have some small amount of personal property, do not seize it. Fifth, if you give them things, give equally to all; do not be biased. [2.73b]

The specific instructions for masters listed exemplify these general comments. The master is to be sympathetic to the physical condition of his servants; he earns one demerit each day he does not provide a servant with sufficient clothing, food, or aid when ill, and he gains one merit each time he attempts to relieve the physical suffering of his servants. The example for this last requirement is the story of a *juren* who gave his quilt to his servant and groom so that they might have protection against the cold [2.73b–74a]. More merit is given for a more exacting requirement: "Eat and drink together with your servants. Be compassionate of their hard labor. When they do wrong, guide them with goodness, do not blame them. For following this prescription for one year, without interruption, take thirty merits." Compassion for the labor of one's servants is illustrated with the story of a Han prefectural official who himself aided his subordinates in the construction of a fortifying wall. Though it was the middle of a hot and humid summer, he refused any refreshments not also offered to the other workers [2.76a].

The *Compendium* devotes particular attention to rules for the appropriate and rational punishment of servants. First, moral persuasion is seen as the best means of correcting one's servants. The model "master" here is a widow who used instruction, teaching shame (*kuichi*) through expressions of disapproval and displeasure, never flogging, as the means of schooling both her children and her servants. Since the servants never witnessed any quarrels within the family, they followed this example, in perfect Confucian form, in their own behavior, and remained at harmony among themselves and devoted to their mistress [2.76b].

In the specific provisions for the correction of servants, there is a similar emphasis on moral suasion and leniency. Masters are urged to be lenient with first offenders, who should not be publicly punished, but privately admonished and given a chance to reform (when sins like petty thievery are thus leniently treated, the master receives fifty merits). There is yet another separate injunction "not to get angry at a servant's wrongs, but to educate him with virtue" (three merits). This prescription is supported with the extraordinary story of a man who allowed the maidservant responsible for the death of his baby son to flee the household unpunished, to escape the murderous wrath of his wife. She was so grateful for his mercy that she prayed that he might have another son. Another son was, of course, the result of her prayers, a son so talented that he achieved the post of minister of finance [2.74a]. So, too, Li Guochang, in his ledger, urges masters to forgive the sins of their servants: one master was rewarded with an extended lifespan for caring for the daughter of a servant who had stolen ten thousand pieces of silver from him, and another was rewarded with an official title for declining to punish a runaway servant.[72]

In all these prescriptions, corporal punishment is not necessarily rejected, but the master is cautioned to be moderate and rational in his use of it. Beating a servant harshly, punishing a servant for careless mistakes, cursing servants, taking one's anger out on them unjustly, and punishing servants for one's own mistakes are all one-demerit offenses, while if one

[72] Li Guochang, *Chongxiu zhiyao*, 6.11b–12a.

beats a servant hard enough to injure him seriously, the penalty is thirty demerits. All these rules encourage rationality and adherence to certain preestablished rules, an attempt to reduce the arbitrariness of the master's control over his servants. Indeed, one hundred merits are given for following just such a rational system: "You should be stern, but fair. If you have set proscriptions, you must follow them; if you have established rules, you must apply them without harshness or laxity" [2.86a–b, 87b, 81a, 79a]. This ledger, then, emphasizes the importance of moral persuasion as the primary means of restricting and instructing servants; if harsher punishments are necessary, they must be carried out according to some rational plan.

But the master's responsibility extends far beyond a commitment to a rational plan of admonition and restraint. The master is also charged with the proper training of his servants, care for them in hardship, the arrangement of suitable marriages for them, and the preservation of their families and their property. First, masters are urged to train their servants in useful skills, not in entertainment or other nonproductive occupations (thirty demerits). This concern extends to ritual and moral education as well: masters are penalized for allowing their servants to be lax about the rules of courtesy, especially to superiors (twenty demerits), and for allowing their female servants too much freedom (ten demerits). Furthermore, they are to see that the children of their servants, if intelligent, are able to continue their education (ten demerits for ignoring this injunction; thirty merits for following it). Second, several items emphasize the importance of seeing that one's servants are satisfactorily married. Arranging a marriage between servants who want to marry each other earns ten merits; matching servants at an appropriate time earns twenty merits, while neglecting to provide a husband for a twenty-year-old maidservant, or a wife for a thirty-year-old male servant, is worth twenty demerits and ten demerits per year respectively. Choosing a suitable mate earns ten merits, while making the choice of a husband for a maidservant on the basis of profit, not suitability, is punished with ten demerits [2.81a–82b, 75b, 76b]. Here Chen is echoing contemporary legal thinking, for during the Kangxi era (1662–1722), legal writers were urging that masters be required by law to marry off their bondservants at reasonably early ages, so that they could start families of their own.[73]

In a variety of other ways, masters are enjoined to treat their servants with a generosity and kindness normally reserved for family members. They are urged not to seize the property of a deceased servant, but to distribute it among other servants, so that the dead man can accumulate merit (thirty demerits for violation, one hundred merits for following this

[73] See, for example, Li Yu, *Zhizhi xinshu*, 14.26a–27b.

prescription). They are urged to care for sick servants (twenty merits or ten demerits) and to be more lenient in their punishment of a servant without a family (fifty merits). When selling a maidservant, they are to be sure that she goes to a good master (thirty merits or demerits). Finally, in a series of proscriptions, masters are urged not to confuse or intimidate their servants with orders too exacting and too harsh (ranging from three to five merits or demerits depending on the situation) [2.81a, 79a, 75b, 82a, 77b, 76b, 73b–74b, 83a–87b].

Though there is clearly a recognition here of the need for greater kindness in the treatment of servants and tenants, it is equally clear that this change does not entail any admission either that servants or tenants should be granted higher status in the society or that their relations with superiors should be eased by changes in their contractual or legal status. The ledger prescriptions are rooted in paternalism, an extension of the rules governing the management of children and family members to servants and tenants. There is no need for an extrafamilial force—i.e., the government—to regulate the relationship; since servants were, after all, "adopted sons and daughters," they would naturally fit into the pattern of the familial hierarchy. The author's goal is to return the master-servant and tenant-landlord relationships to this highly idealized pattern, not to develop some new means of regulation out of the landlord's or master's control. This attitude is explicitly stated in Chen Xigu's ledger; one of his heroes remarks that masters will not have difficulty treating their servants properly if they think of them as children: "It is not difficult to extend one's grace (en) to children" [2.73b–74a].

In the ledgers of the seventeenth and eighteenth centuries, the responsibilities of the elite extend even beyond compassionate treatment of their tenants and servants. As Chen Zhixi had already suggested in his fanciful "Reply of the Gods to a Request for Rain," the gentry have an obligation to their immediate communities as well. This obligation becomes clearest during famine or other periods of economic deprivation. Chen himself presents Ding Bin, one of the wealthier gentry of Jiashan and an official, as a model for this kind of charity:

Ding Qinghui (m. Bin) never tired of taking pleasure in goodness. He was particularly keen on famine relief. During the great flood of 1587, the price of rice rose precipitously. Ding first ordered his servants to take rice and exchange it for cloth. According to the price at the time, each roll of cloth earned four pints of rice. [Ding] spent in all over 1,000 piculs. He also repaired the embankments between the fields, in preparation against flood. It was calculated that he gave altogether 650 piculs of rice.

The next year, in 1588, the harvest was even poorer. [Ding] set up a gruel kitchen to the west of his own household, and everyday several thousand people went to eat there. He also sought out the old and weak, those who could not go, and gave them gruel. This went on for ninety days. That fall there was also a bitter drought, and Ding distributed water to those dying of thirst. His plans were all good policies for famine relief, and they saved the lives of many people.

In the winter the people suffered much from cold. [Ding] searched out all those who did not have enough clothing, registered them, and gave them tickets, admonishing them to save the tickets to hand over in exchange for the cloth they had exchanged [for rice the previous year]. He gave spun cotton and wadded cotton, two rolls of cloth, and four catties of wadded cotton to each person. When all had been passed out, it was calculated that he had distributed over 12,400 piculs of rice, 30,040 rolls of cloth, and 60,080 catties of wadded cotton.

Again in 1608 there was a great flood, and Ding, together with the local officials, petitioned for loans for the needy. Moreover, he urged the officials of Jiangxi and Hubei not to stop the purchase of rice and to open the official treasuries to transport rice in all directions. Again he contributed funds of his own to expand the amount given.

In 1624 there were torrential rains, and [Ding] again opened the granaries to give aid. He distributed a total of 3,000 piculs of rice in four different lots. When it came time to make the adjustment in silver, [Ding] calculated that all of the small householders in the township, those possessing only two or three *mu*, owed 3,000 ounces. He used his own wealth to complete the whole payment.[74]

Here Ding (rewarded, by the way, for all these deeds with long life: he lived to the age of ninety) was taking responsibility for the welfare of his whole community, particularly in times of crisis.

Chen Xigu, in his *Compendium*, also encourages this kind of far-reaching concern for public welfare. In his ledger of charitable deeds, Chen lists, among many smaller acts of one-time generosity, larger community projects that he explicitly makes the responsibility of local officials, local gentry, and "scholars living in the area" [7.25b, 31b]. These members of the local elite should band together to develop projects for relief or community improvement, soliciting aid if necessary from the wealthier households in the area, but managing the programs themselves. Highest merit is given for these projects: one hundred merits reward the construction of charitable schools or the repair or construction of bridges, ferries, and roads. Three hundred merits are awarded to "those in authority who, during years of famine, lead others in making contributions and sincerely developing good methods to aid the people" (more merit may be added if

[74] Chen Zhixi, *Quanjie quanshu*, 5.19b–20b. See *Mingshi*, j. 221, no. 109, vol. 19, pp. 5829–5830, for a biography of Ding Bin.

money is spent) or to anyone who "earnestly carries out a charitable affair, without sparing funds or energy" (if the work continues for a full year, one hundred merits may be added). Finally, one thousand merits, the greatest number, accrue to one who "creates a [charitable] program whose profits never cease" [7.24b–26b, 29b]. Chen sets forth detailed sample programs, including an elaborate plan for the establishment of local granaries (*shecang*) based on Zhu Xi's model [7.31b].[75] Chen himself seems to have been particularly interested in famine relief, for he gives detailed advice on the appropriate form of aid in such crises, including even a recipe for the preparation of gruel:

> In my opinion there are two methods [of distributing rice]. Those who contribute rice should divide the contributions up according to neighborhood. First, two people should be put in charge of the contributions. These men should summon the local gentry to make contributions and to sell rice. The records of population for each family should be investigated, and they should be divided into the poorest and the poor, these two ranks. The poorest should receive eight *ge* [four-fifths of a pint] of rice per day, with the parents receiving the same amount. Wives and children should receive half. The next poorest families should also receive half this amount. A day before [the rice is to be distributed], record the numbers of people and assign them a ticket. The next day at dawn a member from each family will assemble at a certain place to give in the number [and receive his rice]. Distribute rice in this way every ten days.

But Chen complains that this method drew people away from their occupations and thus might encourage popular disturbances. He suggests a safer method:

> Those who distribute gruel [should] gather people together and feed them. The fragrance of the steaming gruel is protection against unexpected disturbances—[thus] there is no [method of distribution] better than that of giving out allotments of gruel. For each picul use fifty to sixty pints of white rice boiled as gruel. When done, place it in a wooden container, and prepare some baskets. Get ten bowls and ten pairs of chopsticks, and prepare a few salted vegetables. Carry all to a public thoroughfare or to the suburbs. Have all the poor who pass by sit down in a row, and give each person a meal. When these are finished, wash the utensils in water borrowed from a neighboring house, so that another group can eat. Each picul will feed approximately fifty to sixty people. Ten piculs will then be enough for five to six hundred people. In this way you can move from neighborhood to neighborhood, without the trouble of gathering people together in one place. You can extend the scope of the aid depending on the cir-

[75] On Zhu Xi's idea of a community granary, see Richard Von Glahn, "Community and Welfare: Zhu Xi's Community Granary in Theory and Practice," pp. 19–25.

cumstances. Nothing is more convenient than this method of distributing gruel. [7.25b–26a]

Chen's method is the best, then, because it relieves the starving without in any way allowing them to threaten the public order.

Although Chen repeatedly insists that scholars and ordinary people can also organize such projects, the exemplary stories accompanying these deeds focus largely on achievements sponsored by local officials: Lu Yijian, while prefect of Binzhou during the reign of Song Zhenzong, was able to persuade the emperor to abolish the tax on agricultural tools and was rewarded with the post of prime minister; Cai Junmo earned a similar reward when, as prefect of Quanzhou, he contributed 140,000 cash of his own funds to build a bridge and construct dikes to protect the city of Luoyang from high tides; and Wang Yong also earned a post for petitioning the emperor Song Taizong (r. 977–997) to reduce the harsh taxes imposed on the Liangzhe region. Pan Gongding, prefect of some unspecified region near Songjiang in the mid-Ming, aided his community by introducing a new industry, the weaving of cloth:

> He taught the women from among the common people and unemployed female workers how to cultivate cotton. He selected four families from Songjiang whose women were good at weaving, and had them live in four different areas, and ordered the *li* captain to lead the people in their *bao* to study with them. After a month, he went to inspect their progress, and rewarded those who had learned. After that they exhorted each other [to greater efforts]. Within the area governed by Pan there were no idle women wandering about.
>
> Pan dreamt that a spirit gave him two cassia branches, saying, "You have led the women of your area to the study of weaving. You have brought benefit to this area. Shangdi presents you with two honorable children; these are symbols of them. The elder son Yunzhe was a *jinshi* of 1565, and the other, Yunduan, was a *jinshi* of 1562. [7.29b–30a]

Chen interprets the benefits of Pan's actions not in economic terms, but in terms of public order and morality: it is not that the handicraft industry will increase the prosperity of the region that counts with him, but the fact that it absorbs the time and attention of otherwise idle womenfolk.

Chen does provide one story that gives those who are not officials a model to follow in their efforts to aid others. This is the case of He Canran, a secretary to the cruel Yao Siren, governor of both Shandong and Henan in the Wanli period. He persuades Yao to memorialize the throne for relief aid during a severe famine and is rewarded with passage of the examination for the *jinshi* degree at the age of forty; he eventually reaches the position of minister in the Ministry of Personnel. He's case is used to assure other scholars or relatively low-ranking members of the elite that they too can exert influence for the good in their local communities:

> If one can exhort heroes and powerful men to do good, the merit for the good deed is doubled. Now heroes have talent and the powerful have influence. . . . The harm they do is great, [yet] the benefit they create is also great. Therefore the sages of the past all associated with and employed heroes and powerful men. Men who [work as] secretaries are used by heroes and powerful men, and in turn they use heroes and powerful men themselves. But while the merits of officials are many, so too their faults are many—they cancel each other out, and merit does not build up. If a secretary has merits but no demerits, he has what is called pure merit. Like the expenditure of a frugal family, the expenses are very small, and it is not difficult to become prosperous. As for officials, when they have finished governing, all the people praise them; they pile up memorials and the court glorifies them; they accumulate wealth and rewards enough to light up the world. [But] then the register of the secret recorder [of merit] is not full. When a secretary is virtuous, he earns no name; hence his is called secret virtue. . . .
>
> Thus the overseer of hell noted that He's resplendent merit was greater than that of governor Yao Siren. Extrapolating from this discussion, all of you who have compassionate minds and are close to strong men, develop a method or strategy, and go with it to the households of the wealthy and high-ranking, for they can all use your ideas to do good. Whoever can devise a strategy will accumulate limitless merit—why can't scholars and ordinary people (*shishu*) also accumulate this merit? [7.31a–b]

Thus the relatively lowly members of local elites should not neglect their opportunities to benefit their communities through the influence they could exert on local officials or local gentry leaders. While they might fail to gain the acclaim accorded officials, their very obscurity assured them of a greater accumulation of secret merit, and thus more substantial rewards from the gods. They, as well as the highest and wealthiest officials and gentry, had responsibilities to their communities.

The morality books and ledgers of the seventeenth century reflect an overriding concern for enforcing an ideal of social hierarchy based on the notion of reciprocity. In a properly ordered world, each status had its own privileges and responsibilities: servants could expect a kind of paternalistic care from their masters in return for hard work and obedience, while officials could expect honor and imperial rewards in return for their devotion to public welfare. The higher the status, the greater the privileges and the heavier the obligations. The participation of heaven and the gods in the network of reciprocity served to correct any failures in the public human sphere—that is, the gods saw to it that everyone was in his or her proper place, and that goodness overlooked by or unknown to men was always, sooner or later, rewarded. In the world of the ledgers, the human hierarchy was an accurate (though sometimes to man's eye rather mystifying) expression of moral order; gods and spirits were constantly working, behind the scenes as it were, investigating human behavior and adjusting status assignments, to see that this was the case.

The ledgers, in their insistence on this ideal of social hierarchy, reflect very clearly what one scholar has called the "crisis consciousness" of the late-Ming and early-Qing elite.[76] For the pattern of relationships presented as a model in the texts little resembled the real conditions of the day. This, after all, was the time when tenants and bondservants were expressing their dissatisfaction with status restrictions through rent-resistance struggles and outright rebellion. The old paternalistic landlord-tenant relationship, idealized as one of "mutual support and mutual nurturance," had broken down as more and more tenants turned to handicraft activities to supplement their income, demanded contractual rights of permanent tenancy, or simply began to refuse to pay their rents. So, too, for the master-servant relationship, the legal fiction that bondservants were simply "adopted" family members wore thinner and thinner as both wealthy and powerful bondservants and poorer agricultural bondservants rose up against their masters, seizing their property and repudiating their contracts of servitude. By the late seventeenth century, the institution of bondservitude was beginning to change radically as landowners began to employ fewer bondservants, using them now largely as household servants, not as agricultural laborers or estate managers. Through the eighteenth-century, decrees of the Yongzheng and Qianlong (r. 1735–1796) emperors further restricted the terms of bondservitude.[77] Thus the ledger authors were trying to impose an old-fashioned, paternalistic ethic on relationships that had both shrunk in economic significance and changed considerably in nature.

Bondservants and tenants were not the only groups who were failing to fit into the ledger authors' vision of an ordered society. What was worse, members of the privileged elite—scholars, officials, and local gentry—were refusing to fulfill the responsibilities for nurturance and community charity commensurate with their place in the social hierarchy.

[76] Okuzaki, *Chūgoku kyōshin jinushi*, pp. 336–516, especially 336–339, 412–421. Okuzaki links this sense of crisis more comprehensively to the major intellectual trends of the late Ming and early Qing; I would use it here in a somewhat narrower sense, to refer simply to the elite awareness of changing social and economic relationships.

Chen Zhixi, for example, in his *Complete Book of Exhortations and Admonitions*, recognizes the precarious hold many elite families had on their status: "In Suzhou wealthy families with tens of thousands of *mu* and houses of a thousand rooms often don't even have any land left to stand on by the time of their second or third generations" (4.3b).

[77] Oyama, "Large Landownership in Jiangnan," pp. 130–147; see also Shih, "Peasant Economy," pp. 167–177.

Even the faith that a landlord or master would care for his own tenants and servants in times of flood and famine no longer held in the late seventeenth century; the central government, through the office of the district magistrate, took on more and more responsibility for relief and charity. Chen Zhixi and Chen Xigu, in their efforts to persuade local elites of the advantages of charitable giving, were clearly fighting this tide of indifference, and trying to reassert for local elites a role of community leadership.

The ledgers were by no means the only texts of the period to reflect elite anxiety about the growing independence and authority of tenants and bondservants and the increasing isolation of landowners, especially absentee landlords, from rural society. Gazetteers describe the breakdown in the relationships, while encyclopedias for daily use and, most particularly, family instructions all reflect the same sense of the precariousness of the gentry position vis-à-vis servants and tenants. Wang Mengji, for example, warned his family not to count too heavily on the helpless dependence of their servants: "Since [our bondservants] have their labor power, how could it be that they could not rely on other [masters]? To say that but for us they would have no means of survival is quite erroneous."[78] To ease what was clearly seen as a potentially tense relationship, the encyclopedias and family instructions urge landlords and masters to deal compassionately with their tenants and servants, and tenants and servants to deal loyally with their landlords and masters. Authors of these texts prescribe rules very similar to those found in the seventeenth-century ledgers: a master should use "kindness and moral influence" in overseeing his servants, though of course status distinctions should be strictly maintained; masters must care for servants in illness, see that they have enough food and clothing, ensure that they are married at reasonable ages. Rational, and preferably noncorporal, methods of punishment should be employed. Servants and tenants in turn should work hard for their superiors, never deserting them for new masters or landlords.[79]

Such prescriptions emphasizing compassionate treatment of tenants and servants are a tacit acknowledgment on the part of the authors of the ledgers and other prescriptive texts that elites, if they hoped to preserve their status, had to adjust their behavior somewhat to the changed social and economic circumstances of the seventeenth and eighteenth centuries. Landlords and masters could no longer assume the absolute control over their tenants and servants that they believed had been possible in previous centuries; gone were the days, as one landlord complained, when "the common people were docile and the masters authoritative."[80] Landlords

[78] Wang Mengji, cited in Hosono, "Minmatsu Shinsho Kōnan," p. 11.
[79] Hosono, "Minmatsu Shinsho Kōnan," pp. 12–19.

and masters had to earn the loyalty of their subordinates through kindness and compassion. Within the rural community they had to work to preserve their position by fulfilling the responsibilities of leadership—caring for the poor, providing relief from famine, setting up regulations for social order, and so forth. Thus, to fulfill their conservative goal, the return to an ideal social hierarchy, the ledger authors had to make some allowance for the shift in economic and social power within Chinese society, and to grant some concessions, as it were, to now more powerful groups. They consistently emphasized not the authoritarian, but the paternalistic principles that were to govern the superior-inferior relationships within the hierarchy. The doctrine of supernatural retribution, whether expressed through a bureaucracy of gods or a cosmic process of action and response, gave the hierarchy moral validity. But it also increased the pressure on those of high status: superiors had to earn and continue to deserve their high status by practicing kindness and compassion in their dealings with tenants and servants, and by providing relief and charity for their communities.

A Pattern for Social Hierarchy: Meritorious Deeds at No Cost

Nowhere is the concern with defining hierarchical distinctions and the rules that preserve them clearer than in Xiong Hongbei's late seventeenth-century ledger, *Meritorious Deeds at No Cost*. This text, unlike the others discussed so far, is explicitly organized by status categories. The 451 deeds of this compact and lightly annotated ledger are listed under twelve sections: local gentry (55 deeds), scholars (32), peasants (21), craftsmen (20), merchants (17), physicians (21), yamen workers (55), women (40), soldiers (22), Buddhist and Daoist monks (20), servants and laborers (22), and people in general (126).

The provisions listed provide a microcosm of the social ideal described at much greater length in ledgers like the *Compendium of Ledgers of Merit and Demerit*. The local rural elites, the gentry and scholars, are given the major leadership roles in the community. Xiong recognizes, however, that their influence is not always used for good; he devotes a great deal of space to proscriptions warning each group not to abuse its particular kind of power. For the gentry this is economic and social power; they are enjoined not to "encroach on others' lands and dispossess them," to "prevent the younger members of your family from oppressing others by taking advantage of your position," and to "prevent your household servants from causing trouble by relying on your influence."

---

[80] See Elvin, *Pattern of the Chinese Past*, pp. 241–244. For roughly the same argument, see Okuzaki, *Chūgoku kyōshin jinushi*, pp. 461–475.

In contrast, the biggest problem for scholars is the abuse of their superior knowledge and intellectual skills; they are encouraged not to "write or post notices that defame other people," not to "write petitions or accusations to high authorities," not to "encourage the spread of immoral and lewd novels," and so forth.[81]

Both gentry and scholars, however, are given positive functions within the community as well. The gentry are seen in several different leadership roles. First, they are mediators between the community and the local official, responsible for informing him of the special problems of the area and for advising him against harmful policies. Second, they are encouraged to settle disputes within the village: "Settle disputes among your neighbors fairly," "persuade others to settle lawsuits through conciliation," and "try to settle complaints and lawsuits among others." But their greatest responsibility seems to lie in the area of education, including moral exhortation and teaching through example. "Take the lead in charitable donations"; "rectify your own conduct and transform the people"; "when villagers commit misdeeds, admonish them boldly and persuade them to desist"; "hold up for public admiration women who are faithful to their husbands and children who are obedient to their parents"; "restrain those who are stubborn and unfilial"; "endeavor to improve manners and customs"—almost one-third of the items encourage the gentry to take responsibility for the moral order of the village.[82]

Not surprisingly, this emphasis is greatly strengthened in the section for scholars. Some of these prescriptions deal with scholars' treatment of their students. Two—"be patient in educating the younger members of poor families" and "if you find yourself with smart boys, teach them sincerity; with children of the rich and high-ranking, teach them decorum and duty"—indicate the ways in which status differences are acknowledged and perpetuated in village schools. Many more, however, give the scholars responsibility for the education and moral training of the whole village. In addition to instruction in the standard virtues of loyalty and filial piety, scholars are urged to "exhort and admonish the ignorant by lecturing to them on the provisions of the local community compact (*xiangyue*) and the public laws," to "publish morality books in which are compiled things useful and beneficial to all," to "explain the teachings of

---

[81] Xiong Hongbei, *Bufeiqian gongdeli*, in Chen Hongmou, *Xunsu yigui*, 4.44a–b. I consulted Sakai Tadao's partial translation in his "Confucianism and Popular Educational Works," pp. 352–361.

The items here warning scholars against writing petitions and defaming people could well be a response to the participation of scholars in many of the urban and rural protest movements of the late sixteenth and seventeenth centuries. See Sakai, *Chūgoku zensho*, pp. 180–196.

[82] Xiong Hongbei, *Bufeiqian gongdeli*, in Chen Hongmou, *Xunsu yigui*, 4.43b–44a.

human nature and principle [i.e., of the Cheng-Zhu school] to those of some understanding; to the uneducated teach the principles of moral retribution," and to "teach the people how to preserve their lives and improve their fate."[83] Scholars are thus responsible for reinforcing government regulations and the Neo-Confucian orthodoxy within the village; the belief in retribution, doubtless because of the moral justification it provides for status distinctions, is to be taught to those too poorly educated to understand the more sophisticated doctrines of the orthodoxy.

But there is also a sense, as in the other fuller ledgers, that these men must cultivate themselves and order their families—following the pattern suggested in the *Greater Learning*—as well as care for the public welfare. The provisions for gentry and scholars thus include many rules for personal conduct or moral cultivation and study: "Do not let yourself be blinded by emotion and personal prejudices," "be tolerant of the mistakes of others," "be willing to listen to things displeasing to your ears," "be loyal to the emperor and filial to your parents," "honor your elder brothers and be faithful to your friends," "respect the writings of the sages and worthies," and so forth. For the gentry there are also several prescriptions covering family affairs; they are urged to be even-handed in their treatment of family members, regardless of economic status, and to restrain the arrogance of their relatives. Several items deal with the master-servant relationship. On the one hand, servants should not be allowed to abuse the master's power or slander his family and friends, while on the other, the master is to be thoughtful in the arrangement of his servants' marriages and is not to force people into servitude. Another prescription in the "people in general" section also provides a guideline for the compassionate treatment of servants: "Do not get angry with household servants when they give you cause for anger, but instead instruct them with kind words."[84]

Members of lower status groups are not burdened with such personal moral responsibilities in *Meritorious Deeds at No Cost*. While they are presumably supposed to follow the general moral prescriptions of the "people in general" section, the deeds exclusively for peasants are almost entirely devoted to relationships with landlords or other peasants. Those focusing on the tenant-landlord relationship urge respect for the landlord's property ("do not take your landlord's seed or crops for your own benefit," "do not steal and sell your master's grain in connivance with his servants"), and loyalty to the landlord even when he is stingy ("do not become lazy and cease being conscientious because you think your landlord does not provide enough food and wine or fails to pay you enough").

[83] Ibid., 4.44a–b.
[84] Ibid., 4.43–44b, 48b–49b.

Many of the deeds address the distruptive potential of tenants within the farming community—the ways in which tenants, by abusing the authority of their landlords, might encroach on a neighbor's land or encourage dissension within the community: "Do not instigate landlords to buy up land"; "do not damage crops in your neighbors' fields by leaving animals to roam at large, relying on your landlord's power and influence to protect you"; "do not encroach beyond the boundaries of your own fields and watercourses, thinking to ingratiate yourself with your landlord"; "do not instigate your landlord to take revenge on a neighbor on the pretext that the neighbor's animals have damaged your crops."[85] The fear reflected in these last prescriptions—the fear that tenants, with or without the collusion of their landlords, would disrupt the community through their primitive techniques of agricultural competition—dominates the ledger for peasants. Again, as with the gentry and scholar ledgers, the focus is on how different statuses function in a community, in particular how the landlord-peasant relationship affects village harmony.

Servants and laborers, however, are to be preoccupied more narrowly with their roles within their master's household. Almost all of the twenty-two deeds in the "servants and laborers" ledger describe how servants should behave before their master or members of his family. Only three items—two warning against gossip about the master's affairs and one against abusing the master's power to bargain prices down—cover the role servants might play in relationships between the household and the community. The prescriptions for behavior within the household emphasize the protection of property ("do not waste your master's grain or material possessions," "do not steal property, or food and drink"), the preservation of household harmony ("do not carry tales and make mischief, to create dissension among the master's relatives," "do not fight with your companions"), and loyalty to the master, even in the face of poor treatment or poverty ("do not wildly curse your master because he has beaten or cursed you," "do not become disloyal to your master because you do not have many clothes or much food").[86]

Meritorious Deeds at No Cost presents a kind of easy summary, almost a crib, to the much more detailed listings and stories of the *Complete Book of Exhortations and Admonitions* or the *Compendium of Ledgers of Merit and Demerit*. The social vision is essentially the same: society is a hierarchy of statuses, each with its own set of benefits and obligations. Both the benefits and the obligations increase and broaden as one moves up the hierarchy, so that the smooth running of this profoundly paternalistic system is dependent on elite acceptance of quite heavy social bur-

[85] Ibid., 4.54a.
[86] Ibid., 4.48b-49a.

dens. The good man is one who accepts the limits of his appointed (and morally justified) status and faithfully fulfills the rules governing that status. Indeed, it is only through such "goodness" that one can hope to advance to a higher status (or to maintain an already high status): the order as a whole is thereby protected, while individual cases of personal advance are sanctioned, always as reflections of moral effort.

Money and "Moral Capital" in the Ledgers of Merit and Demerit

The ledger authors' concern for encouraging social stability is reflected too in their highly ambivalent attitude toward money and property and their use in the process of merit accumulation. The very form and method of the ledgers of merit and demerit suggest some sympathy with at least a crude form of commercial calculation: the ledger user accumulates good deeds just as a merchant accumulates money.[87] One obscure ledger advocate draws the parallel quite clearly when explaining metaphorically the beneficent effects of merit accumulation: "If you take in a thousand strings of cash and expend a hundred, then your income exceeds your expenditures. If you spend a thousand strings and take in one hundred, then your expenditure exceeds your income. When your income is in excess, then you are pleased; when your expenditure is in excess, then you are dissatisfied."[88]

Scholars have also argued that the ledgers encourage a commercial view of goodness, in that a ledger user is called upon to build up a kind of moral capital from which he can draw rewards. Furthermore, since the merit value of each deed varies, he is called upon to plan his actions and to weigh his deeds, in an entrepreneurial style, so that he may set up a full account as efficiently as possible.[89]

Most ledger authors and supporters appear, however, to have been reluctant to emphasize this obvious metaphor. It is almost never used in the seventeenth-century ledgers—a remarkable fact, given the suitability of the comparison. Certainly, one reason was the fear that merit accumulation might be labeled profit seeking. Ledger authors urgently and repeatedly assert that merit will accrue to a doer of good deeds only if he or she does them without thoughts of profit,[90] and any use of a commercial met-

[87] The commercial metaphor, so appropriate to the form of the ledgers of merit and demerit, has no etymological justification: the ge of gongguoge literally means "standard" or "rule." See Sakai, Chūgoku zensho, p. 358.

[88] This passage is attributed to a Cai Shanji. See "Yuanxu xuancun," 2b, in "Xinlu," Riqian chushe. See also Chen Zhixi, Taishang ganying pian (with commentary), Quanjie quanshu, 1.1b–2a.

[89] See, for example, Judith Berling, "Religion and Popular Culture: The Management of Moral Capital in The Romance of the Three Teachings," pp. 211–212.

[90] See, for example, Hu Rongshi, "Tiyao," 2a, Huibian gongguoge.

aphor to describe ledger keeping would certainly undermine this already rather dubious principle by linking it to profit making of the crudest type. But another problem for the ledger authors was their own ambivalence about the relationship between wealth and merit making.

For the very terms of ledger use suggest that wealth can be interpreted as a reflection or emblem of virtue, as a reward for good deeds. If the gods see to it that people get what they deserve in this life, then isn't the luxurious life of the wealthy merchant simply a reward for and advertisement of his goodness? Indeed, occasionally the ledger authors do recount stories of men rewarded for good deeds with wealth. Chen Zhixi even manages to suggest that the fortune of the Wus, one of the great merchant families of Huizhou, was a supernatural reward for an ancestor's virtue and charity.[91] More to the point, wealth is clearly a means to goodness, an aid in the performance of good deeds. Despite the ledger authors' protests that anyone in the community might lead famine relief efforts, it was obviously much easier for wealthy men to organize and fund such merit-earning activities, as ledger authors on occasion acknowledged. Hu Rongshi, when discussing philanthropic and public-works projects, admits that "it rests with the great families and wealthy households (*dajia yinhu*) to take the lead in these activities."[92] Chen Zhixi, in his exhaustive account of Ding Bin's charitable activities, is very conscious of how much is being spent, and it is clear that Ding could not have done nearly as much good if he had not been an extremely wealthy man. And usually the kinds of deeds that require wealth are also ones that yield high merit scores. Chen Xigu's *Compendium* allots one hundred to one thousand merits for deeds that involve considerable expenditures of money [8.25a–26b].

The appearance of ledgers specifically for those who are willing to spend money on merit making also suggests that wealth might be a considerable asset in a man's struggle to be good. Yuan Huang's ledger contains such a section, and most other ledgers award points, usually one merit per one hundred cash, to those who spend money on their virtuous activities. The *Compendium of Ledgers of Merit and Demerit* has a special ledger "Spending Money to Make Merit" ("Feiqian xinggong") for those who can afford to give; it includes deeds such as contributing to the wedding or funeral expenses of clan members, teachers, and friends; rescuing a good person from falling into a lowly position or from having to part from his family; giving aid to the poor, the widowed, and the orphaned in one's neighborhood; establishing schools or orphanages; set-

[91] Chen Zhixi, *Quanjie quanshu*, 8.22a–23b.

[92] Hu Rongshi, *Huibian gongguoge*, 47b–48a, quoted in Chen Xigu, *Huizuan gongguoge*, 7.29a.

ting up winter and summer shelters for the aged and infirm who have no family; providing them with a daily ration of rice and cash; distributing medicine to the ill; setting up gruel kitchens in times of famine; building or repairing bridges and roads; publishing and distributing morality books; and purchasing and releasing animals [8.25b–26b]. Many of the other deeds scattered throughout the other ledgers require some expenditure. There is, then, a tacit admission that wealth may help in merit accumulation, that there is even a direct relationship between the accumulation of "real" capital and the accumulation of moral capital.

But the ledger authors, in their explicit statements about wealth and mercantile activity, are quite hesitant to link the two forms of accumulation. Indeed, their stated attitude toward property and money management reflects the traditional Confucian view of wealth as a potential danger to moral improvement. Some are quite harsh in their condemnation of material accumulation. Chen Zhixi, for example, warns that wealth is "the instrument of ten thousand wrongs" and clearly has reservations about the moral implications of money making: "Few are those who have worked to accumulate wealth without transgressing against righteousness," he writes.[93] Most other ledger authors, however, adopt a more moderate, though still highly qualified, view of the relationship between wealth and moral action. Hu Rongshi, in his *Collection of Ledgers of Merit and Demerit*, best summarizes this more optimistic position: "Wealth (*cai*) is a means of nourishing life. If one values life, then one must value wealth. But righteousness must be where there is wealth."[94] It is this final qualification that shapes most of the ledger authors' views on wealth. Even the ledgers designed for those willing to spend money on merit making warn that attitude and purity of mind are much more important than the amount of the expenditure in earning merit. Chen Xigu advises his readers:

> Whoever uses money to distribute aid must have a mind first, free of stinginess, second, free of any desire for fame, third, free of any expectation of reward, and fourth, free of any sense of self-satisfaction. If he loses this state of mind, then if he is wealthy, even if he spends money on charity every day, he will always feel that he is not doing enough. How can he succeed in earning merit? If he is poor and gives only occasionally, then the ghosts and spirits will feel he has done more than enough. How can the recompense of good fortune not be

[93] Chen Zhixi, *Quanjie quanshu*, 4.26a–27a.

[94] Hu Rongshi, *Huibian gongguoge*, 53b–54a, quoted in Chen Xigu, *Huizuan gongguoge*, 5.21a. The ledger authors use the term "*cai*" (occasionally "*huocai*") in their discussions of wealth. In certain cases, when mercantile activity is the specific subject, it is clear that *cai* refers to money. Otherwise, the authors seem to use it in a very broad sense, to include landed property and possessions as well as money—hence the translation "wealth" used here.

forthcoming? So, then, in using the ledger that records merit according to money spent, you need not adhere completely to the examples given. Simply be constantly aware of whether your mind is sincere or not. [8.25a]

Chen then repeats Yuan Huang's cautionary tale of the woman who earns greater merit contributing two cash to a temple with a sincere mind than she does giving one thousand pieces of silver half-heartedly (see chapter 2). We are to believe that it is the state of mind, not the amount of money, that determines the merit. To reinforce the point, no specific merit points are given for any of the good deeds listed in the ledger "Spending Money to Make Merit." Nor are any stories of recompense told to illustrate the fruits of this kind of virtue: again, the wealthy in particular are to do good without expecting rewards.

Furthermore, in the prescriptions relevant to wealth, the ledger authors consistently urge behavior that elevates honesty and generosity over the accumulation of riches. Yan Maoyou's discussion of rewards associated with wealth focuses, as its title "Recompense Due to Incorruptibility in Regard to Wealth" ("Liancai zhi bao") suggests, on the return of money accidentally or illicitly acquired to its rightful owner and on the destruction of counterfeit money. Those who covet the property of others or who actually steal from others may be punished with sons who cause the ruin of their families, with death by lightening, or with rebirth in animal form—one man, for example, was reborn as a dog in the household of a family whose property he had sought to seize.[95]

Li Guochang devotes more space to money- and property-related deeds, in his "Ledger on Gaining Wealth" ("Lincai ge"), but he too tends to emphasize restraint and strict adherence to moral standards in any commercial or financial transactions: one should always repay money borrowed, be willing to yield one's share when property is divided, avoid deceitful methods of gaining wealth, and guard against avarice. Typical of the kind of behavior that earns reward is that of Cheng Yuwen, a member of a wealthy and powerful family in Nancheng, Jiangxi, during the Chongzhen era (1628–1644). Yuwen alone of his family was sincere and generous: "he did not have the temperament of a slave to wealth." When his father, following the lead of all the other great families of the region, wanted to use an illegally large measure of grain to collect his rents, Yuwen refused to allow this practice, maintaining that to impose an extra burden on the tenants would be an intolerable increase of hardship. The very next day a fire swept through the family compound, killing everyone, but stopping miraculously before it reached Yuwen's household.[96] Li Guochang appropriately ends his ledger with the admonition "know

[95] Yan Maoyou, *Diji lu*, 7.48a–64b; especially 59a.
[96] Li Guochang, *Chongxiu zhiyao*, 8.1b, 5a–b.

when to stop and how to manage on little" (*zhizhi guaying*). A good man, he argues, takes pleasure in whatever economic condition or social status is decreed for him by heaven: "To know what is enough is to be happy, to covet much is to be sad. Those who know what is enough are happy even when poor and lowly, but those who do not know what is enough are sad even when wealthy and honored."[97] Chen Xigu also quite explicitly warns against a single-minded concern for wealth: men who are prosperous enough for their own needs, yet who think only of gaining more and not of aiding others, are penalized one hundred demerits, the highest in his "property" ledger; wealthy men who refuse to practice frugality but devote all their efforts to accumulating more money, lose fifty points [5.33a].

Frugality is the only virtue advocated in the ledgers that could possibly be interpreted as one encouraging the protection and even accumulation of wealth—it is advocated as a means of "protecting one's good fortune" (*xifu*) [5.83b, 30b]. But the accumulation of wealth is valued not as a commercial strategy, but as behavior that will allow one to do more good deeds and more far-reaching good deeds.[98] Indeed, the ledger authors take a strong stand against accumulation for its own sake. Chen Zhixi warns that it is not even a good idea to build up property for one's descendants—a large inheritance encourages laziness and extravagance, and will result in the downfall of the family. He argues that wealth is worth something to its owner only if it is passed on to others:

> The world's wealth is like flowing water. To begin with, it has already passed through many places—today it goes here, then in a moment it flows to another place. Before it comes to me, it is not my water. When it comes to me and I use it to water my fields and to wash away dirt, it is my water. If I hide it and do not use it, again it is not my water. The world's wealth is not my wealth—it only passes through my hands. To begin with, it has already passed through the hands of many people; only now does it come to me. If I use it to revere heaven, to give to others, and to spread goodness, then it is my wealth. If I do not use it, it passes on to other people—how then can it be my wealth?
>
> The wonderful good fortune of wealth does not lie in keeping wealth, but in spreading it about; it does not lie in gaining it for oneself, but in giving it away. Wealth is like thorns. Someone asked: "Thorns injure the body. Money wounds the mind. Are the two the same?" The reply: "They are exactly the same."[99]

In a similar vein, Chen Xigu, in his ledger for those able to expend funds on merit making, suggests that those who have more than they need

[97] Ibid., 8.27a.

[98] Handlin, "Benevolent Societies," pp. 324–325, 330. See Chen Zhixi, *Quanjie quanshu*, 8.3b–4a, for a clear statement of this view.

[99] Chen Zhixi, *Quanjie quanshu*, 4.27a–b.

should first take care of their families, and then move on to broader acts of charity that might benefit "outsiders"—that is, the members of their communities [8.35a–b].

Nowhere is the ledger authors' attitude to the accumulation of wealth clearer than in their stories about merchants and prescriptions for mercantile behavior. Merchants tend to be rewarded for acts of generosity or scrupulous honesty that, however virtuous, are not good for business. For example, Chen Zhixi provides the following model of commercial compassion:

> The father of Li Wenda (m. Xian, 1408–1467) was a wealthy merchant. He had a store of cotton in a warehouse, which he sold to three neighboring merchants for three hundred ounces. A fire started near the warehouse and all of the cotton was consumed. The three merchants were all very upset, and said to each other, "Our capital is exhausted; it will be hard to return home. We might as well go begging." Li overheard them, and called out to them, "Since the goods had not yet been transported to the boat, they were still mine. The goods are lost, but you had paid for them; it is proper for me to return the cost to you. Moreover, my capital is quite large, while yours is small, and if you lost it you would have no livelihood. I could not bear to see that." He returned the three hundred pieces of silver to them.
>
> That night his wife, back at home, dreamt that a man clothed in red gave her a jade child. The next year Xian was born. He reached the rank of grand secretary.[100]

Li's father is not rewarded with greater wealth—that is, greater success as a merchant—but with a son who becomes a famous official, already a hint as to what, in literati eyes, is considered a worthy goal for families engaged in commerce. Obviously there is an irony here: official posts were eagerly sought at least in part because they were potentially very lucrative. Thus while wealth alone was not deemed a suitable reward, it was implicitly accepted as legitimate as long as it was linked to the "proper" status.

Merchants, then, are to be enticed into good (but rarely commercially profitable) behavior with the promise of rewards that would lift them up from their despised status to one highly valued by the literati authors of the ledgers. Another of Chen's stories reflects this position very clearly:

> Prime Minister Yin Min's [1422–1503] father made his living by selling rice cakes. One day he found six hundred ounces of silver, and he buried it so no one would know of it, and planted a tree to mark the place. After several years

---

[100] Chen Zhixi, *Quanjie quanshu*, 6.38a–b. For Li Xian, see Goodrich, *Ming Biography*, vol. 1, pp. 819–822.

had passed and the tree had grown quite large, Yin passed the place and saw a man beneath it, trembling and weeping. He asked what the problem was, and the man replied, "I am a merchant from Shanxi. My business failed, and I had only six hundred pieces of silver left. I thought to return home with it and start another business. I stopped to rest here, and the money all disappeared. I dared not return home to face my parents, so I have been wandering about as a beggar. Now, thinking of all this, I became so sad that I began to tremble." Yin asked the date when this had happened, and found that it coincided with his discovery of the money. Then he said to the man, "Do not weep. Your money is buried beneath the tree." The man then dug down and found the money. He was very surprised and moved; he bowed to Yin and wanted to divide the money with him. Yin smiled and said, "I am simply a poor man who sells rice cakes for a living. If I had coveted money not rightfully mine, why would I not have taken it all before?" The stranger thanked him and left.

That night a spirit appeared to Yin in a dream, saying, "Your secret virtue is very great. You will be given a son who will attain high rank." Afterward Yin had a son, Min, who was secretary in the Ministry of Personnel and who became a grand secretary.

Chen then adds a revealing comment: "In the world every kind of good thought arises because people think little of wealth; all kinds of evil thoughts arise because they value wealth. Wealth is like medicine. It can keep people alive or it can kill them; the difference lies simply in using it well or using it badly."[101]

He proceeds to give examples of how wealth may be used well—largely through charitable activities, by contributing it to the poor, by feeding the hungry, by helping people get married, and so forth. But at the same time that he implicitly acknowledges the moral value money may have, he also explicitly emphasizes the incompatability of commerce and virtue:

Merchants endure all sorts of physical suffering [literally, "they inhale wind and eat snow"] in their single-minded pursuit of profit. If their goods are damaged by fire, disaster falls upon them. They have no leisure for health and happiness. Who cannot pity their poverty? . . . To be a merchant and to have a noble mind, this is truly difficult. . . . Selling rice cakes is a petty trade, requiring little capital and bringing in very few profits. Yin Min's father was by nature content with little—otherwise, how could he have found six hundred pieces of silver and, willing to follow his proper destiny, conceal it from others, until a few years later, he could return it to a poor merchant?

How can one deny that there are gentlemen among men of petty status? I am even willing to humble myself before such men. Generally speaking, those peo-

[101] Chen Zhixi, *Quanjie quanshu*, 6.38b–39a; cited in Okuzaki, *Chūgoku kyōshin ji-nushi*, pp. 464–465. On Yin Min, see *Guochao xianzheng lu*, 24.50a–51b.

ple who value property lightly must value virtue highly. . . . Heaven aids virtuous men, but there is nothing better than the reward for the man who values
property lightly.[102]

There is a clear message here that the occupation of merchant and the
practice of virtue, if not mutually exclusive, are not easily reconciled:
though certain exceptional merchants might be able to rise above their
commercial concerns, it is generally unrealistic to expect too much of
them.

To some extent this attitude is reflected in the specific prescriptions for
merchants listed in the ledgers. *Compendium* author Chen Xigu enjoins
all men to use standard scales for both buying and selling; the reward is
ten merits a year for regular people, twenty for merchants, some indication of the kind of business ethics generally expected of merchants. Merchants are awarded thirty merits a year for charging fair prices to villagers
and poor scholars, one hundred "if you make your livelihood in trade,
and are consistently fair, without quibbling for insignificant advantages" [5.27a]. The merchant ledger of *Meritorious Deeds at No Cost* also
emphasizes fair business practices: "do not deceive ignorant villagers
when fixing the price of goods," "do not use the short measure when
selling and the long measure when buying," "do not deceitfully serve un-
clean dishes or leftover food to customers who are unaware of the fact,"
and so forth. Otherwise, merchants are urged to practice small charities
appropriate to their occupation—that is, they should be generous to the
poor when changing silver for them, forgive small debts, and reduce the
prices of clothing and other basic items when selling them to the poor.[103]
These provisions all suggest a low evaluation of merchant practices and
standards, and a rather limited arena for merchant merit accumulation.[104]

In sum, the seventeenth- and eighteenth-century ledgers of merit and
demerit reflect an ambivalent attitude to the relationship between wealth
and goodness. Certainly, the logic of ledger ideology suggests that wealth
is a reward for goodness, and the ledger authors, in including deeds requiring considerable expenditure (and often earning very high merit
points) in their texts, are acknowledging that it is frequently easier for the
wealthy to do good. But at the same time they are quite explicit in their
doubts about the moral capacities of the wealthy, particularly those
whose wealth is commercial. It is a surprise when a merchant does a good
deed, for after all, not much is to be expected of men devoted to the pursuit of profit. The ledgers certainly do not openly encourage capital ac-

---

[102] Chen Zhixi, *Quanjie quanshu*, 6.39b–40a.

[103] Xiong Hongbei, *Bufeiqian gongdeli*, in Chen Hongmou, *Xunsu yigui*, 4.45b–46a.

[104] For a similar evaluation, see Sakai, "Confucianism and Popular Educational Works,"
pp. 361–362.

cumulation for investment in commerce—on the contrary, wealth is "valuable" only if it is invested morally, in the accumulation of merit.[105]

Furthermore, the ledger authors assume that the only rewards that will attract merchants are those associated with elite status—examination degrees and official posts. These are the achievements of real significance in Chinese society, and thus sufficient to lure even quite wealthy merchants to good behavior. Commercial profits should be used by merchants to get themselves out of their merchant status—a goal it is assumed any merchant would want to attain. Used as the ledgers suggest, money could become a relatively respectable means for merchants to buy themselves into elite status: not through the crude purchase of degrees or offices, but through investment in the values and responsibilities associated with the scholar elite. Certainly, this process is given concrete expression in the merchant biographies of the period, which often describe merchant "purchase" of gentry status through contributions to charities and public works.

What seems to be going on here is an adjustment on the part of the ledger authors to the importance of wealth and the improvement in merchant status that marked the late Ming and the transition to the Qing.[106] They retain the traditional Confucian suspicion of commerce and wealth for its own sake, while tacitly admitting that wealth could be a source of goodness. With this admission of the potential moral value of wealth, they provide (though indirectly) a justification for the accumulation of wealth. It is fair to say, then, that the accumulation of wealth gains a new legitimacy in the morality books and ledgers of the seventeenth century. But it is important to recognize the heavy qualification imposed on this legitimacy: it operates only if the wealth is used morally. Accumulation for economic purposes—what the morality-book authors call "accumulation for its own sake"—is, in fact, perceived as evil. Wealth, especially in its commercial expression, had to be channeled in the proper "Confucian" direction, away from mercantile investment and into the performance of good deeds; only then does the merchant have any chance of attaining what must be his fondest goal—to cease to be a merchant and to become a scholar-official.

Again, the ledger authors are following the sort of conservative impulse that governed their handling of landlord–tenant and master–servant relationships: to preserve the status hierarchy, certain allowances had to be made for inescapable social and economic changes. The greater independence of tenants and bondservants necessitated a greater generosity in the

<hr>

[105] Peterson, *Bitter Gourd*, pp. 74–80; and Okuzaki Hiroshi, "Minmatsu Shinsho no rishoku kihan—kōkakaku no ichisokumen," especially pp. 259–260.

[106] See Handlin, "Benevolent Societies," pp. 330–331.

rules governing their treatment; here the obvious importance of commercial wealth in the seventeenth century requires some provision for its use in socially valuable charitable programs. But in neither case should the hierarchy itself be threatened: the authors of the seventeenth-century ledgers are simply trying to absorb newly powerful social and economic groups into an outdated status hierarchy.

DISTRIBUTION AND USE OF THE LEDGERS OF MERIT AND DEMERIT

If the more comprehensive ledgers of merit and demerit of the seventeenth and eighteenth centuries were indeed designed as comprehensive moral guides to behavior for all the different status levels of society, how did their authors arrange for the actual distribution of the texts? How did they provide for the real application of their instructions? Who was supposed to read the texts, and how were their rules to be transmitted to those who could not read?

The ledgers tell us, usually in a section entitled "education" (*jiaohua*) or "encouraging moral transformation" (*quanhua*), that it was the responsibility of scholars and gentry to perform the important function of transmitting the prescriptions and moral lessons of the morality books to the rest of the population. They were to "endeavor to improve manners and customs" and to "explain books on moral retribution" to the common people.[107] Actual distribution of the ledger texts was encouraged in the ledgers themselves: publication and distribution of morality books was a merit-making activity, earning as many as fifty merits in the *Compendium of Ledgers of Merit and Demerit* [7.73b]. The introduction to the *Collection of Ledgers of Merit and Demerit* gives several examples of scholars who earned rewards in part because of their role in disseminating morality books. Liu Zhu of Kunshan was instructed by the King of Hell and the Mother of the Dipper Star to transmit the *Collection* to the world,[108] and another Kunshan scholar, Zhu Dai, was rewarded for his use and publication of the ledger:

> A scholar from Kunshan, named Zhu Dai, born Taizong, was of a poor family. He reverently practiced the prescriptions in the *Collection of Ledgers of Merit and Demerit* with all his strength, urged that it be printed and circulated, and collected funds for this purpose. When there was a great famine, Zhu set up gruel kitchens in the city. He believed that the merit for keeping people alive, listed in the "charity" ledger, was the greatest, and he urged that people give this kind of aid. . . .
>
> During one of his periods of tireless activity, he became seriously ill. His spirit

---

[107] Xiong Hongbei, *Bufeiqian gongdeli*, in Chen Hongmou, *Xunsu yigui*, 4.43b, 44b.
[108] Hu Rongshi, *Huibian gongguoge*, 5b.

wandered in darkness to a city where he met a scholar clothed in white, followed by a boy clutching a register. The scholar said to Zhu, "You are a good man. Leave this dangerous city immediately. Beyond these walls your sickness will get better." [On following these instructions, Zhu recovered.]

Mr. Xi of Dongting respected Zhu's virtuous works, and invited him to be his teacher. Zhu then urged Xi to print and distribute three hundred copies of this book, and otherwise continued to do good with greater strength.[109]

There is considerable evidence that people actually did fund such efforts at dissemination of the texts: we know, for example, that Yunqi Zhuhong paid for the reprinting and distribution of the *Tract of Taishang on Action and Response* in his youth.[110] A mid-Qing morality book praised a Yan Zhangjing of Songjiang for paying for the printing of as many as 130,000 copies of the *Register of Cinnabar and Cassia (Dangui ji)*, which he had distributed among all the provinces.[111] Other, less wealthy supporters might give more modest amounts; morality books often record the names of such contributors, many of whom paid for the publication of just a page or two of a text.[112]

The language used in the ledgers also suggests that they were written for use by as wide a readership as possible. Though written for the most part in classical Chinese, it is in many cases a classical Chinese so simple as to be accessible to anyone with a rudimentary knowledge of the language; it is in most cases much simpler than the language of Yuan Huang's works. At the least, the ledgers could be used by poorly educated scholars as well as sophisticated thinkers and officials. And since peasants did have some access to a very elementary education in the classical language in the late imperial period, it is possible that some peasants might be able to follow at least the simpler parts of some of the ledger texts.[113]

But it is more likely that the common people were orally instructed in the lessons of the ledgers at public readings and lectures. The clarity in the organization of the ledgers made them easy handbooks for oral moral instruction: deeds were neatly laid out in separate categories, and these were explained fully and simply; illustrative stories were clearly and persuasively narrated. In works as complex as the *Compendium*, classical or

---

[109] Ibid., 6b.

[110] Yunqi Zhuhong, "*Zizhi lu xu*," 1a, *Zizhi lu*, in *Yunqi fahui, ce* 15. 15.

[111] *Ganying pian zhijiang*, 1.6b.

[112] See, for example, the Kangxi edition of Chen Xigu, *Huizuan gongguoge*, "Juanzi xingshi" (in the Naikaku Bunko).

[113] Evelyn Rawski, "Problems and Prospects," p. 400; for a more extended discussion of popular literacy, see her *Education and Popular Literacy*, pp. 81–108, 125–154. By no means all the seventeenth- and eighteenth-century ledgers and morality books were written in a simple style—Yan Maoyou's *Record for Gaining Good Fortune*, for example, is considerably more difficult than Chen Zhixi's *Complete Book of Exhortations and Admonitions*.

other philosophical references were supplied to convince scholarly readers or relatively sophisticated listeners of the validity of the effort. But
even this long text would have been easy to lecture from: the specific
deeds were set off in bolder print, and stories and explanations clearly
marked off for easy selection.

Indeed, some of the longer morality books do contain sections written
in a simple vernacular, presumably to be read aloud or taught to an illit-
erate audience. The *Complete Book of Exhortations and Admonitions*,
for example, contains a vernacular explanation of the Six Maxims by a
Li Changke of Huaian.[114] This text also contains a series of songs in simple classical Chinese that could quite easily be taught to children or illiterates. The subjects of these represent Chen's range of social concerns:
there are relatively difficult songs urging study ("Quanxue ge"), extolling
the pleasures of learning ("Dushu le ge"),[115] and describing elite responsibilities, yet there are also very easy, repetitive songs explaining retributive justice and asserting the importance of keeping to one's place in society. "Lu Pingquan's Song for Awakening the World" ("Lu Pingquan
xingshi ge"), a relatively difficult one, warns the elite against abusing their
position. The first verse, for example, admonishes troublemakers:

> Clever, clever, clever—playing tricks and stirring up trouble all day;
> Such a man is deficient, only satisfying himself.
> When his time comes the King of Hell will take into account
> The one thousand methods he used to gratify his craftiness during life.[116]

The song goes on to point up the dangers of the abuse of power and of
fame- and profit-seeking. Much more accessible is the "Song on Mind and
Fate" ("Xinming ge"), designed to teach the importance of self-cultivation:

> If the mind is good, then fate too will be good;
> Wealth and honor will last through old age.
> If the mind is good and fate is not good,
> Heaven and earth are saving it for you.
> If fate is good and the mind is not good,
> You will die suddenly in the middle of your way.
> If mind and fate are both not good,
> Poor and lowly, you will meet disaster.
> The mind is simply the source of fate,

[114] Chen Zhixi, *Quanjie quanshu*, 3.14a–32a. For a discussion of this kind of literature,
see Victor H. Mair, "Language and Ideology in the Written Popularizations of the *Sacred
Edict*," pp. 325–359.
[115] Chen Zhixi, *Quanjie quanshu*, 3.49b–51a.
[116] Ibid., 3.46a–b. See also "Zhu Wengong dazhangfu ge," in ibid., 3.44b.

The most important thing is to establish the way of benevolence.
Fate is the root of the course of things;
You cannot manage its workings.
If you believe only in fate and do not cultivate the mind,
Yin and *yang* will be out of balance.
If you cultivate the mind and wait for fate,
The creation must recompense you. . . .[117]

Another song, at yet another intellectual level, teaches the value of accepting one's status in society:

Accept your lot, accept your lot.
Accept your lot—everyone reveres these words.
Accept your lot and bide your time.
Accept your lot and listen to heaven's command.
Accept your lot and skillfully manage your life.
Accept your lot and keep to your original place.
Accept your lot and be lenient with others.
Accept your lot and never quarrel.
Accept your lot and appear simple.
Accept your lot and keep your mind calm.
Accept your lot and let opportunities pass.
Throughout your life you will not be sad or melancholy.[118]

The message here is unmistakable; certainly it is cast in a form easy enough for anyone, literate or not, to learn.

Thus, both the contents and the language of many of the seventeenth-century ledgers suggest that their authors made every effort to see that they reached as broad an audience as possible. Clearly, their primary audience was the literate elite, potentially including quite lowly scholars and merchants as well as distinguished officials. These were men who had to be persuaded of the moral validity of the texts, for they were expected to use them in their own self-cultivation and their own family and community interactions—hence the classical allusions and the need to justify the retributive sanction in the prefaces of the ledgers. But then these readers were expected to use the texts in the education of others—hence the inclusion of various forms and styles of writing that might be useful in teaching ledger values. Thus, the ledgers functioned not only as guides to elite behavior, but also as teachers' handbooks for the transmission of approved values.

Below this primary audience was one much harder to define or measure

[117] Chen Zhixi, *Quanjie quanshu*, 3.47b–48a. A much more complex version of the same message is "Wen Wenshan zhengqi ge," *Quanjie quanshu*, 3.37b–38b.
[118] "Tang Huolin sige," in Chen Zhixi, *Quanjie quanshu*, 3.48b.

those, mentioned earlier, whose exposure to simple classical Chinese primers might have given them enough training to make their way through the simply worded prescriptions and stories of some of the ledgers. Finally, even illiterates had access, albeit rather indirect, to the ledgers—they could hear the stories and learn the songs from the real readers of the texts. Thus in theory the ledgers were available, in some form or other, to almost anyone in Chinese society. The wide range of prescriptions in the texts, including sections for special groups (servants, women, craftsmen, the wealthy, and so forth) suggest a very broad intended audience.

There is evidence that the texts did indeed achieve a fairly wide circulation. Authors of the seventeenth- and eighteenth-century ledgers clearly had access to other ledgers, for they quoted extensively from Yan Maoyou's *Record for Gaining Good Fortune*, Chen Zhixi's *Complete Book of Exhortations and Admonitions*, and Hu Rongshi's *Collection of Ledgers of Merit and Demerit*, as well as from more famous earlier texts like the *Tract on Action and Response* and Yuan Huang's *Determining Your Own Fate*. They referred to other morality books and ledgers too, works that they consulted in compiling their own works, but which no longer survive. Li Guochang, who first thought of writing a ledger when a friend showed him his own ledger during a visit to the Fazang Chan monastery in Yixing, Jiangsu, listed fourteen other morality books by title, only six of which are known today.[119] Though the major extant ledgers of the seventeenth and eighteenth centuries were produced in south China, by the early eighteenth century, at least one work, the *Ledger of Merit and Demerit for Spreading Goodness*, had been published in Manchuria. Even within the South, a single text might enjoy a fairly widespread distribution. The *Ledger of Merit and Demerit for Determining Your Own Fate*, for example, was originally published in Wumen, Jiangsu (near Suzhou) in 1747; then in Hangzhou, Zhejiang in 1754; and finally, a quarter of a century later, in Yunnan.[120]

While it is in most cases impossible to discover exactly how the ledgers were transmitted from place to place, it seems likely that Li Guochang's experience—learning of the texts through a friend—provided one common channel. Chan monasteries—both Yuan Huang and Li Guochang were converted to ledger use at such institutions—and other temples were clearly centers for distribution of the texts.[121] And of course, the official

[119] Li Guochang, "Fanli wuze," 1a–2a, *Chongxiu zhiyao*; and Sakai, *Chūgoku zensho*, pp. 383–385.

[120] Sakai, *Chūgoku zensho*, p. 395.

[121] The 1702 edition of the *Huibian gongguoge*, for example, was sponsored by a Daoist monastery; presumably, this institution also distributed copies of the text. See "*Huibian gongguoge* xu," 3b, in *Chongxiu zhiyao*.

network could form one of the most efficient means of disseminating the ledgers throughout China. Yuan Huang, though he learned of the ledgers in Nanjing, kept one himself first at his home in Wujiang, and then brought the system with him to Baodi county, Northern Zhili, where he used it to instruct criminals in self-correction. Thus those in official service could easily take the texts far beyond their point of origin in the south.

How exactly did the authors and supporters of the ledgers believe their texts should be used? Some felt that the texts or abridged versions of them could be employed in the moral education of children, either within the family or in schools. As a child studying at home, the philosopher Peng Dingxiu (1645–1719), for example, was given the *Tract of Taishang on Action and Response* as a textbook by his father.[122] Public admission of transgressions had long been recognized as a way of training school children in the practice of filial piety, sincerity, and reverence for the rules of etiquette;[123] the ledgers simply provided a more precise way of defining and measuring transgressions and of reinforcing positive models. Prescriptions for the education of children ("lesser learning") were included in some of the ledgers, and some whole ledgers were designed exclusively for young men studying for the examinations. Liu Linchang (j.s. 1618) wrote and distributed such a text, the *Ledger for Sagely Merit* (*Shenggong ge*) while an educational intendant in Zhejiang province. Though a whole section of this ledger was devoted to study and examination preparation, Liu was also interested in "regulating in detail the daily behavior" of his students. He recommended that they follow Zhu Xi's rules for the White Deer Grotto Academy, as well as those of his ledgers, to learn behavior appropriate to the different ranks within the family hierarchy.[124]

Educators grasped the instructional value of the ledgers and morality books during the Qing as well. Cui Xuegu suggested that Yan Maoyou's *Record for Gaining Good Fortune* and ledgers of merit and demerit be read and explained to school students in their spare time. We know that such books were used as texts in some schools: Li Zhaoluo (1769–1841) reported that many teachers of his day used the ledgers and Liu Zongzhou's *Manual for Man* instead of the once popular *Lesser Learning* (*Xiaoxue*) of Zhu Xi. Early Qing elementary schools often copied the form of the ledgers in drawing up rules for their students.[125] Chen Hong-

---

[122] Peng Dingqiu, *Nanyun wengao*, 2.1a–6a, in *Wenyun quanji*. See Hummel, *Eminent Chinese*, p. 616; and Handlin, "Benevolent Societies," p. 321.

[123] Wu Pei-yi, "Self-Examination," pp. 23–24.

[124] Liu Linchang, *Shenggong ge*, in *Zhexue zongzhuan*, 6.8b–9b. The only portion of this ledger that survives is the ledger for study ("Dushu ge"). See Sakai, *Chūgoku zensho*, pp. 387–388.

[125] Angela Ki Che Leung, "Elementary Education in the Lower Yangtze Region in the 17th and 18th Centuries," p. 31.

mou (1696–1771), the distinguished provincial official and grand secretary, included two ledgers, the *Ledger for Officials (Dangguan ge)* and *Meritorious Deeds at No Cost*, in his *Five Varieties of Posthumous Instructions (Wuzhong yigui)*, a collection of moral injunctions designed in part for use in village schools. Chen believed that quite young students, including even the sons of peasants, would benefit from education in the hierarchy of prescriptions, organized according to social status, set out in *Meritorious Deeds at No Cost*.[126]

Education through the ledgers was by no means restricted to children, however. Adult education in local study or benevolent societies or in community compacts and public lectures was perceived as perhaps the primary arena for ledger use. Earlier in the Ming, community compacts had already exploited the idea of counting and even measuring the good and bad deeds of its members; Lü Kun's compact included a ledger-like list of good and bad deeds which were assigned very crude values.[127] Although the benevolent societies of the late Ming and early Qing did not necessarily require their members to use ledgers, they often incorporated the general message of the ledgers into their public lectures. Gao Panlong, for example, urged the audience of his benevolent society to practice good behavior on the grounds that it would bring prosperity to them and their whole community. Chen Longzheng referred to the *Tract of Taishang on Action and Response* and another morality book, *Do Good for Secret Merit (Weishan yinzhi)*, in his benevolent society lectures.[128]

Other local societies might actually require that their members use ledgers. Yan Maoyou was the founder of just such a study society, the Yunqi Hui, in Pinghe county. Formed for the discussion of a wide variety of issues—Confucianism, government and economics, literature, history, Buddhism, Daoism, and metaphysics—and for the performance of good works, this society was open to all social and economic levels of the community. The society rules provided that the language used in the discussions be accommodated to the abilities of the less well-educated members, and poorer members were allowed some flexibility in the payment of the society's dues. The Yunqi Hui included only a few degree-holders in its membership rolls: of the thirty-seven listed, only Yan, a *jinshi*, and three other *juren* held degrees.[129]

The ledgers of merit and demerit formed the foundation of the Yunqi

[126] Alexander Woodside, "Some Mid-Qing Theorists of Popular Schools," pp. 11–14.

[127] Lü Kun, *Xiangjia yue*, *Shizheng lu*, 5.22a–25a, 27b–33b, in *Lüzi yishu*. See also Handlin, *Action in Late Ming Thought*, p. 198.

[128] Chen Longzheng's benevolent society rules required that a lecturer talk "in a language accessible to everyone" about the necessity of virtuous behavior. Sakai, "Chūgokushijō no shomin kyōiku to zensho undō," p. 305. See also Handlin, "Benevolent Societies," pp. 313–315, 318–319.

[129] Yan Maoyou, *Yunqi ji, ce* 12, 1a–8b. See Sakai, "Gan Moken," pp. 266–269.

Hui: aspiring members had to submit a completed ledger (*gongguobu*) listing 100,000 good deeds, and only after this document was investigated and found accurate could he be admitted to the society. He had then to confess all his past errors and continue to keep a ledger. An elaborate system of mutual checks operated to ensure honesty: the society was subdivided into five groups, whose members prepared "records of will power" (*yuanlibu*) or "records for nourishing the will" (*yangzhibu*). The group leader checked these records for accuracy and submitted a report on them to the society at large. Small lapses in behavior were allowed, as long as one accepted the correction of fellow members, but grave transgressions brought expulsion.[130] The Yunqi Hui, with its heavy reliance on ledger use, clearly provided one means of disseminating the ledgers among people not necessarily members of the educated elite. But even members of elite scholarly academies might also rely on the ledgers or ledger-like texts; the famous philosopher Li Yong (1627–1705), in his rules for the Guanzhong Academy in Chang'an, stipulated that each member keep a book of "gains and losses" to record his moral and intellectual progress.[131]

By the early Qing, the morality books might also be used much in the way that the *Sacred Edict* (*Shengyu*) was used as a basic text in public lectures (*xuanjiang*), as a means of instructing all the people of a community, not just the members of a special association or school, in proper behavior. *Lectures on Action and Response* (*Ganying pian zhijiang*), originally published in the Kangxi era and frequently republished throughout the Qing, included, in addition to simple explanations in classical Chinese of the *Tract of Taishang on Action and Response*, several suggestions on how to lecture on the text. The author advised:

> When lecturing on the text you must use a summary. The notes and explanations from the past use much elaborate language, and the listeners have a hard time understanding them; so too the lecturer is put to much trouble. Now, just as the Song Confucians in their "collected conversations" used the vernacular, use it in this lecture in order to bring enlightenment to your neighborhood.

---

[130] Yan Maoyou, *Yunqi ji, ce* 12, 11a–b. See Sakai, "Gan Moken," p. 268.

[131] Li Yong, *Erqu ji*, 13.14b; cited in Wu Pei-yi, "Self-Examination," p. 25.

Chen Hu also used his ledger, the *Primer for Sagely Learning*, as a guide to the ethical regulation of his community. A *juren* who never took an official post, Chen lived in retirement in Kunshan county, Jiangsu, farming and leading village cooperative activities like dike-building, land reclamation, and harvesting. Through an unofficial compact he instructed the people in proper familial and community relationships; he recorded the good and bad deeds of the villagers, much as Lü Kun had suggested in his model compact regulations: "On certain days, he would record virtuous deeds as guides to the practice of good, the correction of error, and the sincere extension of knowledge." See "Chen Quean xiansheng zhuang," 1a–4b, *Shengxue rumen shu*; see also Sakai, *Chūgoku zensho*, p. 388.

When virtuous scholars from all over take up this essay to lecture, they should read aloud from the text as little as possible, [rather] summarizing its contents in extemporaneous explanations. Everyone will understand and feel its excellence.[132]

The unknown author then lists a variety of different contexts for lectures on the tract: local society lectures, public lectures to local communities, family lectures, school lectures to students between the ages of 8 and 18, and lectures encouraging virtue.[133] Lectures might be conducted anywhere—in one's neighborhood, in the market, in residential lanes, and in villages before any audience—"scholars, peasants, craftsmen, merchants, physicians, diviners, astrologers, physiognomists, yamen workers and outsiders. Everyone can be reached in the lectures." The author suggested, however, that the rural areas were in special need of such instruction, because for the most part their residents "did not distinguish good and evil." Other special targets were hired laborers and craftsmen: "if they gather to listen, you should add a few sentences directly relevant to their status, to make them feel at ease in their lives."[134]

In these lectures the text of the *Tract* was to be explained (a crib is provided in the *Lectures* text) and illustrative stories and examples from real life told to convince the people. Retribution was acknowledged to be the major prop of the system: it was the means of aiding the people to develop "minds of virtue." Lecturers were urged to use frequent examples of reward and punishment to keep the people interested in the system.[135] Indeed, it was suggested that the lecturers themselves were rewarded for their efforts—Zhou Chi, for example, had his life span extended because of his enthusiastic public lectures on the *Tract*.[136]

Few other texts give instructions as detailed as those found in the *Lectures*, but morality books of the Qing did fairly commonly include lists of suggested methods of transmission. The *Record of Reverence and Belief* (*Jingxin lu*), circulating during the Qianlong period (1736–1796), listed fourteen different methods of circulation, including paying for all or part of the publication and distribution of the text, sending copies with merchants or travelers who were going long distances, and urging others to read the text. Seven different occasions for reciting the text were also

---

[132] *Ganying pian zhijiang*, 1.4a. The first edition we have of this book is a reprint dated 1777, but Sakai argues that it probably first appeared during the Kangxi era. See his "Chūgokushijō no shomin kyōiku," pp. 306–316.

[133] *Ganying pian zhijiang*, 1.4a–6a; Sakai, "Chūgokushijō no shomin kyōiku," pp. 312–315.

[134] *Ganying pian zhijiang*, 1.4b.

[135] Ibid., 1.5a; Sakai, "Chūgokushijō no shomin kyōiku," p. 315.

[136] *Ganying pian zhijiang*, 1.4b. Zhou Chi's story is also told in Chen Zhixi, "Fengchi *Ganying pian* lingyan ji," *Quanjie quanshu*, 1.1a–b.

given: when studying other basic texts like the *Classic of Filial Piety* at school, when seeking emolument or an heir, or when hoping for relief from trouble or illness, to name a few.[137] There were thus actual suggestions for use and distribution right in the texts of the morality books themselves. From the seventeenth century on, there was an increasingly vigorous effort to bring the lessons of the merit-accumulation system to as many people as possible.

Of course, printed suggestions for the distribution of the morality books and ledgers tell us little about the actual use of the ledgers. And because publication of the texts was a means of earning merit, it is impossible to determine demand or use from the number of editions published. Frequent allusions to the idea of merit accumulation (though not to the ledgers themselves) in contemporary vernacular novels, plays, and short stories suggest that knowledge of the system was generally assumed;[138] but again, this knowledge does not necessarily mean actual use. Evidence for real ledger use is scattered and limited; most of the clear-cut cases from the Ming and Qing come, as already discussed, from elite society—and from the relatively high levels of elite society—from men like Yuan Huang, Luo Rufang, Zhou Rudeng, Tao Wangling, and Lu Shiyi. In local gazetteers there are scattered references to ledger use by a somewhat different stratum of the elite: these users were usually relatively obscure local scholars noted largely for their charitable activities or their extraordinary virtue.[139] The proliferation of new titles and the tendency to produce compact, abridged versions of some of the more com-

---

[137] Zhou Dingchen, "Xu," 2b–3b, *(Zengding) Jingxin lu*. The original version of the text, the *Jingxin lu* by Zhou Dingchen, was probably published in 1749 and reprinted at least twice within the next thirty years, once in 1769, and once in 1779. See Sakai, "Chūgoku-shijō no shomin kyōiku," pp. 316–319.

[138] The ledgers of merit and demerit were never, to my knowledge, mentioned by name or title in any late Ming or early Qing vernacular fiction. But the idea of retribution, and more specifically, the concept of keeping moral accounts abound in these works. Chu Ren-huo, the author of the *Romance of the Sui and Tang (Sui Tang yanyi*, 1675), actually sees his own novel as a kind of moral "account book" (*zhangbu*). And some popular morality books—the *Taishang ganying pian* and the *Yinzhi wen*, for example, are mentioned by title in vernacular fiction. See Ogawa Yōichi, "Seiko nishū to zensho" and "Sangen nihyō to zensho"; Ōki Yasushi, "Fū Muryō *Sangen* no hensan ito ni tsuite—toku ni kanzen-chōaku no igi o megutte"; Robert Hegel, *The Novel in Seventeenth-Century China*, p. 204; Qing Xitai, *Daojiao wenhua xintan*, pp. 140–141; P'u Sung-ling, *Strange Stories from a Chinese Studio*, pp. 147–149, 224–225, 304–305, 341–343; Cao Xueqin, *The Story of the Stone*, vol. 1, p. 231; Wilt Idema, *Chinese Vernacular Fiction: The Formative Period*, pp. 34–35, 52–56; and Andrew Plaks, "After the Fall: *Hsing-shih yin-yuan chuan* and the Seventeenth-Century Chinese Novel," pp. 575–579.

[139] See, for example, the *Qujiang xianzhi*, 14.42b, where a Wu Zhonglong, a local scholar (his biography is in the "Rulin" section), is said to have recorded his merits and demerits on a daily basis. I am grateful to Timothy Brook for this reference.

prehensive texts provide more solid evidence that there was a real demand for the books, and particularly for easily usable and portable versions.

Certainly, it is clear that the ledgers of the mid- to late seventeenth and eighteenth centuries were intended for as wide an audience as possible, an audience that included ignorant peasants, laborers, and artisans, who might otherwise not know right from wrong. But persuasive evidence of how well they were known to these people (if they were at all) or of how they might have affected their lives (if they did at all) does not exist for the late Ming and early Qing.[140]

In the seventeenth and eighteenth centuries the ledgers of merit and de-merit became vehicles for the expression of a complete elite social vision. Yuan Huang, absorbed in the process of his own advancement, had un-abashedly embraced merit accumulation as a means of upward mobility; he was perfectly willing to act on his belief in retribution, and he urged

---

[140] It is not until the twentieth century that there is any firm evidence that the texts were consistently used at any level below that of the literate elite. Japanese observers in the 1920s, 1930s, and 1940s reported widespread popular use of the texts: Tachibana Shiraki, visiting Manchuria in 1924, stated that most bookstores in Dairen and Lüshun contained copies of the *Tract of Taishang on Action and Response* and the *Ledger of Merit and Demerit of the Taiwei Immortal*. (See Tachibana, *Shina shakai no kenkyū*, pp. 552–558; and Hattori Unokichi, *Shina kenkyū*, pp. 484–486. See also Yü, *Renewal of Buddhism*, p. 287n.9.) Hatada Takashi claimed that ledgers were the only books owned by the northern Chinese villagers he interviewed for the Mantetsu surveys. (This information was provided in the course of a public discussion at the Tōyō Bunka Kenkyūjo, Tokyo University, November 22, 1982.) Hirano Yoshitarō even gave the books (particularly the *Tract of Taishang*) a major role in the organization of Chinese villages, as the textual foundations for what he called the "communal spirit" (*kyōdōtai*) of rural life. (Hirano, *Hoku-Shi no nōson shakai*, vol. 1, pp. 63–106.) The publication in 1936 of a large collection of morality books, the *Fushou baocang yibaisishizhong*, further attests to the popularity of the texts; this collection, sponsored by the Leshan She, consisted primarily of morality books and ledgers from the Ming and Qing. Apparently the Chinese Communist Party was willing to adopt the ledger form (if not the related religious beliefs) in its campaigns of political education: part of a "merit and demerit register" (*gongguobu*), published in 1947 by the Renmin shudian, survives in the Bureau of Investigation archives in Taiwan. A rhyme on the cover (the only part of the text left) urges the user to record every day his or her merits and demerits, and to look to the day when "the merits will wash away the demerits" and a "new person is self-created." (I am grateful to Joseph Esherick for this reference.)

On Taiwan today there is still a flourishing morality book and ledger industry. On a brief trip to Taiwan in 1982, I collected, from more or less random visits to temples in the Taibei area, several vernacular translations of Yuan Huang's essays on the system (most under the title *Liaofan sixun*; see, for example, Huang Zhihai, *Liaofan sixun baihua jieshi*, 1962) and a ledger for girls and women. Zheng Zhiming, of Shifan Daxue, Taibei, has written a study devoted in part to these modern morality books: *Zhongguo shanshu yu zongjiao* (1988). Gary Seaman has shown that the texts have a role in rural religious life, in his study of temple organization in Pearl Mountain, a Central Taiwan farming community. (See Seaman, *Temple Organization in a Chinese Village*, pp. 51–62.)

others to do the same. His was a system designed for the ambitious individual operating within a dynamic, though strictly hierarchical, social system. Yuan himself identified completely with the ledger user—"Determining Your Own Fate," after all, was an account of his own success with the system.

After Yuan's death, however, the ledger form was taken over, as it were, by men with quite different concerns. Worried over the worsening political situation, a variety of social upheavals, and what they saw as a commercialization of values and a decline in customs, the new ledger authors used the texts to outline the whole network of traditional social relationships that they believed would return society to order. Like Yuan, they accepted the validity of the basic status structure; but unlike Yuan, they believed this structure to be, by the mid- and late seventeenth century, profoundly threatened by social and economic change. As a result, they had become very sensitive to what they perceived as assaults on the status hierarchy. Not primarily interested in encouraging individual advance up a status ladder whose durability and strength they had come to doubt, they adopted a defensive and protective stand: the hierarchy had to be shored up against the "attacks" of rebellious bondservants, disloyal tenants, greedy merchants, and irresponsible gentry.

But how could the hierarchy be protected against the formidable range of forces threatening it in the seventeenth century? First, the belief in supernatural retribution provided a powerful sanction for rules that would preserve the social order. As "gentlemen" themselves, though they probably believed in the operation of some system of "action and response," they could not accept the hope of reward as a ground for moral conduct; rather, this hope became in their hands the way to lure men of only middling abilities to follow the prescriptions in the ledgers. Thus the reward of status advancement could be offered to the person who faithfully observed the requirements of his given place in society: accept your lot happily now, the ledgers say, and you (or, more likely, your descendants) will get your reward later. Furthermore, the doctrine of supernatural retribution could be a powerful sanction for the social hierarchy: the hierarchy became a reflection of the highest moral judgment, that of heaven and the gods, and thus not easily challenged by mere humans.

Second, the ledger authors shaped many of their rules in an attempt to meet some of the needs of the time. They reasserted the paternalistic rules governing the superior-inferior relationships within the hierarchy, emphasizing the mutual dependence that bound each member in these relationships to the other. But in recognition of the growing economic power and independence of tenants and bondservants, they stressed the need for kindness and leniency on the part of landlords and masters. Tacitly, even unconsciously acknowledging that landlords had become more dependent within the relationship, they urged landlords to treat their servants and tenants generously, and they instructed servants and tenants in turn to remain loyal to their masters. Moreover, the ledger authors made room in their system for the new commercial wealth of the seventeenth century: merit could be bought and might even be rewarded with greater wealth.

But despite the adjustments made by the ledger authors to the social and economic changes of the late Ming and early Qing, their books remain essentially conservative documents. It would be inaccurate to suggest that they hoped to freeze the social order and eradicate any movement at all between statuses, for status advancement was one of the rewards they offered for good behavior. But, in contrast to Yuan Huang, these authors did not see status advancement as the focal goal of ledger use—it is rather the "carrot" used to lead people on to good, socially acceptable behavior. The exhaustive provisions of their ledgers and the nature of the conduct they encouraged for different statuses suggest that they were far more interested in containing and inhibiting—or at least very closely regulating—movement within the hierarchy than in encouraging it. Their ideal society consisted of an interlocking hierarchy of statuses defined by specific responsibilities and paternalistically supervised by members of the elite—scholars, officials, and local gentry.

Indeed, in many ways these authors seem to be heirs to the attempts of some Donglin thinkers to assert a "rural hegemony" of local leaders—literati, landlords, and gentry—who would ensure order in their communities by instructing the people in proper behavior, establishing charities for the deserving poor, running relief programs in times of famine, and so forth. Certainly, there is room for cooperation with the district magistrate, as in Chen Xigu's local aid programs, but for the most part the community was seen as a somewhat self-contained unit, cared for and overseen by local leaders, particularly the local gentry. The responsibilities for maintenance of the ideal paternalistic superior-inferior relationship rested most heavily on these men: if they did not perform the duties required of men of their standing by heaven and the gods, the ledger authors suggested, they would lose their privileged status in Chinese society.

Conclusion

THE LEDGERS of merit and demerit are texts that in their very form express certain basic beliefs about moral (and immoral) action and its consequences. As lists of specific deeds to be followed or avoided, they reveal a faith in a prescriptive morality, a goodness formed through the practice of many different, discrete good deeds of varying value. And as texts that promise rewards for good behavior and punishments for evil, they reflect a belief in supernatural retribution, in a heaven and/or an assembly of gods and spirits who watch over men and consciously recompense their acts with good or bad fortune. Founded on a faith in the workings of this higher justice, the ledgers affirm the underlying moral validity of the status quo: man is assured that, however puzzling the actual distribution of rewards and punishments might appear in his limited worldly vision, there is nonetheless a rational and divinely sanctioned system at work to ensure that each person and each family ultimately get their just deserts.

All ledgers of merit and demerit seem to rest on these basic assumptions; they are necessary to the operation of the ledger system. What is remarkable about the history of the ledgers in the period between the Southern Song and the early Qing is the flexibility the form achieved within the limits imposed by this set of shared assumptions. The ledgers went through a series of transformations, each interpreting the basic elements of the texts to a different context and a different conception of their use.

In their earliest known form, the ledgers of merit and demerit operated in a religious context. The appearance of the *Ledger of Merit and Demerit of the Taiwei Immortal* in 1171 capped a long development of what might loosely be called a "system" of merit accumulation, a development that took place largely in the scriptures and apocryphal sutras of medieval Daoist and Buddhist sects. The rewards and punishments of this system were overwhelmingly spiritual and other-worldly: immortality or movement up the ladder of transmigration, or the sufferings of hell or descent into a lower level of reincarnation. The thrust of the system throughout this period was largely deterrent and punitive; by and large, more space was devoted to warning people of the horrors to be suffered for evil deeds than to the blessings consequent upon good ones. The *Ledger of the Taiwei Immortal* itself was directed to a relatively narrow audience, the worshippers of the Immortal Xu Zhenjun. The values expressed in the text certainly reflect the religious concerns and practices of this sect, but they included also more general values—ones protective of family, community, and even national life. They urged cooperation and mutual support as well as worship within the sect during a period of considerable political tension and social disorder.

After the twelfth century there is little evidence for sustained interest in ledger use, though it is clear by the early sixteenth century that some literati were using partial ledgers—ledgers of demerit stripped of the belief in retribution—as guides in their own moral self-cultivation. But the first significant reinterpretation of the full ledger form came in the late sixteenth century at the hands of the Chan monk Yungu and his disciple Yuan Huang. These men made the ledgers instruments of their faith in human power over the contingencies of life; and the texts became the means through which a man could decide his own fate, even the very terms of his material existence in this world. In this new conception of ledger use there was a shift away from the earlier focus on deterrence and the threat of punishment to an emphasis on what positive goods, both moral and material, man could achieve through the proper cultivation of his mind. The ledger user no longer needed to wait until death for an essentially spiritual reward; he could expect examination degrees, sons, and official appointments in his own lifetime as long as he accumulated merit in the proper state of mind. Support for this system was adduced from no less distinguished sources than the earliest of the Confucian Classics. While the *Ledger of Merit and Demerit of the Taiwei Immortal* vaguely claimed the support of the Confucian sages, Yungu and Yuan Huang repeatedly turned to the *Classic of History*, the *Classic of Songs*, the *Classic of Changes*, and *Mencius* (in an unconventional reading) as authorities for their system. Exploiting the ambiguities of the whole range of classical Confucian comments on fate, these men insisted that the system of merit accumulation was Confucian at heart, and therefore perfectly appropriate for the use of scholars and officials.

There was also a shift in intended audience in this new version of the ledgers of merit and demerit. The *Ledger of Merit and Demerit of the Taiwei Immortal* was directed primarily to sect members of any social station, but Yungu's and Yuan Huang's system was designed largely for aspiring officials. It did not preclude use by any social group; indeed, in its insistence on the power of the individual to change fate, it encouraged upward mobility within the Chinese status hierarchy. But in the "Confucian" justification it provided for merit accumulation, in the rewards offered, and even in the stories used to illustrate the process of reward, the system reflected an overwhelming interest in a very "official" definition of success, one accessible only to men with at least some rudimentary education in the Confucian canon.

The popularity of Yungu's and Yuan Huang's version of the ledger system seems to have rested on its use as an aid to morally legitimized upward mobility into scholar-official status. As such, it is perhaps not surprising that it was bitterly attacked by the more conservative Confucian thinkers of the day. The ledgers were perceived as threats to the sanctity of the orthodox Neo-Confucian curriculum: they suggested that success in the examinations depended on divine reward for merit accumulation, and not exclusively on one's understanding of the Confucian canon. Furthermore, while claiming sanction in Confucian texts and principles, the merit-demerit system relied heavily on "heterodox" Daoist and Buddhist notions of retribution as well—it certainly contradicted the classic Confucian injunction that man do good for its own sake, not for material profit. Thus by offering hope of advancement through what was seen as a dubious means, it threatened the supposed moral purity and homogeneity of the scholar-official elite.

How subversive, in fact, was Yuang Huang's message? By urging ledger users to follow the dictates of their minds over conventional opinion in making moral choices, as Yuan did in his essay "Accumulating Goodness," he could be seen as a man willing to undermine generally accepted notions of good behavior. Some of his illustrative stories portray good men questioning the judgment of their official superiors or allowing the "hidden laws" of the merit-demerit system to shape their official policies (as Yuan Huang himself did in trying to lower the tax rate in Baodi). But, though Yuan might make claims for the independence of individual moral judgment, his heroes all followed fairly conventional behavior, and the deeds listed in his *Ledger* were, if anything, supportive rather than disruptive of conventional morality and social order. Those heroes who questioned official behavior were depicted, not as rebels against an unjust system, but rather as men who, to preserve the purity of correct official standards of behavior, were rebuking those who were simply unfit for their posts.

Yuan Huang's ledger system was in its own way fundamentally supportive not only of conventional moral rules but also of existing institutions and status distinctions. By claiming, in Yuan Huang's own words, that "Success in the Examinations Depends Entirely on Secret Virtue," it reaffirmed the value of the civil service examination system as a tool for distinguishing virtuous candidates for official service. And by explaining puzzling cases of examination failure as cases of personal moral failure (particularly as failures in sincerity), it provided a rational, moral basis for understanding the workings of the civil service system—indeed, it even suggested that the system operated with the backing of the gods themselves.

Furthermore, Yungu's and Yuan Huang's ledger system, like the

Ledger of the Taiwei Immortal before it, implied at least implicit support for the existing status structure as a whole. The poor peasant "deserved" his lowly place because he had inherited demerits, or because he had bad karma, or because he was not sincere in his accumulation of merit. So, too, the wealthy official "deserved" his position in society, if not because of his own virtues, then because of those of his forebearers. By defining specific deeds that purported to lead one to elite status, the ledgers assumed the correctness of accepted social and moral standards and directed the ambition of those dissatisfied with their status toward conformity to these standards through the relatively safe and socially beneficial channel of merit accumulation.

Thus neither Yungu nor Yuan Huang, despite the attacks leveled against them, can be seen as men intent on challenging in any significant way the terms of the Chinese social hierarchy. Their system, it is true, encouraged individual upward mobility in its vigorous assertion that man could decide his own fate, but it never called into question the validity of the social structure as a whole. It simply made a virtue, even a moral necessity, of what was already a principle of Chinese social organization, the possibility of movement between different social stations. Since status groups were not closed, it had long been possible, albeit difficult, for the lowly to move up the status ladder; now, said Yungu and Yuan Huang, it was a moral obligation, for status advancement reflected growth in moral stature. Indeed, it is hard to imagine a more optimistic moral affirmation of both the validity of the social hierarchy and the benefits of upward mobility: both were perfect mirrors of a moral order sanctioned by the Confucian sages as well as the Buddhist and Daoist gods.

It is not surprising, then, that Yuan Huang's *Ledger* became popular at a time perceived as one of intense social competition and rapid status change: it provided the individual with a practical, and purportedly Confucian, guide for navigating his own (and his family's) course through what appeared to be rough waters indeed. We can understand why Yuan's system would find its most vocal supporters among Taizhou school thinkers: Yuan's championing of the human mind or moral will as the source of man's fate suited their own identification of the mind as a great creative power.

But as the social, political, and intellectual situation changed, the new ledgers produced in the course of the seventeenth century, though perhaps inspired by the success of Yungu's and Yuan Huang's *Ledger*, were nonetheless quite different in both form and focus. As lengthy and detailed compendia of social rules for all occasions, contexts, and statuses, they were now primarily moral guidebooks, handbooks for a lifetime of good behavior. Produced by scholars whose intellectual sympathies tended to lie with orthodox Neo-Confucian teachings, these texts did not so much celebrate the transformative power of the human mind as advise the careful performance of cut-and-dried prescriptions for virtue.

These ledgers were still based, of course, on the belief in retribution—that is, on the understanding that the gods would reward good behavior and punish evil. But the sanction of retribution was presented now rather uneasily by the ledger authors—it was necessary, they claimed, as a prod to good behavior for people of only middling abilities. The true gentleman, however, who did good for its own sake, did not need such "cheap" encouragement. Here the objection leveled against the selfish, profit-seeking motive behind Yuan Huang's ledger system was answered, but in the process the ledgers were made into texts designed to some extent to shape popular behavior, to entice and frighten the ignorant into following rules of behavior set by members of the scholar elite.

Even in those cases where the ledger authors themselves seemed to trust in the operation of supernatural retribution—few, indeed, denied outright the force of retribution—there was a shift in what were seen as the social implications of the system. Retribution was interpreted now as a belief that first and foremost affirmed the status quo. Although Yuan Huang accepted the existing social hierarchy, he encouraged upward mobility within it. But, in the course of the seventeenth century, it was the preservation of the levels of the social structure as they were occupied at "this" moment—the status quo in a very literal sense—that became the message of the ledgers. Both Yuan Huang and his successors would have agreed that each person's status was a reflection of his (and his family's) moral worth, but while Yuan drew from this principle the lesson that the better one was the higher one rose, his successors focused on a different interpretation: if each man's status was a reflection of his moral worth, they argued, he could best fulfill his moral destiny, the lot heaven had given him, by accepting his place and humbly following the moral and social prescriptions associated with it. Thus the ledgers of the seventeenth and eighteenth centuries would serve to contain or inhibit social mobility, or at least to regulate it closely by suggesting that the gods demanded sincere acquiescence to the strict rules for good behavior listed in the ledgers. A ledger user might well, as in Yuan Huang's system, be rewarded with status advancement for his acquiescence, but his reward was likely to be in the form of a kind of secular "salvation"—examination degrees and official posts for his descendants, perhaps a posthumous title, but not necessarily anything to be enjoyed in this life. And in these later ledgers other types of rewards supplemented Yuan Huang's overwhelming preference for status benefits, so that now a ledger user might be rewarded with deification or spiritual salvation, prizes that would not advance his social standing in this world.

The shift in ledger meaning analyzed here is never openly acknowledged, and was perhaps never recognized by the later seventeenth- and eighteenth-century authors of the texts. They claimed that they were carrying on the work of Yuan Huang and frequently named him in their works as the major interpreter of the system. They adopted his advice on proper ledger use and relied on many of the same stories and citations introduced by Yuan to explain merit accumulation. Their texts were still very much ledgers of merit and demerit, grounded in the sanction of divine retribution and consisting of lists of rules for behavior.

There was also little change in the specific values expressed in the rules for behavior in the later ledgers. While it is true that the later texts provide many more prescriptions than Yuan Huang's *Ledger*, they did not in any significant way contradict or undermine the ethical values set forth in the earlier text. In fact, little in the way of specific value change can be observed in the ledgers throughout the whole segment of their history treated here. Of course, individual ledgers expressed different authorial concerns—the *Ledger of Merit and Demerit of the Taiwei Immortal* and Yunqi Zhuhong's *Record of Self-Knowledge*, for example, not surprisingly tended to emphasize Daoist and Buddhist practices respectively.[1] But the ledger deeds otherwise by and large reflect social and moral values generally accepted within Chinese society—preservation of the rules of the five relationships; personal cultivation of the qualities of self-restraint, frugality, and humility; reverence for the spirits; acceptance of hierarchical social relationships; acts of charitable giving; and so forth.

What differentiated later seventeenth- and eighteenth-century ledgers from Yuan Huang's, then, was the shift in ledger ideology, the change in the way the texts expressed different visions of the relationship between moral practice and social place. Both affirmed the moral validity of the Chinese social hierarchy, but Yuan Huang urged advance up the hierarchy through moral cultivation, while the later authors encouraged a kind of individual stasis through fulfillment of the duties defined by one's heaven-given allotment. For Yuan, the possibility of advancement through the performance of good deeds was the emblem, as it were, of the moral character of the status system. But for his successors, it was the harmony that would inevitably result if each status performed its duties that revealed the moral reason underlying the system.

It would be a mistake, certainly, to exaggerate the implications of the social ideology underlying either message. However much Yuan Huang's work might have disturbed conservative scholars, he was producing a guide to individual and familial success, not a document for widespread social or even moral change. On the other hand, his successors in ledger production cannot be dismissed as reactionaries simply devoted to the

---

[1] Yü, *Renewal of Buddhism*, p. 120.

suppression of the ambitions of those of low status. These ledger authors were disturbed by what they perceived as a general decline in moral standards and widespread social upheaval; what they proposed as a remedy was the strengthening of status hierarchy, a reinforcement through the ledgers of merit and demerit of the values defining all different status distinctions, and hence a containment or strict regulation of mobility. If they emphasized the responsibilities of servants and tenants to obey their masters and landlords and accept peacefully their allotted place in society, they stressed no less the even heavier obligations the elite—scholars, officials, and larger property-holders—had to ensure the well-being and security of their social inferiors. Indeed, as one would expect from defenders of a paternalistic system, these men blamed their peers for many of the problems they saw about them, and so placed the greatest burden for their solution on the elite. Their ledgers can be read as full and specific expressions of a social ideology for the local elite, an ideology that explained existing status divisions in terms highly flattering to this elite, and at the same time, using the threat of downward mobility, encouraged members of the elite to engage in charitable action.

Not surprisingly, the shift in ledger ideology that occurred over the course of the Ming-Qing transition period roughly followed the major developments in contemporary elite interests, mirroring to a large extent the changes in intellectual orientations and social concerns that marked the seventeenth and eighteenth centuries. Yuan Huang publicized his ledger system late in the sixteenth century, just toward the end of the period that marked the great intellectual flowering of the Ming. True, there was growing concern among "pure critics" like the Donglin affiliates about both the decline in central political competence and what was seen as the moral corruption of the "wilder" followers of Wang Yangming. But the Taizhou school and the movement for popular education were still vigorous. Carried away by the idea that "any man could become a sage" (or in more mundane terms, any man could become an official), many thinkers, particularly those sympathetic to Taizhou claims, were willing to accept the ledgers as guides to the achievement of "sagehood" or official status in a highly competitive civil service system.

But as the century progressed, the corruption of the political order, now increasingly dominated by eunuchs and venal officials, and the precariousness of the social order, now more frequently rent by popular uprisings, began to absorb the attention of more members of the scholar-official elite. The founding of the Donglin Academy provided the Taizhou school with perhaps its greatest intellectual and political challenge. From the early seventeenth century on, the dominant thinkers of the day—men like Gu Xiancheng, Gao Panlong, and Liu Zongzhou—urged a return, if not to all the teachings of the Neo-Confucian orthodoxy strictly defined, at least to the more rigorous form of moral discipline associated with the orthodoxy.

As the increasingly weak central government proved itself incompetent to preserve order, first in the face of widespread smaller incidents of violence, and later before the great rebellions of Li Zicheng and Zhang Xianzhong, local elites stepped in to restore order in some areas. Community compacts, famine relief, charitable societies for the care of orphans and the poor, and local public works efforts were all examples of the practical "statecraft" methods employed by at least some of the local gentry to restore a degree of order in the absence of effective central control. The leaders of these local efforts, particularly those affiliated with the Donglin partisans, often used a version of the belief in cosmic retribution—the theory of action and response—to encourage such community action. Thus Chen Longzheng, in exhorting members of his benevolent society, suggested that maintenance of elite status is a cosmic "response" to the human "action" of charitable giving.

It was in this context that most of the surviving seventeenth- and eighteenth-century ledgers were created. The ledgers now became local, almost group productions, in contrast to Yuan Huang's individual effort. The new texts were written most frequently by private scholars who were aided editorially and financially by local residents, often lower-degree holders or entirely obscure people. An informal official interest in the ledgers was maintained through sponsorship by government officials, often friends of the ledger authors. In their prefaces, these sponsors usually pointed up the stabilizing influence of the ledgers, their value as textbooks for the behavioral definition of status distinctions.

After the fall of the Ming in 1644, scholars and officials were even more devoted to the cause of political and social stability. Blaming late-Ming figures like Yuan Huang and Li Zhi for encouraging moral laxity and social and political corruption, the forces they felt had led to the Ming downfall, they gradually turned back to the more conservative moral teachings of the Cheng-Zhu school of Neo-Confucianism as guides to the revitalization of the social order. They were determined to reestablish a stable system, an interlocking hierarchy of statuses governed by solid "traditional" values and thus able to resist disintegration. Again, the ledgers were one of several tools employed to this end. Men whose more conservative political and intellectual affiliations suggest that they might have sided with Liu Zongzhou in his attack on Yuan Huang's *Ledger* became the new champions of the ledgers, albeit ledgers quite different in their message from Yuan Huang's. The change in ledger form, from rough lists of deeds to fuller and more comprehensive treatments of deeds applicable to all situations and occupational levels, reflects their new interest in educating people in values supportive of social stability.

The progress of the ledgers over the course of the Ming-Qing transition from guides for the upwardly mobile to handbooks for comprehensive moral and social instruction also reveals much of the flexibility and diversity of elite beliefs, even of elite ideology. Nowhere are these qualities clearer than in the shifting value and meaning assigned to the belief in retribution expressed in the ledgers. Yuan Huang, in asserting his faith in a quantitative retribution mediated by (largely Buddhist) gods and spirits, was championing a belief associated in the minds of the strictest Neo-Confucians with "heterodox" Buddhist and Daoist doctrines and popular superstitions. Yet it is clear that Yuan was by no means the first or the only Chinese literatus to hold such a belief; we have seen that the view of supernatural retribution presented in the *Tract of Taishang on Action and Response* and the *Ledger of Merit and Demerit of the Taiwei Immortal* certainly did not lack the support of some of the more imposing Confucian scholars of the Southern Song. And it is easy enough to find scholar-officials contemporaneous with Yuan Huang who shared his belief in a system of retribution operated by a bureaucracy of spirits.[2]

Thus it would be simplistic and misleading to treat Yuan Huang's work, particularly his *Determining Your Own Fate*, as a crude mixture of "popular" superstition (i.e., the belief in supernatural retribution) and elite values (i.e., the desire to succeed in the examinations and the need to find sanction for any system of belief in the Classics). The kind of retribution Yuan Huang described was not the exclusive preserve of the common people. This particular belief had long been part of the elite tradition; it simply occupied a somewhat more ambiguous place in that tradition as a concept repudiated in orthodox Neo-Confucianism. Since scholars and officials were dependent for their bread and butter on mastery of this orthodoxy, naturally it assumed pride of place in their writings and policies. But it clearly never altogether eclipsed other beliefs, and for many scholars it seemed to have been quite easy to accept the orthodox Mencian requirement that the gentleman did good without thought of reward, while cherishing too a belief in a retribution organized by a celestial bureaucracy. What was new and perhaps a little startling about Yuan Huang's work was that he tried to identify the two strains, to suggest in fact that Mencius himself shared both beliefs.

Of course, Yuan Huang's task was not really as wrongheaded as some of his critics would have had us believe. To be sure, two of the most popular Confucian Classics, the *Analects* and the *Mencius*, urge man not to consider the possibility of retribution. But other texts—indeed, many other texts—within the canon accept and even emphasize the operation of supernatural retribution. Yuan Huang was quite within his rights in

[2] For examples, see Wu Pei-yi, "Self-Examination," pp. 22–38.

quoting the *Classic of Songs*, the *Classic of History*, the *Classic of Changes*, and the *Spring and Autumn Annals* in support of the belief in retribution. Certainly, the *Chronicle of Zuo* too is full of stories reflecting a belief in supernatural retribution—that is, one run by gods and spirits. Thus the very richness of the Confucian tradition itself allowed in a sense for a diversity of beliefs not always clearly supported by the civil service orthodoxy.

But even those conservative scholars who repudiated the particular kind of retribution envisioned by Yuan Huang were not necessarily willing to abandon faith in some form of action-and-response cycle in operation between earth and heaven. As we have seen, these men accepted a naturalistic form of cosmic retribution: whenever a person acted or had a thought, his "cosmic pneuma" or *qi* moved, naturally moving or influencing the *qi* around him. Through an infinite series of such movements, the consequences of the original thought or deed were returned, not to the man himself, but to his general vicinity. Thus heaven "responded" to human actions in a naturalistic way, independent of the necessary intervention of ghosts and spirits. There was no way that insincere good deeds might mistakenly be rewarded by a careless or corrupt celestial bureaucrat here; this "godless" retribution was automatic and completely objective. Individual selfishness was discouraged, for this system did not always reward good individuals with specific material benefits; at most it ensured that a kind of general prosperity would develop in a community that had stimulated good, "positive" movements of *qi*. This particular view of retribution was one that emphasized the importance of individual moral responsibility for general betterment: since the individual could not expect immediate, specifically personal rewards, he did good in the hopes of bringing a return of favorable *qi* to his environment, essentially in the hopes of bringing order to his world (a world that included, of course, him and his own family). Though obviously very different from Yuan Huang's vision of an individualized, precisely measured retribution, this view nonetheless did assert that heaven would return material benefits for good behavior, and as such was used by men like Gao Panlong and Chen Longzheng to encourage charitable activities. It is this use of cosmic retribution as the basis for an elite social ideology that was given detailed expression in the late-Ming and early-Qing ledgers of merit and demerit.

The belief in retribution forms a kind of continuum within Chinese religious and intellectual history, a continuum ranging from faith in a precisely measurable supernatural retribution engineered by a vast bureaucracy of aggressive divine "officials" to acceptance of an essentially unmeasurable, somewhat abstract cosmic process of action and response. It is impossible, however, to identify any one point on this continuum with any particular point on the Chinese social continuum. The belief in a finely calculated supernatural retribution, for example, is frequently labeled "popular," in the sense of "held by the common people." Yet, as we have seen, members of the elite, such as Yuan Huang, eagerly embraced this belief. Moreover, support for this belief could be found in many texts of the "elite" Confucian canon, as Yuan Huang himself was quick to point out. Thus, "popular" and "elite" are basically meaningless as descriptions of beliefs and ideas. That is, there are few beliefs that can, with any confidence, be tied exclusively to any one level in the social hierarchy.

Nor are the terms "popular" and "elite" justified as designations of the social provenance of beliefs and ideas. We might be tempted to assume that the "superstitious" faith in the Three Towers, the Lord of the North Bushel Star, and the Three Worm Spirits set forth in the *Tract of Taishang on Action and Response* was derived from the "popular Buddhist and Daoist" religion of the peasantry. Yet the first evidence for belief in these spirits can be found in the astronomical sections of the earliest histories of China—texts by and for the elite—where they are accepted as parts of the heavenly bureaucracy. Of course, these texts cannot unquestioningly be taken to represent the ultimate source of this belief either; after all, the presence of a belief or idea in an "elite" text does not necessarily make that belief or idea the creation of the elite. In this case, and indeed in many others, we simply do not know enough about the real origins of a belief to link it conclusively to either "the people" or "the elite."

It seems more reasonable, in this study at least, to think rather in terms of cultural "appropriation"—that is, to focus on the different interpretations and varied uses of the same idea, here the belief in retribution, without attempting to associate the idea itself rigidly (and inaccurately) with any one social group.[3] Thus Yuan Huang first appropriated the belief,

---

[3] This concept is taken from the French historian Roger Chartier. He explains the value of the concept of "appropriation" as follows: "It has enabled me to avoid identifying various cultural levels merely on the basis of a description of the objects, beliefs, or acts presumed to have been proper to each group. Even in *ancien régime* societies, many of these were shared by several different social groups, although the uses to which they were put may not have been identical. A retrospective sociology has long held that unequal distribution of material objects is the prime criterion of cultural differentiation. Here, this theory yields to an approach that concentrates on differentiated uses and plural appropriation of the same goods, the same ideas, and the same actions. A perspective of this sort does not ignore differences—even socially rooted differences—but it does shift the place in which this identification takes place. It is less interested in describing an entire body of material in social terms (for example, designating books printed in Troyes and sold by peddlers as 'popular' literature); it instead aims at a description of the practices that made for differing and strongly characteristic uses of the cultural materials that circulated within a given society." Chartier, *The Cultural Uses of Print in Early Modern France*, pp. 6–7.

James Watson's study of Tian Hou and Prasenjit Duara's analysis of Guandi apply generally the same approach in the field of Chinese history. See Watson, "Standardizing the

reinterpreting it as a sanction for upward mobility. His Taizhou supporters embraced it for a slightly different reason—for the emphasis it placed on the power of the individual mind as a transformative force. The Donglin thinkers again appropriated the concept and accepted the operation of action and response as an incentive to community reform. Finally, the seventeenth- and eighteenth-century ledger authors, while dismissing the idea of retribution as a "popular" misconception, nonetheless relied rather heavily on it in their efforts to encourage social stability. If evidence existed about the nonelite responses to and use of the ledgers in the late Ming and early Qing, we would doubtless discover a new and different series of appropriations, reinterpretations, and uses.

This approach also allows us to see more clearly the absorptive powers and relative flexibility of the Confucian intellectual tradition, qualities that help to explain its endurance and strength. The history of the ledgers of merit and demerit in the sixteenth and seventeenth centuries can be interpreted as the gradual appropriation of a system based originally on "heterodox" Daoist and Buddhist beliefs into the Confucian tradition.[4] In the process, it was transformed from a system that encouraged mobility and social advance (and thus might be disruptive of social order) into one that was supportive of stability, even social stasis. By the late seventeenth century, then, the ledgers, once texts of rather doubtful origin and suspect use, had become comprehensive reflections of an elite vision of social order. At every step in the process of transformation, the ledger authors were able to justify their work through reference to principles of the Confucian tradition—to the concept of retribution found in the early Confucian Classics, to Confucian notions of action and response, and even to a Confucian conception of elite leadership, to the idea that "gentlemen" may have to use rewards and punishments to persuade their moral and intellectual inferiors to behave properly.

Gods: The Promotion of T'ien Hou ("Empress of Heaven") along the South China Coast, 960–1960"; Duara, "Superscribing Symbols: The Myth of Guandi, Chinese God of War."

[4] While the different interpretations and uses of retribution did arouse some controversy among late-Ming and early-Qing intellectuals, on the whole the differences seem to have been tolerated. Despite Zhang Lixiang's concern over the purity of examination studies, no scholar was ever punished in any significant way for keeping a ledger of merit and demerit. Even Yuan Huang, the most notorious elite upholder of the "superstitious" view of retribution, though he was certainly never honored as a Confucian scholar, was never actively persecuted for his belief. Okuzaki does suggest that Yuan Huang's impeachment in 1593 may have been based in part on an accusation of heterodoxy (see *Chūgoku kyōshin jinushi*, pp. 176–179), but it is not clear what role his use of a ledger had in this charge.

Extant Morality Books and Ledgers of Merit and Demerit Published in the Seventeenth and Eighteenth Centuries

THIS LIST is not intended to be exhaustive; it gives, in a rough chronological order, the morality books and ledgers I consulted.[1] The asterisk (*) marks the ledgers; the others are all morality books containing ledgers.

> *Liming pian* (written in 1600, first published in 1607),[2] by Yuan Huang (1533–1606; j.s. 1586)
>
> *Zizhi lu (preface 1606), compiled by Yunqi Zhuhong (1535–1615)[3]
>
> *Diji lu* (written around 1622, first published in 1631), compiled by Yan Maoyou (j.s. 1634)
>
> *Guyi hui* (preface 1634), compiled by Tao Ting and Tao Gong
>
> *Riqian chushe* (published between 1631 and 1641?)[4]
>
> *Quanjie quanshu* (written in 1639, preface 1641), compiled by Chen Zhixi
>
> *Chongxiu zhiyao (prefaces 1666 and 1667; also known as *Guang gongguoge xinpian*, New edition of the Expanded Ledgers of Merit and Demerit), compiled by Li Guochang (completed by his son Li Yuanxing)
>
> **Huibian gongguoge* (prefaces 1671), compiled by Hu Rongshi (d. 1695)
>
> **Huizuan gongguoge* (written between 1671 and 1687; preface 1688), compiled by Chen Xigu (1634–1687; j.s. 1676)
>
> *Shenggong ge (date unknown), compiled by Liu Linchang (j.s. 1618)[5]
>
> **Shengxue rumen shu* (date unknown), compiled by Chen Hu (1613–1675; j.s. 1642)
>
> **Bufeiqian gongdeli* (late seventeenth century), compiled by Xiong Hongbei[6]
>
> **Zuibi Tang sanshiliu shan* (late seventeenth century), compiled by Li Erjing
>
> *Dangui ji* (preface 1703), compiled by Yan Zheng and Yan Yunlu
>
> *Tongshan lu* (preface 1706), author unknown
>
> *Gongguoge jiyao (preface 1717), compiled by Li Shida
>
> **Guangshan pian gongguoge* (preface 1721), compiled by Lu Fudan (?)

[1] I have drawn most of the information here from Sakai, *Chūgoku zensho*, pp. 378–398; and his "Kōkakaku no kenkyū," pp. 59–76. I list the earliest of the preface dates only.

[2] Okuzaki, *Chūgoku kyōshin jinushi*, p. 314.

[3] Yü, *Renewal of Buddhism*, pp. 118–124.

[4] See Sakai, *Chūgoku zensho*, p. 382.

[5] This ledger does not survive in its complete form; only the section on study remains.

[6] Sakai, "Confucianism and Popular Educational Works," p. 348.

Wenchang dijun gongguoge (preface 1724), author unknown
Yu Xujie gongguoge (preface 1734), compiled by Huang Zhengyuan
Liming gongguoge (prefaces 1747 and 1748), compiled by Xu Ben (j.s. 1718)
Jingxin lu (preface 1749), compiled by Zhou Dingchen
Chenzhong lu (preface 1763), by Jiang Wenlan

Glossary

The glossary does not include any names or titles that appear in Sources Cited.

A Ji　阿寄
"Aiwu ge"　愛物格
anfen　安分
anshen (*liming*)　安身(立命)
anxin (*liming*)　安心(立命)
baigong　百工
"Baiyi Guanyin jingzhou"　白衣關音經呪
bao　報
Bao Ping　包憑
bazi　八字
Beidou shenjun　北斗神君
benming　本命
benshu　本數
"Bian nü wei er pusa qiao"　變女為兒菩薩巧
Binzhou　濱州
budong nian　不動念
budong xin　不動心
cai　財
Cai Fangbing　蔡方炳
Cai Junmo　蔡君謨
Cai Maode　蔡懋德
Cai Shanji　蔡善繼
"Caiyong gujin shumu"　採用古今書目
canding　參訂
Cao Delin　曹德麟
ce　册
Changzhou　長洲
Chen Xianzhang　陳獻章
cheng　誠
Cheng-Zhu　程朱
"Chengguo"　成過
Chenghua　成化
chengyi zhi xue　誠意之學
chixin　恥心
Chongde　崇德

Chongzhen 崇禎
chuan 傳
Chuan jiabao quanji sanji 傳家寶全集三集
Chun'an 淳安
chūshō jinushi sō 中小地主層
cijiao 慈教
Ciyun 慈雲
cong ci niantou budong chu 從此念頭不動處
cong lishang gaiguo 從理上改過
cong shishang gaiguo 從事上改過
cong xinshang gaiguo 從心上改過
"Congguo baixing zhu zhi" 叢過百行主之
Cui Xuegu 崔學古
Cui Ziyu 催子玉
cunshen 存神
cunxin 存心
"Daguo wulun zhu zhi" 大過五倫主之
dajia yinhu 大家殷戶
dan 但
Dan jing 丹經
dangguan gongguoge 當官功過格
dangxia 當下
Dangxia yi 當下繹
Daojia 道家
Daojian 搗堅
dasheng 大乘
datong 大同
dawu weixin 大悟惟心
"Daxue richeng" 大學日程
dazhong 大眾
de 德
Deng Yu 鄧禹
Di 帝
"*Diji lu* xu" 廸吉錄序
Ding Bin 丁賓
Ding Gaiting 丁改亭
Ding Qinghui 丁清惠
dingming 定命
Dong 董
Donglin 東林
Dongta 東塔
doulao hui 斗栳會
Doumu 斗母

Dunhuang 敦煌
"Dushu ge" 讀書格
"Dushu le ge" 讀書樂歌
en 恩
Faben 法本
Fahui 法會
Faju jing 法句經
faming 發明
Fan Zhongyan 范仲淹
Fang Yizhi 方以智
Fanli 凡例
"Fanli wuze" 凡例五則
fashen 法身
Fazang 法藏
"Feiqian gongdeli" 費錢功德例
"Feiqian xinggong" 費錢行功
fen 分
Feng Kaizhi 馮開之
foxing 佛性
fu 福
"Fu ganying wuze" 附感應五則
Fu She 復社
Fu Xi 伏義
fulu 附錄
funü 婦女
"Gaiguo" 改過
"Gaiguo shuo" 改過說
ganying 感應
"*Ganying pian* xu" 感應篇序
"*Ganying pian zhu* xiaoyin" 感應篇註小引
Gao Panlong 高攀龍
Gaozong 高宗
ge 格
Ge Hong 葛洪
gewu 格物
Gezhi pian 格致篇
gezhi zhi xue 格致之學
gong 功
gong 公
gongde 功德
gongfu 工夫
gongguobu 功過簿
gonguoge 功過格

"Gongguoge xu" 功過格序
"Gongguoge xuyan" 功過格緒言
gongjian 公鑑
gonglun 公論
gongmen 公門
gongsheng 貢生
Gu Xichou 顧錫疇
Guangshan 光山
guangyi 廣義
guanjian 官鑑
Guanyin 觀音
Guanzhong 關中
Gui Hong 歸泓
Gui Shengmai 歸聖脉
Guian 歸安
guo 過
guobao 果報
Gushi 固始
Hainan 海南
Hangzhou 杭州
hao 毫
hao 號
hao 釐
haochiang 豪強
haonu 豪奴
Hatada Takashi 旗田巍
He Canran 賀燦然
He Shengxiu 賀聖修
He Zhengong 何眞公
hemu 和睦
Hetu jiming fu 河圖記命符
Hong Mai 洪邁
Hongwu 洪武
Hu Jiagui 胡甲桂
Hu Jinchen 胡晉臣
Huaian 淮安
Huainanzi 淮南子
Huang Lao 黃老
Huang Tingjian 黃庭堅
Huang Zhengyuan 黃正元
Huangdi 黃帝
Huangji jingshi 皇極經世
"Huangji shu zhengchuan" (or "-zhuan") 皇極數正傳

Huanyu 幻余
Huayan 華嚴
Huayan jing 華嚴經
"*Huibian gongguoge* xu" 彙編功過格序
Huikong 慧空
Huineng 惠能
huishi xiangli 回事向理
huixiang 迴向
Huixiang Dangui ji 繪像丹桂籍
Huizhou 徽州
hundun kaiji 混沌開基
hundun ligen 混沌立根
huocai 貨財
Huzhou 湖州
inga hō-ō 因果報應
ji 紀
ji 幾
Ji Chunyuan 計春元
Ji Maoxun 紀懋勳
"Ji Xianzu Juquan yishi" 記先祖菊泉遺事
Jiading 嘉定
Jiajing 嘉靖
"Jia'nan pian" 家難篇
Jianding 檢訂
Jiangyin 江陰
jianmin 賤民
jiansheng 監生
Jianwen 建文
jiaohua 教化
jiaojie 交接
Jiaomin bangwen 教民榜文
"Jiapu shi jiazhu" 家僕事家主
Jiashan 嘉善
Jiaxing 嘉興
"Jiaxun" 家訓
jiguo ge 紀過格
Jin 晉
Jin Ping Mei 金瓶梅
Jin Shiqi 金世祺
Jindan 金丹
jing 敬
"Jingming daoshi Jingyang Xu Zhenjun zhuan" 淨明道師旌陽許眞君傳
Jingming ji gongguobu 淨明記功過簿

Jingming Zhongxiao Dao　淨明忠孝道
Jingshan　京山
jingsheng　敬聖
Jingshi gongguoge　警世功過格
jingshi zhiyong　經世致用
Jingtu　淨土
Jingyang　旌陽
jingzuo　靜坐
"Jinlun ge"　盡倫格
jinshen　縉紳
jinshi　進士
Jinsi lu　近思錄
Jintan　金壇
jinwei yi yi dingming　謹威儀以定命
Jinxi　金谿
"Jishan"　積善
jishan　積善
jiuji　救濟
jiyi　積義
ju　住
juan　卷
"Juanzi xingshi"　捐梓姓氏
Jueshi mingyan shier lou　覺世名言十二樓
jujing　聚精
juntian junyi　均田均役
juren　舉人
Kangxi　康熙
kaozheng　考證
"Kedi quanping yinde"　科第全憑陰德
keji fuli　克己復禮
Kong　孔
kuanxia　寬下
kuichi　愧恥
Kunshan　崑山
kyōdōtai　共同体
Laozi　老子
letian anming　樂天安命
li　理
li　禮
Li Changling　李昌齡
Li Dami　李大泌
Li Hao　李郛
Li Jian'an　李漸菴

Li Le 李樂
Li Ruding 李如鼎
Li Wenda 李文達
Li Xian 李賢
Li Yuanxing 李元行
Li Zhiji 李知幾
Li Zicheng 李自成
"Liancai shi bao" 廉財之報
liangmin 良民
Liangzhe 兩浙
liangzhi 良知
Liao Yingzhao 廖應召
Liaodong 遼東
Liaofan 了凡
Liaofan sixun 了凡四訓
Liji 禮記
lijia 里甲
liming 立命
"Liming wen xu" 立命文序
liming zhi xue 立命之學
Lin Chun 林春
Lin Han 林釬
Lin Zengzhi 林增志
"Lincai ge" 臨財格
Linchuan 臨川
Lingbao 靈寶
Lingbao jingming dongshen shangpin jing 靈寶淨明洞神上品經
Lingbao jingming xinxiu jiulaoshen yinfumo mifa
　靈寶淨明新修九老神印伏魔秘法
Lingbao jingming yuanxing qianshi 靈寶淨明院行遣式
Liu Daxia 劉大夏
Liu Ju 劉聚
Liu Mengzhen 劉夢震
Liyang 溧陽
Lizong 理宗
Lu 魯
Lu Guangzu 陸光祖
Lü Liuliang 呂留良
Lu Pingquan 陸平泉
Lu Shusheng 陸樹聲
Lu-Wang 陸王
Lu Xiangshan 陸象山
Lü Yijian 呂夷簡

Lun Xuechou da　論學酬答
Luo Rufang　羅汝芳
Lüshi chunqiu　呂氏春秋
Lüshun　旅順
Ma Jun　馬俊
Macheng　麻城
Mantetsu　滿鉄
Mao Shan　茅山
Maoshi huowen　毛詩或問
Meizhou　眉州
ming　命
ming　名
ming ze buke mian　命則不可免
mingyun　命運
"Minzhi pian"　民職篇
Mu　穆
mu　畝
neidan　內丹
nian　念
nimen baixing　你們百姓
nongjia　農家
Pan Gongding　潘恭定
Pan Yunduan　潘允端
Pan Yunzhe　潘允哲
Pei Du　裴度
Pinghe　平和
Poxie ji　破邪集
pubei gongyi　僕婢工役
puti huixiang　菩提迴向
qi　氣
Qi Biaojia　祁彪佳
Qian Guangju　錢廣居
Qian Shisheng　錢士升
Qianlong　乾隆
"Qianxu lizhong"　謙虛利中
qijia zhi xue　齊家之學
Qin Hongyou　秦弘祐
qingshi　卿士
qiongli　窮理
Qiongzhou　瓊州
qishu　氣數
Qixia　棲霞
Qu Rangong　瞿然恭

quanhua 勸化
"*Quanjie quanshu* shu" 勸戒全書叙
"*Quanjie quanshu* xiaoyin" 勸戒全書小引
"Quanshan pian" 勸善篇
"Quanxue ge" 勸學歌
Quanzhen 全眞
Quanzhou 泉州
Quwei zhai wenji 去僞齋文集
rendao 人道
"Renji tu" 人極圖
Renpu 人譜
Rizhi lu 日知錄
"*Rizhi lu* xu" 日知錄序
Rulin 儒林
sanbao 三寶
sanguan 三官
sanming 三命
sanshi 三世
Sanshi shen 三尸神
Santai 三台
sengdao 僧道
shan'e baoying zhi shuo 善惡報應之說
Shang 商
Shangcheng 商城
Shangdi 上帝
shanggu 商賈
Shangqing 上清
shangtian mingshu 上天命數
shanshu 善書
Shao Shigao 邵式誥
Shao Yong 邵雍
She 攝
shecang 社倉
shejian 奢儉
Shen Wending 申文定
Shen Yunzuo 沈雲祚
shendu 愼獨
sheng 聖
"Shengong miaoji zhenjun" 神功妙濟眞君
Shengxue zongzhuan 聖學宗傳
Shengyu 聖語
Shengyu liuyan jie 聖語六言解
shengyuan 生員

shenhuan 紳宦

shi 市

Shi Chengjin 石成金

shiduan fa 十段法

Shijie gongguoge 十戒功過格

shiren 士人

shixing 士行

Shizheng lu 實政錄

Shizong 世宗

shizu 士卒

shouchi 受持

shouming 壽命

shu 數

Shuihu zhuan 水滸傳

shumin 庶民

Shun 舜

Shunde 順德

Shunzhi 順治

shuyin 署印

si 私

siguo zhi shen 司過之神

Siming 司命

Song Qi 宋乞

"Songguo fa" 訟過法

Songling 松陵

su 俗

Su Rulin 蘇汝霖

suan 算

sui 歲

Sui Tang yanyi 隋唐演義

suiming 隨命

"Suixin tuoluoni" 隨心陀羅尼

suming 宿命

Sun Hong 孫鈜

Sun Qi 孫琪

Taicangzhou 太倉州

Taihu 太湖

"Taiji tushuo" 太極圖說

Taiping Dao 太平道

Taishang baofu 太上寶筏

Taishang dongxuan lingbao yebao yinyuan jing
太上洞玄靈寶業報因緣經

Taishang ganying jingzhuan jiyao 太上感應經傳輯要

Taishang ganying pian 太上感應篇
Taishang ganying pian jijie 太上感應篇集解
Taishang ganying pian jingzhuan 太上感應篇經傳
Taishang ganying pian shuyan 太上感應篇疏衍
Taishang ganying pian tushuo 太上感應篇圖說
Taishang ganying pian xinzhu 太上感應篇新註
Taishang ganying pian zhu 太上感應篇注
Taishang ganying pian zhujiang zheng'an huibian
    太上感應篇註講證案彙編
Taishang ganying pian zhuzheng hebian 太上感應篇註證合編
Taishang lingbao jingming dongshen shangpin jing
    太上靈寶淨明洞神上品經
Taishang lingbao jingming feitian duren jingfa
    太上靈寶淨明飛天度人經法
Taishang lingbao jingming rudao pin 太上靈寶爭明入道品
Taishang lingbao zhutian neiyin ziran yuzi 太上靈寶諸天內音自然玉字
Taiwei xianjun gongguoge 太微仙君功過格
Taiyi 太一
Taiyuan 太原
Taizhou 泰州
"Tang Huolin sige" 湯霍林四歌
Tang Qisheng 湯其升
Tang Taizong 唐太宗
Tao Ningzuo 陶寧祚
Tao Shiling 陶奭齡
Taozhuang 陶莊
Tiancao 天曹
Tianfu 天府
"Tianguan" 天官
tianming 天命
Tianqi 天啓
Tianshi 天師
Tiantai 天台
"Tianwen" 天文
Tianxia diyizhong haoshu 天下第一種好書
"Tiyao" 提要
Tongcheng 桐城
tongshan hui 同善會
"Tongshan hui jiangyu" 同善會講語
"Tongshan hui xu" 同善會序
Tu Kangxi 屠康僖
Tu Shufang 屠叔方
tuan 團

waidan 外丹
Wairen pian 外任篇
Wanli 萬歷
wang 忘
Wang Anshi 王安石
Wang Chong 王充
Wang Daokun 王道焜
Wang Daoquan 王道全
Wang He 王賀
Wang Huai 王淮
Wang Jiazhen 王家禎
Wang Kun 王坤
Wang Mengji 王孟箕
Wang Menglan 王夢蘭
Wang Wensu 王文肅
Wang Younian 王有年
Wang Yuan 王原
Wang Zhidao 王志道
wangfa 王法
wanghua 王化
wangqi 望氣
wei 未
Wei Chengrun 魏呈潤
Wei Zhongxian 魏忠賢
"Weiguo duzhi zhu zhi" 微過獨知主之
weiguo weimin 為國為民
Weishan yinzhi 為善陰隲
Weixin 唯心
weixin 畏心
weixin liming 唯心立命
"Weixue pian" 為學篇
Wen Tiren 溫體仁
"Wen Wenshan zhengqi ge" 文文山正氣歌
Wen Zhenmeng 文震孟
Wenchang 文昌
wenyan 文言
wo ming zai wo, buzai tian 我命在我, 不在天
wu 無
Wu Liufang 吳六房
Wu Mao 吳毛
Wu Meiquan 吳默泉
Wu Zhouhong 吳周紘
Wudoumi Dao 五斗米道

Wujiang　吳江

wujue zhi jue　無覺之覺

Wumen　吳門

wunian　無念

wushan er zhishan xin zhi ti ye　無善而至善心之體也

wushan wu'e　無善無惡

wushan you'e　無善有惡

wushan zhi shan　無善之善

wusi wulü　無思無慮

Wusong　吳淞

Wutai　五台

wuwei er wei　無為而為

wuxin　無心

wuxin weizhu　悟心為主

"Wuyun lun"　五運論

wuzhuo　五濁

Xia Jiansuo　夏建所

xian　咸

"Xianguo jiuyong zhu zhi"　顯過九容主之

xiang　相

Xiangjia yue　鄉甲約

xiangshen　鄉紳

"Xiangshen jiaju yixing zhi bao"　鄉紳家居懿行之報

xiangyue　鄉約

xiaocai　效財

xiaoshun　孝順

Xiaoxin zhai zhaji　小心齋劄集

xiaoxue　小學

Xiaoyao　逍遙

xiaren　下人

Xici　繫辭

xifu　惜福

xin　心

Xingkong　性空

Xingshen lu　省身錄

"Xingxin ji"　省心紀

xingxing　性行

Xinhui　新會

Xinjian　新建

"Xinlu"　心錄

Xiong Mian'an baoshan bufeiqian gongdeli　熊勉菴寶善不費錢功德例

Xishan yinshi Yuzhen Liu xiansheng zhuan　西山隱士玉眞劉先生傳

"Xiushen ge"　修身格

xiushen zhi xue 修身之學
Xiuzhen shishu 修眞十書
xu 虛
xu 序
Xu Fuyuan 許孚遠
Xu Sian 徐思菴
Xu Sun 許孫
Xu Xingzhi 徐行志
Xu Zhenjun 許眞君
Xu Zhenjun shihan ji 許眞君石函記
"Xu Zhenjun zhuan" 許眞君傳
xuanjiang 宣講
xuanmen 玄門
xuanpin zhi men 玄牝之門
Xue Xuan 薛瑄
Xuehai 學海
Xunsu yigui 訓俗遺規
Xunzi yan 訓子言
Xunzi yu 訓子語
Yan Tiaoyu 嚴調御
Yang Maoren 楊茂仁
Yang Maoyuan 楊茂元
Yang Qiyuan 楊起元
Yang Shouchen 楊守陳
Yang Shouzhi 楊守阯
Yang Zicheng 楊自懲
yangqi 養氣
yangqi 陽氣
yangsheng 養生
yangzhibu 養志簿
Yangzhou 揚州
Yao 堯
Yao Shisheng 姚士升
Yao Siren 姚思仁
Yaoxiu keyi jielü chao 要修科儀戒律鈔
Ye Zhiji 葉之奇
Yi Yin 伊尹
yijia 醫家
Yin 鄞
Yin Min 尹旻
Yin Qiuming 殷秋溟
yi'nan 義男
yinci 淫祠

Yi'nei jie 易內戒
yinguo 因果
"Yinguo qiqing zhu zhi" 隱過七情主之
yinlü 陰律
"Yinsong xingshi" 印送姓氏
yi'nü 義女
yinyuan 因緣
yinzhi 陰隲
Yinzhi lu 陰隲錄
Yinzhi wen 陰隲文
yitian liangzhu 一田兩主
yitiao bianfa 一條鞭法
Yixing 宜興
Yongfeng 永豐
Yongle 永樂
yongxin 勇心
Yongzheng 雍正
You Minggui 游名桂
You Xuanzi 又玄子
youxia 游俠
Yu Yue 俞樾
Yuan Cai 袁采
Yuan Hao 袁顥
Yuan Ren 袁仁
Yuan Shun 袁順
Yuan Xiang 袁祥
Yuan xiansheng Sishu xun'er sushuo 袁先生四書訓兒俗說
Yuan Yan 袁儼
yuanlibu 願力簿
Yuanshi jiaxun 袁氏家訓
Yuanshi shifan 袁氏世範
Yuanshi tianzun 元始天尊
Yuanshi wuliang duren shangpin miaojing tongyi
　元始無量度人上品妙經通義
"Yuanxu xuancun" 原序選存
"Yueling" 月令
yufu yufu 愚夫愚婦
Yulong Wanshou Gong 玉隆萬壽宮
yun 運
Yungu 雲谷
"Yungu xiandashi zhuan" 雲谷先大師傳
Yunjian 雲間
Yunqi hui 雲起會

"Yunqi zonglun" 運氣總論
"Yuren ge" 與人格
zaoming 造命
zaoming 遭命
Zaoshen 竈神
zengzhu 增註
Zhang Jue 張角
Zhang Jun 張浚
Zhang Juzheng 張居正
Zhang Qi 張圻
Zhang Shiren 張士任
Zhang Weiyan 張畏巖
Zhang Xianzhong 張獻忠
zhangbu 帳簿
Zhangzhou 漳州
Zhao Bian 趙抃
Zhao Qi 趙岐
Zhao Shiyan 趙世延
Zhao Xiong 趙雄
Zhao Yuedao 趙閱道
Zhe Xiang 折像
Zhenda 眞大
Zheng Chenggong 鄭成功
Zheng Danquan 鄭旦泉
Zheng Liang 鄭梁
Zheng Qingzhi 鄭淸之
Zheng Xiu 鄭秀
zhengming 正命
Zhengren hui 證人會
"Zhengren yaozhi" 證人要旨
zhengshi 徵事
Zhengxing bian 證性編
Zhenzong 眞宗
Zhi Dalun 支大綸
Zhi Li 支立
Zhi Songzi jing 赤松子經
zhiguan 止觀
zhiping zhi xue 治平之學
Zhixin pian 治心篇
zhizhi 致知
zhizhi guaying 知止寡營
Zhong Lijin 鍾離瑾
zhongsheng huixiang 衆生回向

Zhou Chi 周箎
Zhou Dunyi 周敦頤
Zhou Lianggong 周亮工
Zhu Dai 朱岱
Zhu Di 朱棣
Zhu Shangbao 諸尚寶
Zhu Taizong 朱泰宗
"Zhu Wengong dazhangfu ge" 朱文公大丈夫歌
Zhunti 準提
"Zhunti zhou" 準提呪
zi 字
Zibo Zhenke 紫柏眞可
Zigong 子工
Zilu 子路
Zitong 梓潼
"Zixu" 自序
zonglun 總論
zongshi 宗師
Zou Wang 鄒望
Zou Yuanbiao 鄒元標
Zuo zhuan 左傳
Zuofei 昨非
zuqin 租親

Sources Cited

Akizuki Kan'ei 秋月觀暎. *Chūgoku kinsei Dōkyō no keisei—Jōmeidō no kisoteki kenkyū* 中國近世道教の形成—浄明道の基礎的研究. Tokyo: Sōbunsha, 1978.

———. "Jōmeidōkyōgaku kanken—Ju, Butsu, Dō sankyō kankei o chūshin ni" 浄明道教學管見—儒佛道三教關係を中心に, *Tōhō shūkyō* 東方宗教 35 (1970): 20–35.

Araki Kengo 荒木見悟. *Minmatsu shūkyō shisō kenkyū—Kan Tōmei no shōgai to sono shisō* 明末宗教思想研究—管東溟の生涯とその思想. Tokyo: Sōbunsha, 1972.

Atwell, Williams. "From Education to Politics: The Fu She." In *The Unfolding of Neo-Confucianism*, edited by William Theodore de Bary, 333–367. New York: Columbia University Press, 1975.

———. "Notes on Silver, Foreign Trade, and the Late Ming Economy," *Ch'ing-shih wen-t'i*, 3.8 (December 1977): 1–33.

Baicheng 稗乘. 1618. Reprinted in *Baibu Congshu jicheng* 百部叢書集成. Taibei: Yiwen yinshuguan, 1967.

Baodi xianzhi 寶坻縣志. 1745.

Beizhuan ji 碑傳集. Edited by Qian Yiji 錢儀吉. 1983.

Berling, Judith. "Religion and Popular Culture: The Management of Moral Capital in *The Romance of the Three Teachings*." In *Popular Culture in Late Imperial China*, edited by David Johnson, Andrew Nathan, and Evelyn Rawski, 188–218. Berkeley and Los Angeles: University of California Press, 1985.

Birdwhistell, Anne D. *Transition to Neo-Confucianism: Shao Yung on Knowledge and Symbols of Reality*. Stanford: Stanford University Press, 1989.

Bodde, Derk. *Essays on Chinese Civilization*, edited by Charles LeBlanc and Dorothy Borei. Princeton: Princeton University Press, 1981.

Bokenkamp, Stephen R. "Sources of the Ling-pao Scriptures." In *Tantric and Taoist Studies in Honour of R. A. Stein*, edited by Michel Strickmann, vol. 2, 434–486. Mélanges chinois et bouddhiques, vol. 21. Brussels: Institut Belge des Hautes Études Chinoises, 1983.

Boltz, Judith. *A Survey of Taoist Literature, Tenth to Seventeenth Centuries*. China Research Monograph 32. Berkeley: Institute of East Asian Studies, University of California, 1987.

Brokaw, Cynthia J. "Yuan Huang (1533–1606) and the Ledgers of Merit and Demerit." *Harvard Journal of Asiatic Studies* 47.1 (June 1987): 137–195.

Busch, Heinrich. "The Tung-lin Academy and Its Political and Philosophical Significance." *Mounmenta Serica* 14 (1949–1955): 1–163.

Cao Xueqin. *The Story of the Stone*. Vol. 1: *The Golden Days*. Translated by David Hawkes. Baltimore: Penguin Books, 1973.

Carus, Paul, and D. Z. Suzuki, trans. *T'ai Shang Kan-Ying P'ien*. 1906. Reprint. LaSalle, Ill.: Open Court Publishing Company, 1950.

Chan, Albert. *The Glory and Fall of the Ming Dynasty*. Norman: University of Oklahoma Press, 1982.

Chan, Wing-tsit. *A Source Book in Chinese Philosophy*. Princeton: Princeton University Press, 1963.

Chang, Carson. *The Development of Neo-Confucian Thought*. 2 vols. New York: Bookman Associates, 1962.

Chartier, Roger. *The Cultural Uses of Print in Early Modern France*. Princeton: Princeton University Press, 1987.

Chen Hu 陳瑚. *Shengxue rumen shu* 聖學入門書. In *Jiguo zhai congshu* 記過齋叢書, *ce* 1, edited by Su Yuansheng 蘇源生. Tongzhi edition.

Chen Jian 陳堅. *Taishang ganying ling pian tushuo* 太上感應靈篇圖說. 1324. In *Wulin wangzhe yizhuo houbian* 武林往哲遺箸後編, *ce* 76, edited by Nan Lizhong 男立中. 1875–1900.

Chen Longzheng 陳龍正. *Jiting quanshu* 幾亭全書. 1665.

Chen Yuan 陳垣. *Nan Songchu Hebei xin Daojiao kao* 南宋初河北新道教考. Beijing: Zhonghua shuju, 1962.

Chen Xigu 陳錫嘏. *Huizuan gongguoge* 彙纂功過格. 1828.

Chen Zhixi 陳智錫. *Quanjie quanshu* 勸戒全書. 1641. Held by the Naikaku Bunko.

Chü Tung-tsu. *Law and Society in Traditional China*. Paris: Mouton and Company, 1961.

Coyle, Michael. "Book of Rewards and Punishments." In *Chinese Civilization and Society: A Sourcebook*, edited by Patricia Ebrey, 71–74. New York: The Free Press, 1981.

Daozang 道藏. Shanghai: Shangwu yinshuguan, 1923–1926.

Daozang jiyao 道藏輯要. Edited by He Longxiang 賀龍驤 and Peng Hanran 彭瀚然. Chengdu: Erxian An, 1906. Reprint. Taibei: Kaozheng shuju, 1971.

Daozang zimu yinde 道藏字目引得. Harvard-Yenching Institute Sinological Index Series no. 25. Beijing: Harvard-Yenching Institute, 1935. Photocopy reprint. Taibei: Ch'eng Wen Publishing Company, 1966.

de Bary, William Theodore. "Individualism and Humanitarianism in Late Ming Thought." In *Self and Society in Ming Thought*, edited by William Theodore de Bary and the Conference on Late Ming Thought, 145–247. New York: Columbia University Press, 1970.

———. "Neo-Confucian Self-Cultivation and the Seventeenth-Century 'Enlightenment,'" In *The Unfolding of Neo-Confucianism*, edited by William Theodore de Bary, 141–216. New York: Columbia University Press, 1975.

Dennerline, Jerry. *The Chia-ting Loyalists: Confucian Leadership and Social Change in Seventeenth-Century China*. New Haven: Yale University Press, 1981.

Dimberg, Ronald. *The Sage and Society: The Life and Thought of Ho Hsin-yin*. Monographs of the Society for Asian and Comparative Philosophy, no. 1. Honolulu: The University Press of Hawaii, 1974.

Dong Yang 董瑒. "Liuzi nianpu" 劉子年譜. In Liu Zongzhou, *Liuzi quanshu*, 40.1a–52b (vol. 6, pp. 3487–3722).

Dong Zhongshu 董仲舒. *Chunqiu fanlu* 春秋繁露. 17 *juan*. Sibu beiyao edition.

Doré, Henry. *Researches into Chinese Superstitutions*. 13 vols. Translated by M. Kennelly and L. F. McGreal. Shanghai: T'usewei Printing Press, 1914. Reprint. Taibei: Ch'eng-wen Publishing Company, 1966–1967.

Duara, Prasenjit. "Superscribing Symbols: The Myth of Guandi, Chinese God of War." *Journal of Asian Studies* 47.4 (November 1988): 778–795.

Dunstan, Helen. "The Late Ming Epidemics: A Preliminary Survey." *Ch'ing-shih wen-t'i* 3.3 (November 1975): 1–59.

Eberhard, Wolfram. *Guilt and Sin in Traditional China*. Berkeley and Los Angeles: University of California Press, 1967.

Ebrey, Patricia. *Family and Property in Sung China: Yuan Ts'ai's Precepts for Social Life*. Princeton: Princeton University Press, 1984.

Elman, Benjamin A. *From Philosophy to Philology: Intellectual and Social Aspects of Change in Late Imperial China*. Harvard East Asian Monographs, no. 110. Cambridge: Council on East Asian Studies, Harvard University, 1984.

Elvin, Mark. *The Pattern of the Chinese Past*. Stanford: Stanford University Press, 1973.

Feng Congwu 馮從吾. "Shanli tushuo" 善利圖說. In *Shaoxu ji* 少墟集. Siku quanshu zhenben, 5th series. Photo reprint of Wen Yuan Ge copy. Taibei: Shangwu yinshuguan, 1974.

Fisher, T. S. "Accommodation and Loyalism: The Life of Lü Liu-liang (1629–1683)," parts 1, 2, and 3. *Papers on Far Eastern History*, no. 15 (March 1977): 97–104; no. 16 (September 1977): 107–145; and no. 18 (September 1978): 1–42.

Franke, Herbert, ed. *Sung Biographies*. 4 vol. Weisbaden: Franz Steiner Verlag GMBH, 1976.

Freeman, Michael D. "From Adept to Worthy: The Philosophical Career of Shao Yung." *Journal of the American Oriental Society* 102.3 (July–October 1982): 477–492.

Fu Yiling 傅衣凌. *Mingdai Jiangnan shimin jingji shitan* 明代江南市民經濟試探. Shanghai: Shanghai renmin chuban she, 1963.

———. *Ming-Qing shidai shangren ji shangye ziben* 明清時代商人及商業資本. Beijing: Renmin chuban she, 1956.

Fujian tongzhi 福建通志. 1871.

Fuma Susumu 夫馬進. "Dōzenkai shōshi—Chūgoku shakai fukushi shijō ni okeru Minmatsu Shinsho no ichizuke no tame ni" 同善會小史—中国社会福祉史上における明末清初の位置づけのために, *Shirin* 史林 65.4 (1982): 37–76.

Fung Yu-lan. *A History of Chinese Philosophy*. 2 vols. Translated by Derk Bodde. Princeton: Princeton University Press, 1952.

Fushou baocang yibaisishizhong 福壽寶藏一百四十種. Edited by Leshan She 樂善社. Shanghai: Dazhong shuju, 1936.

Fuzhou fuzhi 福州府志. 1876.

Ganying pian zhijiang 感應篇直講. 1856. Reprint. 1925.

Gao Panlong 高攀龍. *Gaozi yishu* 高子遺書. Edited by Chen Longzheng. 1876.

Gernet, Jacques. *China and the Christian Impact: A Conflict of Cultures*. Translated by Janet Lloyd. Cambridge: Cambridge University Press, 1985.

Goodrich, L. Carrington, and Chaoying Fang, eds. *Dictionary of Ming Biography, 1368–1644.* 2 vols. New York: Columbia University Press, 1976.

Graham, Angus Charles. *Two Chinese Philosophers: Ch'eng Ming-tao and Ch'eng Yi-ch'uan.* London: Lund Humphries, 1958.

Greenblatt, Kristin Yü. "Chu-hung and Lay Buddhism in the Late Ming." In *The Unfolding of Neo-Confucianism,* edited by William Theodore de Bary, 93–140. New York: Columbia University Press, 1975.

Grove, Linda, and Joseph Esherick. "From Feudalism to Capitalism: Japanese Scholarship on the Transformation of Chinese Rural Society." *Modern China* 6.4 (October 1980): 397–438.

Gu Xiancheng 顧憲成. *Gu Duanwen Gong yishu* 顧端文公遺書. 1694–1698.

Gu Yanwu 顧炎武. *Tianxia junguo libing shu* 天下郡國利病書. Sibu congkan xubian, vols. 279–328.

Guan Zhidao 管志道. *Cong xianwei suyi* 從先維俗議. Photocopy of Ming edition. In *Taikun xianzhe yishu shouji* 太崑先哲遺書首集, edited by Yu Qing'en 俞慶恩. 1928.

Gui Youguang 歸有光. *Zhenchuan xiansheng ji* 震川先生集. Kangxi era edition. Shanghai: Shanghai guji chubanshe, 1981.

Gujin tushu jicheng 古今圖書集成. Edited by Chen Menglei 陳夢雷 and Jiang Tingxi 蔣廷錫. Shanghai: Gujin tushu jicheng ju, 1884.

Guo yu 國語. Sibu congkan edition.

Guochao qixian leizheng (chubian) 國朝耆獻類徵(初編). Edited by Li Huan 李桓. 1890.

Guochao xianzheng lu 國朝獻徵錄. Edited by Jiao Hong 焦竑. 1616. Facsimile reproduction. Taibei: Xuesheng shuju, 1965.

Hamashima Atsutoshi 濱島敦俊. *Mindai Kōnan nōson shakai no kenkyū* 明代江南農村社会の研究. Tokyo: Tōkyō Daigaku shuppansha, 1982.

Han shu 漢書. By Ban Gu 班固. Beijing: Zhonghua shuju, 1962.

Handlin, Joanna. *Action in Late Ming Thought: The Reorientation of Lü K'un and Other Scholar-Officials.* Berkeley and Los Angeles: University of California Press, 1983.

———. "Benevolent Societies: The Reshaping of Charity During the Late Ming and Early Ch'ing." *Journal of Asian Studies* 46.2 (May 1987): 309–337.

Hanshan Deqing 憨山德清. *Hanshan dashi mengyou ji* 憨山大師夢遊集. Edited by Tong Qiong 通炯 and Liu Qixiang 劉起相. 1859. Reprint. Hong Kong: Xiangfang Fojing liutong chu, 1965.

Harrell, Stevan. "The Concept of Fate in Chinese Folk Ideology." *Modern China* 13.1 (January 1987): 90–109.

Hattori Unokichi 服部宇之吉. *Shina kenkyū* 支那研究. Tokyo: Meiji shuppansha, 1917.

Hegel, Robert. *The Novel in Seventeenth-Century China.* New York: Columbia University Press, 1981.

Henderson, John. *The Development and Decline of Chinese Cosmology.* New York: Columbia University Press, 1984.

Hirano Yoshitarō 平野義太郎. *Hoku-Shi no sonraku shakai* 北支の村落社会, vol. 1. Tokyo: Kankoku chōsa happyō, 1944.

Ho, P'ing-ti. *The Ladder of Success in Imperial China*. New York: Columbia University Press, 1971.

Hosono Kōji 細野浩二. "Minmatsu Shinsho Kōnan ni okeru jinushi doboku kankei—kakun ni mirareru sono shintenkai o megutte" 明末清初江南における地主奴僕関係—家訓にみられるその新展開をめぐって. *Tōyō gakuhō* 東洋學報 50.3 (December 1967): 1–36.

Hou Ching-lang. *Monnaies d'offrande et la notion de trésorie dans la religion chinoise*. Paris: Collège de France, Institut des hautes études chinoises, 1975.

Hou Han shu 後漢書. By Fan Ye 范曄. Beijing: Zhonghua shuju, 1965.

Hou Wailu 侯外庐, Zhao Jibin 赵紀彬, and Du Guoxiang 杜国庠. *Zhongguo sixiang tongshi* 中國思想通史. 5 vols. Beijing: Renmin chubanshe, 1960.

Hsi, Angela Ning-jy Sun. "Social and Economic Status of the Merchant Class of the Ming Dynasty, *1368–1644*." Ph.D. diss., University of Illinois at Urbana-Champaign, 1974.

Hu Rongshi 胡溶時. *Huibian gongguoge* 彙編功過格. 1702. Reprint. 1885.

Hua Yuncheng 華允誠. "Gao Zhongxian Gong nianpu" 高忠憲公年譜. In Gao Panlong, *Gaozi yishu, ce* 8, 1a–36b. 1876.

Huang Chin-shing. "The Lu-Wang School in the Ch'ing Dynasty: Li Mu-t'ang." Ph.D. diss., Harvard University, 1983.

Huang, Ray. *1587, A Year of No Significance: The Ming Dynasty in Decline*. New Haven: Yale University Press, 1981.

———. "The Lung-ch'ing and Wan-li Reigns, 1567–1620." In *The Cambridge History of China*. Volume 7: *The Ming Dynasty, 1368–1644*, part 1, edited by Frederick W. Mote and Denis Twitchett. Cambridge: Cambridge University Press, 1988, pp. 511–584.

Huang Tsung-hsi (Huang Zongxi). *The Records of Ming Scholars by Huang Tsung-hsi*. Edited by Julia Ching, with Chaoying Fang. Honolulu: University of Hawaii Press, 1987.

Huang Zhengyuan 黃正元. *Yu Xujie gongguoge* 御虛階功過格. 1734.

Huang, Zhihai 黃智海. *Liaofan sixun baihua jieshi* 了凡四訓白話解釋 Taibei: Taiwan yinjingchu, 1962.

Huang Zongxi 黃宗羲. *Mingru xuean* 明儒學案. 2 vols. Sibu beiyao edition. Reprint. Taibei: Zhonghua shuju, 1960.

Hui Dong 惠棟. *Taishang ganying pian zhu* 太上感應篇注. In *Yueya tang congshu* 粵雅堂叢書. 1853. Facsimile reproduction. Taibei: Huawen shuju, 1965.

Hummel, Arthur. *Eminent Chinese of the Ch'ing Period*. Washington, D.C.: U.S. Government Printing Office, 1943.

Huo Tao 霍韜. *Huo Weiya jiaxun* 霍渭涯家訓. In *Hanfen lou miji* 涵芬樓秘笈, 2d collection. Jingji guge edition. Reprint. Shanghai: Shangwu yinshuguan, 1917.

Hymes, Robert. "Not Quite Gentlemen? Doctors in Sung and Yuan." *Chinese Science* 8 (1987): 9–76.

———. *Statesmen and Gentlemen: The Elite of Fu-Chou, Chiang-Hsi, in Northern and Southern Sung*. Cambridge: Cambridge University Press, 1986.

Idema, Wilt. *Chinese Vernacular Fiction: The Formative Period*. Leiden: E. J. Brill, 1974.

Inahata Koichirō 稲畑小一郎. "Shimei shinsō no tenkai" 司命信想の展開. *Chū-goku bungaku kenkyū* 中国文学研究 5 (December 1979): 1–15.

Inoue Susumu 井上進. "Fukusha no gaku" 復社の學. *Tōyōshi kenkyū* 東洋史研究 44.2 (September 1985): 40–70.

Ishikawa Umejirō 石川梅次郎. *Inshitsu roku* 陰隲錄. Tokyo: Meitoku shuppan-sha, 1970.

Jan, Yun-hua. "A Comparative Study of 'No-Thought' ('Wu-Nien') in Some Indian and Chinese Buddhist Texts." *The Journal of Chinese Philosophy* 16.1 (March 1989): 37–58.

Jiang Wenlan 江文瀾. *Chenzhong lu* 晨鐘錄. 1763. Held by the Naikaku Bunko.

Jing Junjian 经君健. "Guanyu Qingdai nubi zhidu de fange wenti" 关于清代奴婢制度的几个问题, *Jingji yanjiusuo jikan* 经济研究所集刊 5 (1983): 60–178.

Julien, Stanislas. *Le Livre des Récompenses et des Peines*. Paris: Oriental Transla-tion Fund, 1835.

Kasoff, Ira. *The Thought of Chang Tsai (1020–1077)*. Cambridge: Cambridge University Press, 1984.

Keightley, David N. *Sources of Shang History: The Oracle-Bone Inscriptions of Bronze Age China*. Berkeley and Los Angeles: University of California Press, 1978.

Kubo Noritada 窪德忠. "Chūgoku no sanshi shinkō to Nihon no kōshin shin-kō 中國の三尸信仰と日本の庚申信仰. *Tōhōgaku ronshū* 東方學論集 3 (September 1955): 1–54.

———. *Dōkyō shi* 道教史. Tokyo: Yamagawa shuppansha, 1977.

———. "Kōshin shinkō to Hokuto shinkō" 庚申信仰と北斗信仰. *Minzokuga-ku kenkyū* 民族学研究 21.3 (August 1957): 21–27.

Lau, D. C., trans. *Confucius: The Analects*. New York: Penguin Books, 1979.

———. *Mencius*. New York: Penguin Books, Ltd., 1970.

Legge, James, trans. *The Chinese Classics*. 5 vols. Hong Kong: Hong Kong University Press, 1960.

———. "The Thai Shang Tractate of Actions and Their Retributions." In *The Sacred Books of the East*, edited by Max Muller, vol. 39, 233–246. Oxford: Oxford University Press, 1980.

Leung, Angela Ki Che. "Elementary Education in the Lower Yangtze Region in the 17th and 18th Centuries." Paper presented at the Conference on Education and Society in Late Imperial China, Montecito, California, June 8–14, 1989.

———. "Organized Medicine in Ming-Qing China: State and Private Medical Institutions in the Lower Yangzi Region." *Late Imperial China* 8.1 (June 1987), 134–166.

Li Banghua 李邦華. *Huangming Li Zhongwen xiansheng ji* 皇明李忠文先生集. 1726.

Li Erjing 李日景. *Zuibi tang sanshiliu shan* 醉筆堂三十六善. In *Tanji congshu erji* 檀几叢書二集, edited by Wang Zhuo 王晫 and Zhang Chao 張潮. 1697.

Li Fu 李紱. *Mutang chugao* 穆堂初稿. 1740.

Li Guochang 李國昌. *Chongxiu zhiyao* 崇修指要. Preface dated 1667. Held in the Naikaku Bunko.

Li Shi 李石. *Fangzhou ji* 方舟集. Sikuquanshu zhenben edition.

———. *Leshan lu* 樂善錄. Jingyin sibu shanben zongkan, 1. Song Shaoding edition. Photolithographic copy. Taibei, 1971.

Li Shida 李士達. *Gongguoge jiyao* 功過格輯要. 1717.

Li Xinchuan 李心傳. *(Jianyan yilai) Chaoye zaji* (建炎以來) 朝野雜記. In *Wuying dianju zhenban shu* 武英殿聚珍版書, edited by Jin Jian 金簡, *ce* 208–218. Qianlong edition.

Li Yong 李顒. *Erqu ji* 二曲集. 1694. Facsimile reprint. Taibei: Shangwu yinshu guan, 1973.

Li Yu 李漁. *Li Yu quanji* 李漁全集. 15 vols. Edited by Helmut Martin. Taibei: Chengwen chuban she, 1970.

———. *Zizhi xinshu erji* 資治新書二集. 1667.

Li Zhi 李贄. *Cang shu* 藏書. 2 vols. Beijing: Zhonghua shuju, 1959.

———. *Xu fen shu* 續焚書. Beijing: Zhonghua shuju, 1959.

Liang Fang-chung. *The Single Whip Method of Taxation in China*. Translated by Wang Yü-ch'üan. Cambridge: Chinese Economic and Political Studies, Harvard University, 1956.

Liang Ruyuan 梁汝元 (He Xinyin 何心隱). *He Xinyin ji* 何心隱集. Beijing: Zhonghua shuju, 1981.

Ling Xiqi 淩錫祺. "Zundao xiansheng nianpu" 尊道先生年譜. In Lu Shiyi, *Lu Futing xiansheng yishu, ce* 1, 1a–19b. 1889.

Liu Linchang 劉麟長. *Shenggong ge* 聖功格. In *Zhexue zongzhuan* 浙學宗傳. 1638. In the Naikaku Bunko.

Liu Ts'un-yan. "Yuan Huang and His 'Four Admonitions,'" *Journal of the Oriental Society of Australia* 5.1 and 2 (December 1967): 108–132.

Liu Zongzhou 劉宗周. *Liuzi quanshu* 劉子全書. Zhonghua wenshi congshu, no. 57. 1824. Facsimile reprint. Taibei: Huawen shuju, 1968.

Lu Fudan 魯復旦 (?). *Guangshan pian gongguoge* 廣善篇功過格. 1721.

Lü Kun 呂坤. *Lüzi yishu* 呂子遺書. Edited by Wang Qinglin 王慶麟 and Su Yumei 栗毓美. 1827.

Lü Liuliang 呂留良. *Lü Wancun xiansheng sishu jiangyi* 呂晚村先生四書講義. 1686.

Lu Shiyi 陸世儀. *Futing xiansheng wenchao* 桴亭先生文鈔. In *Lu Chen erxiansheng wenchao* 陸陳二先生文鈔. 1876.

———. *Lu Futing xiansheng yishu* 陸桴亭先生遺書. 1889.

Lunyu yinde 論語引得. Harvard-Yenching Sinological Index Series Supplement 16. Beijing: Harvard-Yenching Institute, 1940. Photocopy reprint. Taibei: Ch'eng Wen Publishing Company, 1966.

McDermott, Joseph. "Bondservants in the T'ai-hu Basin During the Late Ming: A Case of Mistaken Identities." *Journal of Asian Studies* 40.4 (August 1981): 675–701.

Mair, Victor. "Language and Ideology in the Written Popularizations of the *Sacred Edict*." In *Popular Culture in Late Imperial China*, edited by David Johnson, Andrew Nathan, and Evelyn Rawski, 325–359. Berkeley and Los Angeles: University of California Press, 1985.

Martinson, Paul Varo. "*Pao Order and Redemption: Perspective on Chinese Religion and Society Based on a Study of the Chin P'ing Mei*." Ph.D. diss., University of Chicago, 1973.

Maspero, Henri. *Taoism and Chinese Religion*. Translated by Frank A. Kierman, Jr. Amherst: University of Massachusetts Press, 1981.

Matsuda, Shizue. "Li Yu: His Life and Moral Philosophy as Reflected in His Fiction." Ph.D. diss., Columbia University, 1978.

Mengzi yinde 孟子引得. Harvard-Yenching Institute Sinological Index Series Supplement 17. Beijing: Harvard-Yenching Institute, 1941. Photocopy reprint. Taibei: Ch'eng Wen Publishing Company, 1966.

Ming shi 明史. Compiled by Zhang Tingyu 張廷玉 et al. Beijing: Zhonghua shuju, 1974.

Mingdai chizhuan shukao fuyinde 明代勅撰書考附引得. Harvard-Yenching Institute Sinological Index Series Supplement 3. Beijing: Harvard-Yenching Institute, 1932. Photocopy reprint. Taibei: Ch'eng Wen Publishing Company, 1966.

Mingren zizhuan wenchao 明人自傳文鈔. Edited by Du Lianzhe 杜聯喆. Taibei: Yiwen yinshuguan, 1976.

Mizoguchi Yūzō 溝口三雄. "Iwayuru Tōrinha jinshi no shisō—zenkindaiki ni okeru Chūgoku shisō no tenkai—(jō)" いわゆる東林派人士の思想—前近代期における中國思想の展開(上). *Tōyō bunka kenkyūjo kiyo* 東洋文化研究所紀要 75 (March 1978): 111–341.

Mori Masao. "The Gentry in the Late Ming—An Outline of the Relations between the *Shih-ta-fu* and Local Society." *Acta Asiatica*, no. 38 (1980): 31–53.

———— 森正夫. "Jūroku-jūkaseiki ni okeru kōsei to jinushi denko kankei" 十六-十八世紀における荒政と地主佃戸關係. *Tōyōshi kenkyū* 東洋史研究 27.4 (March 1969): 69–111.

————. *Nuhen to kōso* 奴変と抗租. Nagoya, 1980–1981.

Nakamura Hajime 中村元. "Inga" 因果. In *Inga. Bukkyō shisō* 佛教思想 3. Edited by Bukkyō shisō kenkyūkai 佛教思想研究会. Tokyo: Heirakuji shoten, 1978.

Nanfeng xianzhi 南豊縣志. 1873.

Nanxun zhi 南潯志. 1923.

Needham, Joseph, and Wang Ling. *Science and Civilization in China*. Vol. 2: *History of Scientific Thought*. Cambridge: Cambridge University Press, 1956.

Nishimura Kazuyo 西村かずよ. "Mindai no doboku" 明代の奴僕. *Tōyōshi kenkyū* 東洋史研究 38.1 (June 1979): 24–50.

Nishizawa Karō 西澤嘉朗. *Inshitsu roku no kenkyū* 陰隲錄の研究. Tokyo: Hachikumo shoten, 1946.

Nivison, David. *The Life and Thought of Chang Hsueh-ch'eng (1738–1801)*. Stanford: Stanford University Press.

Ogawa, Yōichi 小川陽一. "*Sangen nihyō* to zensho" 三言二拍と善書. *Nihon Chūgoku gakkaihō* 日本中國學會報 32 (1980): 183–195.

————, "*Seiko nishū* to zensho" 西湖二集と善書. *Tōhō shūkyō* 東方宗教 51 (1978): 16–34.

Okada, Takehiko 岡田武彦. "Chō Yōen to Roku Futei" 張楊園と陸桴亭. *Teoria* テオリア, no. 9 (December 1965): 1–30.

————. "Wang Chi and the Rise of Existentialism." In *Self and Society in Ming Thought*, edited by William Theodore de Bary, 121–144. New York: Columbia University Press, 1970.

Ōki, Yasushi 大木康. "Fū Muryō *Sangen* no hensan ito ni tsuite—toku ni kanzen-chōaku igi o megutte—馮夢龍三言の編纂意圖について—特に勸善懲惡の意義をめぐって. *Tōhōgaku* 東方學 69 (1985): 105–118.

Okuzaki Hiroshi 奧崎裕司. *Chūgoku kyōshin jinushi no kenkyū* 中國鄉紳地主の研究. Tokyo: Kyūko shoin, 1978.

———. "Chūgoku Mindai no kasō minshū no ikikata—zensho ni arawareta ichisokumen—" 中国明代の下層民衆の生き方—善書にあらわれた一側面—. *Senshū shigaku* 專修史学 13 (April 1981): 22–50.

———. "Minmatsu Shinsho no rishoku kihan-kōkakaku no ichisokumen" 明末清初の利殖規範—功過格の一側面. In (*Sakuma Shigenan Kyōju taishu kinen*) *Chūgokushi tojishi ronshū* (佐久間重男教授退休記念)中国史·陶磁史論集. Tokyo: Ryōgen, 1983.

Ono Kazuko 小野和子. "Tōrinha to sono seiji shisō" 東林派とその政治思想. *Tōhō gakuhō* 東方學報 (Kyoto), no. 28 (March 1958): 249–282.

Oyama Masaaki. "Large Landownership in the Jiangnan Delta Region during the Late Ming–Early Qing Period." In *State and Society in China: Japanese Perspectives on Ming-Qing Social and Economic History*, Edited by Linda Grove and Christian Daniels, 101–163. Tokyo: Tokyo University Press, 1984.

Oyanagi Shigeta 小柳司氣太. *Rō-Sō no shisō to Dōkyō* 老莊の思想と道教. Tokyo: Shinhoku shoten, 1942.

Peele, Thomas Benjamin, Jr. "Liu Tsung-chou's *Jen-pu*." M.A. thesis, University of California at Berkeley, 1978.

Peng Dingchiu 彭定求. *Nanyun wengao* 南畇文稿. In *Nanyun quanji* 南畇全集. 1881.

Peng Shaosheng 彭紹升. *Jushi zhuan* 居士傳 Liuli jingfang edition, 1775. Photocopy. Taibei.

Peterson, Willard. *Bitter Gourd: Fang I-chih and the Impetus for Intellectual Change*. New Haven: Yale University Press, 1979.

Pi Xirui 皮錫瑞. *Jingxue lishi* 經學歷史. Taibei: Heluo tushu chubanshe, 1973.

Plaks, Andrew. "After the Fall: *Hsing-shih yin-yuan chuan* and the Seventeenth-Century Chinese Novel." *Harvard Journal of Asiatic Studies* 45.2 (December 1985): 543–580.

P'u Sung-ling. *Strange Stories from a Chinese Studio*. Translated by Herbert Giles. London: Thomas La Rue, 1925.

Qian Mu 錢穆. *Zhuzi xinxuean* 朱子新學案. 5 vols. Taibei: Sanmin shuju, 1971.

Qiantang xianzhi 錢塘縣志. 1718.

Qing Xitai 卿希泰. *Daojiao wenhua xintan* 道教文化新探. Chengdu: Sichuan renmin chubanshe, 1988.

Qingpu xianzhi 青浦縣志. 1781–1785.

Quanzhou fuzhi 泉州府志. 1763.

Qujiang xianzhi 曲江縣志. 1638.

Rawski, Evelyn. *Agricultural Change and the Peasant Economy of South China*. Cambridge: Harvard University Press, 1972.

———. "Economic and Social Foundations of Late Imperial Culture." In *Popular Culture in Late Imperial China*, edited by David Johnson, Andrew

Nathan, and Evelyn Rawski, 3–33. Berkeley and Los Angeles: University of California Press, 1985.

———. *Education and Popular Literacy in Ch'ing China*. Ann Arbor: University of Michigan Press, 1979.

———. "Problems and Prospects." In *Popular Culture in Late Imperial China*, edited by David Johnson, Andrew Nathan, and Evelyn Rawski, 399–418. Berkeley and Los Angeles: University of California Press, 1985.

Riqian chushe 日乾初撰. Late Ming edition in the Naikaku Bunko.

Robinet, Isabelle. *La Révélation du Shangqing dans l'Histoire du Taoisme*. 2 vols. Publications de l'École Française d'Extrême-Orient 137. Paris: École Française d'Extrême-Orient, 1984.

———. "Original Contributions of *Neidan* to Taoism and Chinese Thought." In *Taoist Meditation and Longevity Techniques*, edited by Livia Kohn in cooperation with Yoshinobu Sakade, 297–330. Ann Arbor: Center For Chinese Studies, University of Michigan, 1989.

Ropp, Paul S. *Dissent in Early Modern China: Ju-lin wai-shih and Ch'ing Social Criticism*. Ann Arbor: University of Michigan Press, 1981.

Ruian xianzhi 瑞安縣志. 1809.

Saeki Yūichi 佐伯有一. "Minmatsu no Tōshi no hen—iwayuru 'nuhen' no seikaku ni kanren shite" 明末の董氏の變 — いわゆる'奴變'の性格に関連して. *Tōyōshi kenkyū* 東洋史研究 16.1 (June 1957): 26–57.

Sakai Tadao 酒井忠夫. *Chūgoku zensho no kenkyū* 中國善書の研究. Tokyo: Kōbundō, 1960.

———. "Chūgokushijō no shomin kyōiku to zensho undō" 中国史上の庶民教育と善書運動. In *Chūsei Ajia kyōikushi kenkyū* 中世アジア教育史研究, edited by Taga Akigorō 多賀秋五郎, 294–323. Tokyo: Kokusho kankōkai, 1980.

———. "Confucianism and Popular Educational Works." In *Self and Society in Ming Thought*, edited by William Theodore de Bary, 331–366. New York: Columbia University Press, 1970.

———. "Gan Moken no shisō ni tsuite" 顔茂猷の思想について. In *Kamada Hakushi kanreki kinen rekishigaku ronsō* 鎌田博士還暦記念歴史學論叢, 259–273. Tokyo: Kokusho kankōkai, 1969.

———. "Minmatsu Shinsho no shakai ni okeru taishūteki dokushojin to zensho. seigen" 明末清初の社会における大衆的読書人と善書・清言. In *Dōkyō no sōgōteki kenkyū* 道教の総合的研究, edited by Sakai Tadao, 370–393. Tokyo: Kokusho kankōkai, 1977.

———. "Yōmeigaku to Mindai no zensho" 陽明學と明代の善書. In *Yōmeigaku taikei* 陽明學大系, vol. 1, 341–363. Tokyo: Meitoku shuppansha, 1971.

Seaman, Gary. *Temple Organization in a Chinese Village*. Taibei: Orient Cultural Service, 1978.

Shih, Chin. "Peasant Economy and Rural Society in the Lake Tai Area, 1368–1840." Ph.D. diss., University of California at Berkeley, 1981.

Shimada Kenji 島田虔次. *Chūgoku ni okeru kindai shii no zasetsu* 中國における近代思惟の挫折. Tokyo: Chikuma shobō, 1949.

Shimizu Taiji 清水泰次. "Mindai ni okeru shūkyō yōgō to kōkakaku" 明代における宗教融合と功過格. *Shichō* 史潮 6.3 (October 1936): 29–55.

Siku quanshu zongmu 四庫全書總目. Compiled by Ji Yun 紀昀 et al. Taibei: Yiwen yinshu guan, 1957.

Soymié, Michel. "Notes d'iconographie chinoise: les acolytes de Ti-tsang," parts 1 and 2. *Arts Asiatiques* 14 (1966): 45–78; and 16 (1967): 141–170.

Stein, Rolf A. "Religious Taoism and Popular Religion from the Second to Seventh Centuries." In *Facets of Taoism: Essays in Chinese Religion*, edited by Holmes Welch and Anna Seidel, 53–81. New Haven: Yale University Press, 1979.

Strickmann, Michel. *Le Taoisme du Mao Chan: Chronique d'une Révélation*. Paris: Collège de France, Institut des hautes études chinoises, 1968.

Sung, Z. D. *The Text of the Yi King and Its Appendixes*. Translated by James Legge. Shanghai: China Modern Education Company, 1935.

Suzhou fuzhi 蘇州府志. 1883.

Tachibana Shiraki 橘樸. *Dōkyō to shinwa densetsu—Chūgoku no minken shinkō* 道教と神話傳說—中國の民間信仰. Tokyo: Kaizōshaban, 1948.

———. *Shina shakai kenkyū* 支那社会研究. Tokyo: Nippon hyōronsha, 1941.

Taicang zhouzhi 太倉州志. 1919.

Takao Giken 高雄義堅. "Mindai ni taisei saretaro kōkakaku shisō" 明代に大成されたろ功過格. *Ryūkoku Daigaku ronsō* 龍谷大學論叢, no. 244 (June 1922): 12–25.

Tanaka Masatoshi. "Popular Uprisings, Rent Resistance, and Bondservant Rebellions in the Late Ming." In *State and Society in China: Japanese Perspectives on Ming–Qing Social and Economic History*, edited by Linda Grove and Christian Daniels, 165–214. Tokyo: Tokyo University Press, 1984.

T'ang Chün-i. "The T'ien-ming [Heavenly Ordinance] in Pre-Ch'in China." *Philosophy East and West* 11.4 (January 1962): 195–218; and 12.1 (April 1962): 29–49.

Tang Junyi (T'ang Chün-i) 唐君毅. *Zhongguo zhexue yuanlun: Daolun pian* 中國哲學原論: 導論篇. Jiulong: Xinya shuyuan yanjiusuo, 1966.

Tao Ting 陶珽 and Tao Gong 陶珙. *Guyi hui* 穀詒彙. Early Qing edition in the Naikaku Bunko.

Tao Wangling 陶望齡. *Gongguoge lun* 功過格論. Undated and unpaginated manuscript in the Library of Congress.

Tjan, Tjoe Som, trans. *Po Hu T'ung: The Comprehensive Discussions in the White Tiger Hall*. 2 vols. Leiden: E. J. Brill, 1949.

Tong, James. "Collective Violence in a Premodern Society: Rebellions and Banditry in the Ming Dynasty (1368–1644)." Ph.D. diss., University of Michigan, 1985.

Tongshan lu 同善錄. 1718.

Tsurumi Naohiro. "Rural Control in the Ming Dynasty." In *State and Society in China: Japanese Perspectives on Ming–Qing Social and Economic History*, edited by Linda Grove and Christian Daniels, 245–277. Tokyo: Tokyo University Press, 1984.

Tu Long 屠隆. *Hongbao ji* 鴻苞集. 1610.

Tu, Wei-ming. *Neo-Confucian Thought in Action: Wang Yang-ming's (1472–1509)*. Berkeley and Los Angeles: University of California Press, 1976.

———. "Subjectivity in Liu Tsung-chou's Philosophical Anthropology." In *Indi-*

vidualism and Holism: Studies in Confucian and Taoist Values, edited by Donald J. Munro, 215–238. Ann Arbor: Center for Chinese Studies, University of Michigan, 1985.

Uchiyama Toshihiko 內山俊彦. "Kandai no ōhō shisō" 漢代の應報思想. *Tōkyō Shina gakuhō* 東京支那學報 6 (June 1960): 17–23.

Van Gulik, Robert. *Sexual Life in Ancient China*. Leiden: E. J. Brill, 1974.

Von Glahn, Richard. "Community and Welfare: Zhu Xi's Community Granary in Theory and Practice." Paper for the Workshop on Sung Dynasty Statecraft in Thought and Action, Scottsdale, Arizona, January 5–12, 1986.

Wakeman, Frederic, Jr. "China and the Seventeenth-Century Crisis." *Late Imperial China* 7.1 (June 1986): 1–26.

———. "The Price of Autonomy: Intellectuals in Ming and Ch'ing Politics," *Daedalus*, Spring 1972, 35–70.

Waley, Arthur. *Ballads and Songs from Tun-huang*. London: George Allen and Unwin, 1960.

———, trans. *The Book of Songs*. New York: Grove Press, 1960.

Wang Anshi 王安石. "Zhongjian Jingyang ciji" 重建旌陽祠記. In *Xiaoyao shan Wanshou gongzhi* 逍遙山萬壽宮志, edited by Jin Guixing 金桂馨 and Qi Fengyuan 漆逢源, j. 15, 6b–7b. 1878.

Wang Ch'ung (Wang Chong). *Lun-heng: Miscellaneous Essays of Wang Ch'ung*. 2 vols. Translated by Alfred Forke. New York: Paragon Book Gallery, 1962.

Wang Daokun 汪道昆. *Taihan fumo* 太函副墨. 1633. Held by the National Central Library in Taibei.

Wang Fuzhi 王夫之. *Du Tongjian lun* 讀通鑑論. Beijing: Zhonghua shuju, 1975.

Wang Gen 王艮. *Wang Xinzhai quanji* 王心齋全集. 1468.

Wang Ji 王畿. *Wang Longxi xiansheng quanji* 王龍谿先生全集. 1882.

———. "Yuan Canbo xiaozhuan" 袁參坡小傳. In *Yuanshi congshu* 袁氏叢書, edited by Yuan Huang. Wanli edition held in the Naikaku Bunko.

Wang Ming 王明. *Baopuzi neipian jiaoshi* 抱朴子內篇校釋. Beijing: Zhonghua shuju, 1980.

Wang Yangming 王陽明 (m. Shouren 守仁). *Chuanxi lu* 傳習錄. In *Yangming quanshu* 陽明全書. Sibu beiyao edition.

———. *Instructions for Practical Learning and Other Neo-Confucian Writings by Wang Yang-ming*. Translated and edited by Wing-tsit Chan. New York: Columbia University Press, 1963.

———. *The Philosophical Letters of Wang Yang-ming*. Translated and edited by Julia Ching. Columbia: University of South Carolina Press, 1972.

Watson, Burton, trans. *The Complete Works of Chuang Tzu*. New York: Columbia University Press, 1968.

Watson, James. "Standardizing the Gods: The Promotion of T'ien Hou ("Empress of Heaven") Along the South China Coast." In *Popular Culture in Late Imperial China*, edited by David Johnson, Andrew J. Nathan, and Evelyn Rawski, 292–324. Berkeley and Los Angeles: University of California Press, 1985.

Webster, James, trans. *The Kan Ying Pien*. Shanghai: Presbyterian Mission Press, 1918. Reprint. Taibei: Ch'eng Wen Publishing Company, 1971.

Wei Qingyuan 韦庆远, Wu Qiyan 吴奇衍, and Lu Su 鲁素. *Qingdai nubi zhidu* 清代奴婢制度. Beijing: Zhongguo renmin daxue chubanshe, 1982.

Welch, Holmes. *Taoism: The Parting of the Way*. Boston: Beacon Press, 1957.

Wenchang dijun gongguoge 文昌帝君功過格. Taibei, 1938.

Whitaker, P. K. "A Buddhist Spell." *Asia Major*, n.s. 10, part 1 (1963): 9–22.

Wiens, Mi Chu. "Lord and Peasant: The Sixteenth to the Eighteenth Century." *Modern China* 6.1 (January 1980): 3–39.

———. "Socioeconomic Change during the Ming Dynasty in the Kiangnan Area." Ph.D. diss., Harvard University, 1973.

Woodside, Alexander. "Some Mid-Qing Theories of Popular Schools." *Modern China* 9.1 (Jaunary 1983): 3–36.

Wu, Pei-yi. "Self-Examination and Confession of Sins in Traditional China." *Harvard Journal of Asiatic Studies* 39.1 (June 1979): 5–38.

Wu Yuancui 伍袁萃. *Manlu pingzheng* 漫錄評正. Wanli edition.

Wujiang xianzhi 吳江縣志. 1747.

Xie Guozhen 謝國楨. *Qingchu nongmin qiyi ziliao jilu* 清初農民起義資料輯錄. Shanghai: Xinzhishi chubanshe, 1956.

Xie Zhaozhe 謝肇淛. *Wuza zu* 五雜组. Ming Wanli edition.

Xiong Hongbei 熊弘備. *Bufeiqian gongdeli* 不費錢功德例. In *Wuzhong yigui* 五種遺規, edited by Chen Hongmou 陳宏謀, 4.43a–51a. Sibu beiyao edition.

Xu Ben 徐本. *Liming gongguoge* 立命功過格. 1770 edition.

Xu Jie 徐階. *Shijing tangji* 世經堂集. Wanli edition.

Xu Ke 徐珂. *Qingbai leichao* 清稗類鈔. Shanghai: Shangwu yinshuguan, 1928.

Xu Zhonglin 許仲琳 (attrib.). *Fengshen yangyi* 封神演義. 2 vols. Hong Kong: Zhonghua shuju, 1976.

Yamamoto Makoto 山本命. *Minjidai Jugaku no ronrigakuteki kenkyū* 明時代儒学の倫理学的研究. Tokyo: Risōsha, 1974.

Yamane Yukio. "Reforms in the Service Levy System in the Fifteenth and Sixteenth Centuries." In *State and Society in China: Japanese Perspectives on Ming–Qing Social and Economic History*, edited by Linda Grove and Christian Daniels, 279–310. Tokyo: Tokyo University Press, 1984.

Yamanoi Yū 山井湧. *Min Shin jidai no kenkyū* 明清時代の研究. Tokyo: Tōkyō Daigaku shuppansha, 1980.

———. "Shushi no shisō ni okeru ki" 朱子の思想における気. In *Ki no shisō—Chūgoku ni okeru shizenkan to ningenkan no tenkai* 気の思想—中国における自然観と人間観の展開, edited by Onozawa Seiichi 小野沢精一, Fukunaga Mitsuji 福永光司, and Yamanoi Yū. Tokyo: Tōkyō Daigaku shuppankai, 1978.

Yampolsky, Philip B. *The Platform Sutra of the Sixth Patriarch*. New York: Columbia University Press, 1967.

Yan Maoyou 顔茂猷. *Diji lu* 廸吉錄. 1886 edition.

———. *Yunqi ji* 雲起集. Late Ming edition in the Naikaku Bunko.

Yan Zheng 顔正 and Yan Yunlu 顔雲麓. *Dangui ji* 丹桂籍. Edited by Zhao Songyi 趙松一. 1749.

Yang Dongming 楊東明. *Shanju gongke* 山居功課. 1624.

Yang Lien-sheng. "The Concept of *Pao* as a Basis for Social Relationships in

China." In *Chinese Thought and Institutions*, edited by John King Fairbank, 3–23. Chicago: University of Chicago Press, 1957.

Yang Xiong 揚雄. *Yangzi fayan* 揚子法言. Sibu beiyao edition.

Yin xianzhi 鄞縣志. 1877.

Yoshioka Yoshitoyo 吉岡義豊. *Dōkyō no kenkyū* 道教の研究. Kyoto: Hōzo-kan, 1952.

———. *Dōkyō to Bukkyō* 道教と佛教. Vol. 2. Tokyo: Toshima shobō, 1970.

Yü, Chün-fang. *The Renewal of Buddhism in China: Chu-hung and the Late Ming Synthesis*. New York: Columbia University Press, 1981.

Yü, Ying-shih. "Life and Immortality in the Mind of Han China." *Harvard Journal of Asiatic Studies* 25 (1964–1965), 80–122.

Yuan Huang 袁黃. *Lianghang zhai wenji* 兩行齋文集. 1624.

———. *Liaofan xiansheng sishu shanzheng jianshuyi* 了凡先生四書刪正兼疏意. Ming edition held in the Naikaku Bunko.

———. *Liming pian* 立命篇. 1607.

———. *Qisi zhenquan* 祈嗣眞詮, in *Congshu jicheng chubian*.

———, ed. *Yuanshi congshu* 袁氏叢書. Wanli edition in the Naikaku Bunko.

Yuan Zhong 袁衷. *Tingwei zalu* 庭幃雜錄. Edited by Qian Xiao 錢曉. In *Congshu jicheng chubian*.

Yuhang xianzhi 餘杭縣志. 1808.

Yunqi Zhuhong 雲棲袾宏. *Zizhi lu* 自知錄. In *Yungqi fahui* 雲棲法彙. Nanjing: Jingling kejing chu, 1897.

Zha Jizuo 查繼佐. *Zuiwei lu* 罪惟錄. Sibu congkan edition.

Zhang Lixiang 張履祥. *Yangyuan xiansheng quanji* 楊園先生全集. 2 vols. Edited by Tao Lian 桃璉 and Wan Huquan 萬斛全. 1818. Reprint. Taibei: Huanqiu shuju, 1964.

Zhang Xuecheng 章學誠. *Zhangshi yishu* 章氏遺書. 1922. Reprint. Taibei: Hansheng chubanshe, 1973.

Zhangzhou fuzhi 漳州府志. 1796.

Zhen Dexiu 眞德秀. *Xishan xiansheng Zhen Wenzhong Gong wenji* 西山先生眞文忠公文集. Sibu congkan chubian yinben, vol. 68.

Zheng Zhiming 鄭志明. *Zhongguo shanshu yu zongjiao* 中國善書與宗教. Taibei: Taiwan Xuesheng shuju, 1988.

Zhou Dingchen 周鼎臣. *(Zengding) Jingxin lu* (增訂)敬信錄. 1749. Reprint. Wenxin Tang, 1779.

Zhou Rudeng 周汝登. *Dongyue zhengxue lu* 東越證學錄. 1605.

Zhouyi yinde 周易引得. Harvard-Yenching Institute Sinological Index Series 10. Beijing: Harvard-Yenching Institute, 1935. Photocopy reprint. Taibei: Ch'eng Wen Publishing Company, 1966.

Zhu Guozhen 朱國楨. *Yongchuang xiaopin* 湧幢小品. In *Biji xiaoshuo daguan* 筆記小說大觀.

Zhu Xi 朱熹. *Sishu jizhu* 四書集注. Sibu beiyao edition.

———. *Zhu Wengong zhengxun* 朱文公政訓. In *Congshu jicheng chubian*.

———. *(Yuzuan) Zhuzi quanshu* (御纂)朱子全書. Compiled by Li Guangdi 李光地. 1714.

———. *Zhuzi yishu* 朱子遺書. Facsimile reproduction of Kangxi edition in the National University Library, Taiwan. Taibei: Yiwen yinshuguan, 1969.

———. *Zhuzi yulei* 朱子語類. Compiled by Li Jingde 黎靖德. Beijing: Zhonghua shuju, 1986.

Zhuangzi yinde 莊子引得. Harvard-Yenching Sinological Institute Series Supplement 20. Beijing: Yenching University Press, 1947. Reprint. Cambridge: Harvard University Press, 1956.

Index

academic degrees, purchase of, 5
"Accumulating Goodness," 95
action: and response, 29, 29n–30n, 42, 53, 92, 138–57, 167, 240; spontaneous, 19, 20, 116
agricultural laborers, economic independence of, 63
alchemy, external, 48; internal, 48, 71
Aleni, Guilio, 158
Analects, 104
Annotated General Catalogue of the Siku quanshu, 70
Avalokiteśvara, 82n

Bao Ping, 103n
Baopuzi. See *Master Who Embraces Simplicity*
baoying, 53, 92, 167
benevolent societies, 23, 141–42, 145–48, 222
Biographies of Lay Monks, 72
bondservants. See servants, bondservants
Buddhism: acts of faith in, 35; causation in, 143; Chan, 20, 63, 73, 77, 78, 83, 84, 93, 116, 220; conversion of Confucians to, 93; criticism of, 121, 138–40, 145; fate in, 77, 78, 84; goal of, 35; influence of on merit system, 40, 41–42, 77–95 passim; influence of on Neo-Confucianism, 20; influence on Yuan Huang, 77–95 passim, 72–74, 105, 106–7, 168, 237; Jingtu sect, 78n; ledgers used in, 62–63; merit accumulation in, 25, 32, 229; practices of in ledgers, 234; Pure Land sect, 62–63; retribution in, 30–31, 52, 116, 138–39, 167, 231; spirits in, 239; Three Treasures, 72; Tiantai school, 73; Weixin sect, 78n; and Yuan family, 71–72. See also transmigration
Bufeiqian gongdeli. See *Meritorious Deeds at No Cost*
bureaucracy, supernatural. See gods and spirits, bureaucracy of

Cai Fangbing, 160n

Cai Maode, 160n
Categorized Conversations of Master Zhu, 55, 123. See also Zhu Xi
causation, 31, 53, 138, 140, 143, 167. See also retribution
charity, 30, 146n, 153
Chen Hongmou, 221–22
Chen Hu, 161n, 223n
Chen Longzheng, 23–24, 74n, 138, 144–56 passim, 187, 222, 236
Chen Xianzhang, 162n
Chen Xigu, 157–71 passim, 178–83, 184, 186, 191, 192–200, 202, 208–14 passim. See also *Compendium of Ledgers of Merit and Demerit*
Chen Zhixi, 157, 158–59, 163, 176–77, 183–90 passim, 196–97, 202, 208–14 passim, 220. See also *Complete Book of Exhortations and Admonitions*
Cheng Yi, 17n, 42. See also Neo-Confucianism, Cheng-Zhu school
Cheng Yuwen, 210–11
Chenzhong lu. See *Record of Enlightenment*
children, role of. See family hierarchy
Chinese Communist Party, ledgers used by, 226n
Chongzhen emperor, 11
Chong xiu zhiyao. See *Essentials of Self-Cultivation*
Christianity, opposition to, 158
Chronicle of Zuo, 36, 40, 238
civil service examination: Classics in, 70, 73; and Confucianism, 55, 56, 68, 73; education for, 18; ledgers used by candidates, 110; morality of, 69; purchase of degrees, 5; qualifications for taking, 65n; value of, 94, 231; and Yuan Huang, 75–76, 80, 81, 86, 87–88, 94, 107, 148, 150; Zhu Xi's influence on, 56
Classic of Changes: action and response in, 29n–30n, 42; goodness in, 33, 42, 81, 148; retribution in, 31, 42, 53, 81, 107, 138, 238; and Yuan Huang, 71, 81, 107, 230, 238

The Ledgers of Merit and Demerit

Social Change and Moral Order in Late Imperial China

CYNTHIA J. BROKAW

The ledgers of merit and demerit were a type of morality book that achieved sudden and widespread popularity in China during the sixteenth and seventeenth centuries. Consisting of lists of good and bad deeds, each assigned a certain number of merit or demerit points, the ledgers offered the hope of divine reward to users "good" enough to accumulate a substantial sum of merits. By examining the uses of the ledgers during the late Ming and early Qing periods, Cynthia Brokaw throws new light on the intellectual and social history of the late imperial era.

The ledgers originally functioned as guides to salvation for twelfth-century Daoists and Buddhists, but Brokaw shows how the literati of turbulent sixteenth-century China began to use them as aids in the struggle for official status through civil service examinations. The author describes how the responses of some Confucian thinkers to the popularity of the ledgers not only refined the orthodox Neo-Confucian method of self-cultivation but also revealed the serious ambiguity of the classic Confucian understanding of the relationship between fate and human action. Finally, she demonstrates that by the end of the seventeenth century the